Komomo Confiserie

Volume 4

Story & Art by Maki Minami

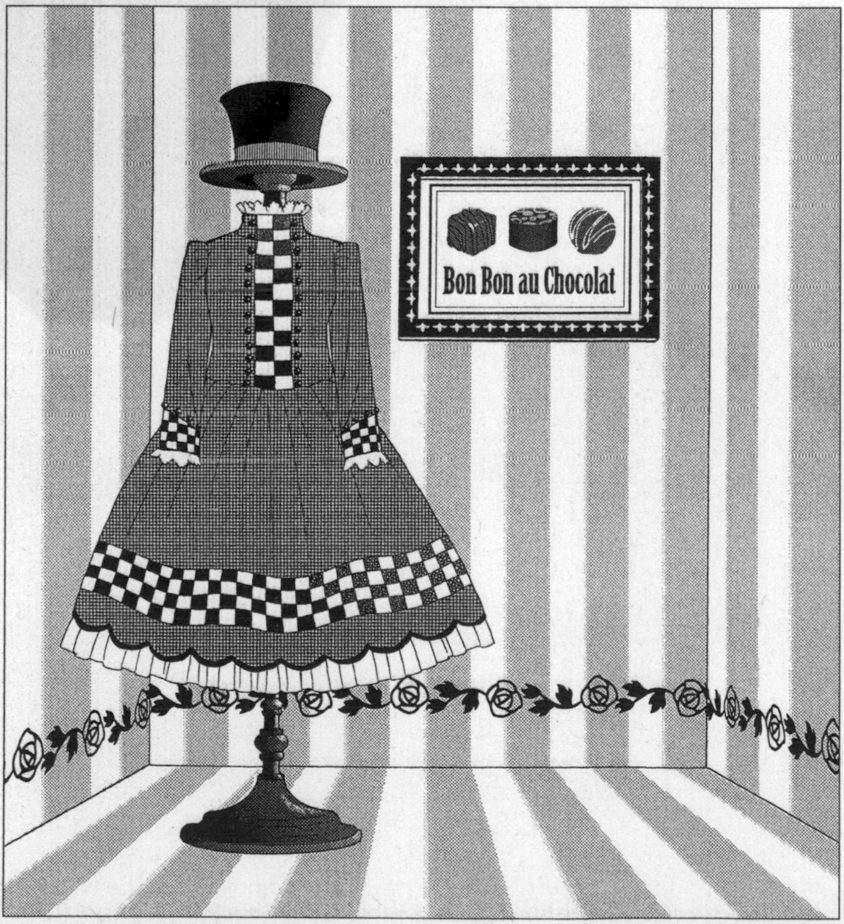
Bon Bon au Chocolat

Komomo Confiserie

CONTENTS

Chapter 18 003

Chapter 19 033

Chapter 20 065

Chapter 21 095

Chapter 22 125

Chapter 23 155

Bonus Pages 186

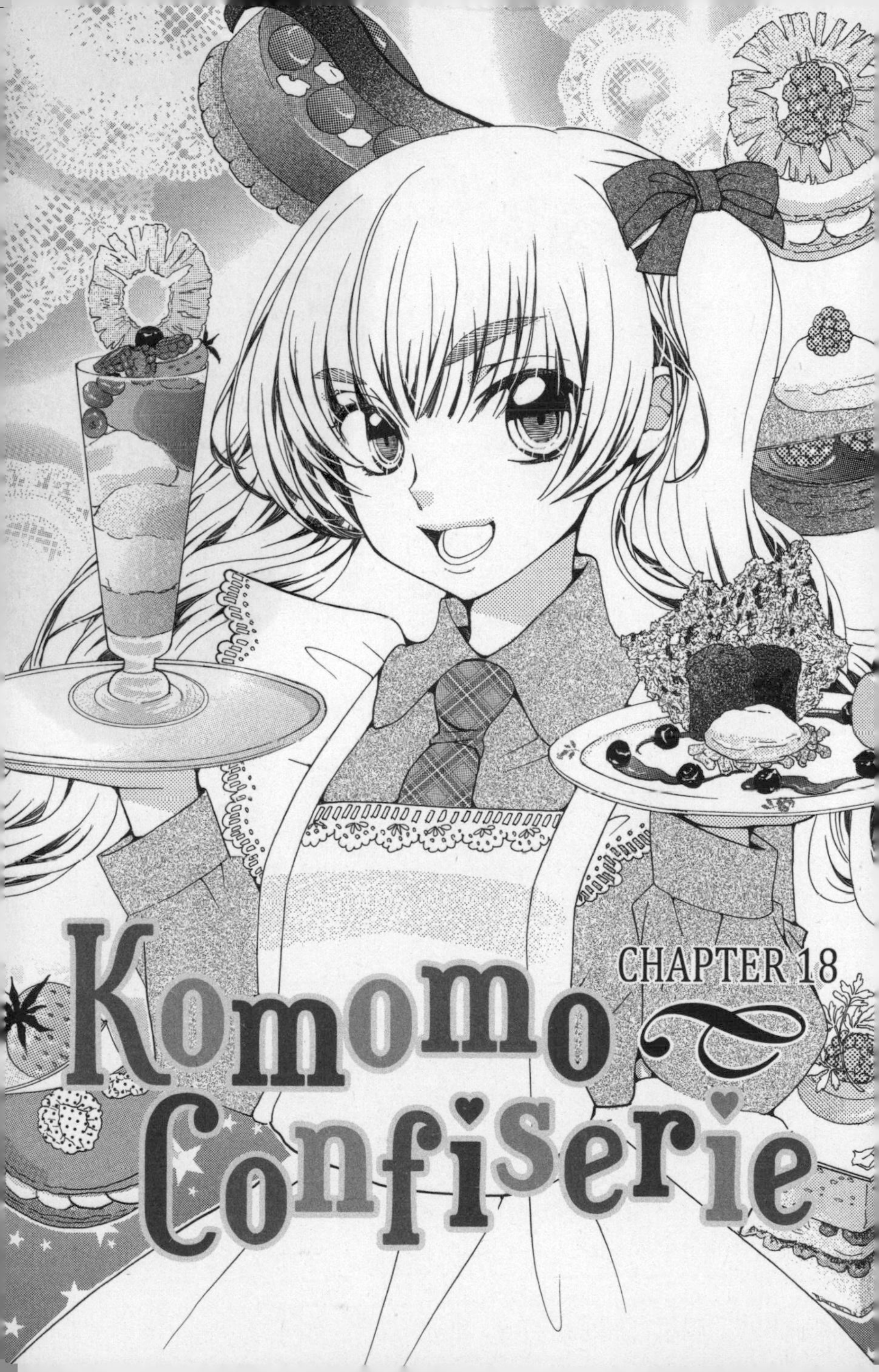
CHAPTER 18
Komomo Confiserie

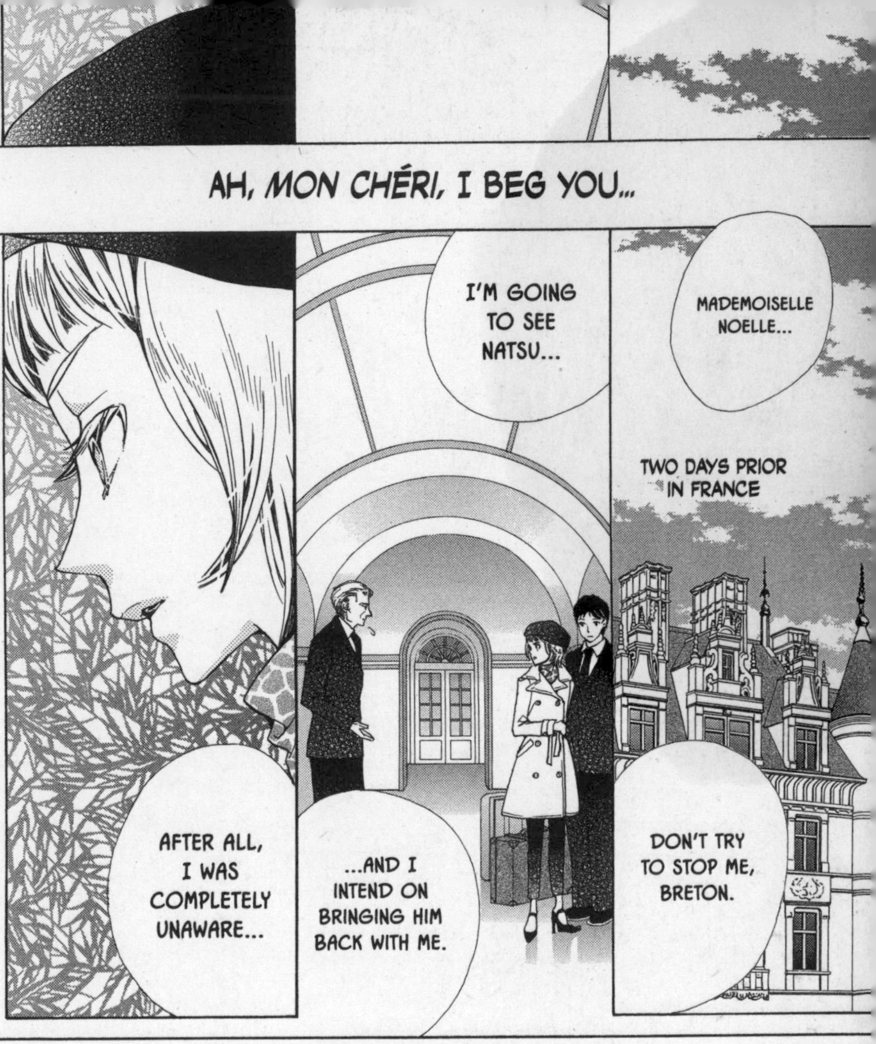
AH, MON CHÉRI, I BEG YOU...
MADEMOISELLE NOELLE...
TWO DAYS PRIOR IN FRANCE
DON'T TRY TO STOP ME, BRETON.
I'M GOING TO SEE NATSU...
...AND I INTEND ON BRINGING HIM BACK WITH ME.
AFTER ALL, I WAS COMPLETELY UNAWARE...

1

• Cover •

This time the theme is chocolate bonbons. They're little chocolates with something in the middle. I like the ones with praline or caramel inside. On Valentine's Day, I get to eat bonbons you can't usually find in Japan by an overseas chocolatier. I really look forward to it every year! Back to the cover: I used some color tones I don't usually use. The character on the back, Mitsuru, is new and appears in this volume.

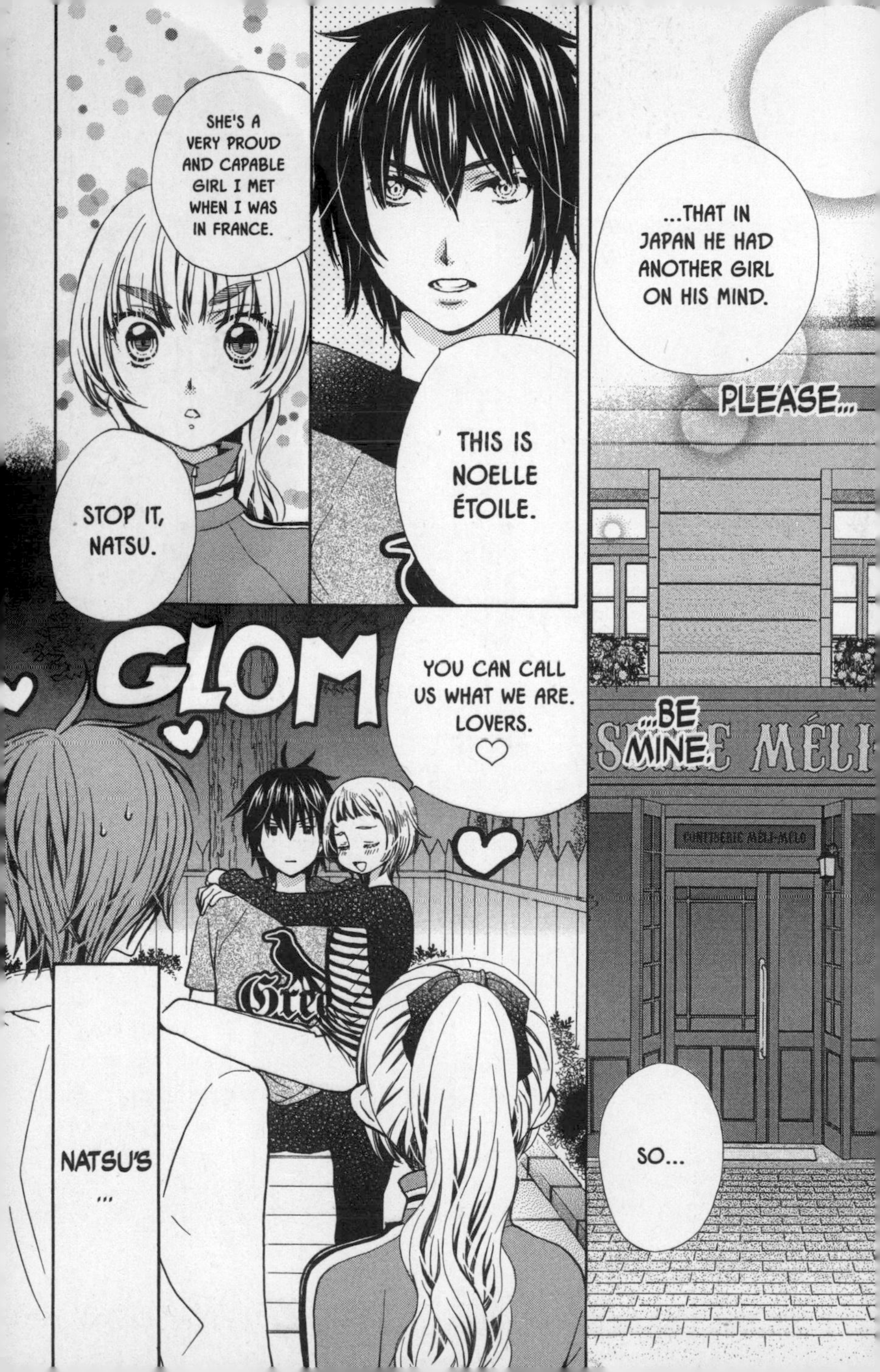
...THAT IN JAPAN HE HAD ANOTHER GIRL ON HIS MIND.
PLEASE...
...BE MINE.
SO...
THIS IS NOELLE ÉTOILE.
SHE'S A VERY PROUD AND CAPABLE GIRL I MET WHEN I WAS IN FRANCE.
STOP IT, NATSU.
YOU CAN CALL US WHAT WE ARE. LOVERS.
GLOM
NATSU'S ...

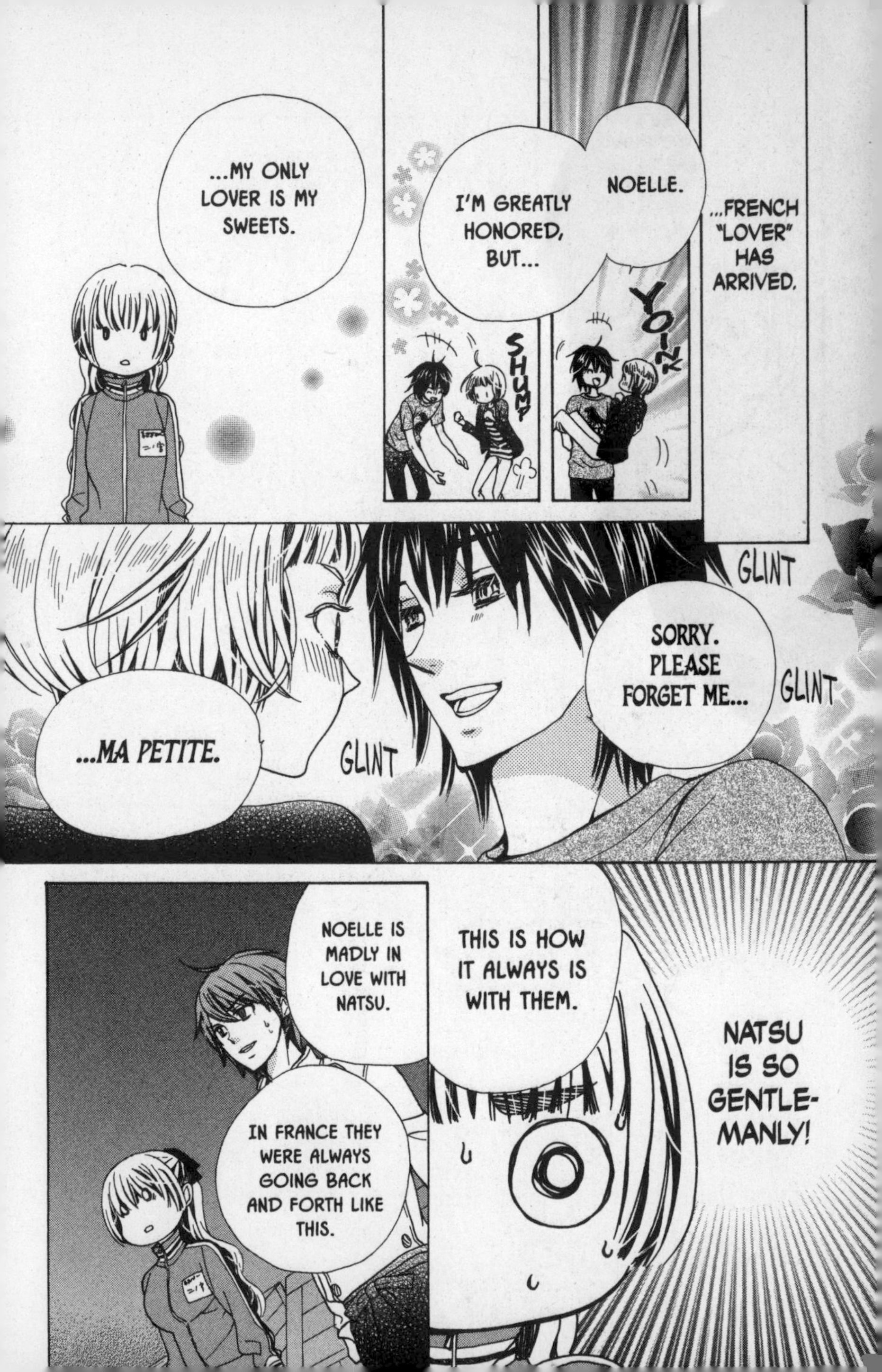
...FRENCH "LOVER" HAS ARRIVED.
YOINK
NOELLE.
SHUMP
I'M GREATLY HONORED, BUT...
...MY ONLY LOVER IS MY SWEETS.
GLINT
SORRY. PLEASE FORGET ME...
GLINT
...MA PETITE.
GLINT
NATSU IS SO GENTLE-MANLY!
THIS IS HOW IT ALWAYS IS WITH THEM.
NOELLE IS MADLY IN LOVE WITH NATSU.
IN FRANCE THEY WERE ALWAYS GOING BACK AND FORTH LIKE THIS.

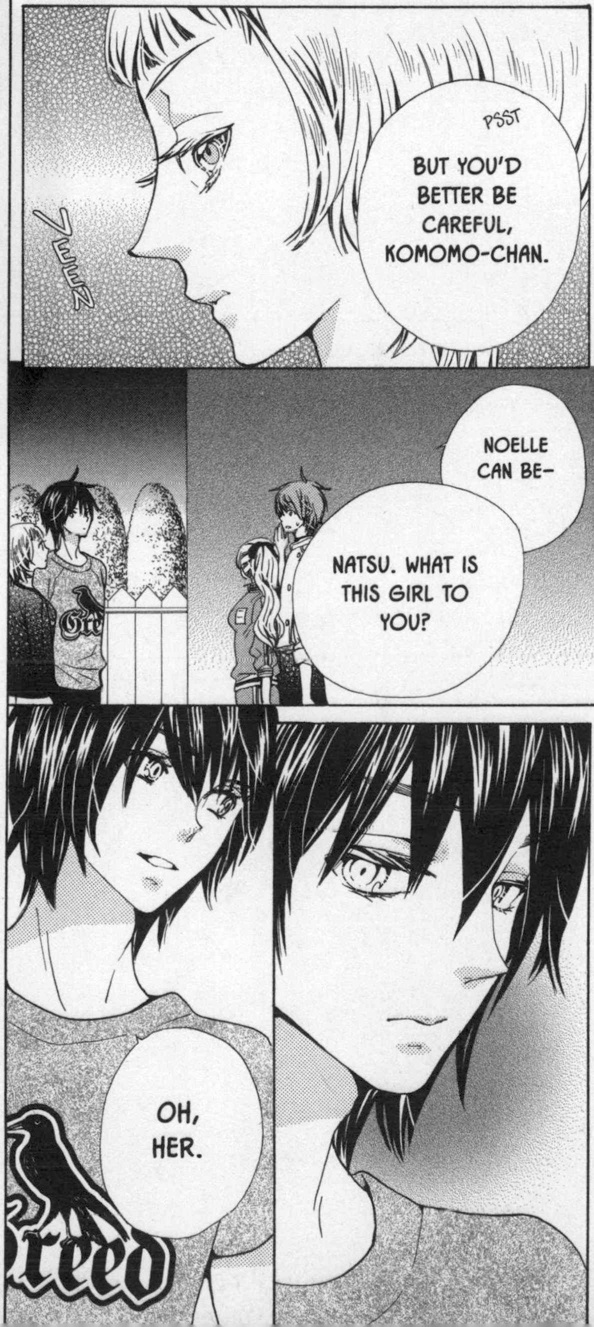
PSST
BUT YOU'D BETTER BE CAREFUL, KOMOMO-CHAN.
VEEN
NOELLE CAN BE—
NATSU. WHAT IS THIS GIRL TO YOU?
OH, HER.

• Greetings •

Hello and nice to meet you!!

I'm Maki Minami, and this is volume 4 of *Komomo Confiserie*.

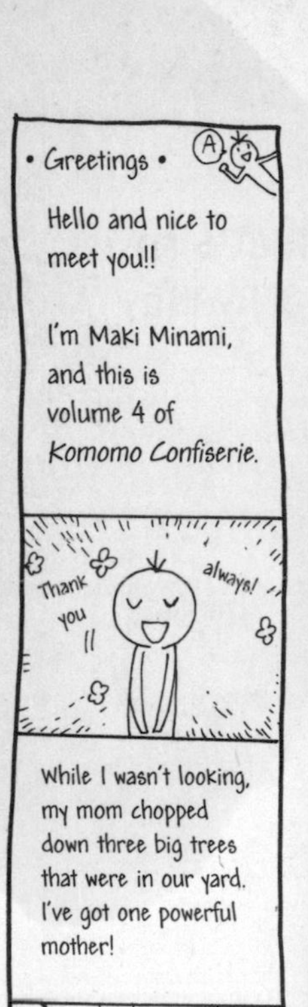
Thank you!!
always!

While I wasn't looking, my mom chopped down three big trees that were in our yard. I've got one powerful mother!

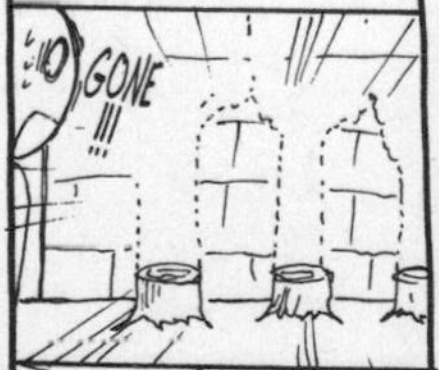
!!
GONE!!!

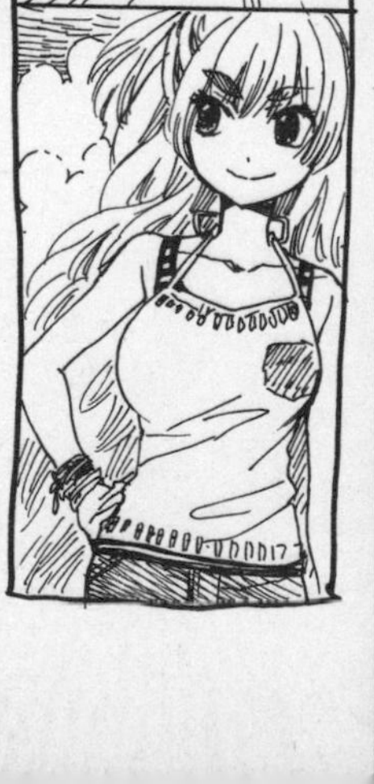

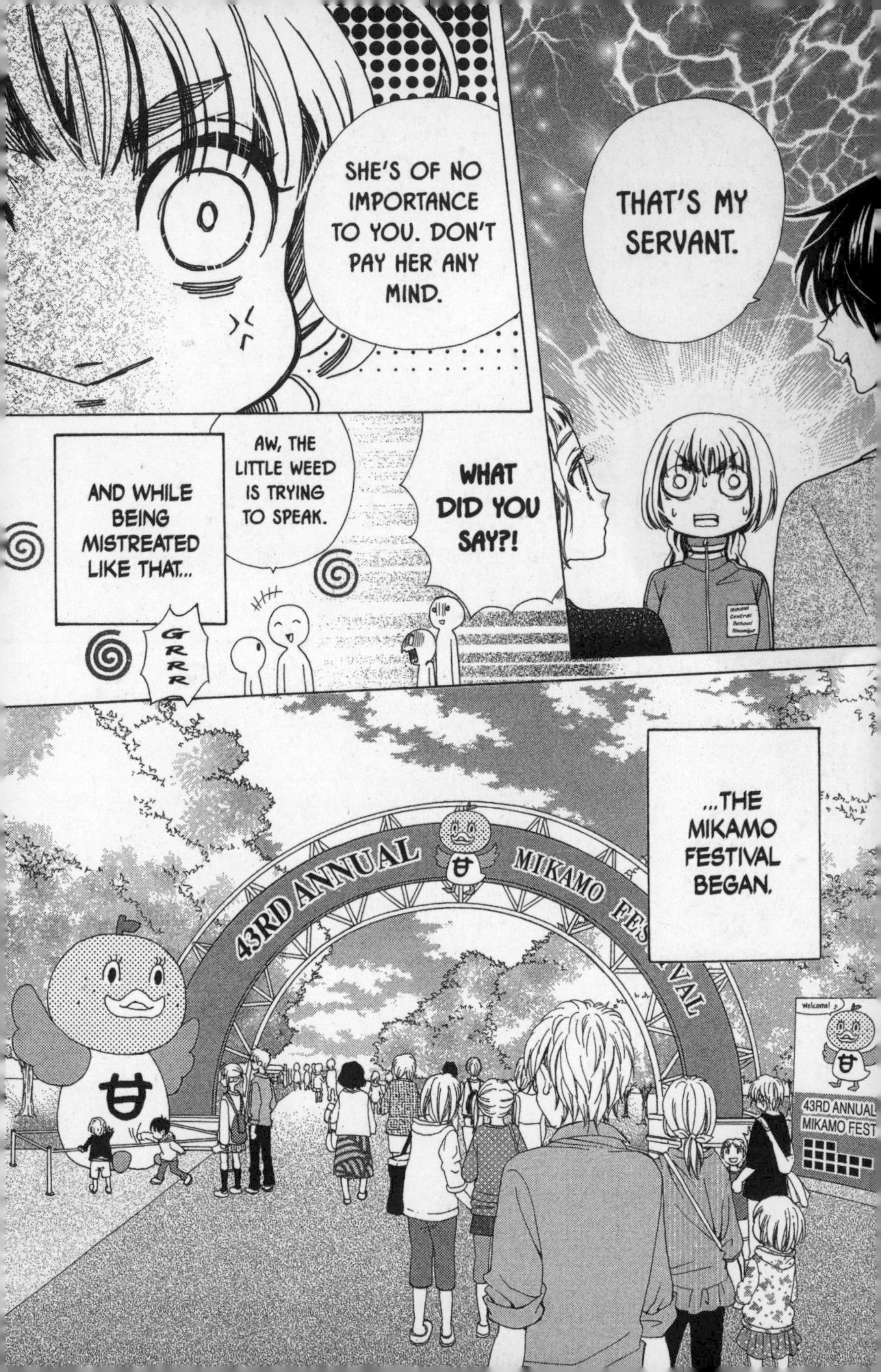
THAT'S MY SERVANT.
SHE'S OF NO IMPORTANCE TO YOU. DON'T PAY HER ANY MIND.
WHAT DID YOU SAY?!
AW, THE LITTLE WEED IS TRYING TO SPEAK.
AND WHILE BEING MISTREATED LIKE THAT...
GRRR
...THE MIKAMO FESTIVAL BEGAN.
43RD ANNUAL MIKAMO FESTIVAL
Welcome!
43RD ANNUAL MIKAMO FEST

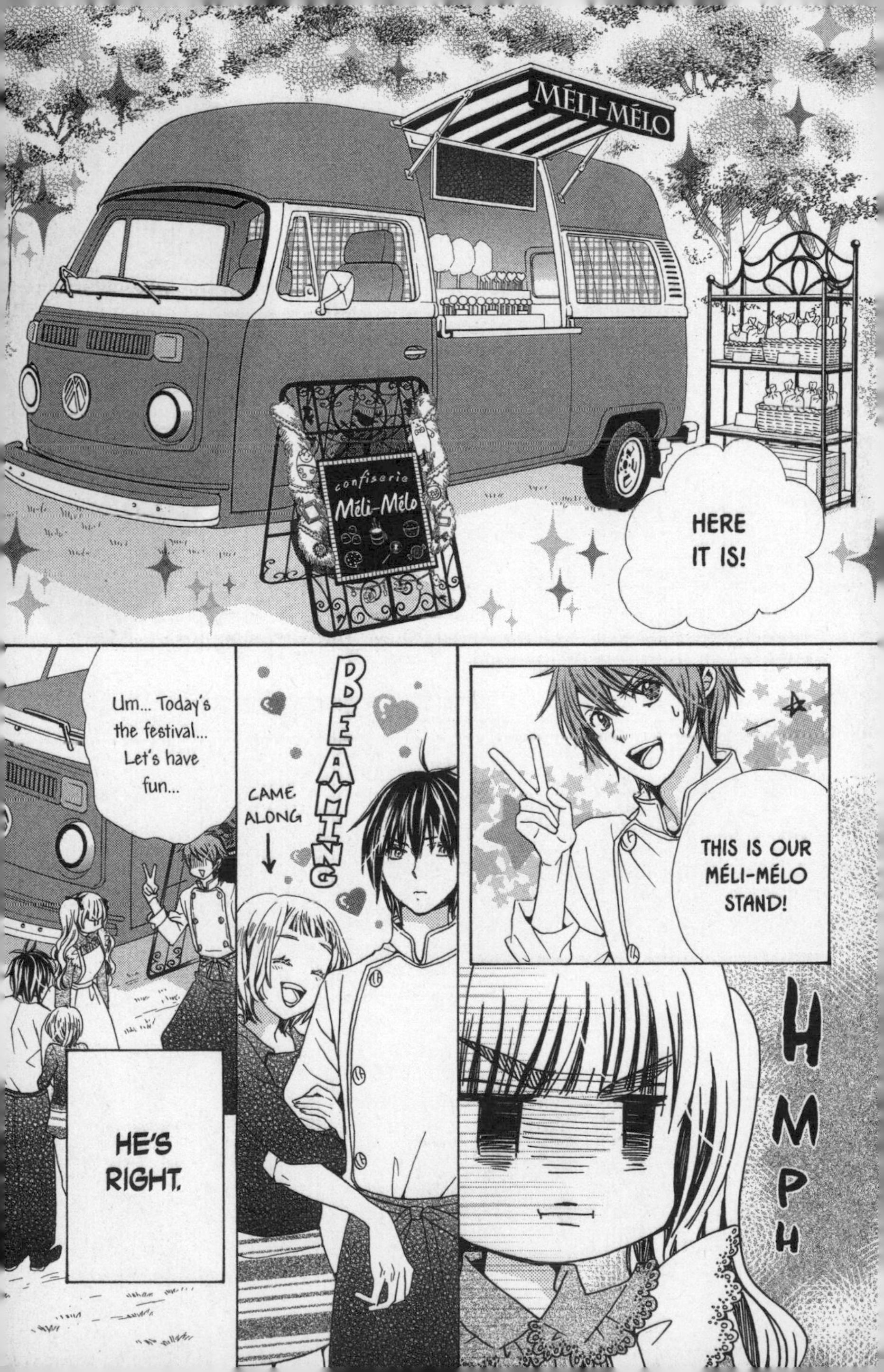
MÉLI-MÉLO
confiserie
Méli-Mélo
HERE IT IS!
THIS IS OUR MÉLI-MÉLO STAND!
HMPH
BEAMING
CAME ALONG
Um... Today's the festival... Let's have fun...
HE'S RIGHT.

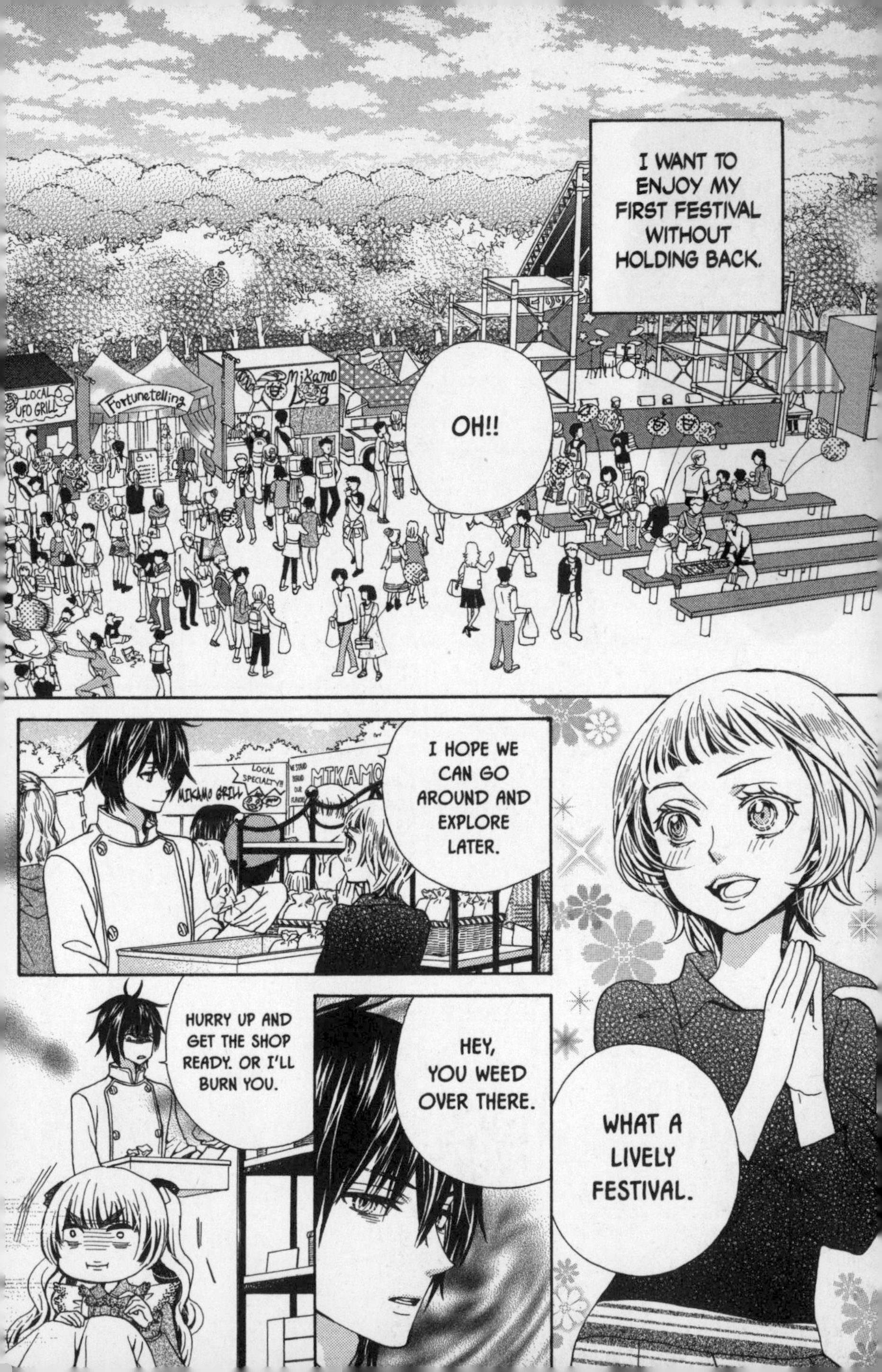
I WANT TO ENJOY MY FIRST FESTIVAL WITHOUT HOLDING BACK.
OH!!
LOCAL UFO GRILL
Fortunetelling
WHAT A LIVELY FESTIVAL.
I HOPE WE CAN GO AROUND AND EXPLORE LATER.
LOCAL SPECIALTY!!
MIKAMO GRILL
HEY, YOU WEED OVER THERE.
HURRY UP AND GET THE SHOP READY. OR I'LL BURN YOU.

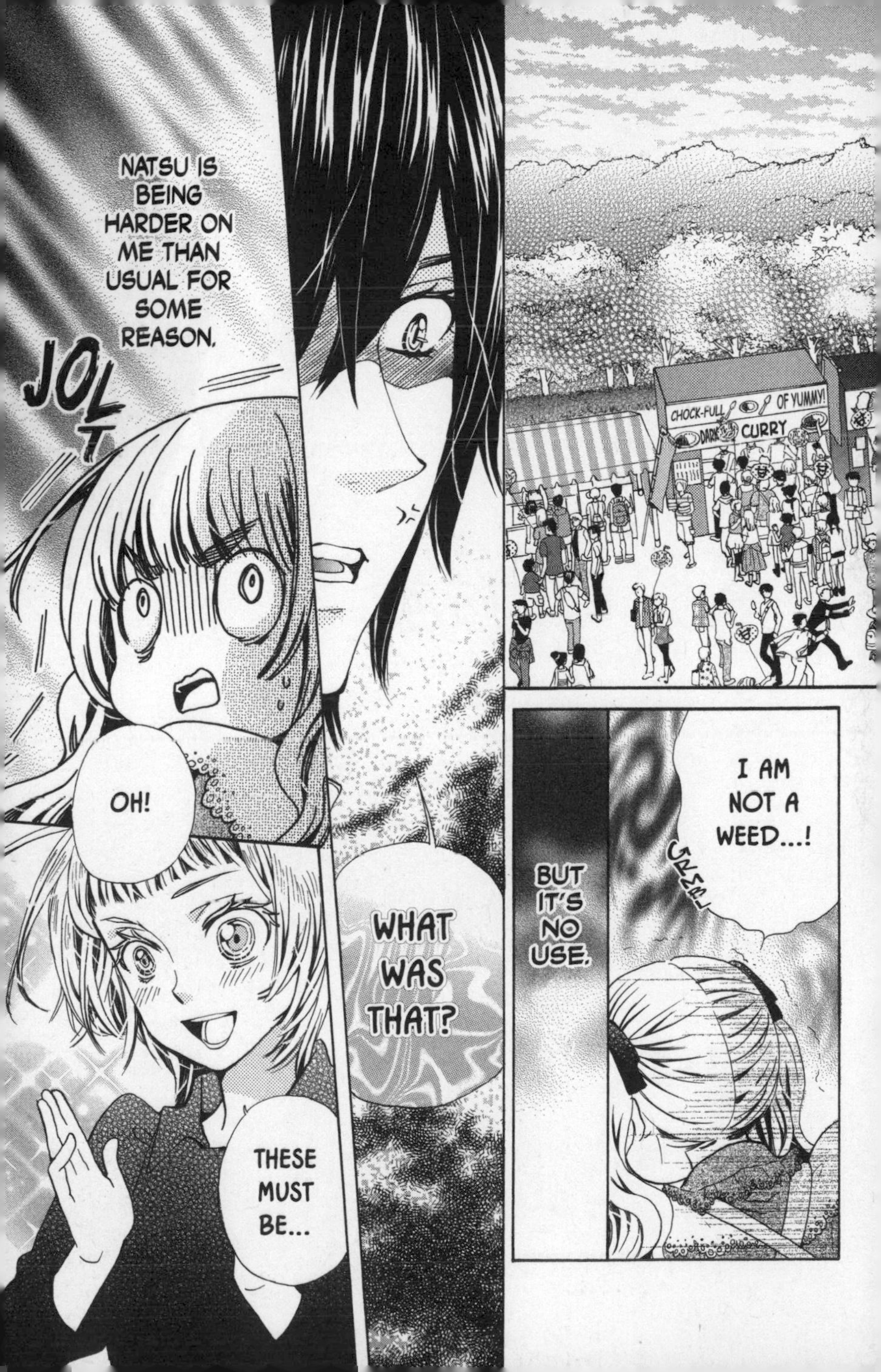
CHOCK-FULL OF YUMMY!
DARK CURRY
I AM NOT A WEED...!
GRMBL
BUT IT'S NO USE.
WHAT WAS THAT?
NATSU IS BEING HARDER ON ME THAN USUAL FOR SOME REASON.
JOLT
OH!
THESE MUST BE...

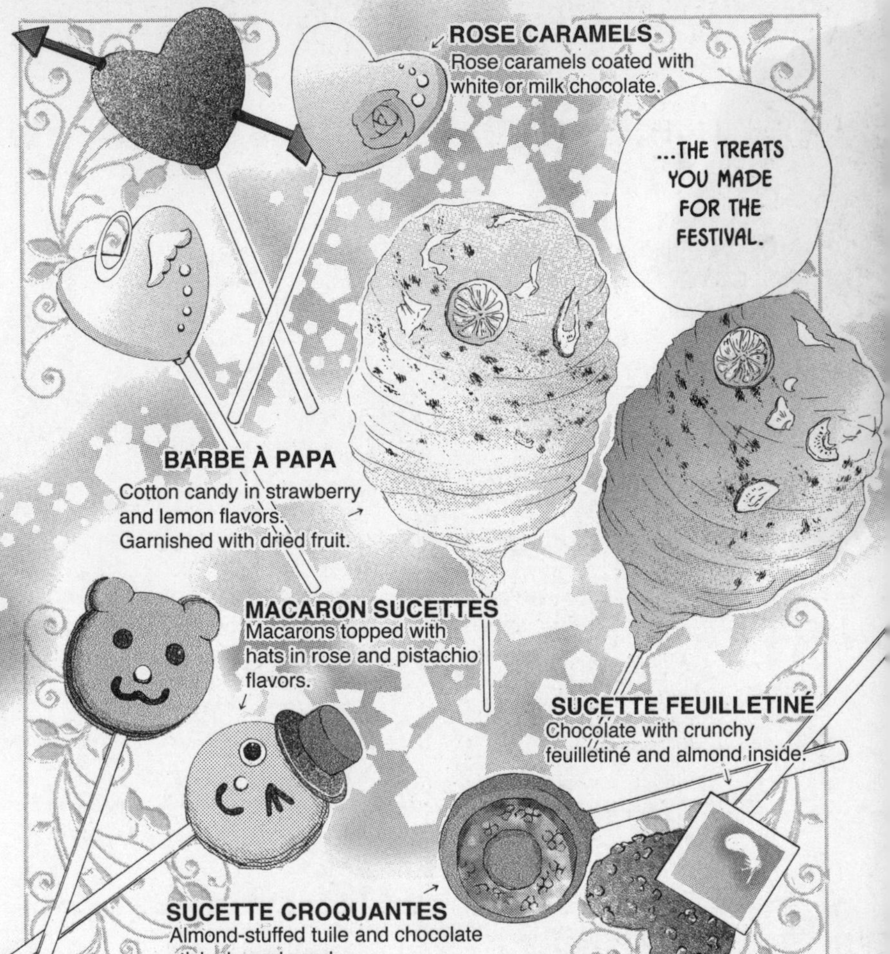
ROSE CARAMELS
Rose caramels coated with white or milk chocolate.
...THE TREATS YOU MADE FOR THE FESTIVAL.
BARBE À PAPA
Cotton candy in strawberry and lemon flavors. Garnished with dried fruit.
MACARON SUCETTES
Macarons topped with hats in rose and pistachio flavors.
SUCETTE FEUILLETINÉ
Chocolate with crunchy feuilletiné and almond inside.
SUCETTE CROQUANTES
Almond-stuffed tuile and chocolate stick-shaped candy.

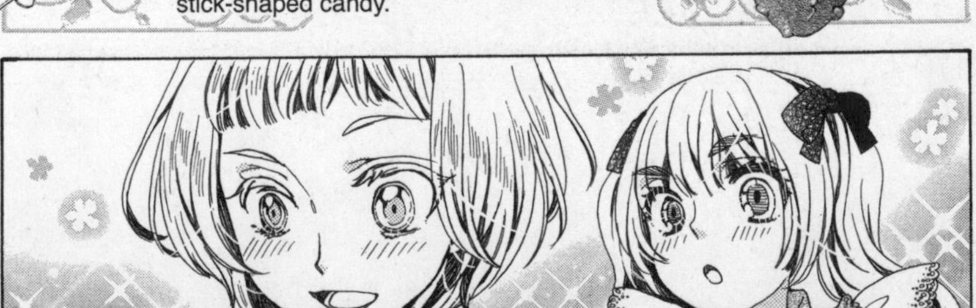

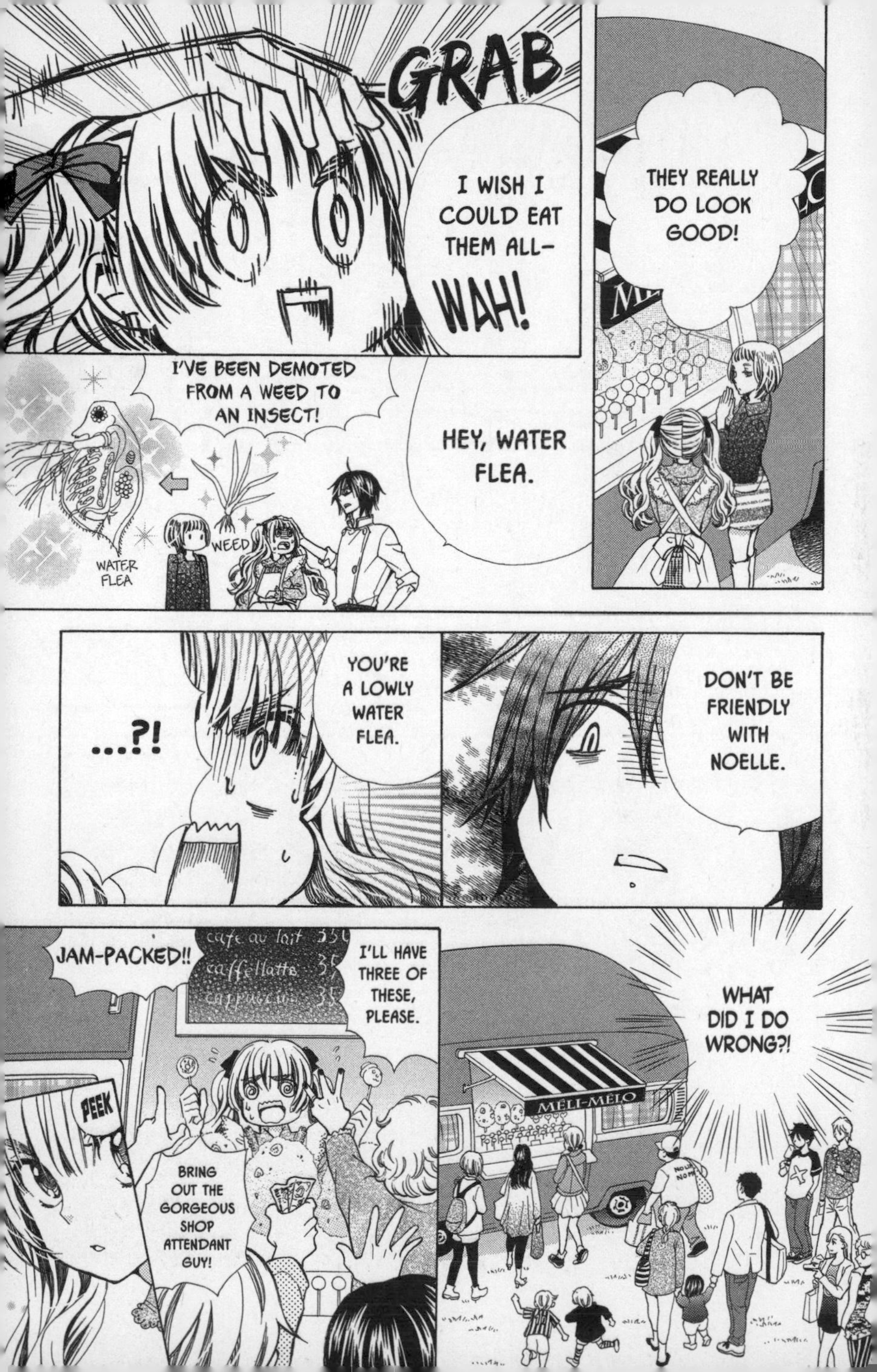
THEY REALLY DO LOOK GOOD!
GRAB
I WISH I COULD EAT THEM ALL—
WAH!
HEY, WATER FLEA.
I'VE BEEN DEMOTED FROM A WEED TO AN INSECT!
WEED
WATER FLEA
DON'T BE FRIENDLY WITH NOELLE.
YOU'RE A LOWLY WATER FLEA.
...?!
WHAT DID I DO WRONG?!
MÉLI-MÉLO
I'LL HAVE THREE OF THESE, PLEASE.
JAM-PACKED!!
PEEK
BRING OUT THE GORGEOUS SHOP ATTENDANT GUY!

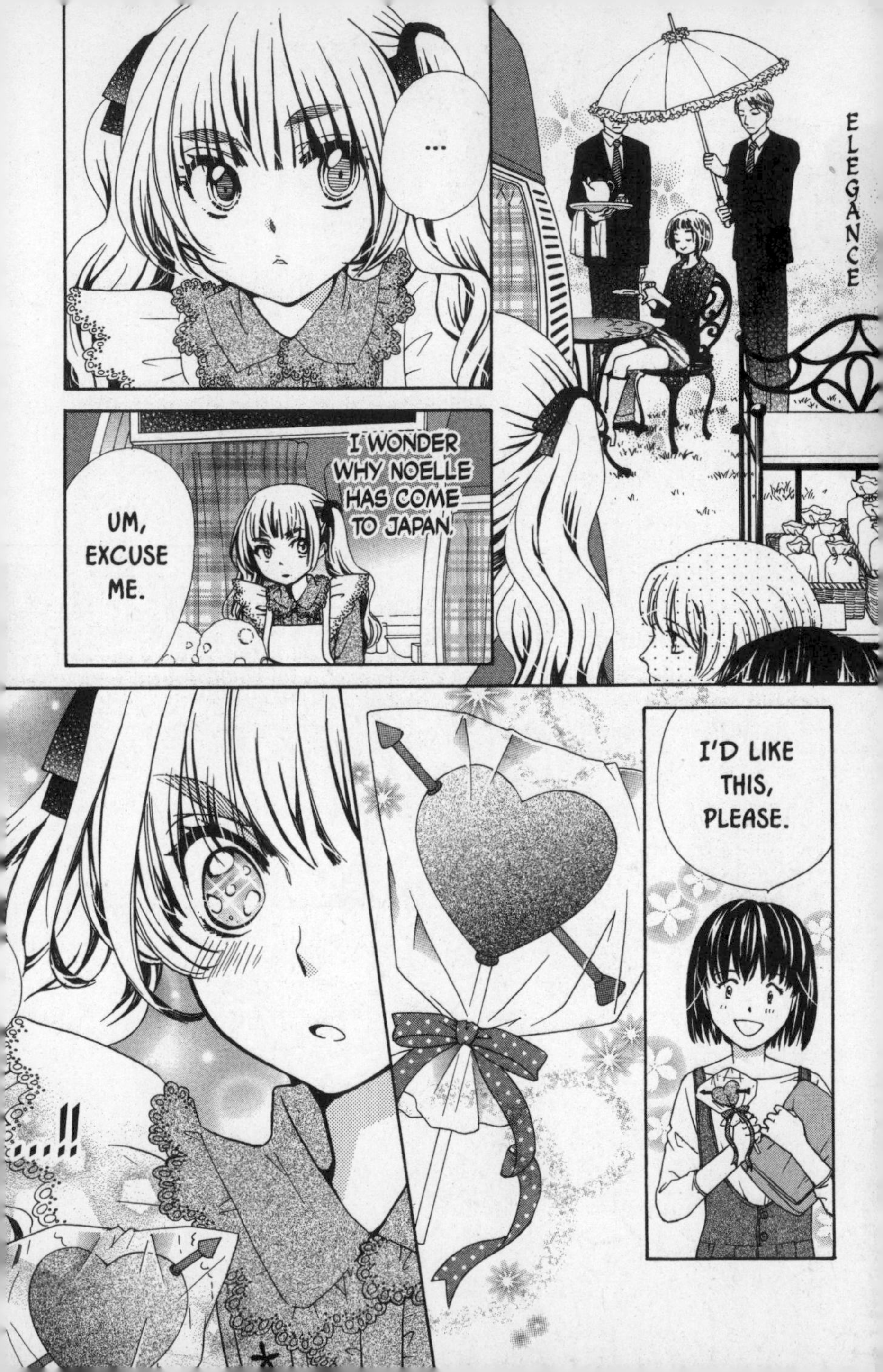
ELEGANCE
...
I WONDER WHY NOELLE HAS COME TO JAPAN.
UM, EXCUSE ME.
I'D LIKE THIS, PLEASE.
...!!

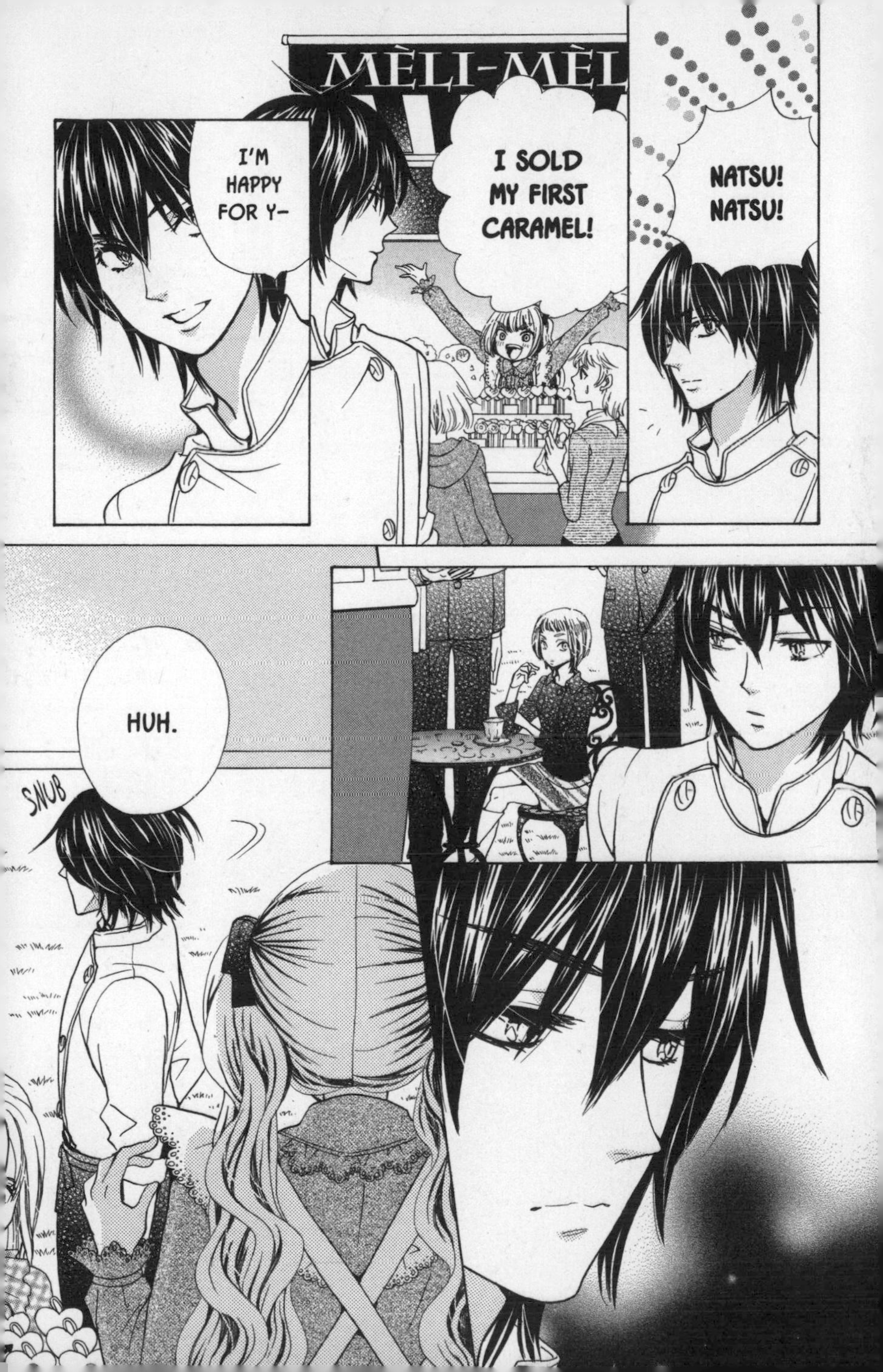
NATSU! NATSU!
MÈLI-MÈL
I SOLD MY FIRST CARAMEL!
I'M HAPPY FOR Y–
HUH.
SNUB

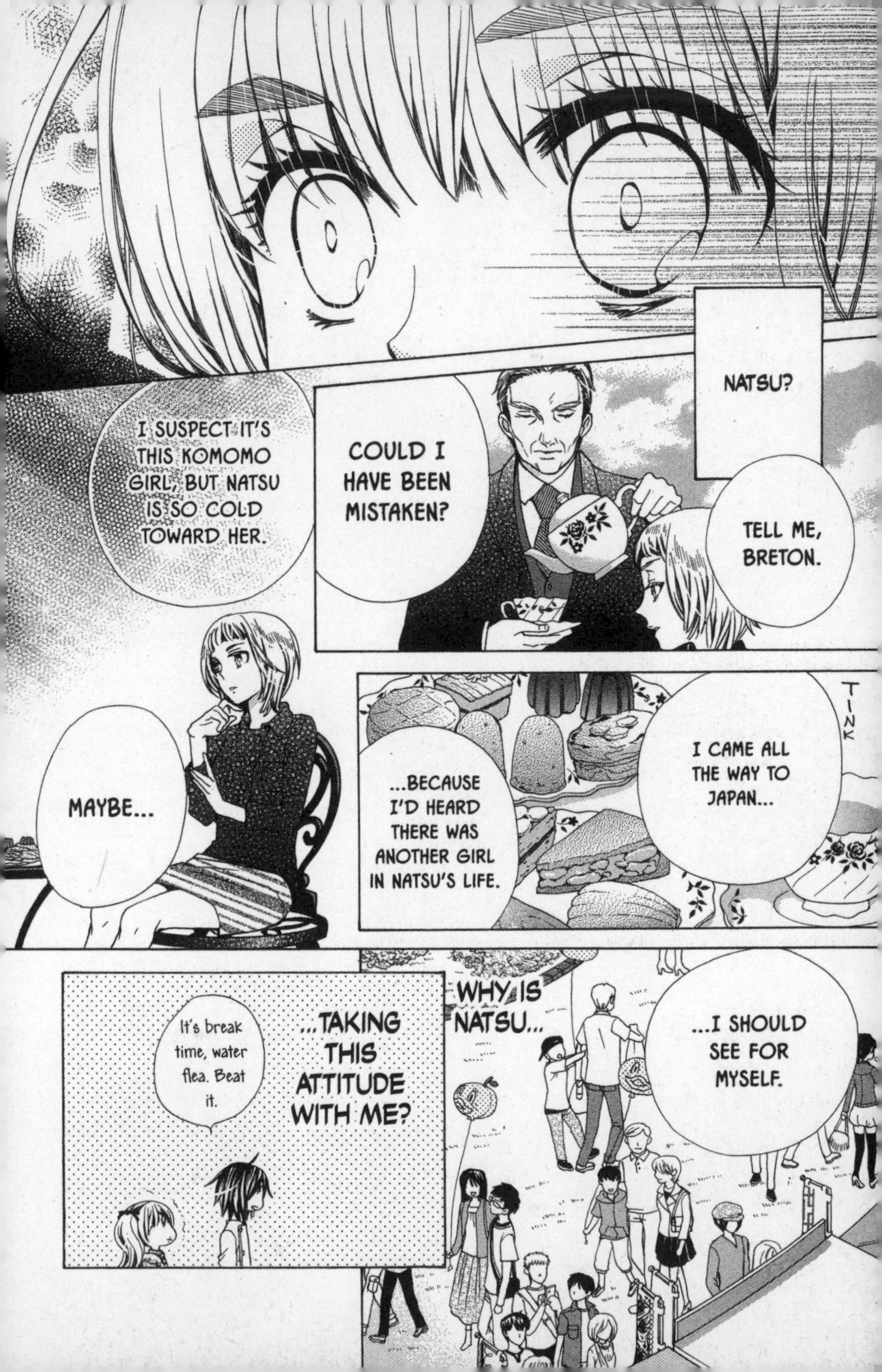
NATSU?
TELL ME, BRETON.
COULD I HAVE BEEN MISTAKEN?
I SUSPECT IT'S THIS KOMOMO GIRL, BUT NATSU IS SO COLD TOWARD HER.
TINK
I CAME ALL THE WAY TO JAPAN...
...BECAUSE I'D HEARD THERE WAS ANOTHER GIRL IN NATSU'S LIFE.
MAYBE...
...I SHOULD SEE FOR MYSELF.
WHY IS NATSU...
...TAKING THIS ATTITUDE WITH ME?
It's break time, water flea. Beat it.

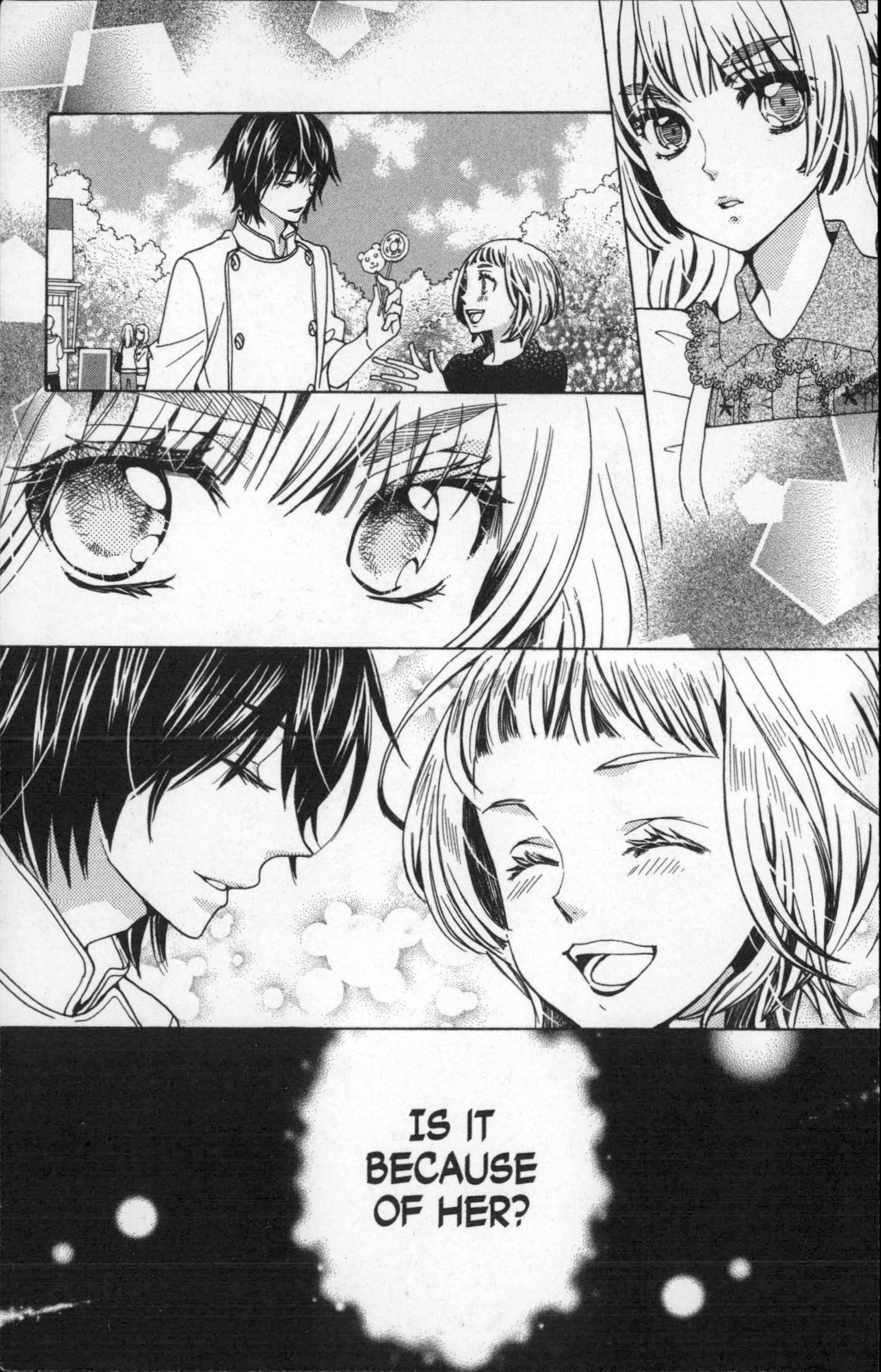
IS IT BECAUSE OF HER?

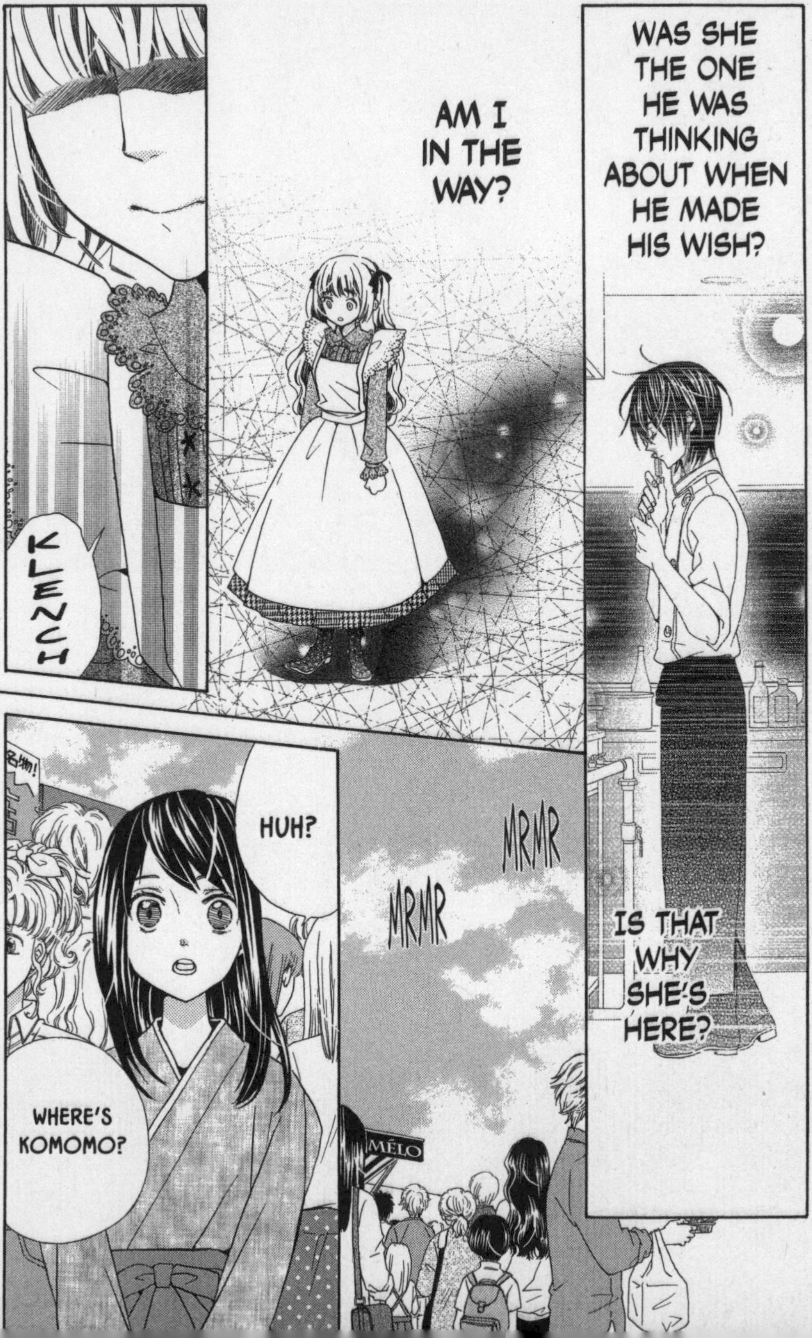
WAS SHE THE ONE HE WAS THINKING ABOUT WHEN HE MADE HIS WISH?
IS THAT WHY SHE'S HERE?
AM I IN THE WAY?
KLENCH
MRMR
MRMR
MÉLO
HUH?
WHERE'S KOMOMO?

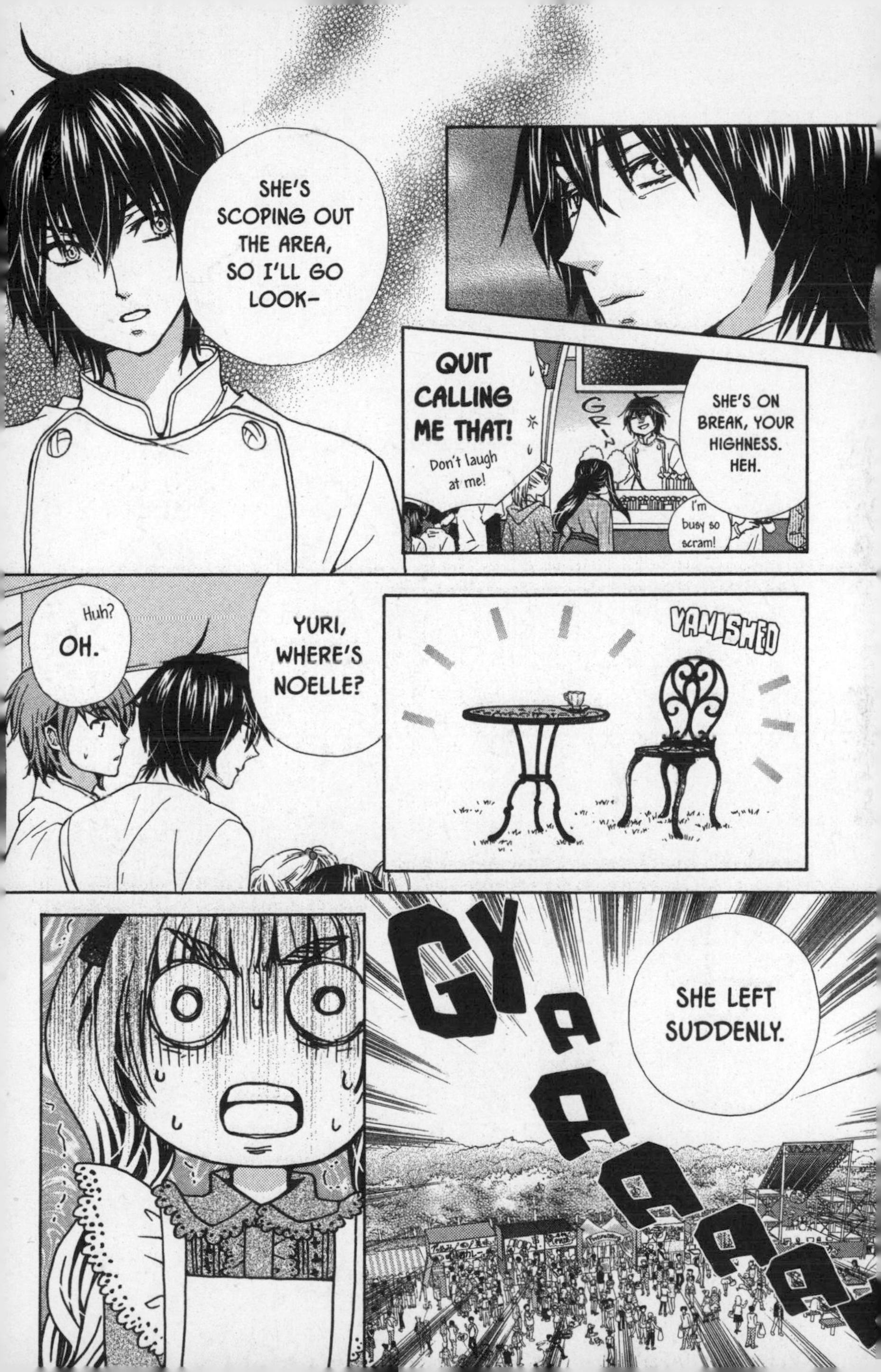
SHE'S ON BREAK, YOUR HIGHNESS. HEH.
I'm busy so scram!
GRIN
QUIT CALLING ME THAT!
Don't laugh at me!
SHE'S SCOPING OUT THE AREA, SO I'LL GO LOOK–
VANISHED
YURI, WHERE'S NOELLE?
Huh?
OH.
SHE LEFT SUDDENLY.
GYAAAAAA

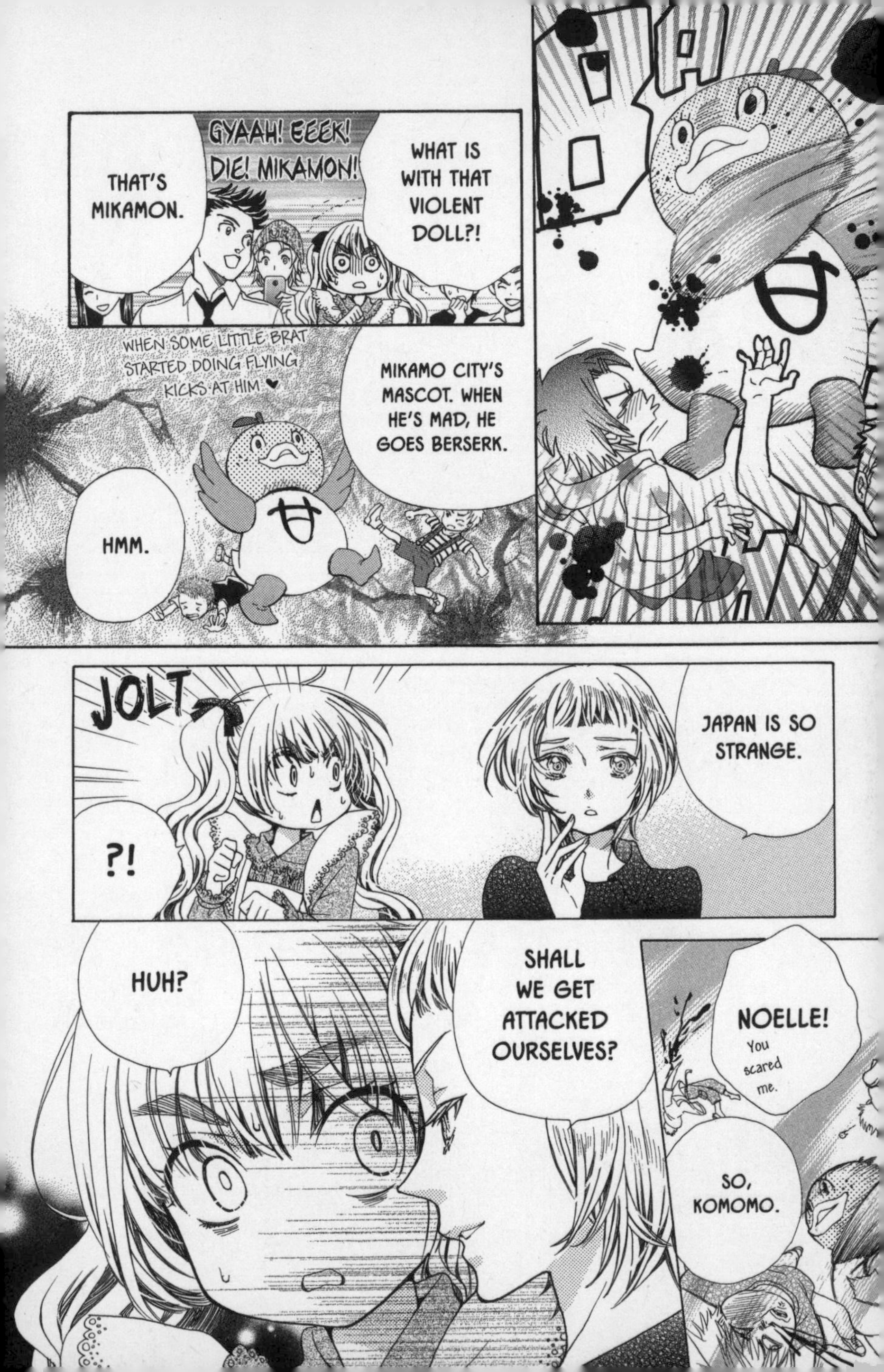
WHAT IS WITH THAT VIOLENT DOLL?!
GYAAH! EEEK! DIE! MIKAMON!
THAT'S MIKAMON.
MIKAMO CITY'S MASCOT. WHEN HE'S MAD, HE GOES BERSERK.
WHEN SOME LITTLE BRAT STARTED DOING FLYING KICKS AT HIM ♥
HMM.
JAPAN IS SO STRANGE.
JOLT
?!
NOELLE!
You scared me.
SO, KOMOMO.
SHALL WE GET ATTACKED OURSELVES?
HUH?

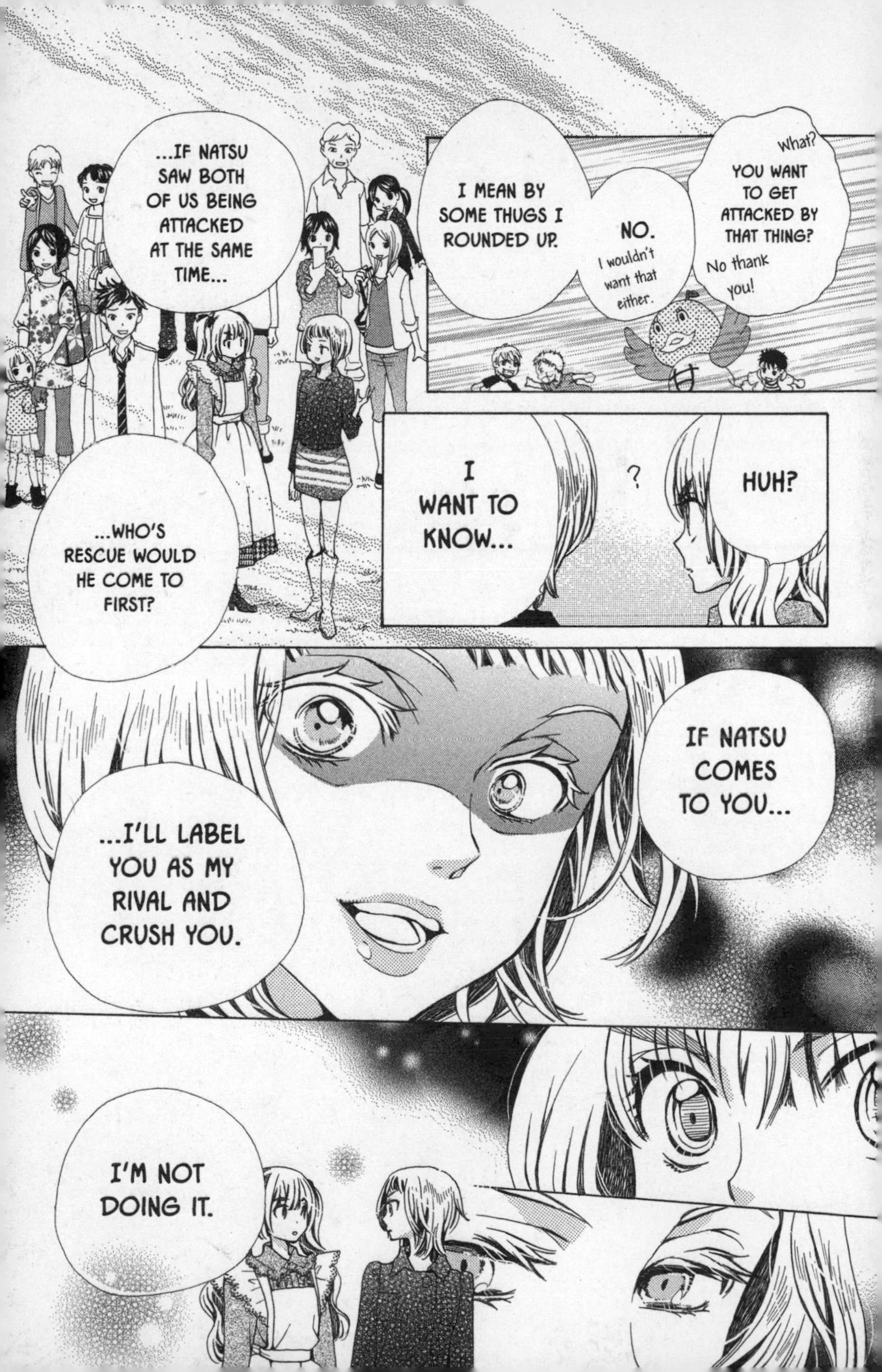
What?
YOU WANT TO GET ATTACKED BY THAT THING?
No thank you!
NO.
I wouldn't want that either.
I MEAN BY SOME THUGS I ROUNDED UP.
HUH?
?
I WANT TO KNOW...
...IF NATSU SAW BOTH OF US BEING ATTACKED AT THE SAME TIME...
...WHO'S RESCUE WOULD HE COME TO FIRST?
IF NATSU COMES TO YOU...
...I'LL LABEL YOU AS MY RIVAL AND CRUSH YOU.
I'M NOT DOING IT.

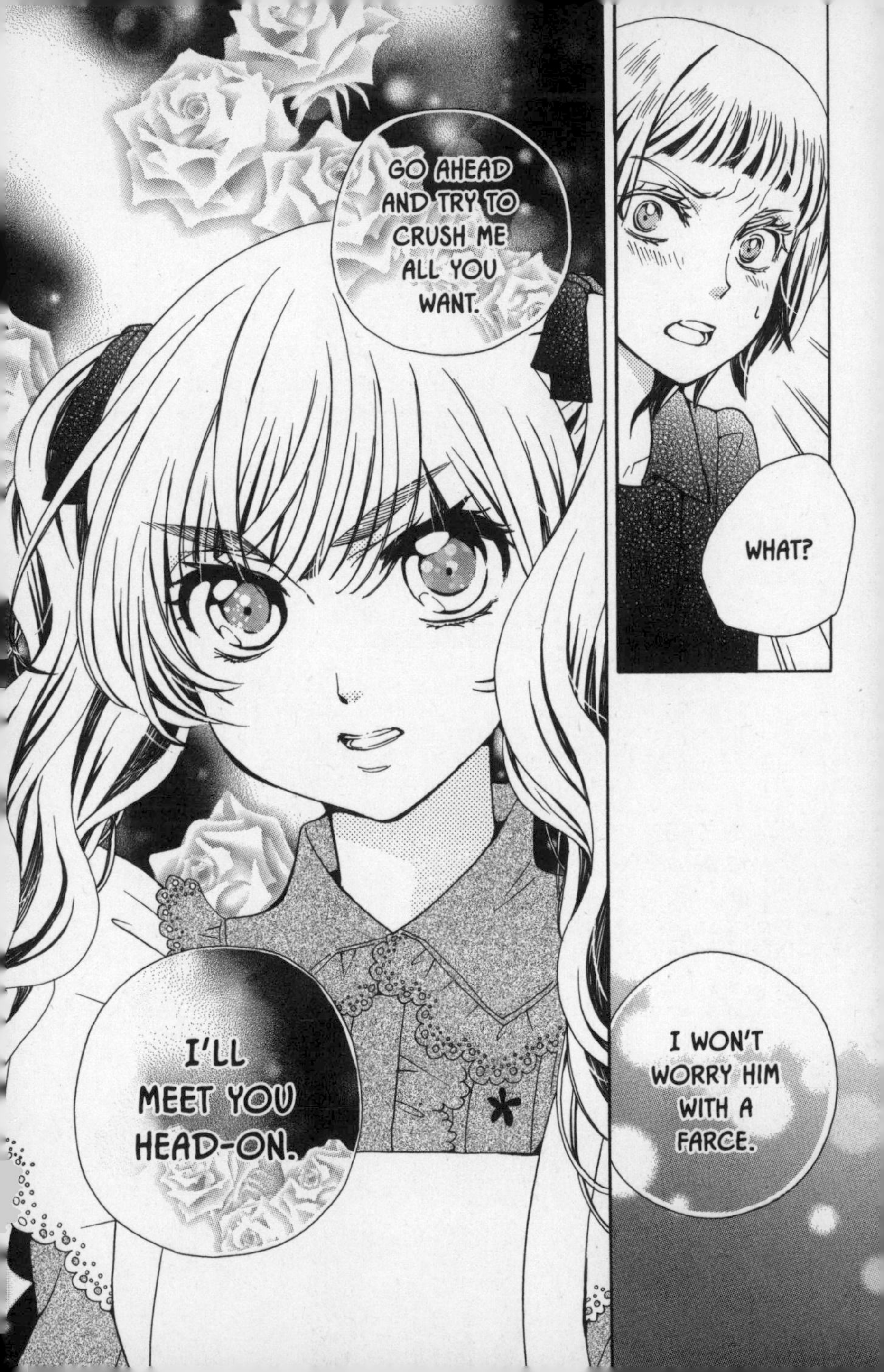
WHAT?
I WON'T WORRY HIM WITH A FARCE.
GO AHEAD AND TRY TO CRUSH ME ALL YOU WANT.
I'LL MEET YOU HEAD-ON.

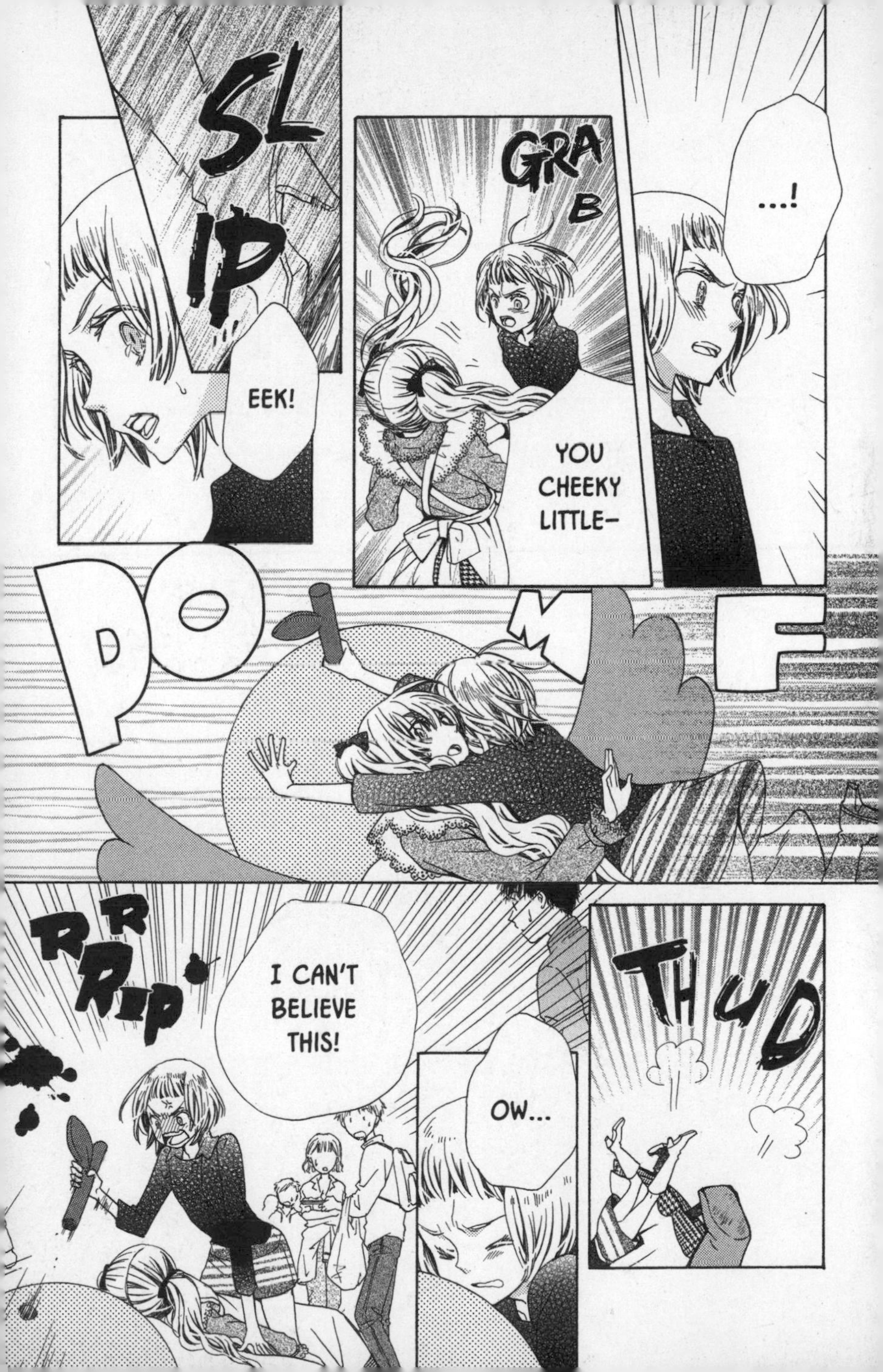
...!
GRAB
YOU CHEEKY LITTLE—
SLIP
EEK!
POMF
THUD
OW...
RRRIP
I CAN'T BELIEVE THIS!

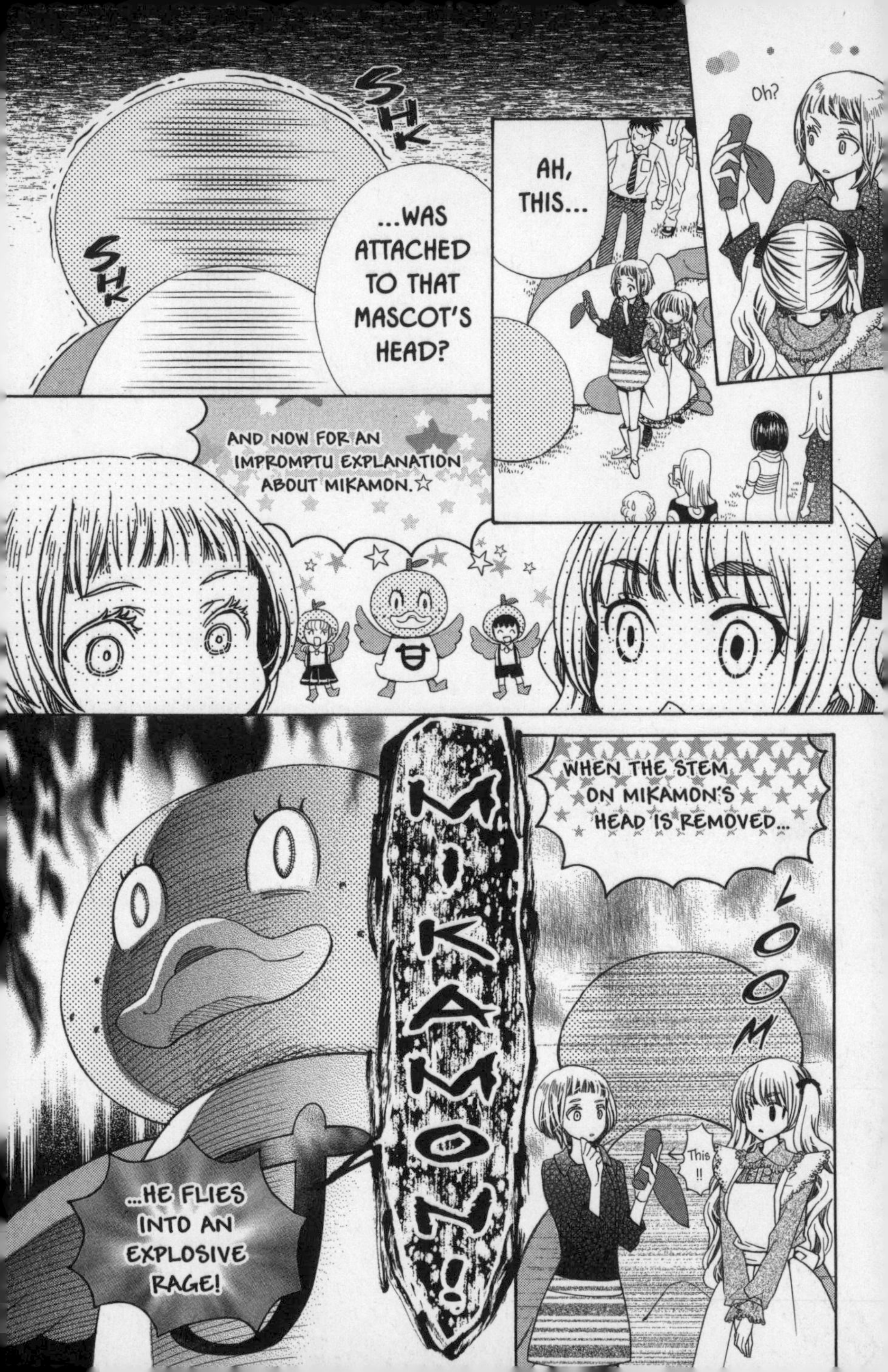
Oh?
AH, THIS...
SHK
SHK
...WAS ATTACHED TO THAT MASCOT'S HEAD?
AND NOW FOR AN IMPROMPTU EXPLANATION ABOUT MIKAMON.☆
WHEN THE STEM ON MIKAMON'S HEAD IS REMOVED...
VOOOM
This !!
MIKAMON!!
...HE FLIES INTO AN EXPLOSIVE RAGE!

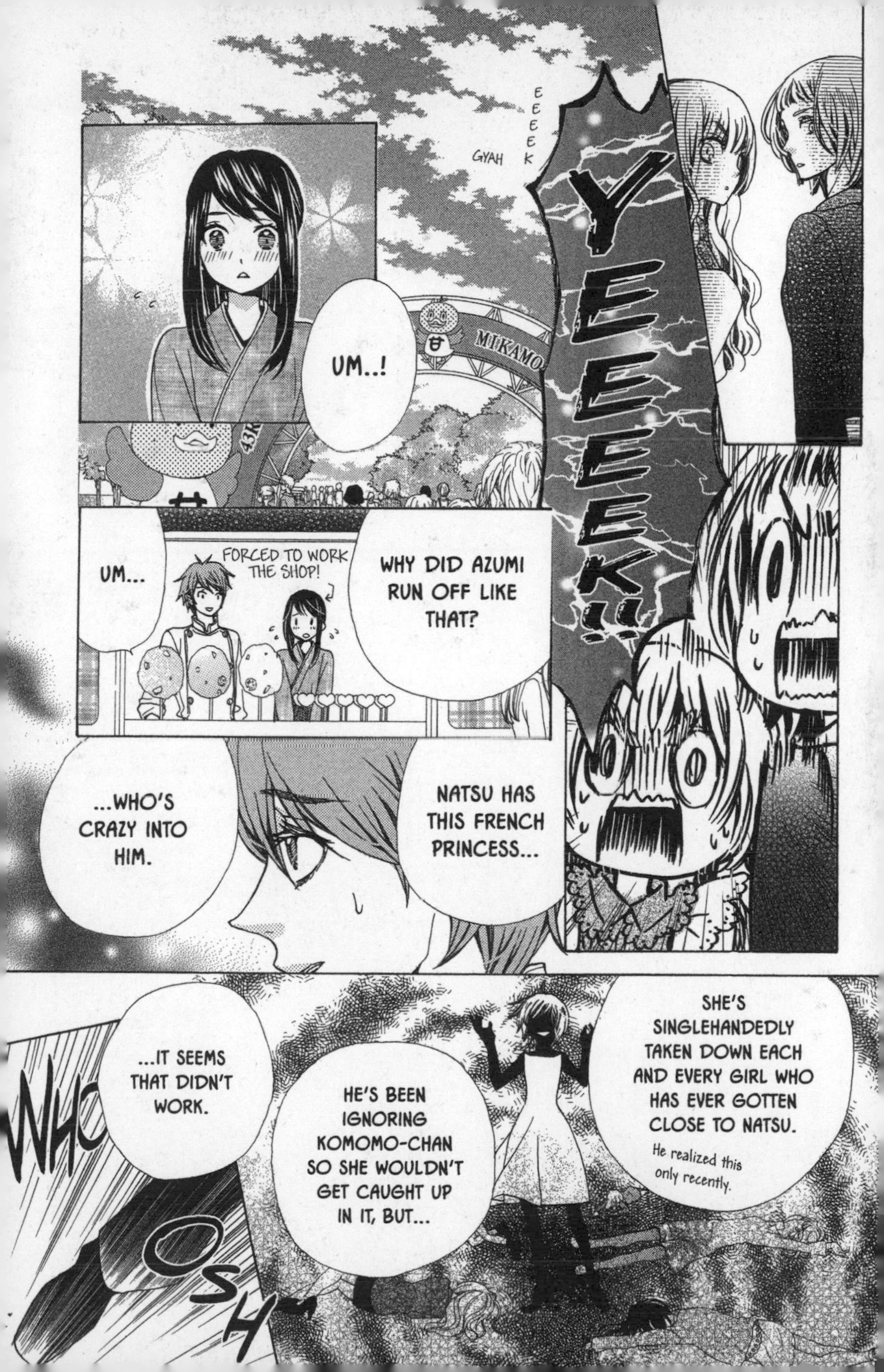
YEEEEEEK!!
EEEEK
GYAH
UM..!
WHY DID AZUMI RUN OFF LIKE THAT?
UM...
FORCED TO WORK THE SHOP!
NATSU HAS THIS FRENCH PRINCESS...
...WHO'S CRAZY INTO HIM.
SHE'S SINGLEHANDEDLY TAKEN DOWN EACH AND EVERY GIRL WHO HAS EVER GOTTEN CLOSE TO NATSU.
He realized this only recently.
HE'S BEEN IGNORING KOMOMO-CHAN SO SHE WOULDN'T GET CAUGHT UP IN IT, BUT...
...IT SEEMS THAT DIDN'T WORK.
WHOOSH

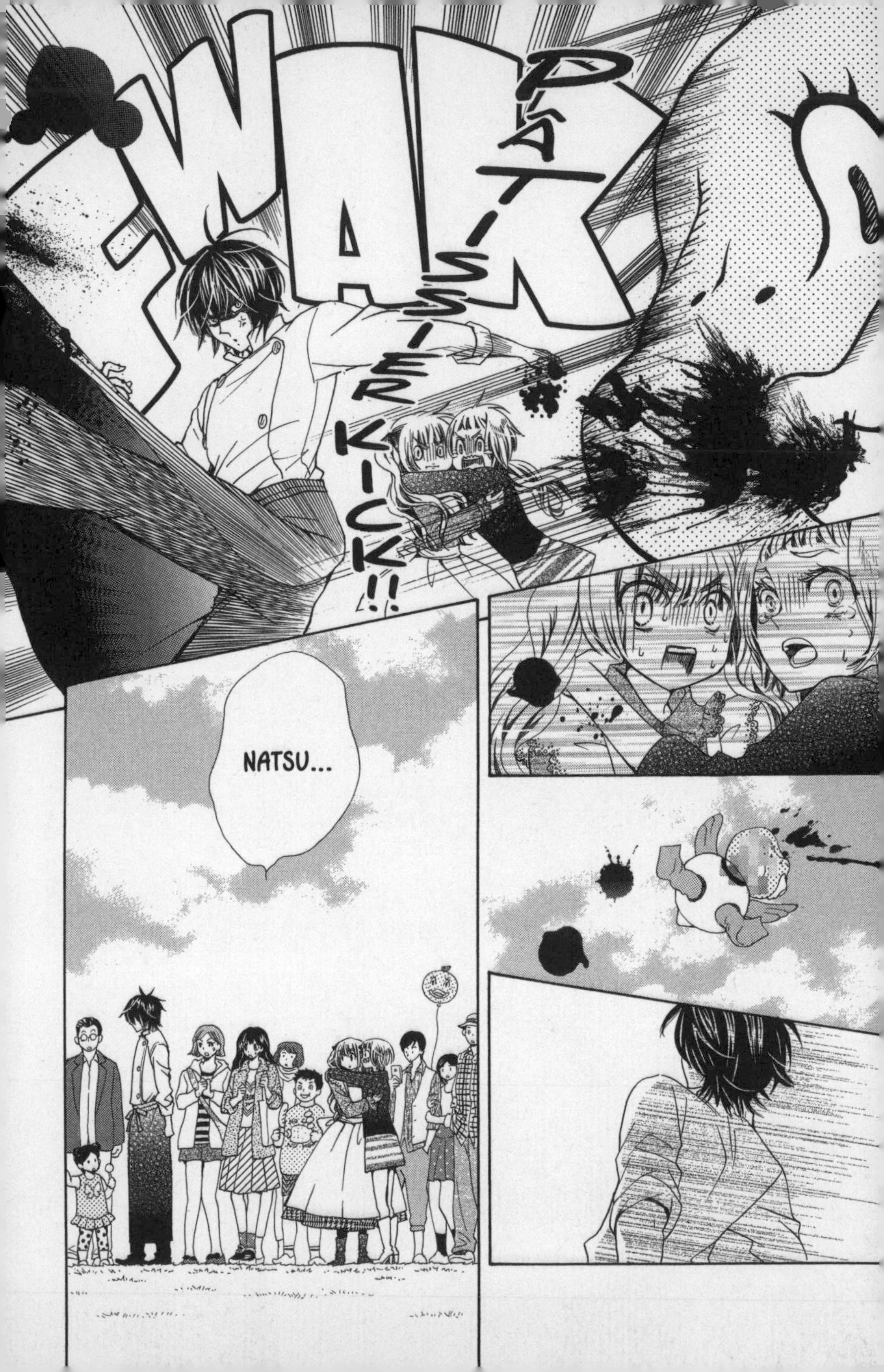
WAK
PATISSIER KICK!!
NATSU...

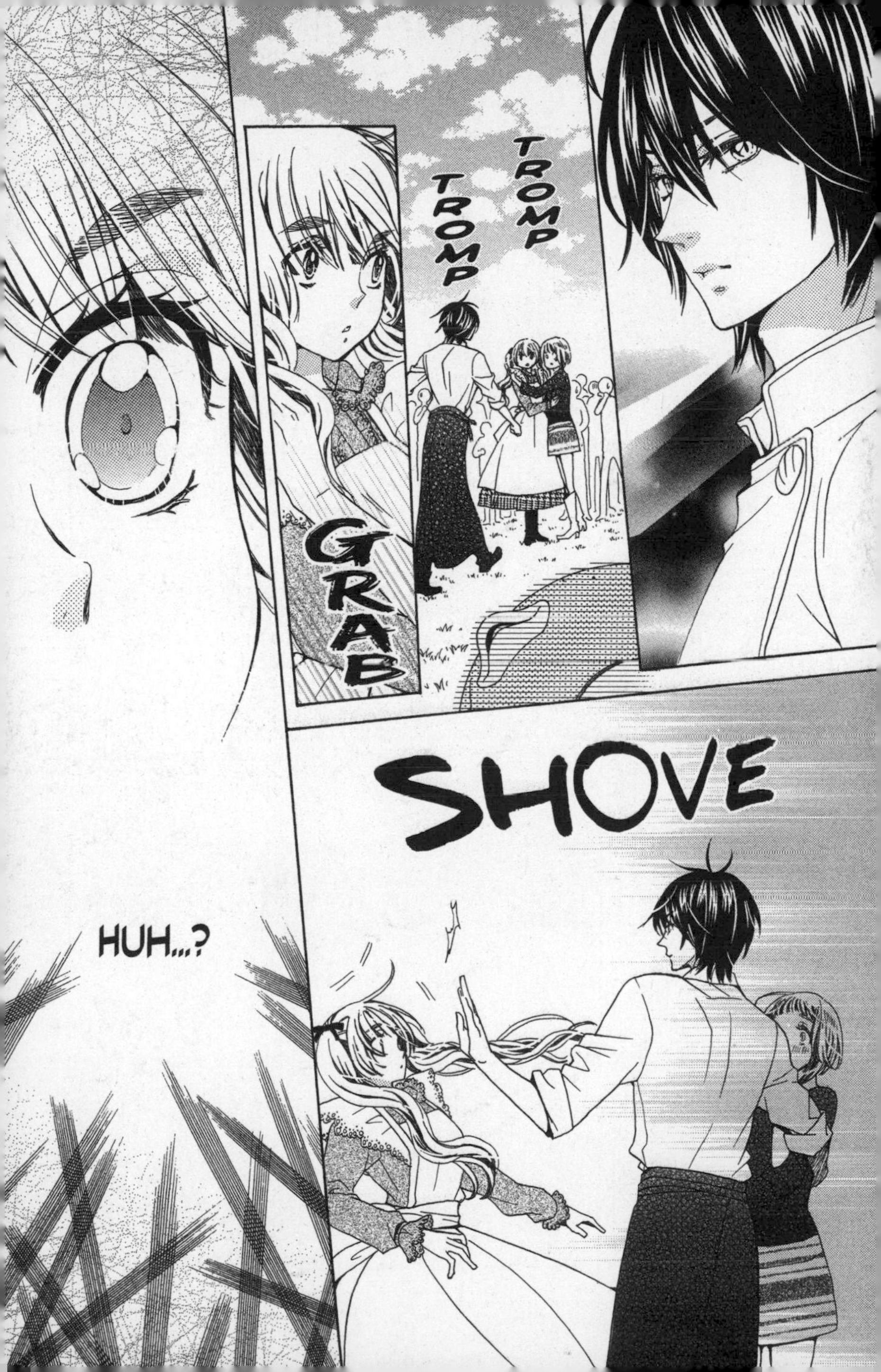
TROMP
TROMP
GRAB
SHOVE
HUH...?

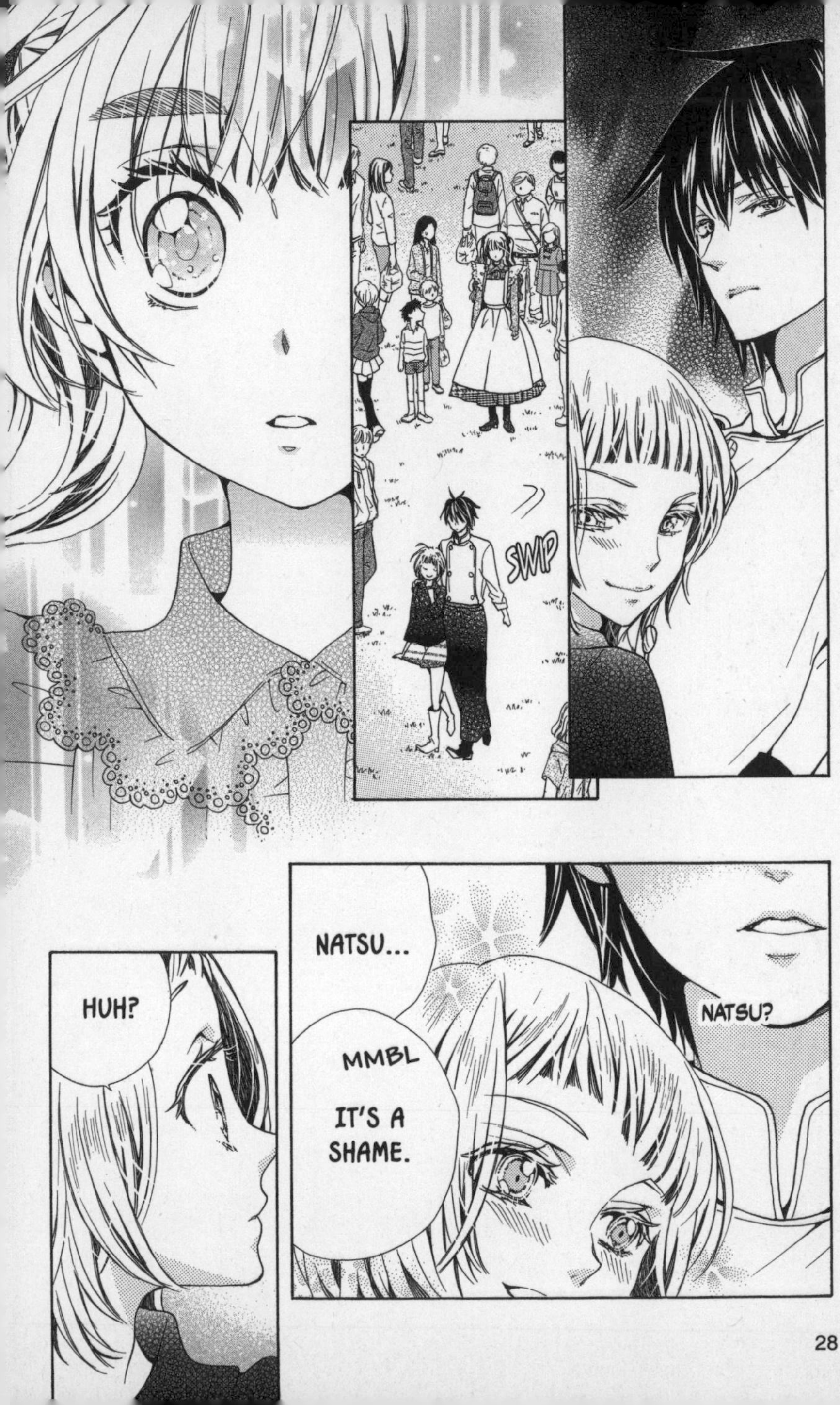
SWIP
NATSU...
NATSU?
MMBL
IT'S A SHAME.
HUH?

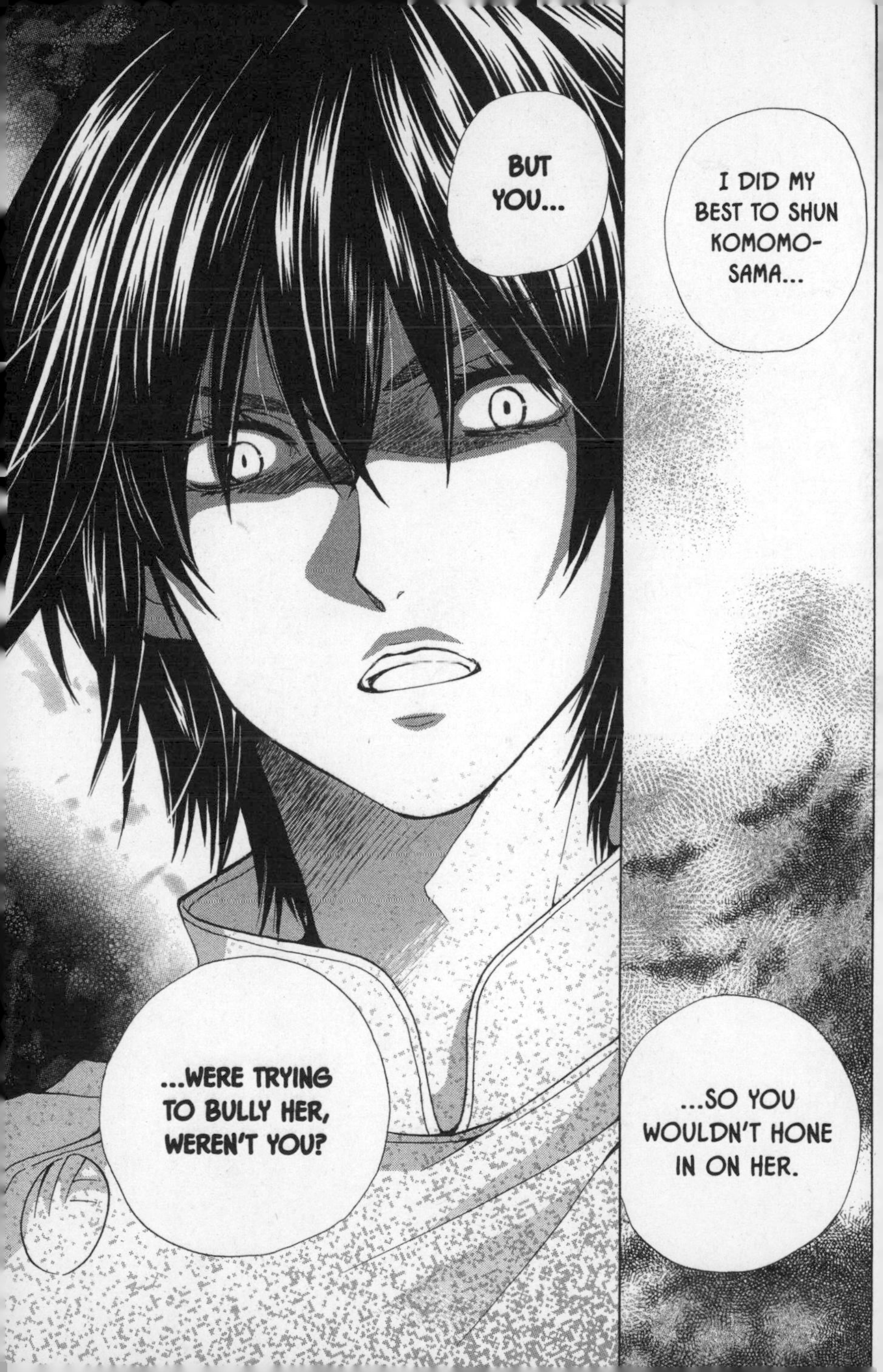
I DID MY BEST TO SHUN KOMOMO-SAMA...
...SO YOU WOULDN'T HONE IN ON HER.
BUT YOU...
...WERE TRYING TO BULLY HER, WEREN'T YOU?

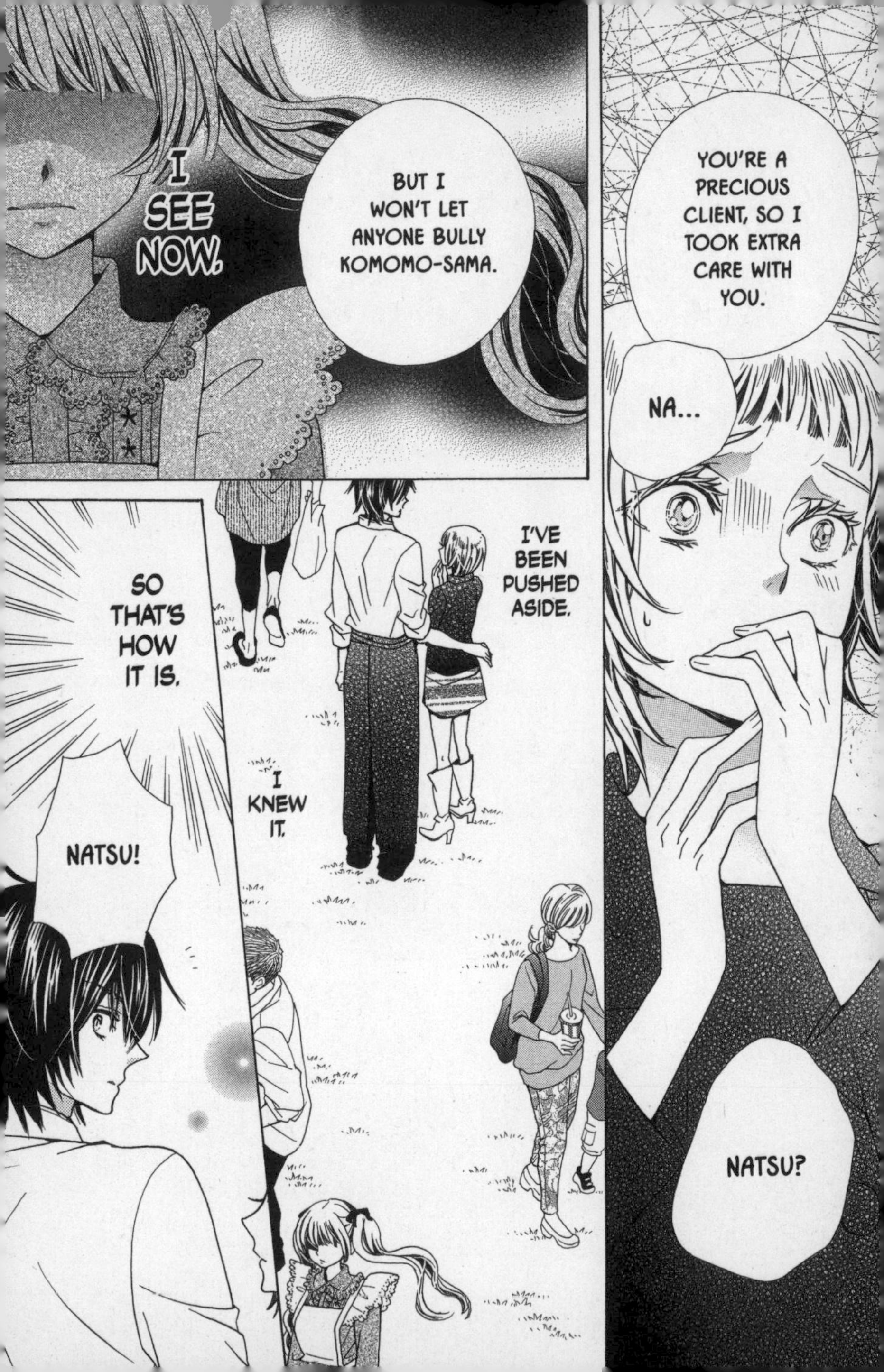
YOU'RE A PRECIOUS CLIENT, SO I TOOK EXTRA CARE WITH YOU.
NA...
NATSU?
BUT I WON'T LET ANYONE BULLY KOMOMO-SAMA.
I SEE NOW.
I'VE BEEN PUSHED ASIDE.
I KNEW IT.
SO THAT'S HOW IT IS.
NATSU!

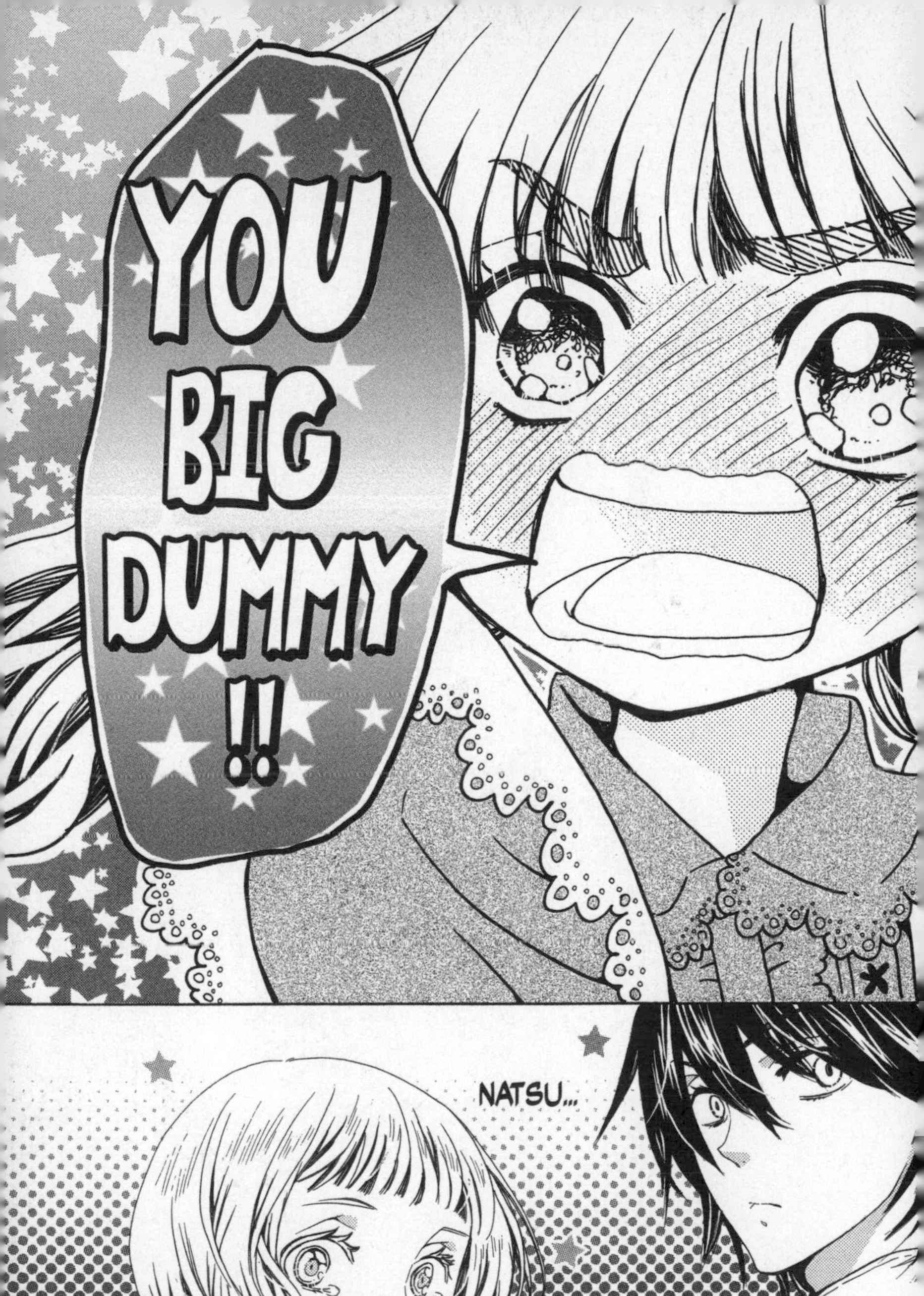
YOU BIG DUMMY!!
NATSU...

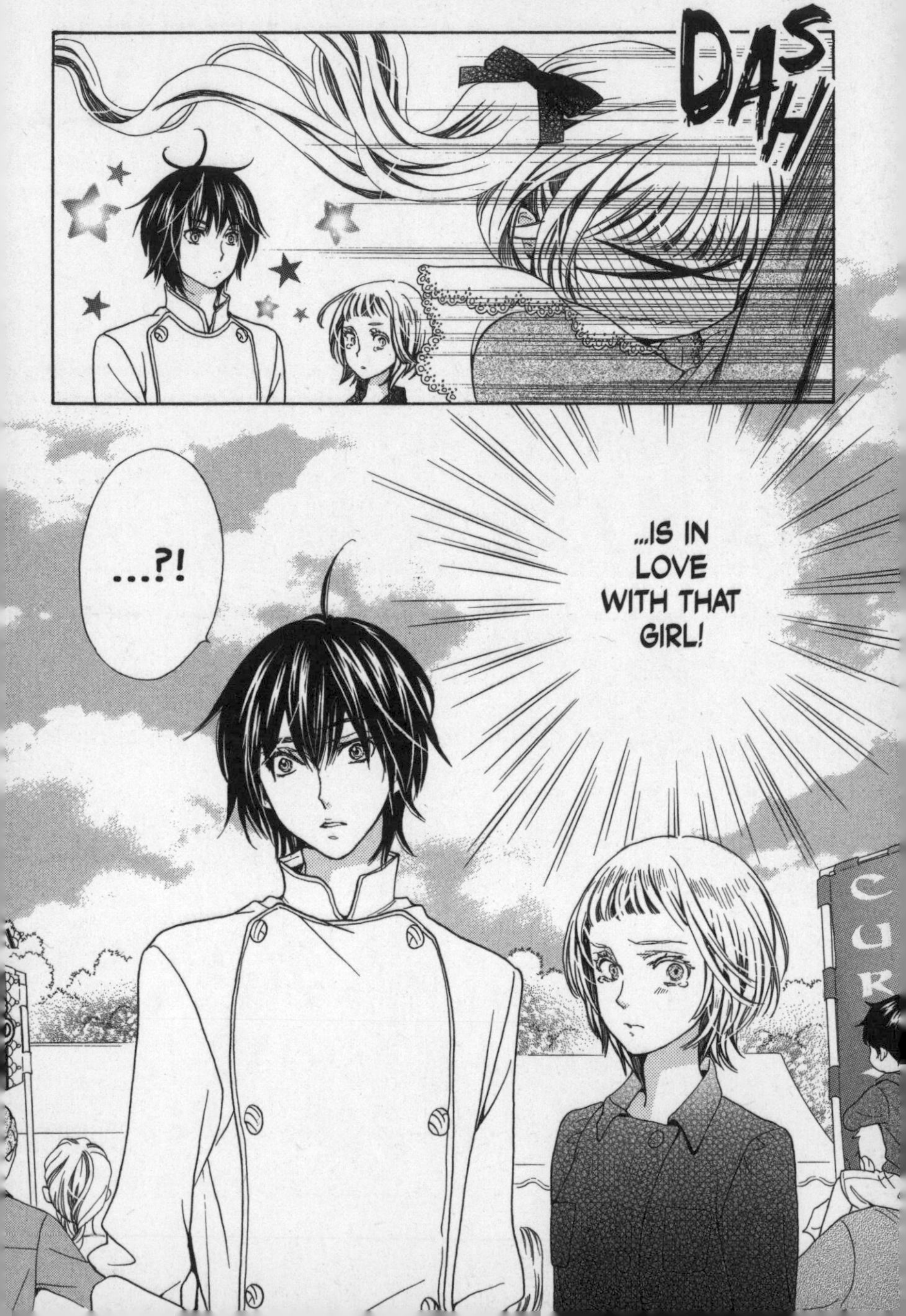
DASH
...IS IN LOVE WITH THAT GIRL!
...?!

CHAPTER 19

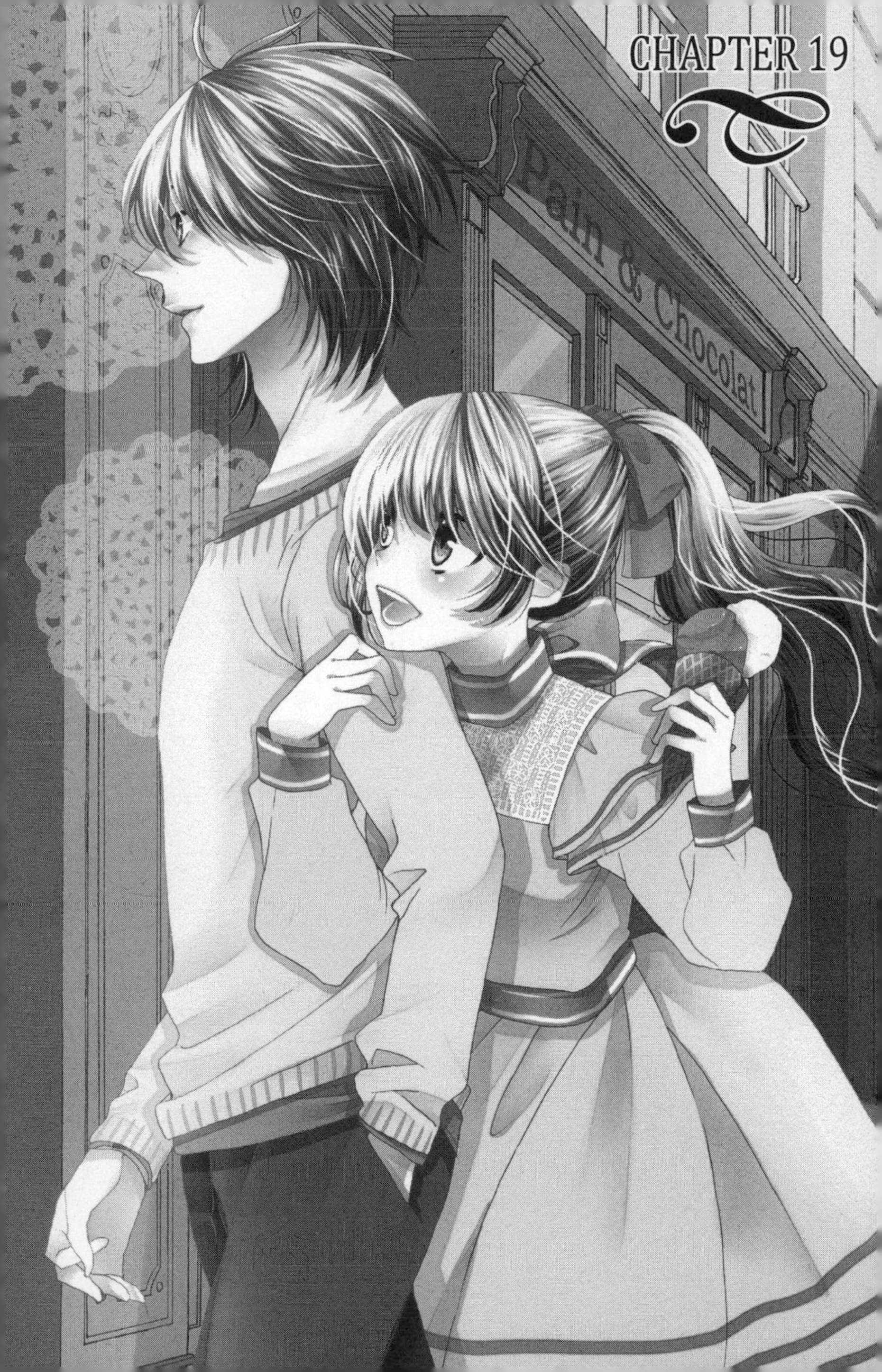
Pain & Chocolat

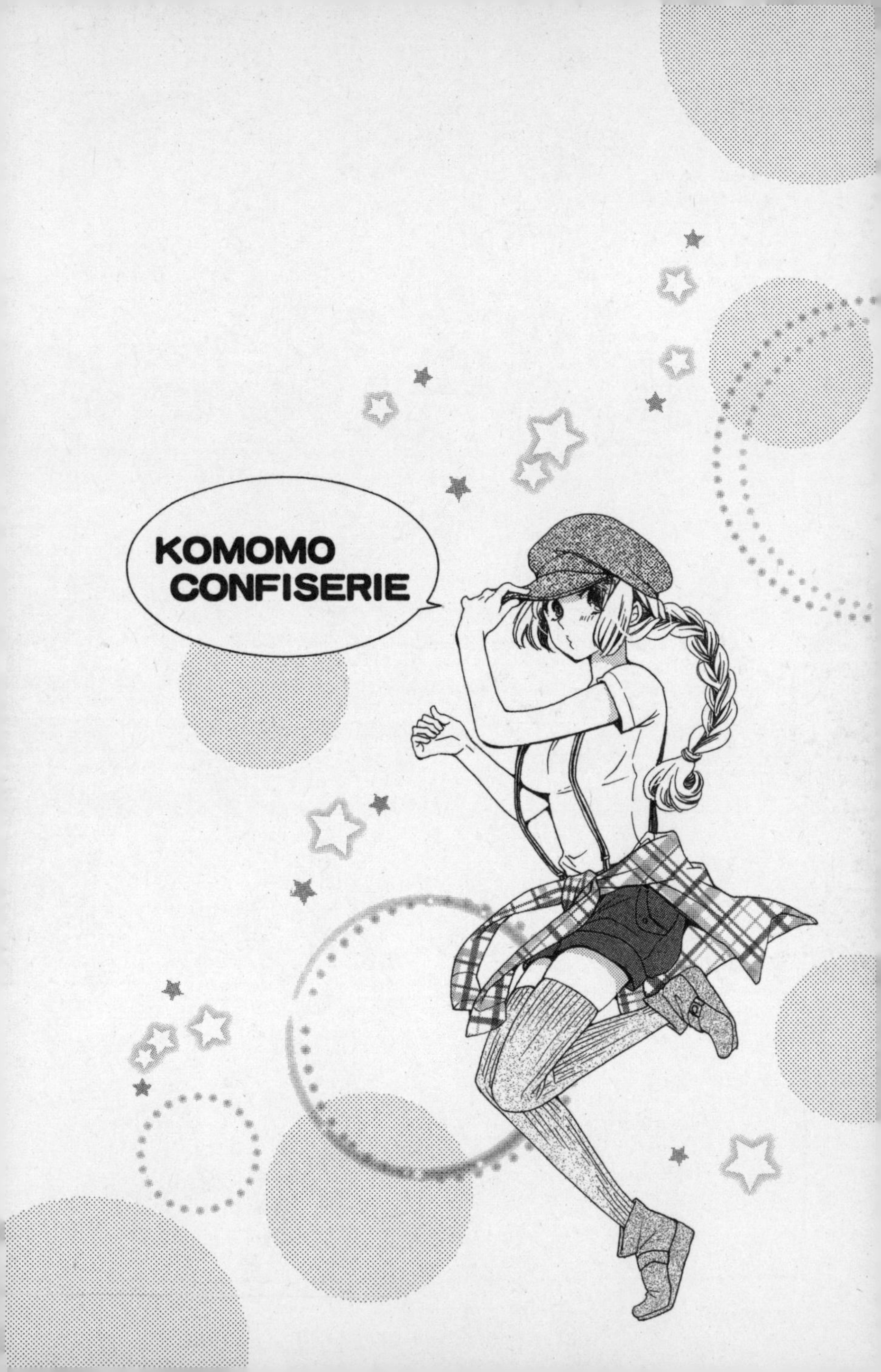
KOMOMO CONFISERIE

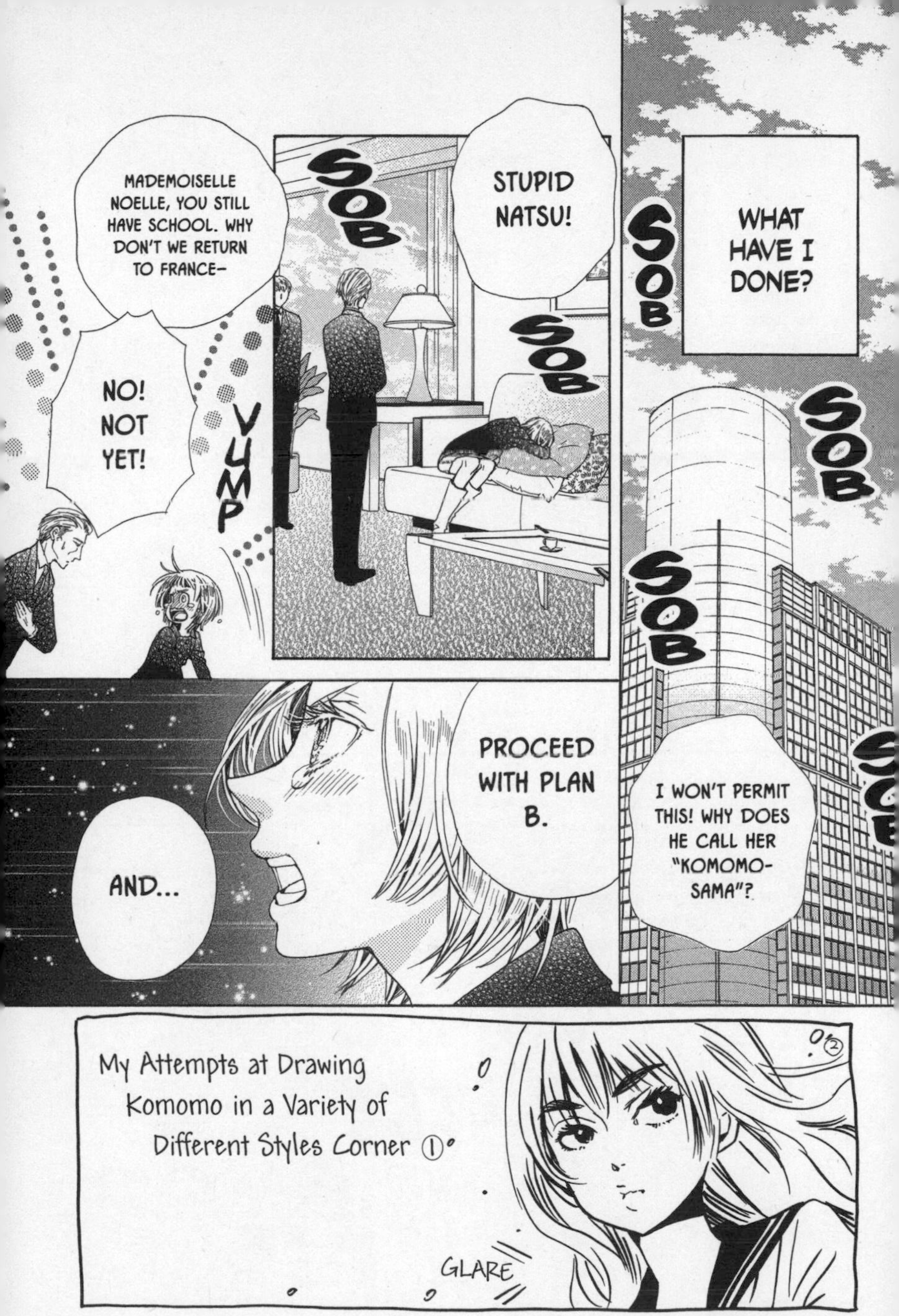
WHAT HAVE I DONE?
SOB
SOB
SOB
SOB
I WON'T PERMIT THIS! WHY DOES HE CALL HER "KOMOMO-SAMA"?
STUPID NATSU!
SOB
SOB
MADEMOISELLE NOELLE, YOU STILL HAVE SCHOOL. WHY DON'T WE RETURN TO FRANCE–
NO! NOT YET!
VUMP
PROCEED WITH PLAN B.
AND...
My Attempts at Drawing Komomo in a Variety of Different Styles Corner ①
GLARE

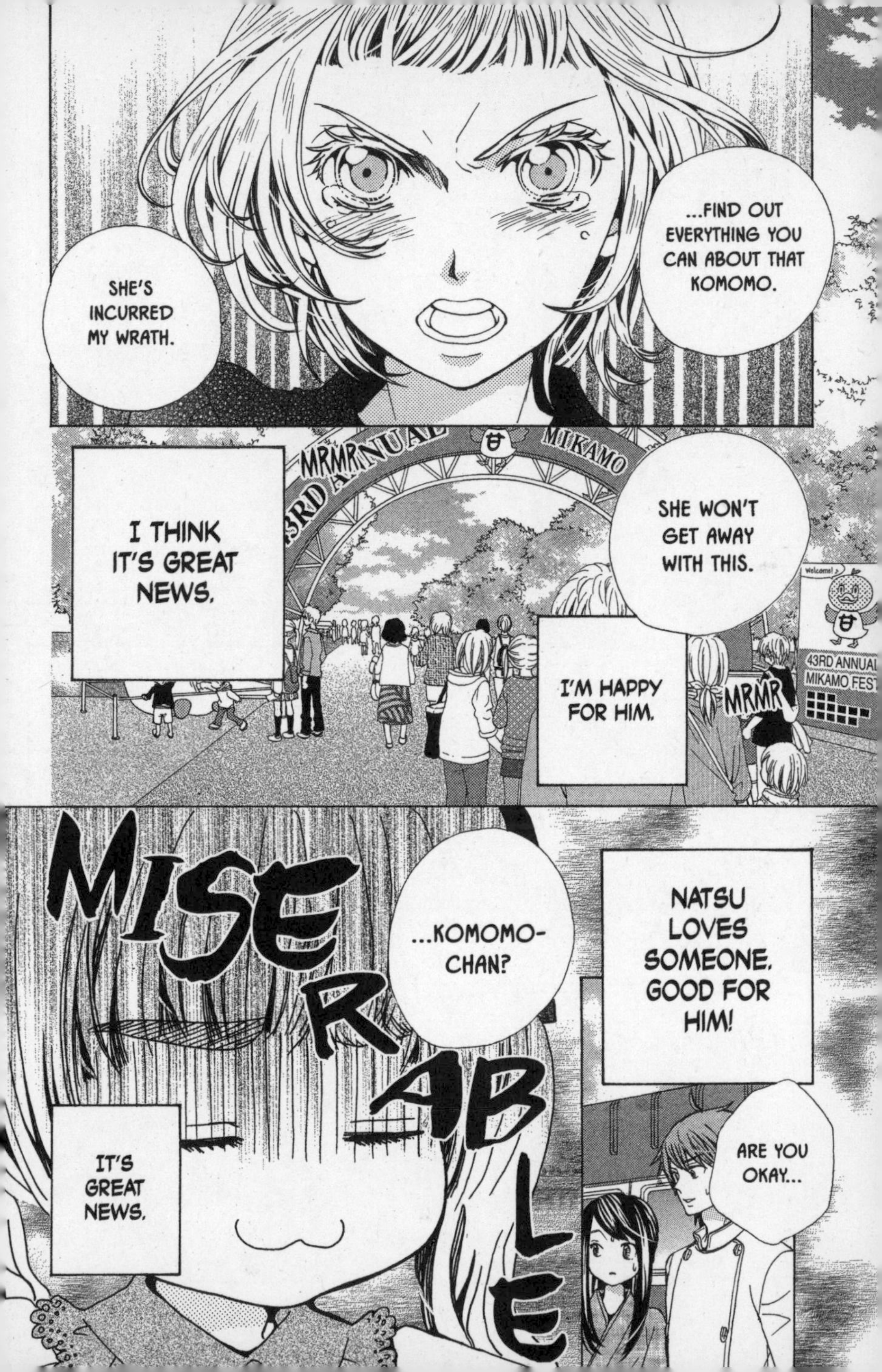
...FIND OUT EVERYTHING YOU CAN ABOUT THAT KOMOMO.
SHE'S INCURRED MY WRATH.
MIKAMO
43RD ANNUAL
MRMR
SHE WON'T GET AWAY WITH THIS.
I THINK IT'S GREAT NEWS.
Welcome!
43RD ANNUAL MIKAMO FEST
MRMR
I'M HAPPY FOR HIM.
NATSU LOVES SOMEONE. GOOD FOR HIM!
...KOMOMO-CHAN?
MISERABLE
ARE YOU OKAY...
IT'S GREAT NEWS.

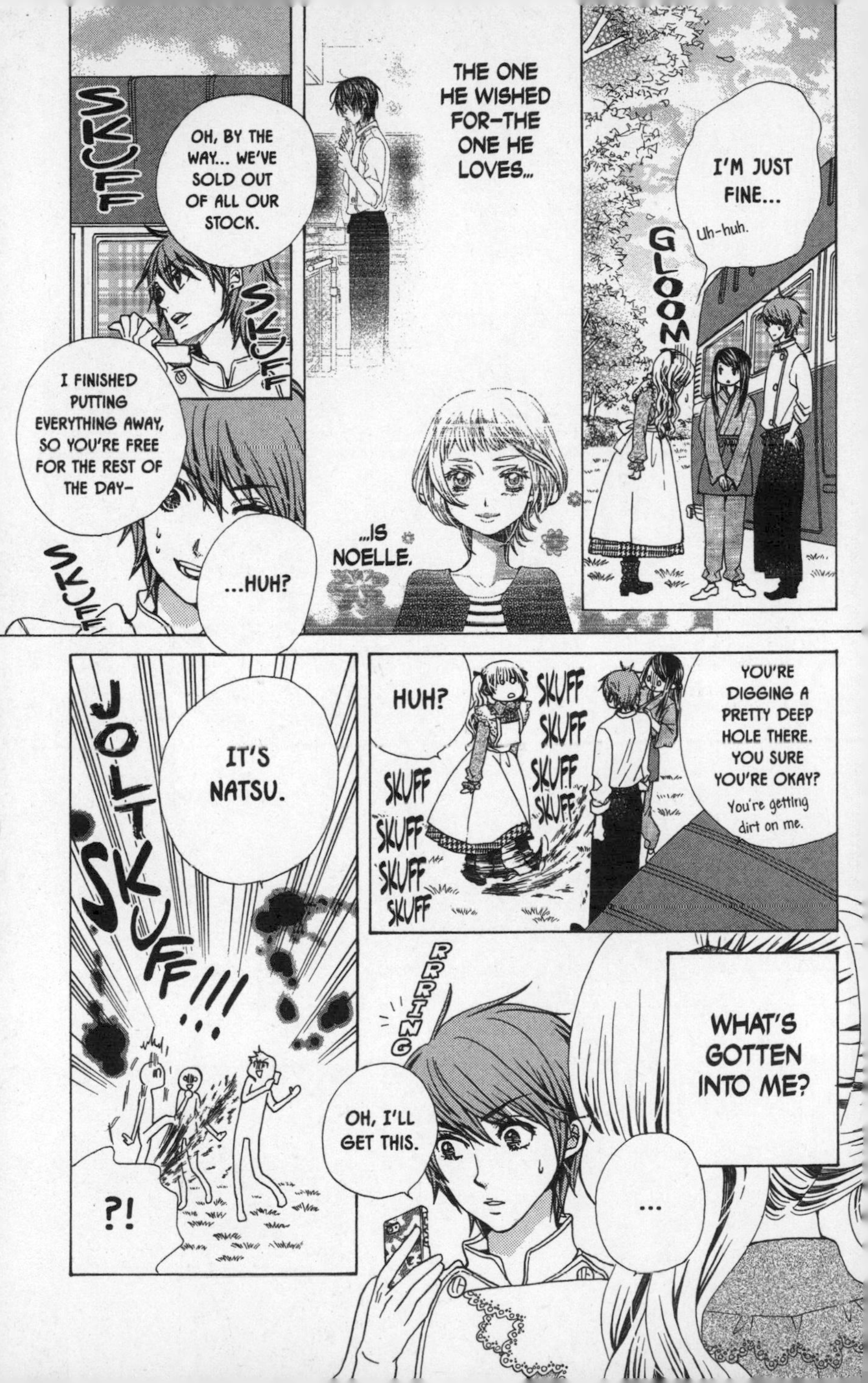
I'M JUST FINE...
Uh-huh.
GLOOM
THE ONE HE WISHED FOR—THE ONE HE LOVES...
...IS NOELLE.
SKUFF
OH, BY THE WAY... WE'VE SOLD OUT OF ALL OUR STOCK.
SKUFF
I FINISHED PUTTING EVERYTHING AWAY, SO YOU'RE FREE FOR THE REST OF THE DAY–
...HUH?
SKUFF
YOU'RE DIGGING A PRETTY DEEP HOLE THERE. YOU SURE YOU'RE OKAY?
You're getting dirt on me.
HUH?
SKUFF SKUFF SKUFF SKUFF
SKUFF SKUFF SKUFF SKUFF
WHAT'S GOTTEN INTO ME?
...
RRRING
OH, I'LL GET THIS.
IT'S NATSU.
JOLT
SKUFF!!!
?!

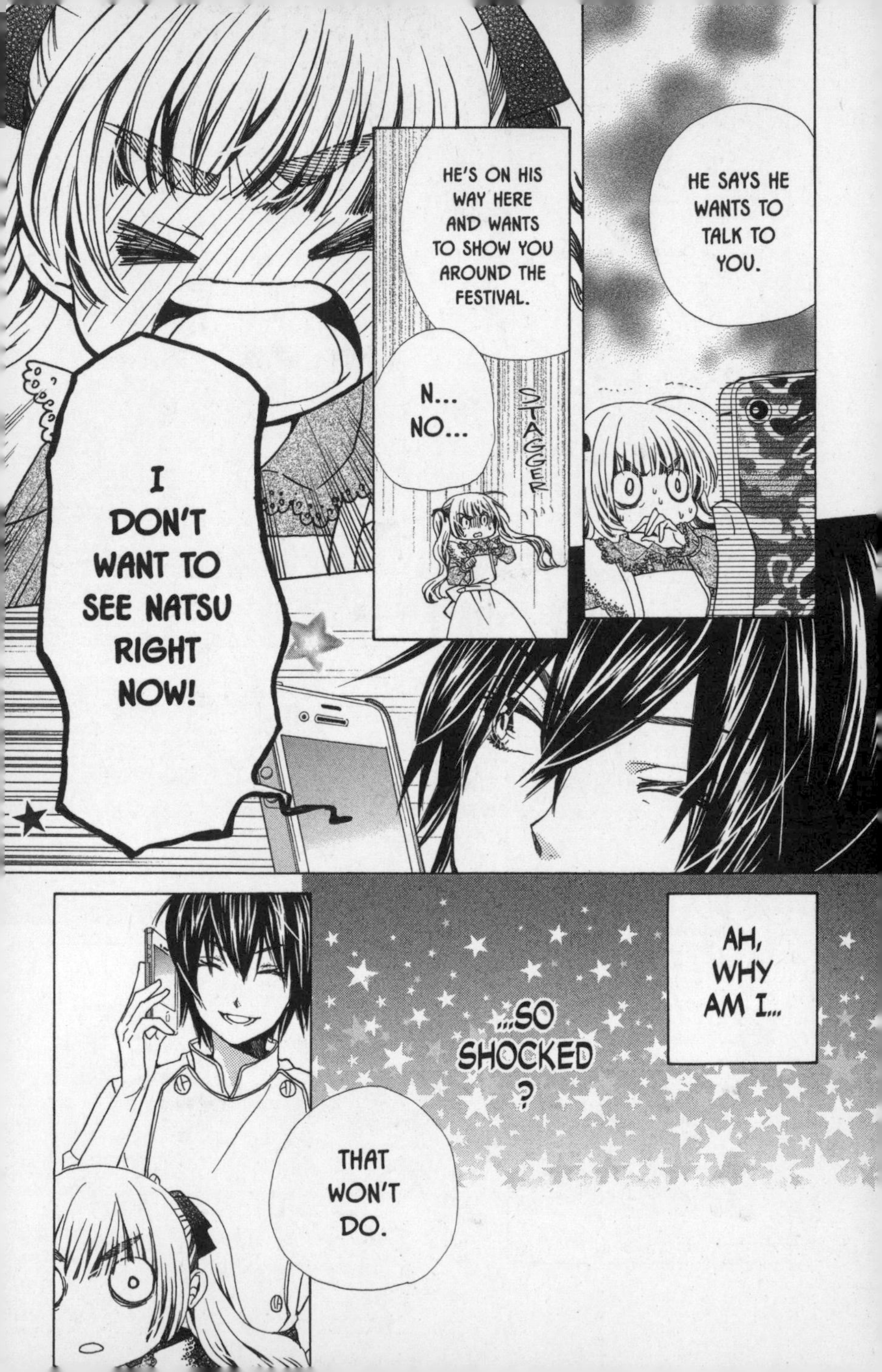
HE SAYS HE WANTS TO TALK TO YOU.
HE'S ON HIS WAY HERE AND WANTS TO SHOW YOU AROUND THE FESTIVAL.
N... NO...
STAGGER
I DON'T WANT TO SEE NATSU RIGHT NOW!
AH, WHY AM I...
...SO SHOCKED?
THAT WON'T DO.

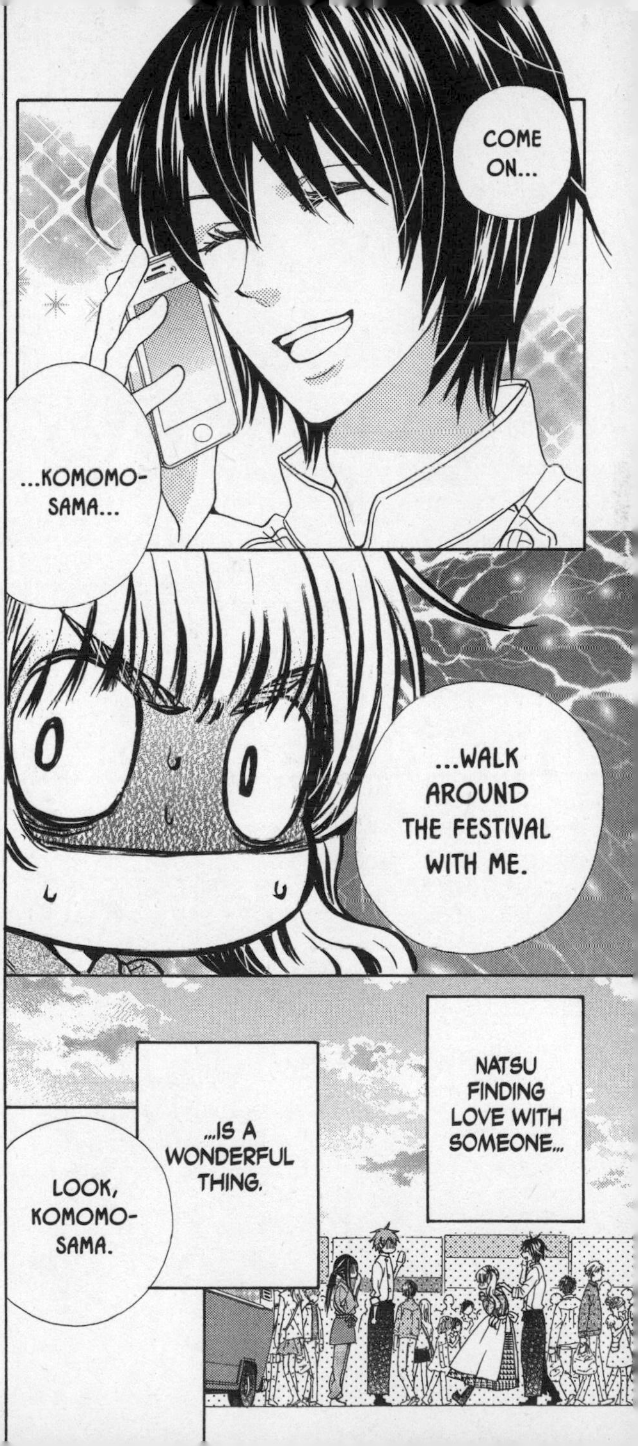
COME ON...
...KOMOMO-SAMA...
...WALK AROUND THE FESTIVAL WITH ME.
NATSU FINDING LOVE WITH SOMEONE...
...IS A WONDERFUL THING.
LOOK, KOMOMO-SAMA.

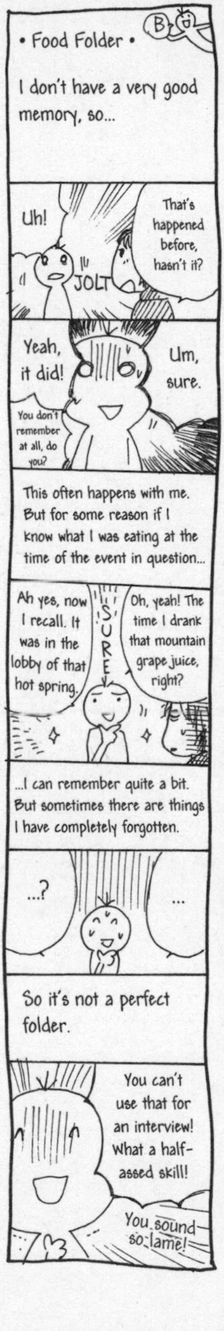
• Food Folder •
B
I don't have a very good memory, so...
That's happened before, hasn't it?
Uh!
JOLT
Um, sure.
Yeah, it did!
You don't remember at all, do you?
This often happens with me. But for some reason if I know what I was eating at the time of the event in question...
Oh, yeah! The time I drank that mountain grape juice, right?
SURE
Ah yes, now I recall. It was in the lobby of that hot spring.
...I can remember quite a bit. But sometimes there are things I have completely forgotten.
...
...?
So it's not a perfect folder.
You can't use that for an interview! What a half-assed skill!
You sound so lame!

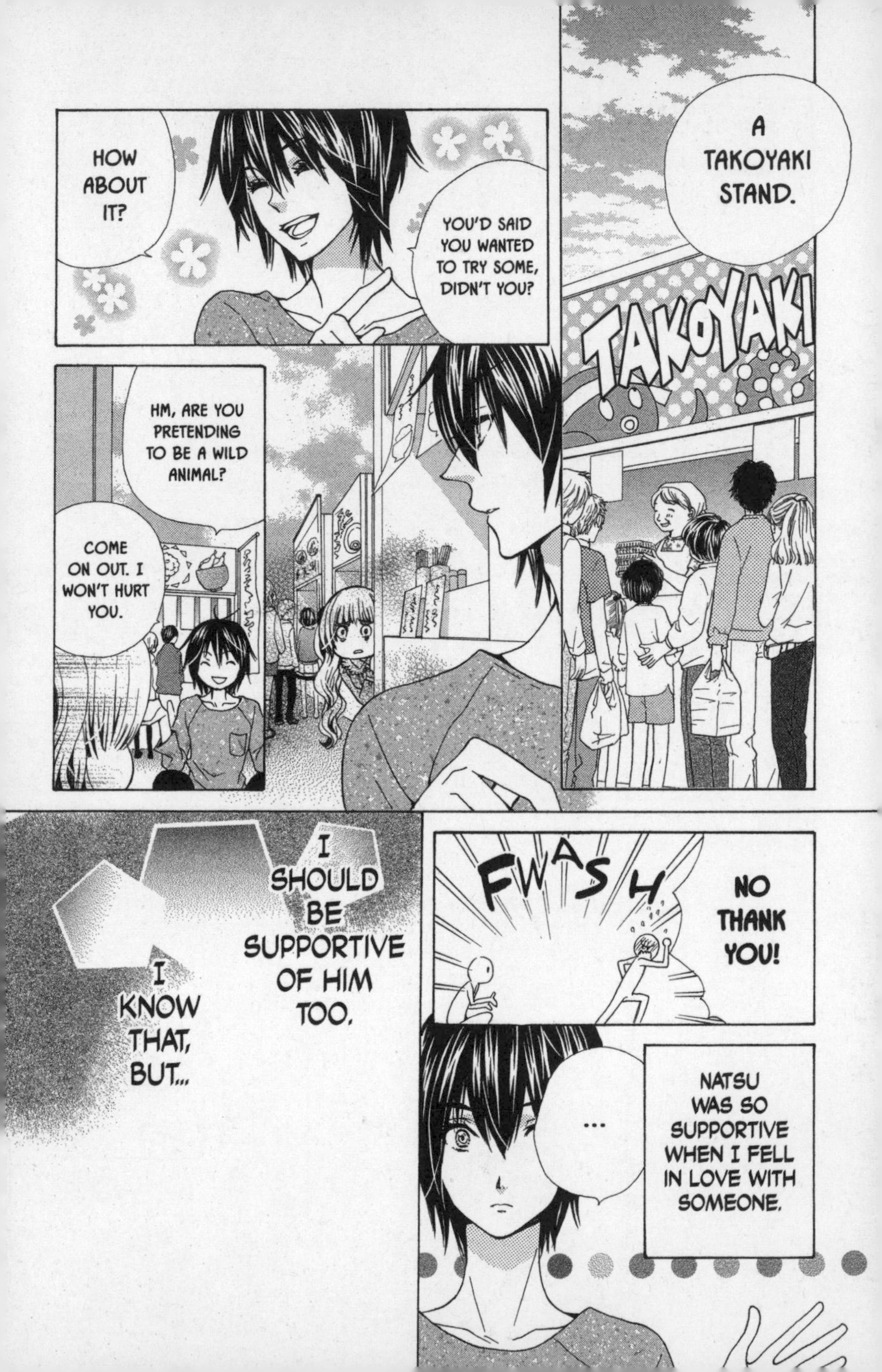
A TAKOYAKI STAND.
TAKOYAKI
YOU'D SAID YOU WANTED TO TRY SOME, DIDN'T YOU?
HOW ABOUT IT?
HM, ARE YOU PRETENDING TO BE A WILD ANIMAL?
COME ON OUT. I WON'T HURT YOU.
NO THANK YOU!
FWASH
NATSU WAS SO SUPPORTIVE WHEN I FELL IN LOVE WITH SOMEONE.
...
I SHOULD BE SUPPORTIVE OF HIM TOO.
I KNOW THAT, BUT...

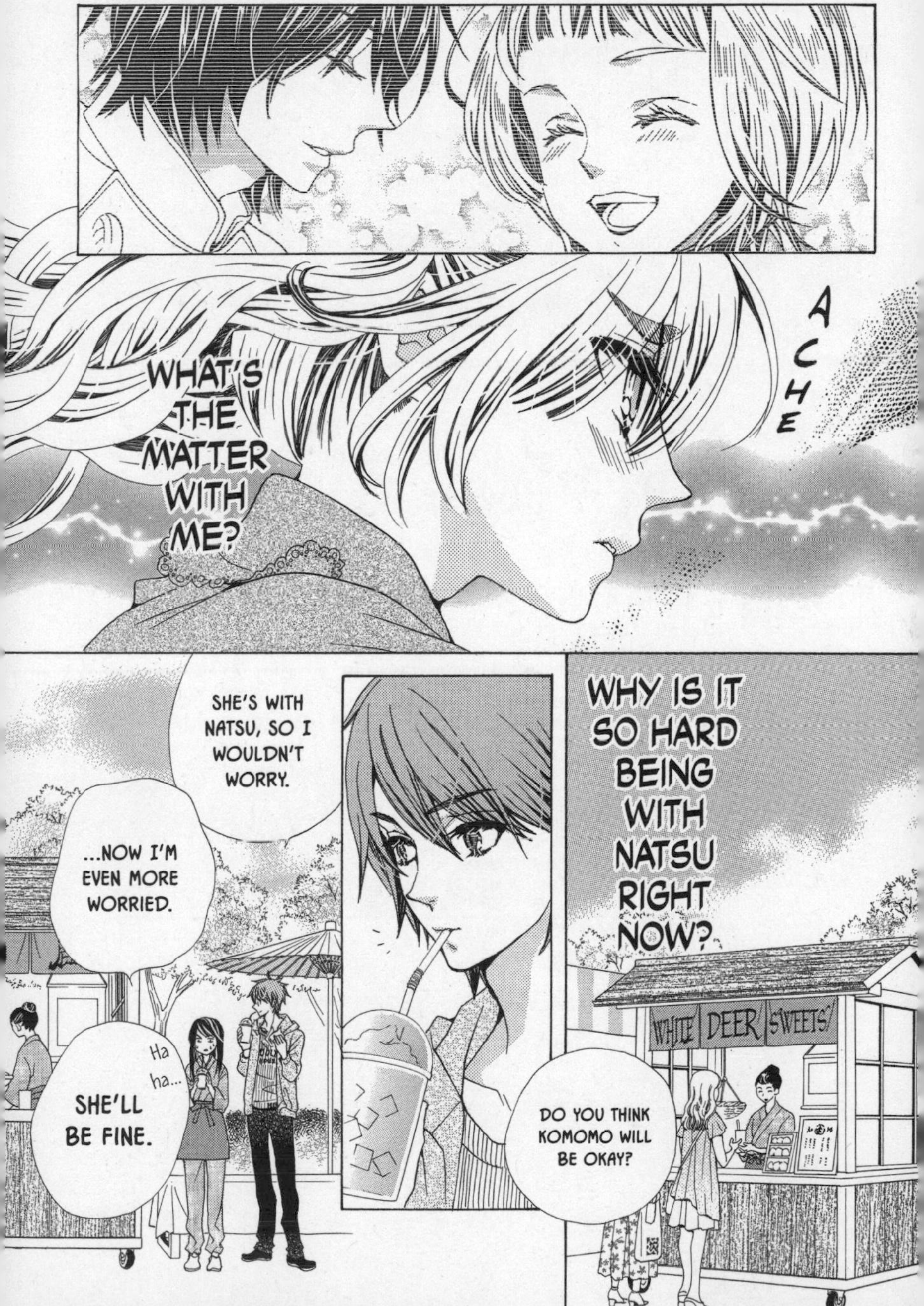
ACHE
WHAT'S THE MATTER WITH ME?
WHY IS IT SO HARD BEING WITH NATSU RIGHT NOW?
WHITE DEER SWEETS
DO YOU THINK KOMOMO WILL BE OKAY?
SHE'S WITH NATSU, SO I WOULDN'T WORRY.
...NOW I'M EVEN MORE WORRIED.
Ha ha...
SHE'LL BE FINE.

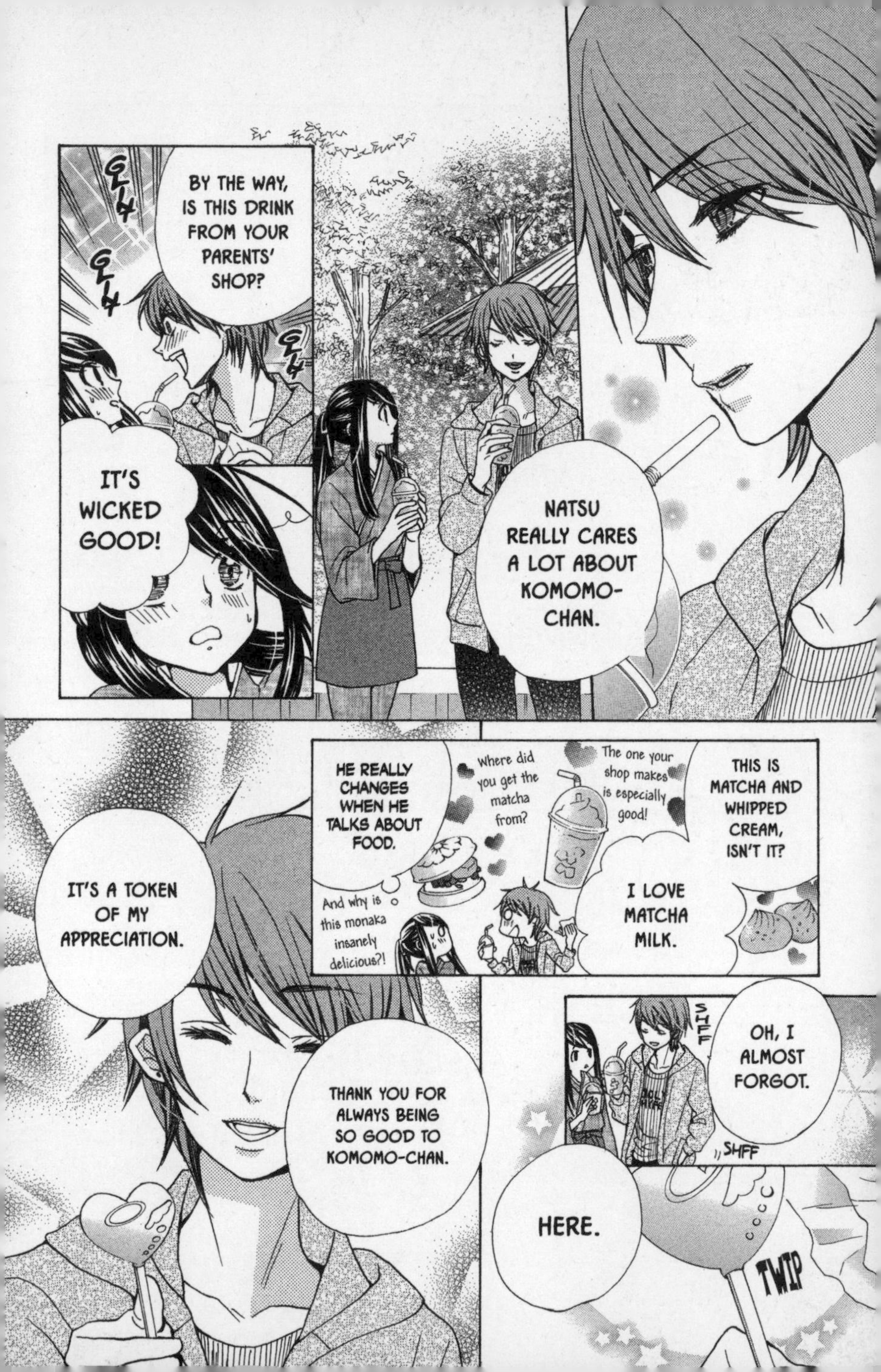

NATSU REALLY CARES A LOT ABOUT KOMOMO-CHAN.
BY THE WAY, IS THIS DRINK FROM YOUR PARENTS' SHOP?
IT'S WICKED GOOD!
THIS IS MATCHA AND WHIPPED CREAM, ISN'T IT?
The one your shop makes is especially good!
I LOVE MATCHA MILK.
Where did you get the matcha from?
HE REALLY CHANGES WHEN HE TALKS ABOUT FOOD.
And why is this monaka insanely delicious?!
OH, I ALMOST FORGOT.
SHFF
SHFF
HERE.
TWIP
THANK YOU FOR ALWAYS BEING SO GOOD TO KOMOMO-CHAN.
IT'S A TOKEN OF MY APPRECIATION.

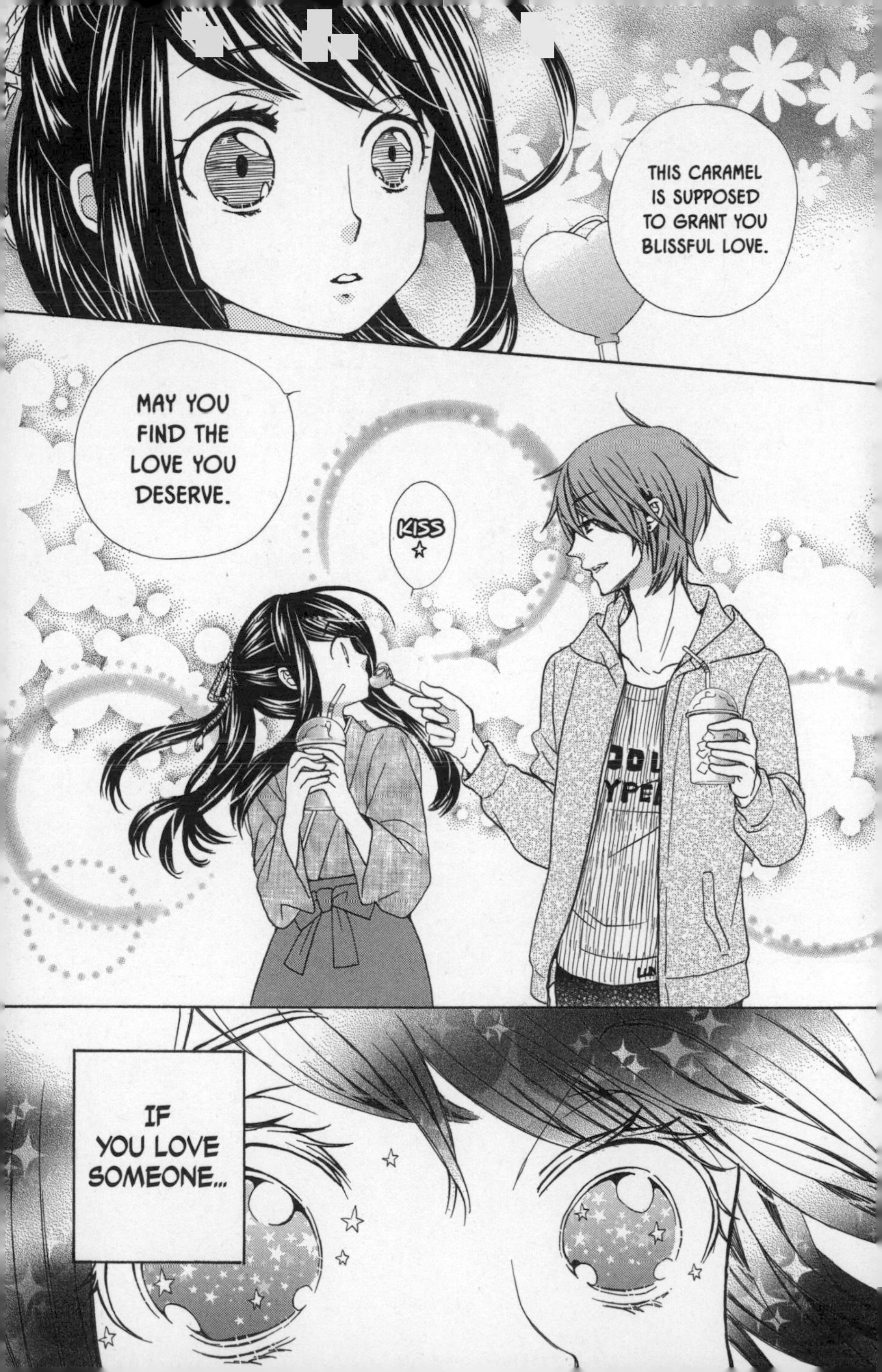
THIS CARAMEL IS SUPPOSED TO GRANT YOU BLISSFUL LOVE.
MAY YOU FIND THE LOVE YOU DESERVE.
KISS ☆
IF YOU LOVE SOMEONE...

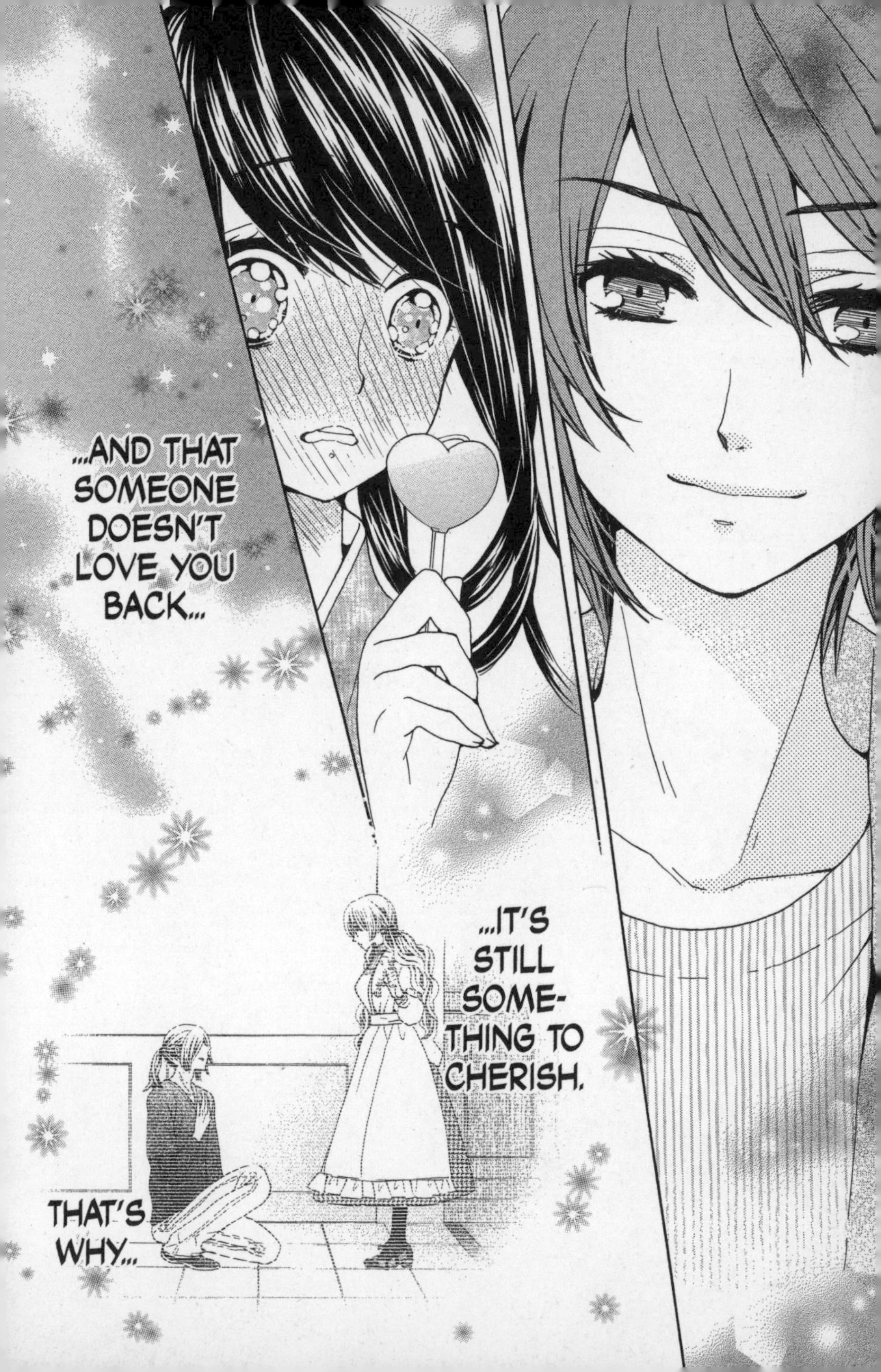
...AND THAT SOMEONE DOESN'T LOVE YOU BACK...
...IT'S STILL SOME-THING TO CHERISH.
THAT'S WHY...

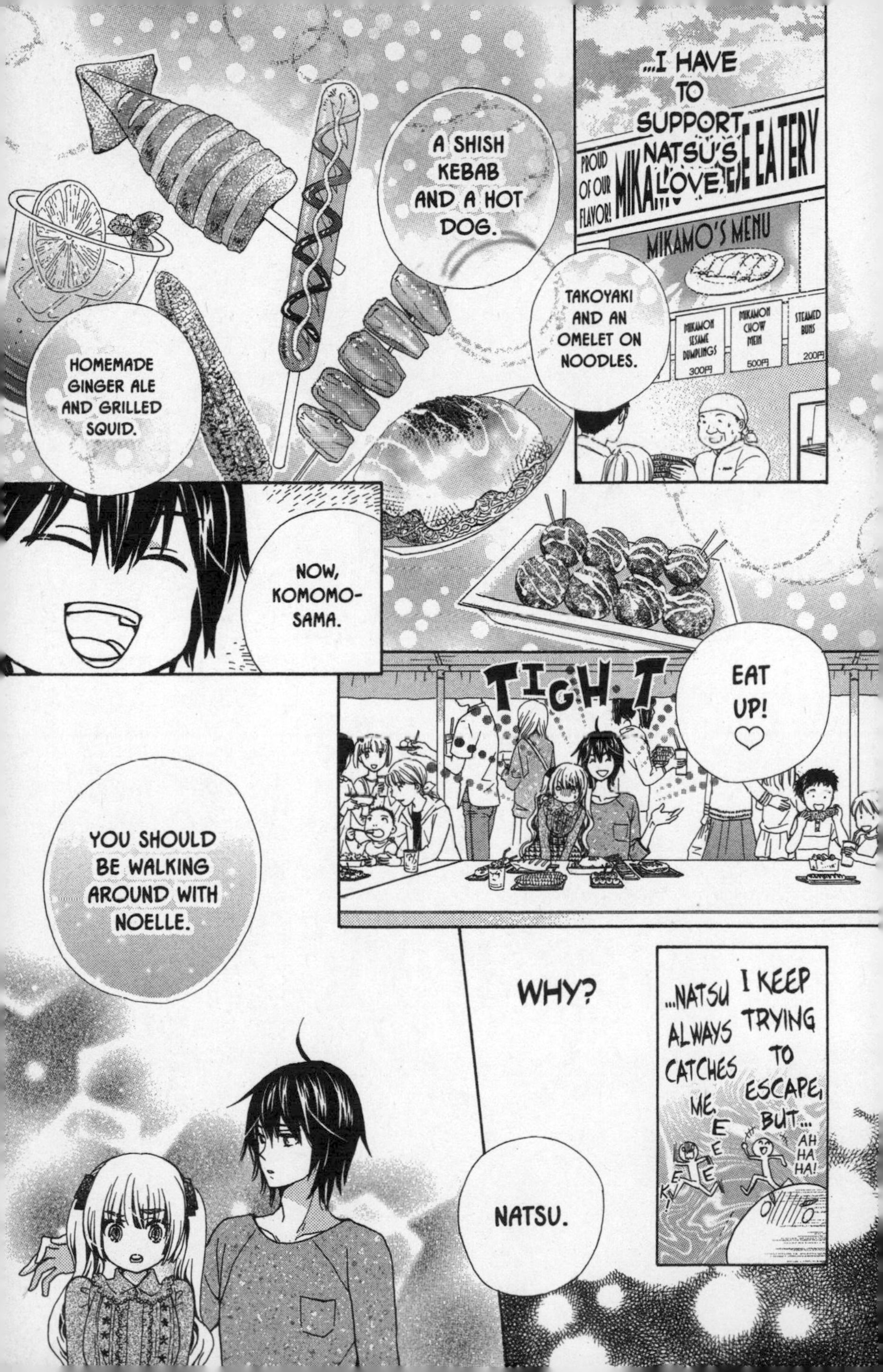
PROUD OF OUR FLAVOR!
MIKA... EATERY
...I HAVE TO SUPPORT NATSU'S LOVE.
MIKAMO'S MENU
STEAMED BUNS 200円
MIKAMON CHOW MEIN 500円
MIKAMON SESAME DUMPLINGS 300円
A SHISH KEBAB AND A HOT DOG.
TAKOYAKI AND AN OMELET ON NOODLES.
HOMEMADE GINGER ALE AND GRILLED SQUID.
NOW, KOMOMO-SAMA.
TIGHT
EAT UP! ♡
YOU SHOULD BE WALKING AROUND WITH NOELLE.
I KEEP TRYING TO ESCAPE, BUT...
...NATSU ALWAYS CATCHES ME.
AH HA HA!
EEEEK!
WHY?
NATSU.

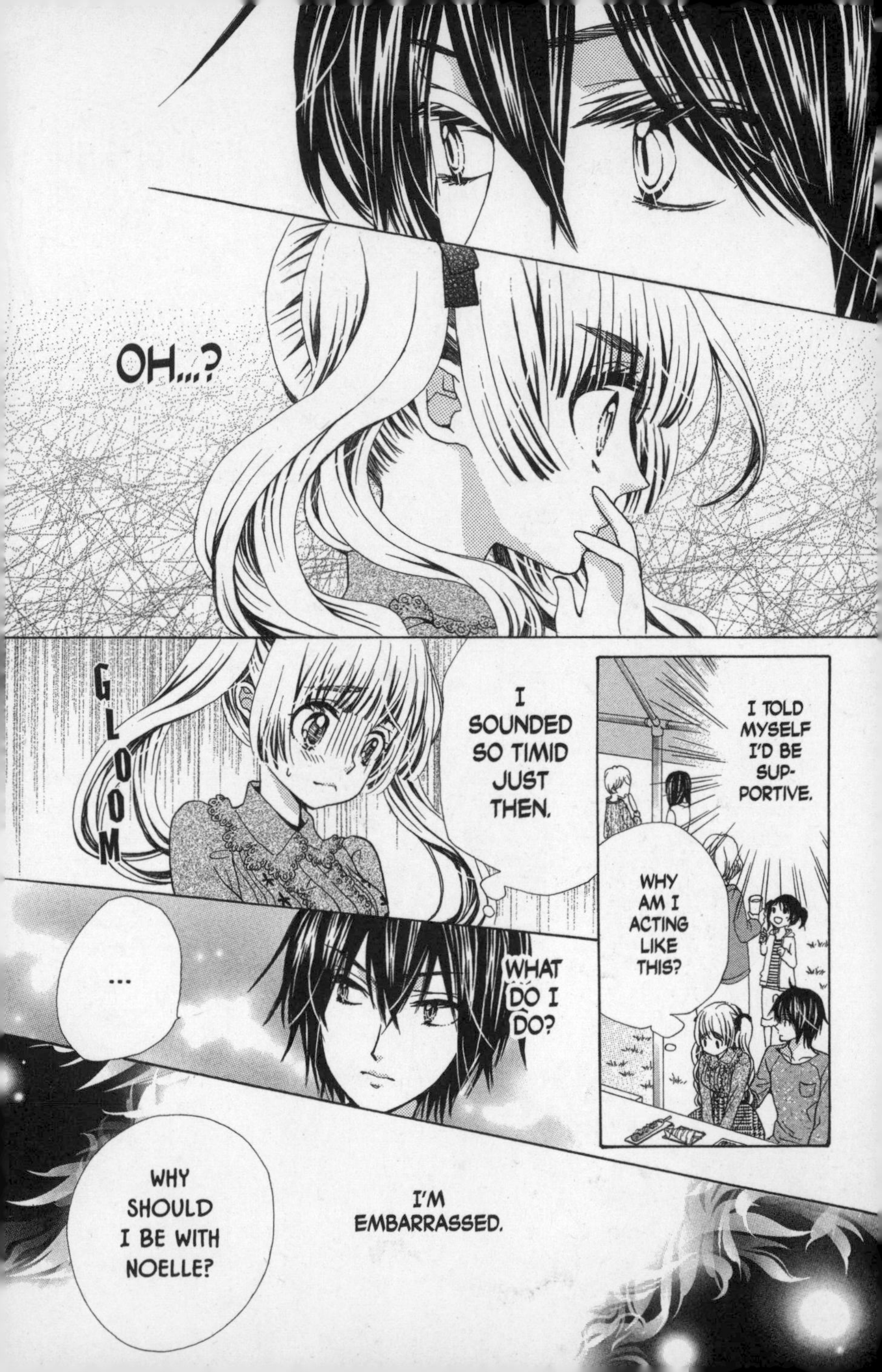
OH...?
I TOLD MYSELF I'D BE SUP-PORTIVE.
WHY AM I ACTING LIKE THIS?
I SOUNDED SO TIMID JUST THEN.
GLOOM
WHAT DO I DO?
...
I'M EMBARRASSED.
WHY SHOULD I BE WITH NOELLE?

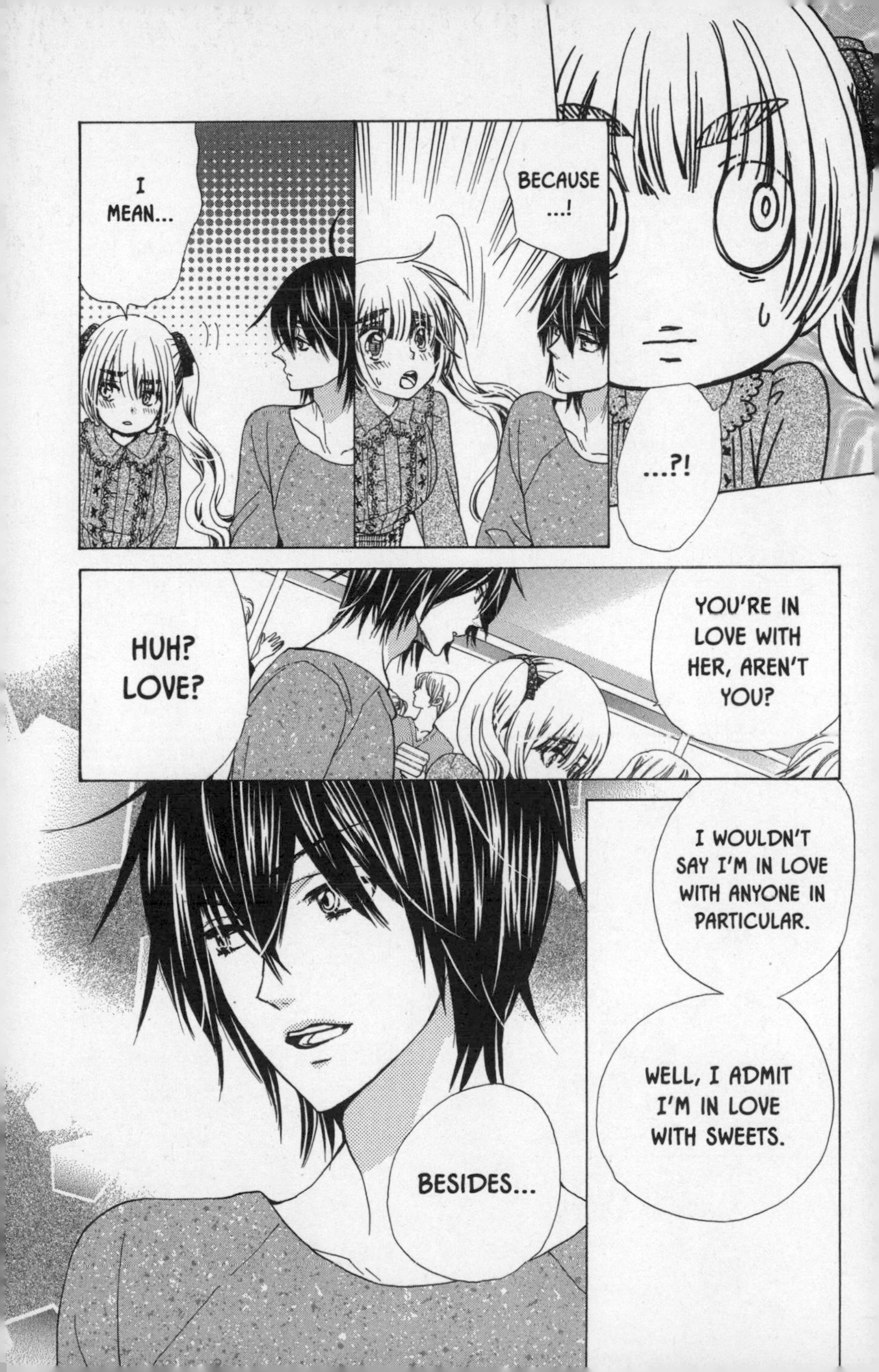
...?!
BECAUSE ...!
I MEAN...
YOU'RE IN LOVE WITH HER, AREN'T YOU?
HUH? LOVE?
I WOULDN'T SAY I'M IN LOVE WITH ANYONE IN PARTICULAR.
WELL, I ADMIT I'M IN LOVE WITH SWEETS.
BESIDES...

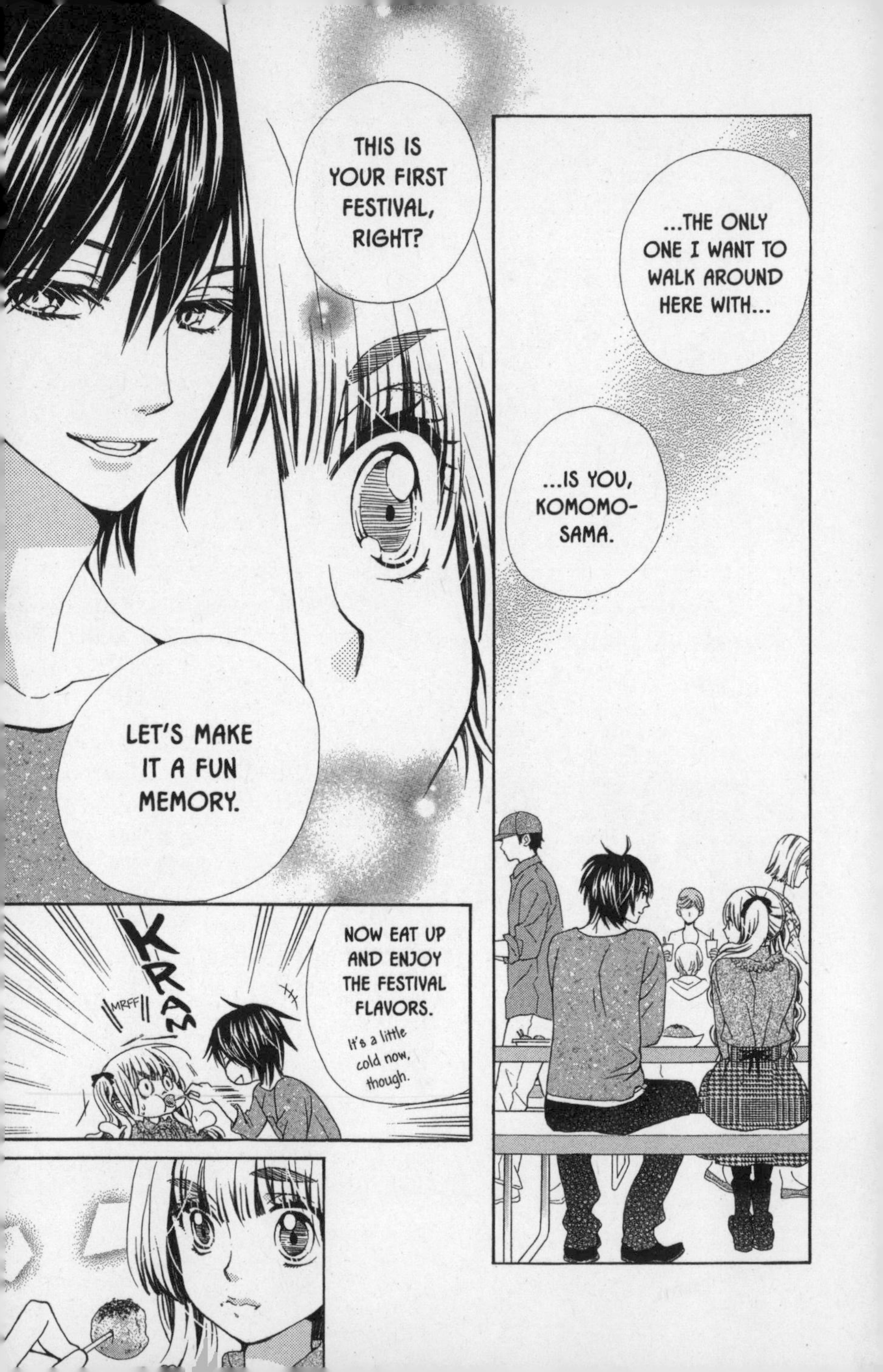
...THE ONLY ONE I WANT TO WALK AROUND HERE WITH...
...IS YOU, KOMOMO-SAMA.
THIS IS YOUR FIRST FESTIVAL, RIGHT?
LET'S MAKE IT A FUN MEMORY.
NOW EAT UP AND ENJOY THE FESTIVAL FLAVORS.
It's a little cold now, though.
KRAM
MRFF

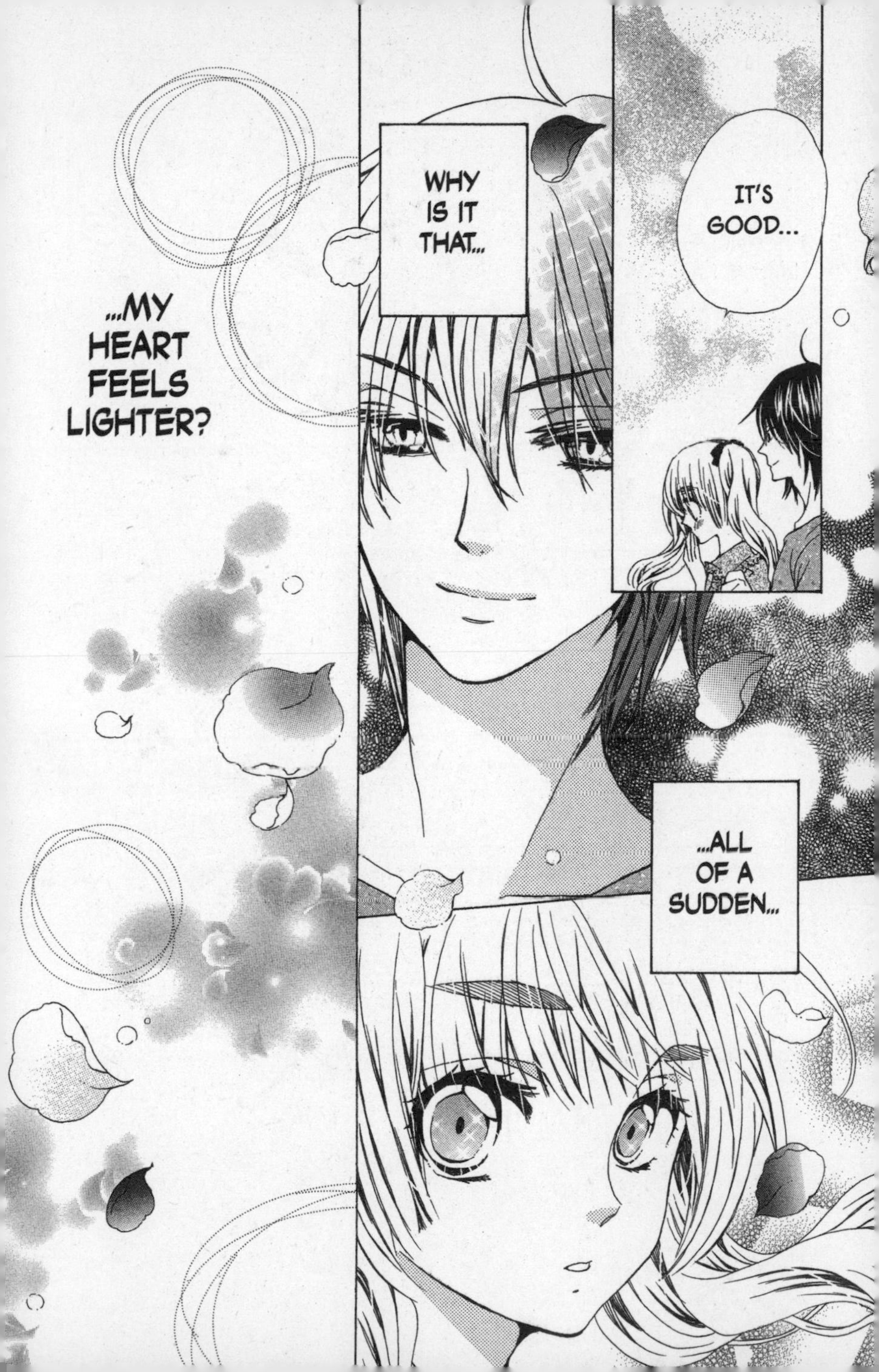
IT'S GOOD...
WHY IS IT THAT...
...ALL OF A SUDDEN...
...MY HEART FEELS LIGHTER?

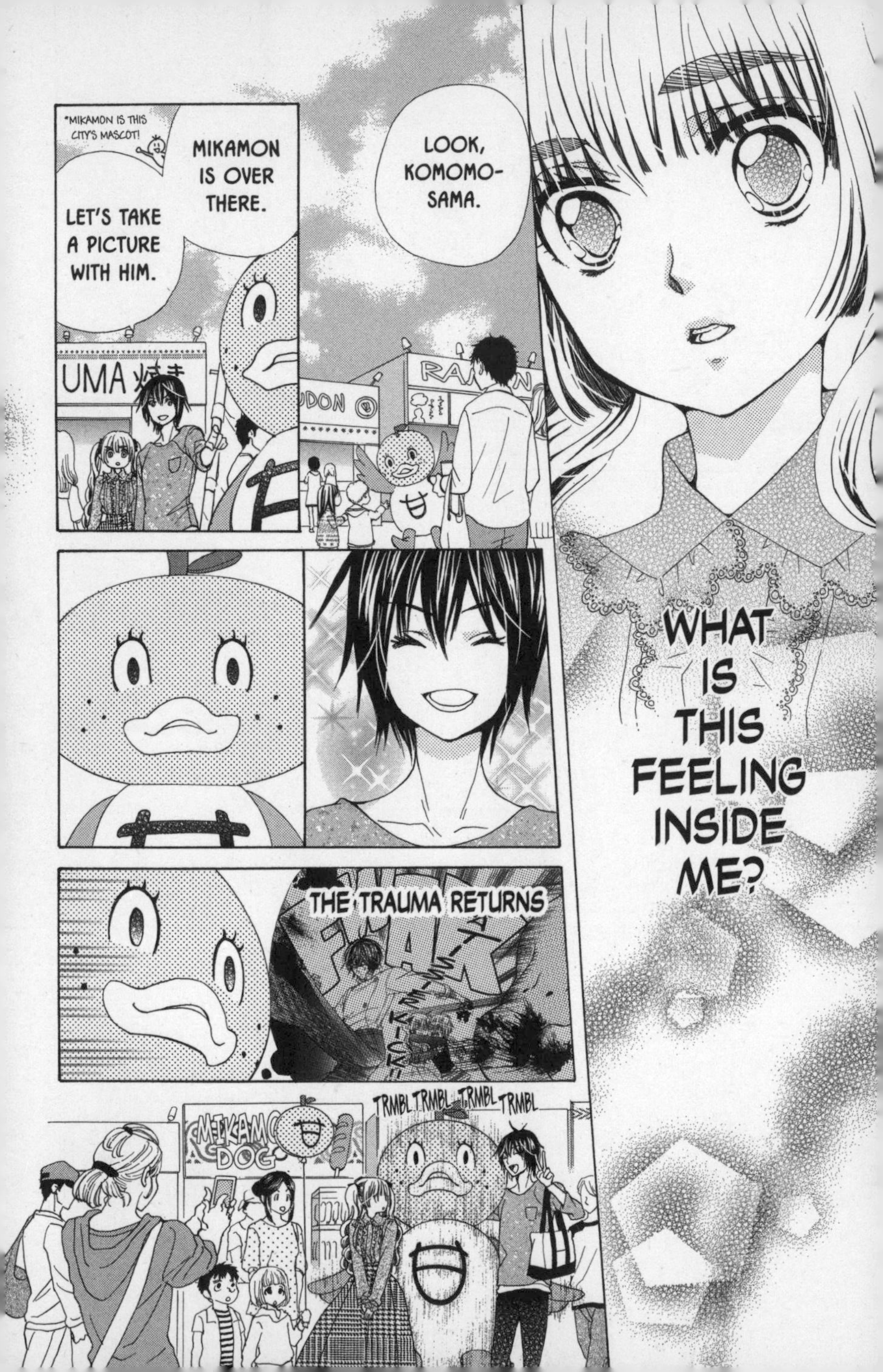
WHAT IS THIS FEELING INSIDE ME?
LOOK, KOMOMO-SAMA.
MIKAMON IS OVER THERE.
*MIKAMON IS THIS CITY'S MASCOT!
LET'S TAKE A PICTURE WITH HIM.
UMA 焼き
UDON
THE TRAUMA RETURNS
TRMBL TRMBL TRMBL TRMBL

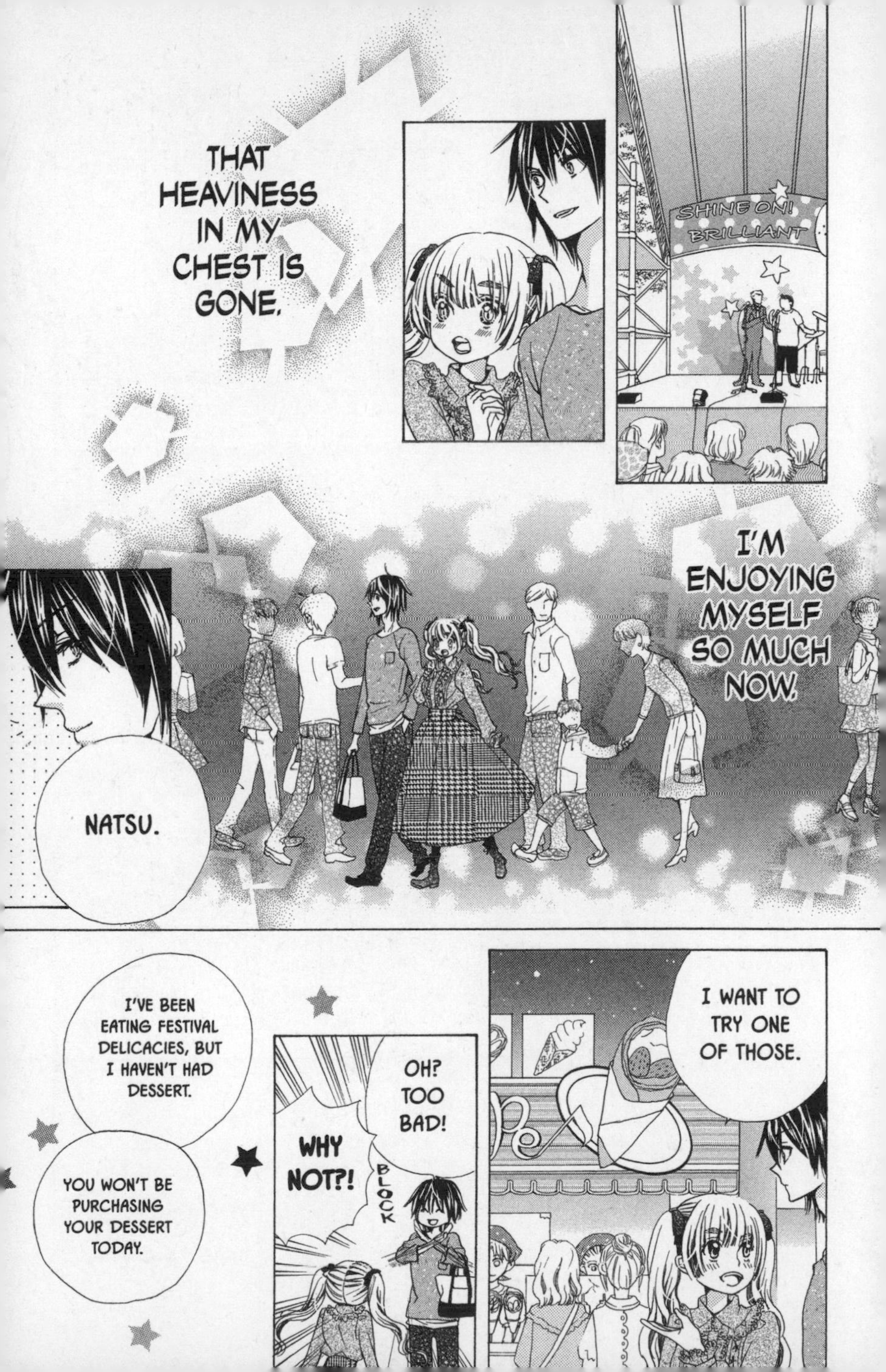
SHINE ON! BRILLIANT
THAT HEAVINESS IN MY CHEST IS GONE.
I'M ENJOYING MYSELF SO MUCH NOW.
NATSU.
I WANT TO TRY ONE OF THOSE.
OH? TOO BAD!
WHY NOT?!
BLOCK
I'VE BEEN EATING FESTIVAL DELICACIES, BUT I HAVEN'T HAD DESSERT.
YOU WON'T BE PURCHASING YOUR DESSERT TODAY.

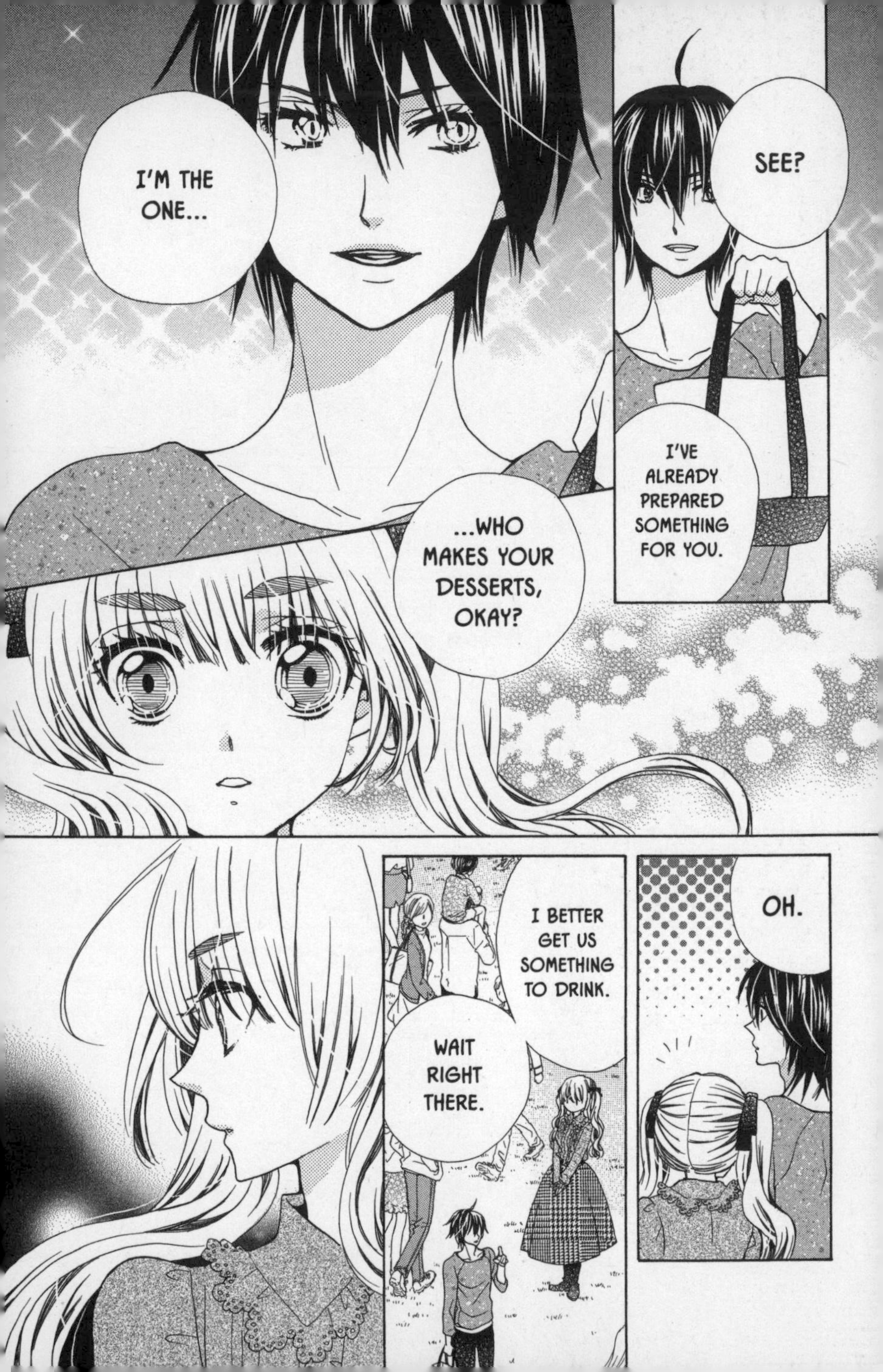
SEE?
I'VE ALREADY PREPARED SOMETHING FOR YOU.
I'M THE ONE...
...WHO MAKES YOUR DESSERTS, OKAY?
OH.
I BETTER GET US SOMETHING TO DRINK.
WAIT RIGHT THERE.

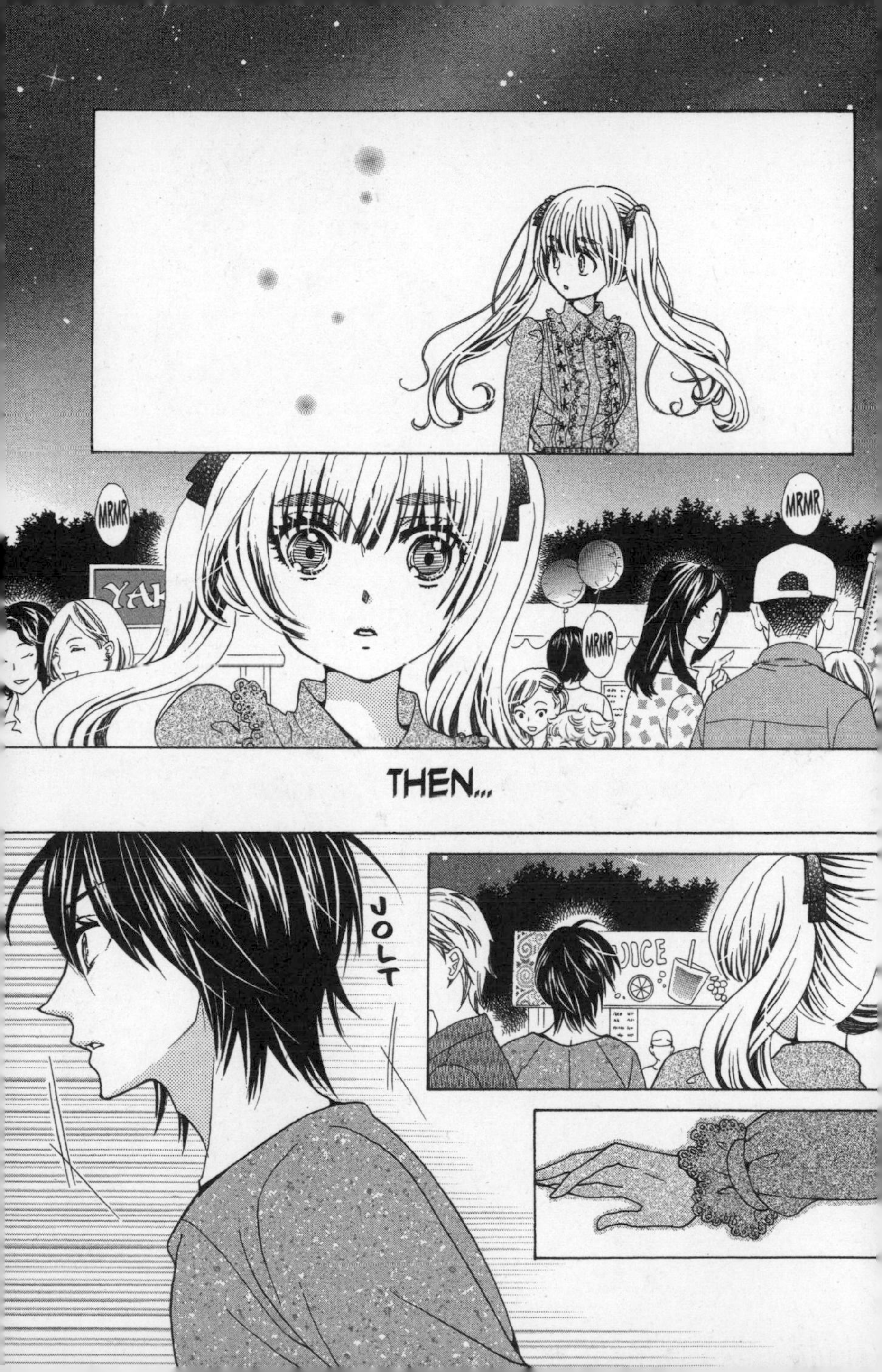
MRMR
MRMR
MRMR
YAK
THEN...
JOLT

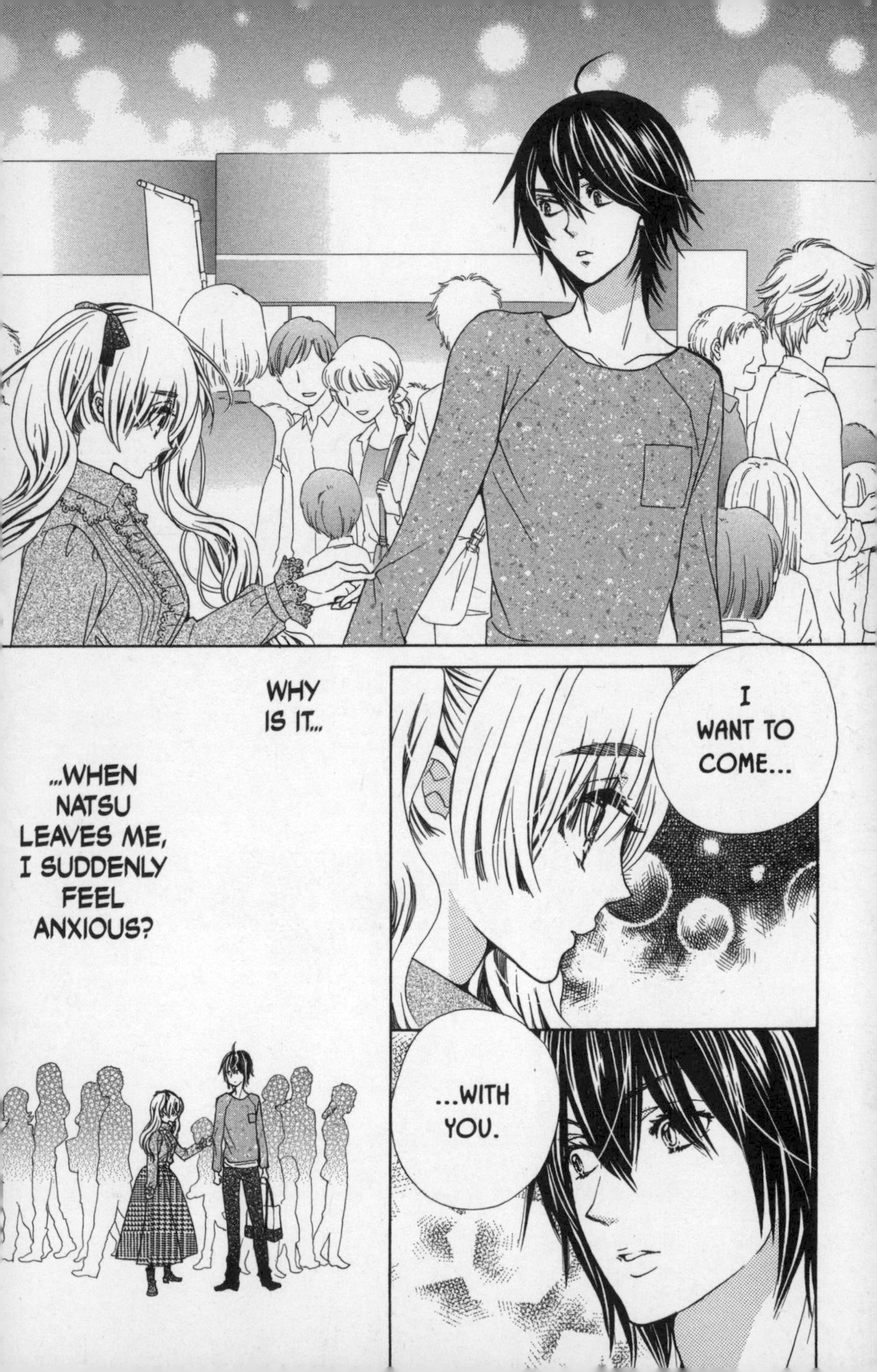
I WANT TO COME...
...WITH YOU.
WHY IS IT...
...WHEN NATSU LEAVES ME, I SUDDENLY FEEL ANXIOUS?

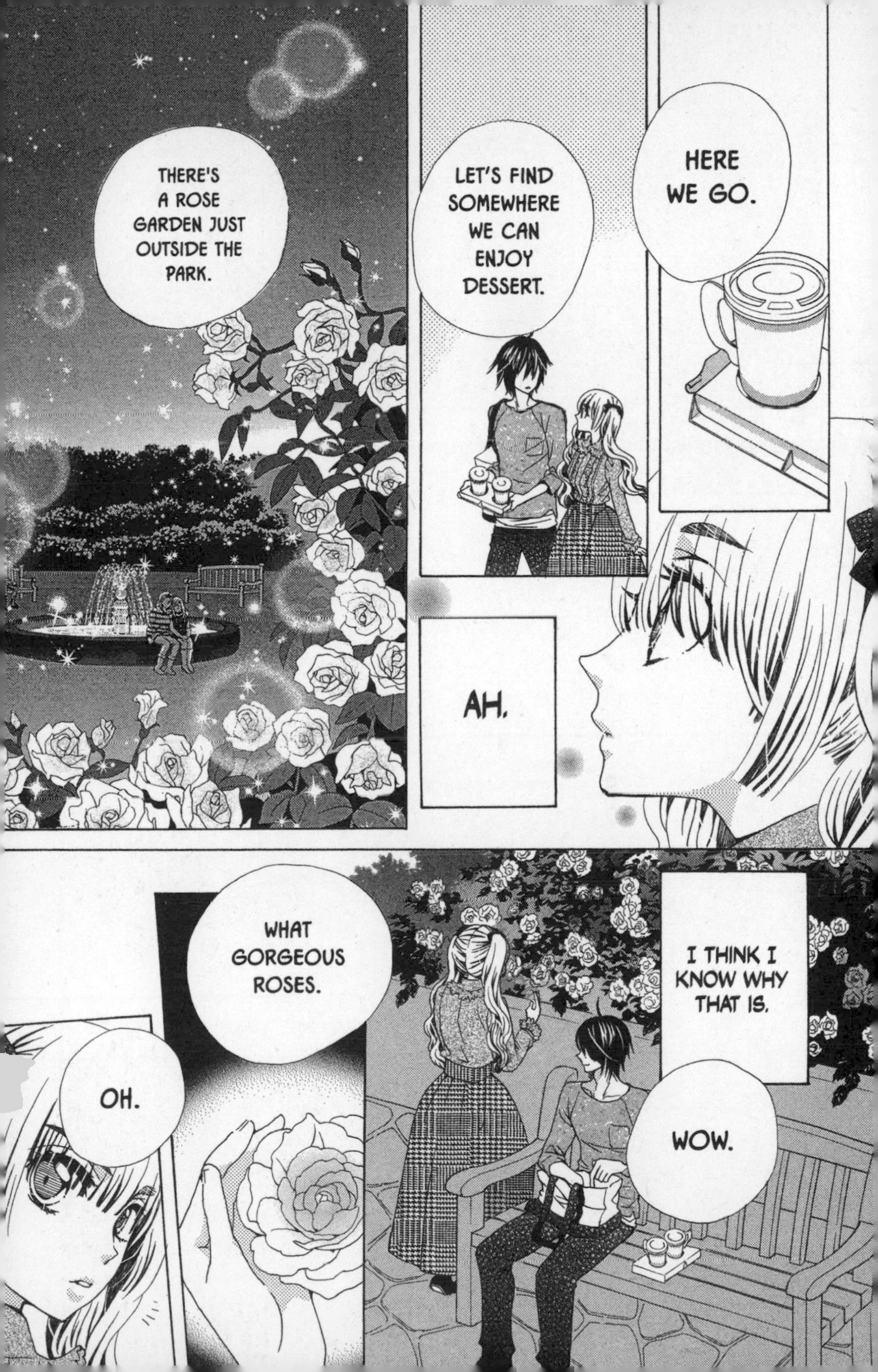
HERE WE GO.
LET'S FIND SOMEWHERE WE CAN ENJOY DESSERT.
AH.
THERE'S A ROSE GARDEN JUST OUTSIDE THE PARK.
I THINK I KNOW WHY THAT IS.
WOW.
WHAT GORGEOUS ROSES.
OH.

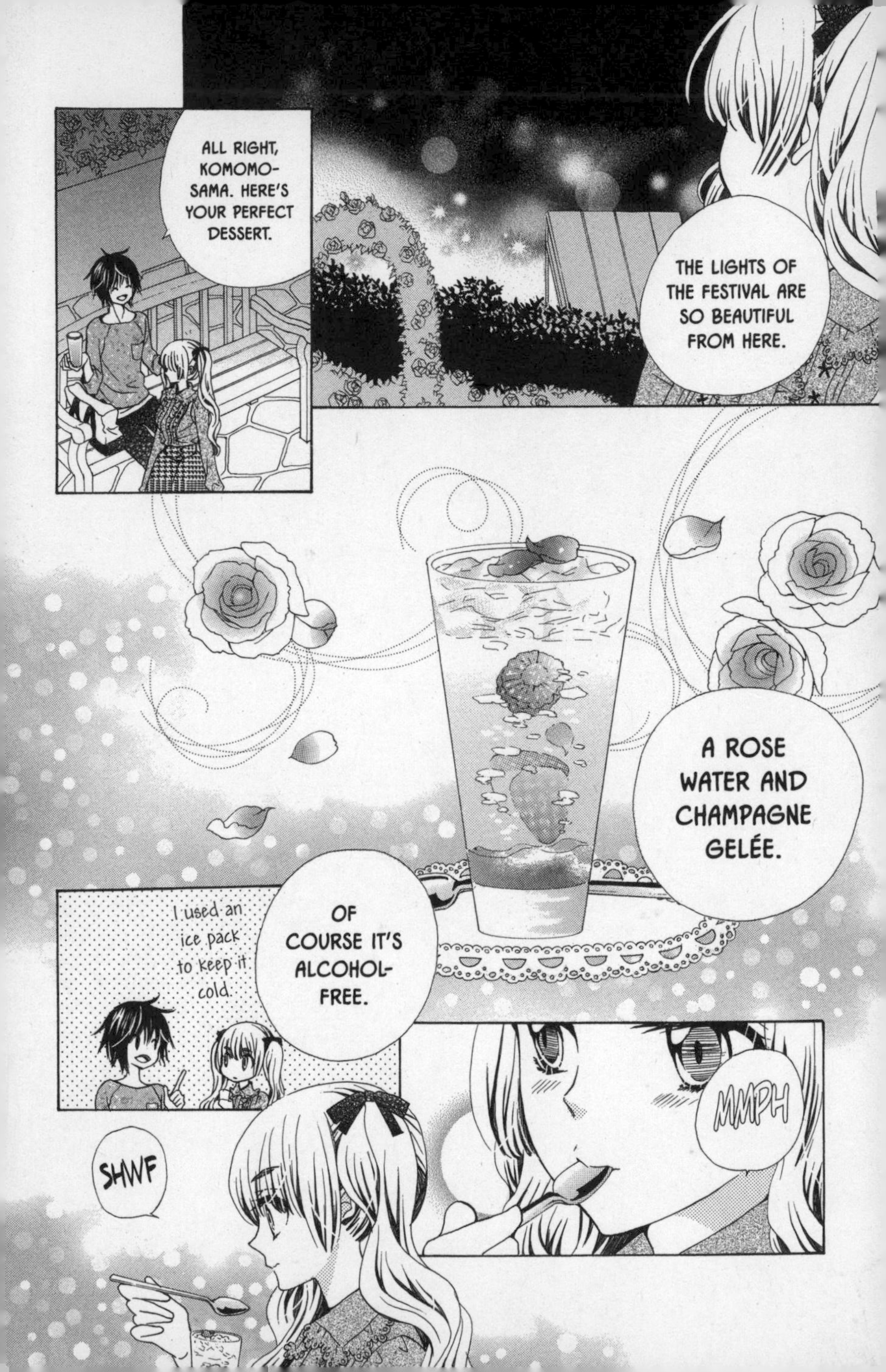

THE LIGHTS OF THE FESTIVAL ARE SO BEAUTIFUL FROM HERE.
ALL RIGHT, KOMOMO-SAMA. HERE'S YOUR PERFECT DESSERT.
A ROSE WATER AND CHAMPAGNE GELÉE.
OF COURSE IT'S ALCOHOL-FREE.
I used an ice pack to keep it cold.
MMPH
SHWF

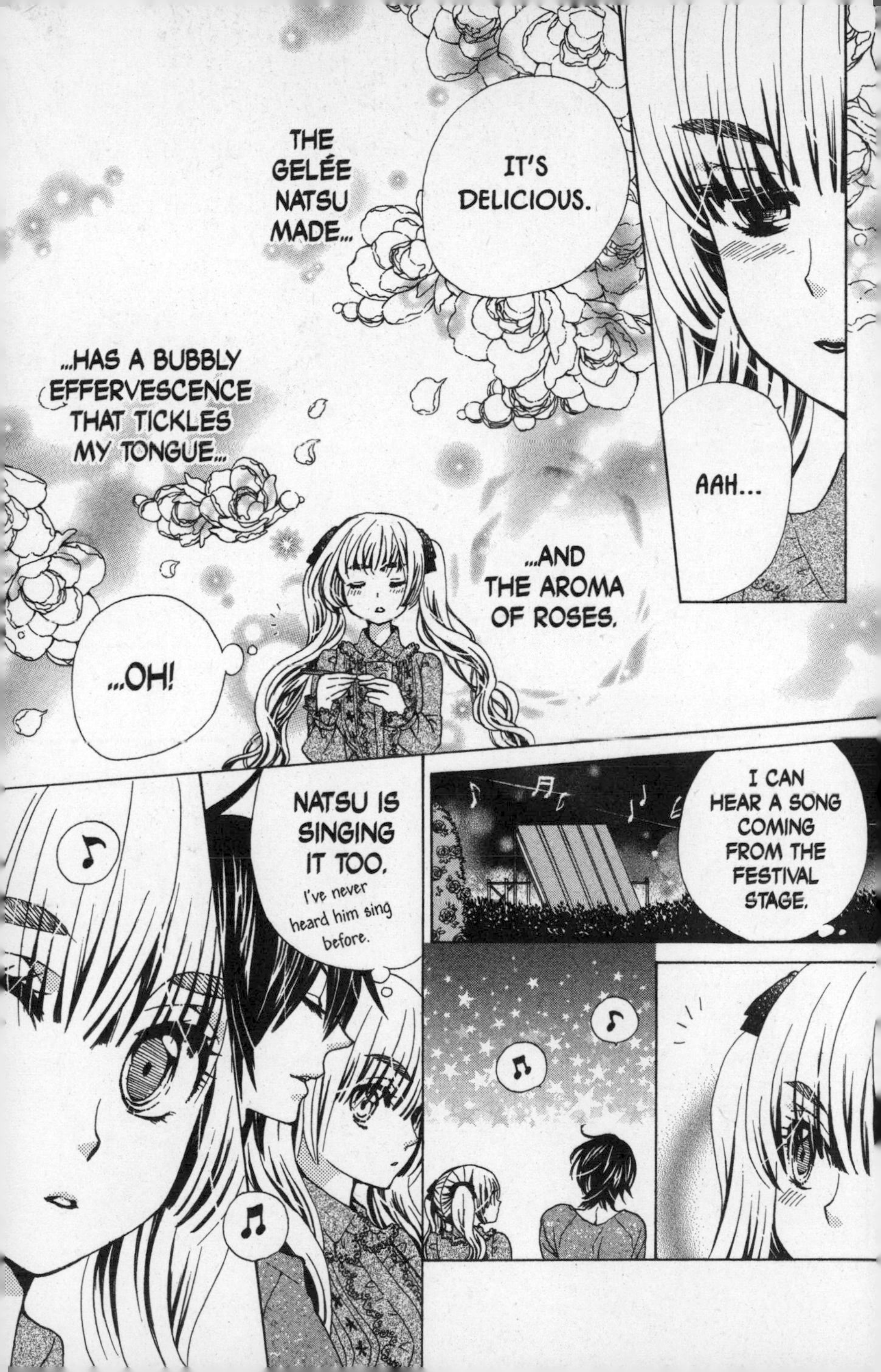
IT'S DELICIOUS.
AAH...
THE GELÉE NATSU MADE...
...HAS A BUBBLY EFFERVESCENCE THAT TICKLES MY TONGUE...
...AND THE AROMA OF ROSES.
...OH!
I CAN HEAR A SONG COMING FROM THE FESTIVAL STAGE.
NATSU IS SINGING IT TOO.
I've never heard him sing before.

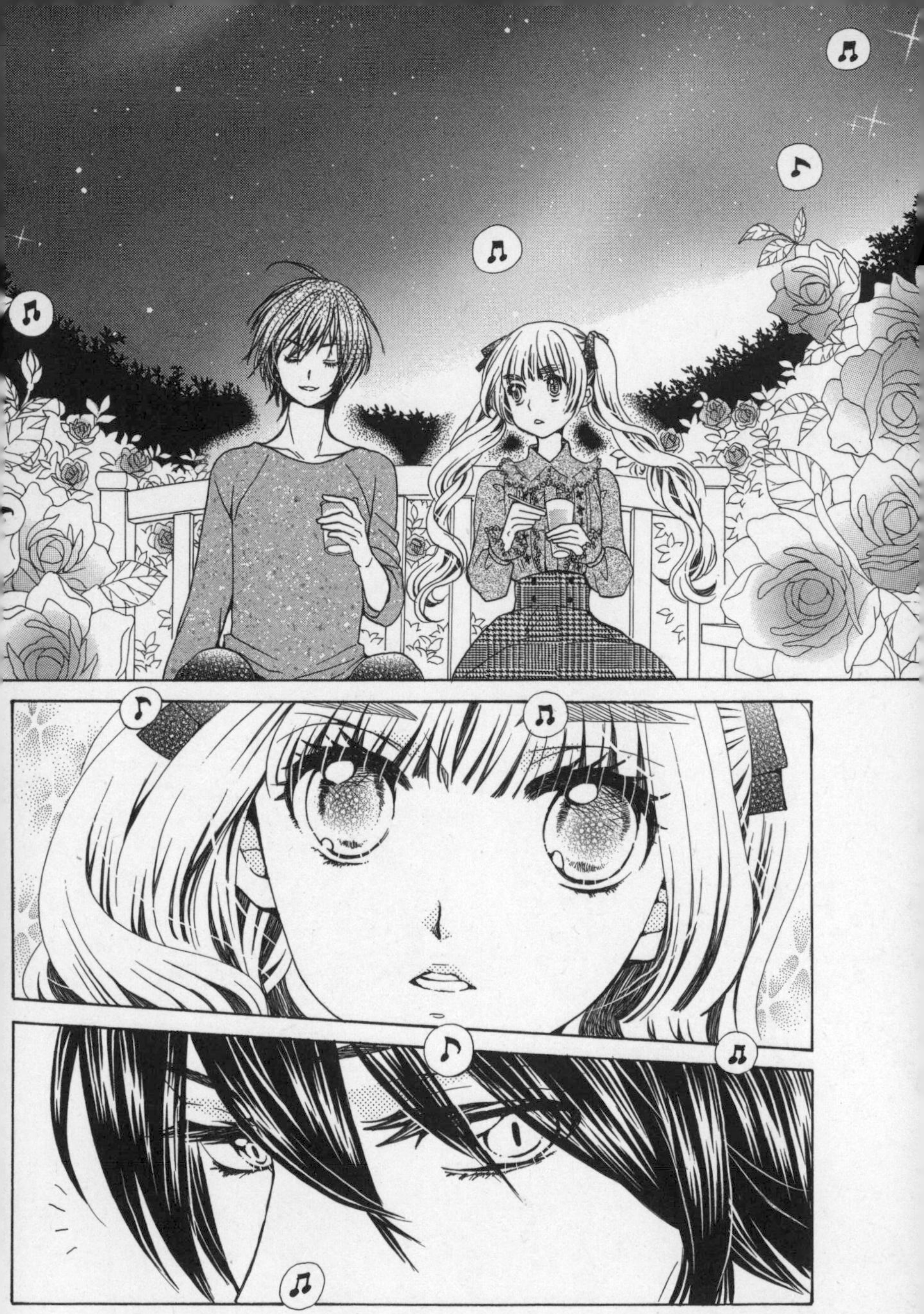

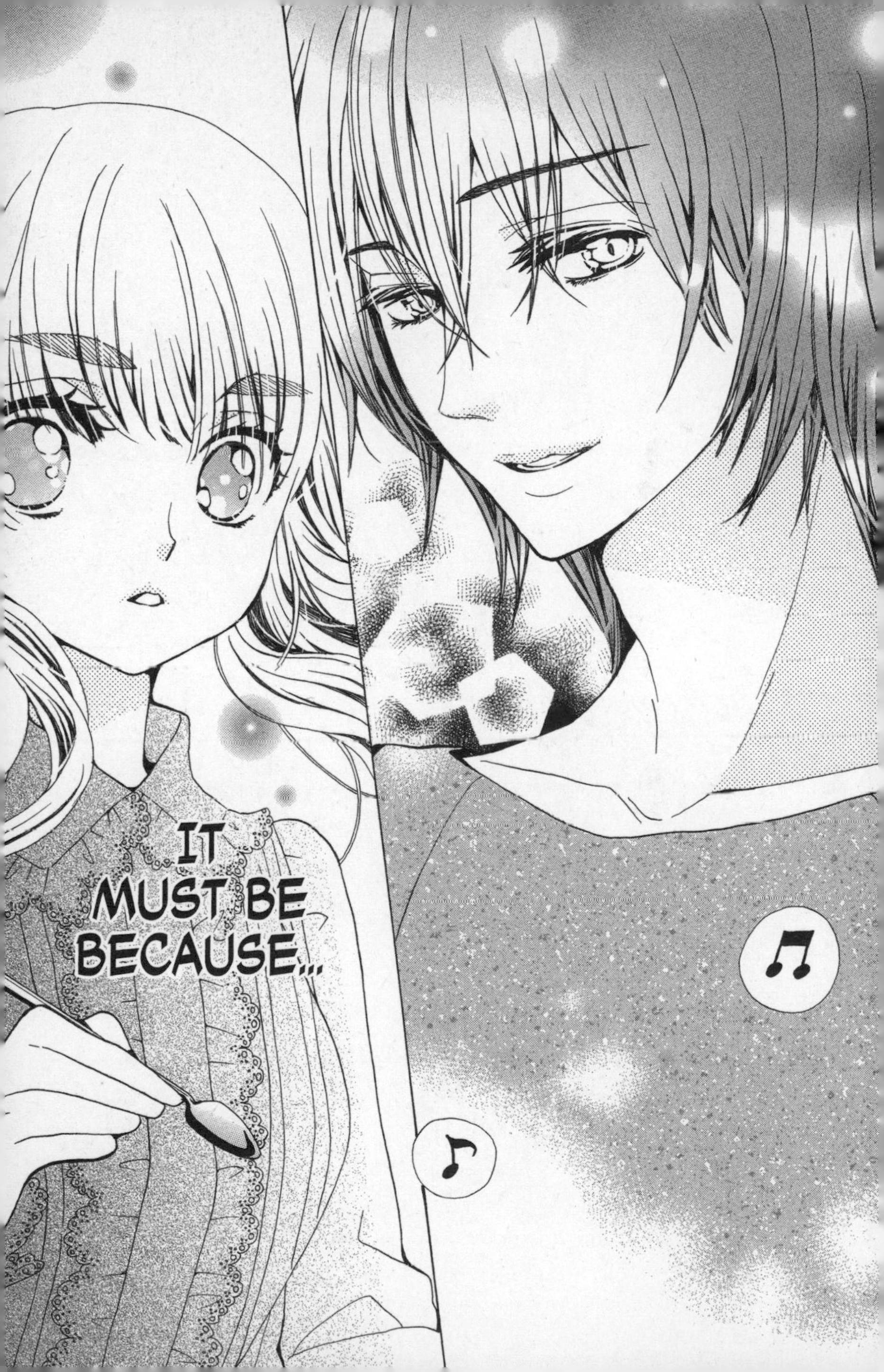
IT MUST BE BECAUSE...
♫
♪

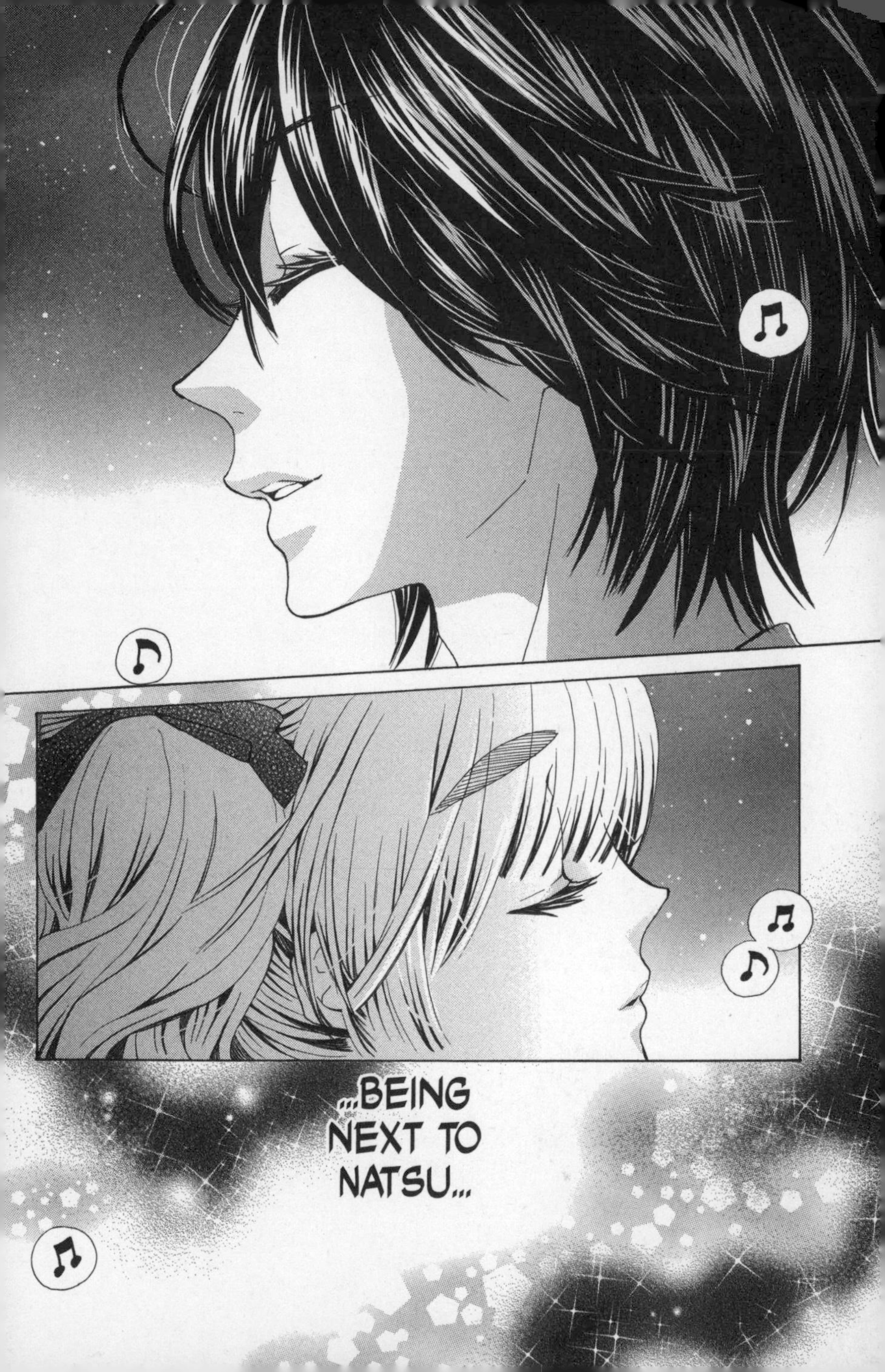
...BEING NEXT TO NATSU...

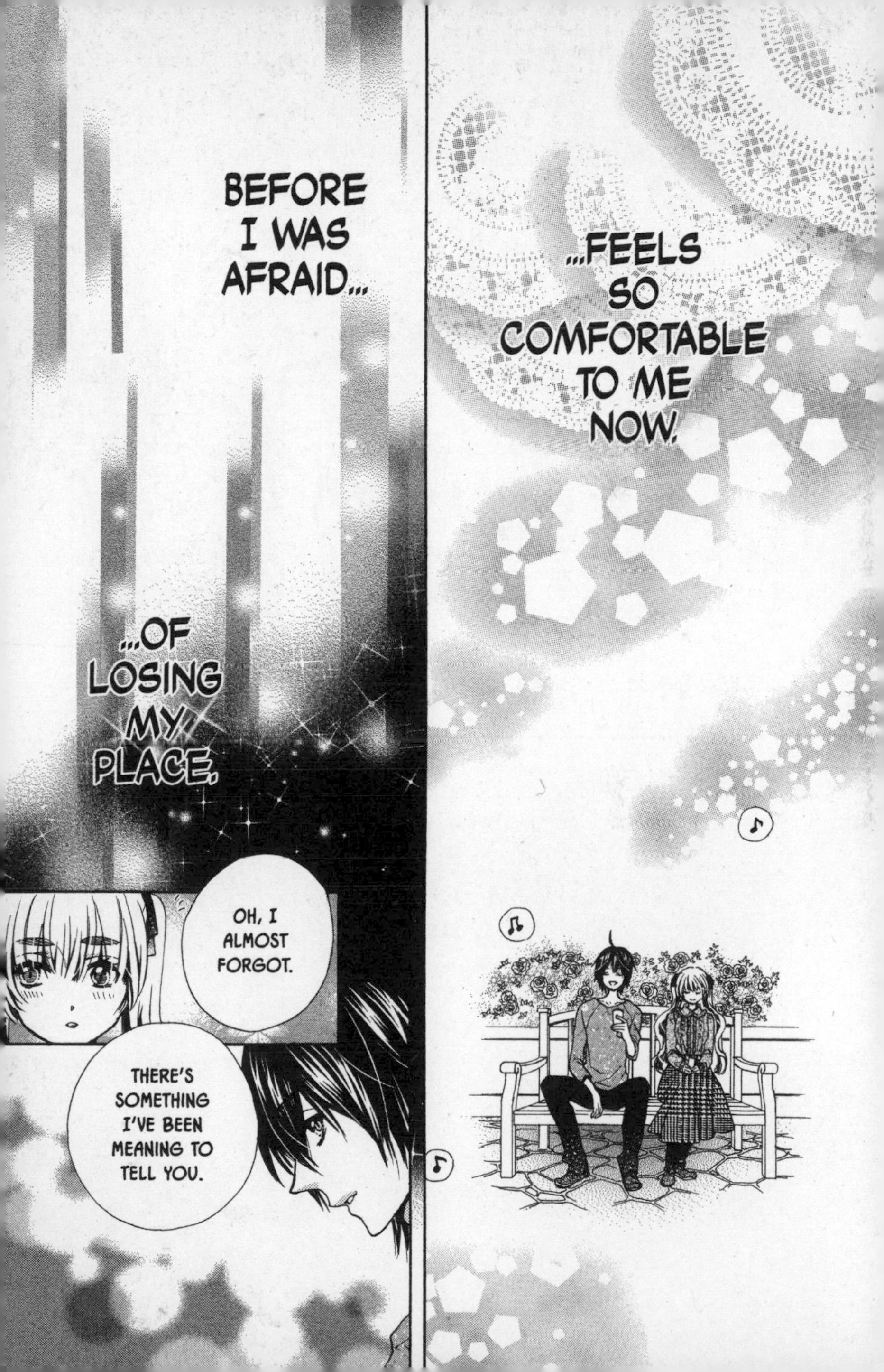
...FEELS SO COMFORTABLE TO ME NOW.
BEFORE I WAS AFRAID...
...OF LOSING MY PLACE.
OH, I ALMOST FORGOT.
THERE'S SOMETHING I'VE BEEN MEANING TO TELL YOU.

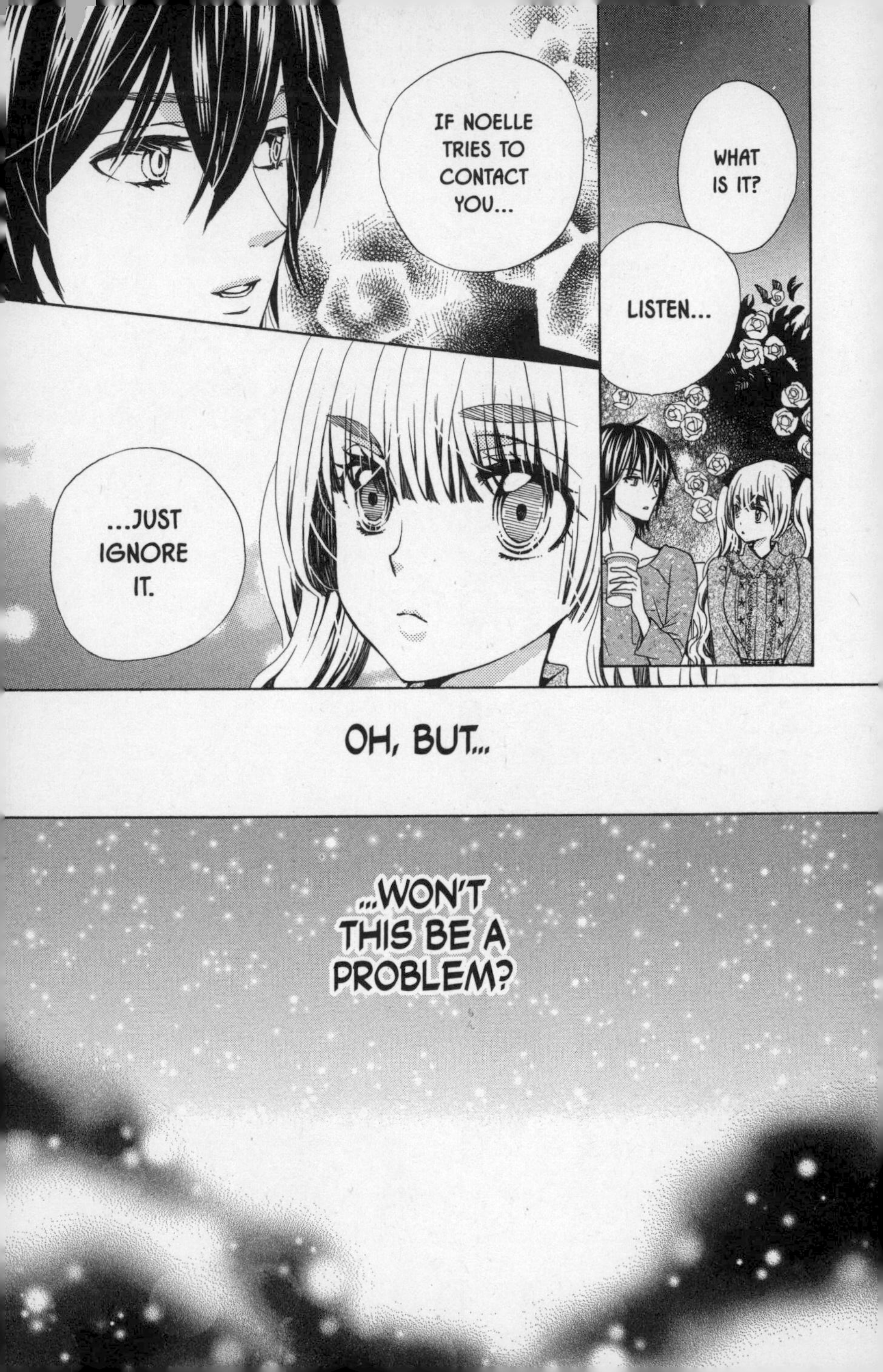
WHAT IS IT?
LISTEN...
IF NOELLE TRIES TO CONTACT YOU...
...JUST IGNORE IT.
OH, BUT...
...WON'T THIS BE A PROBLEM?

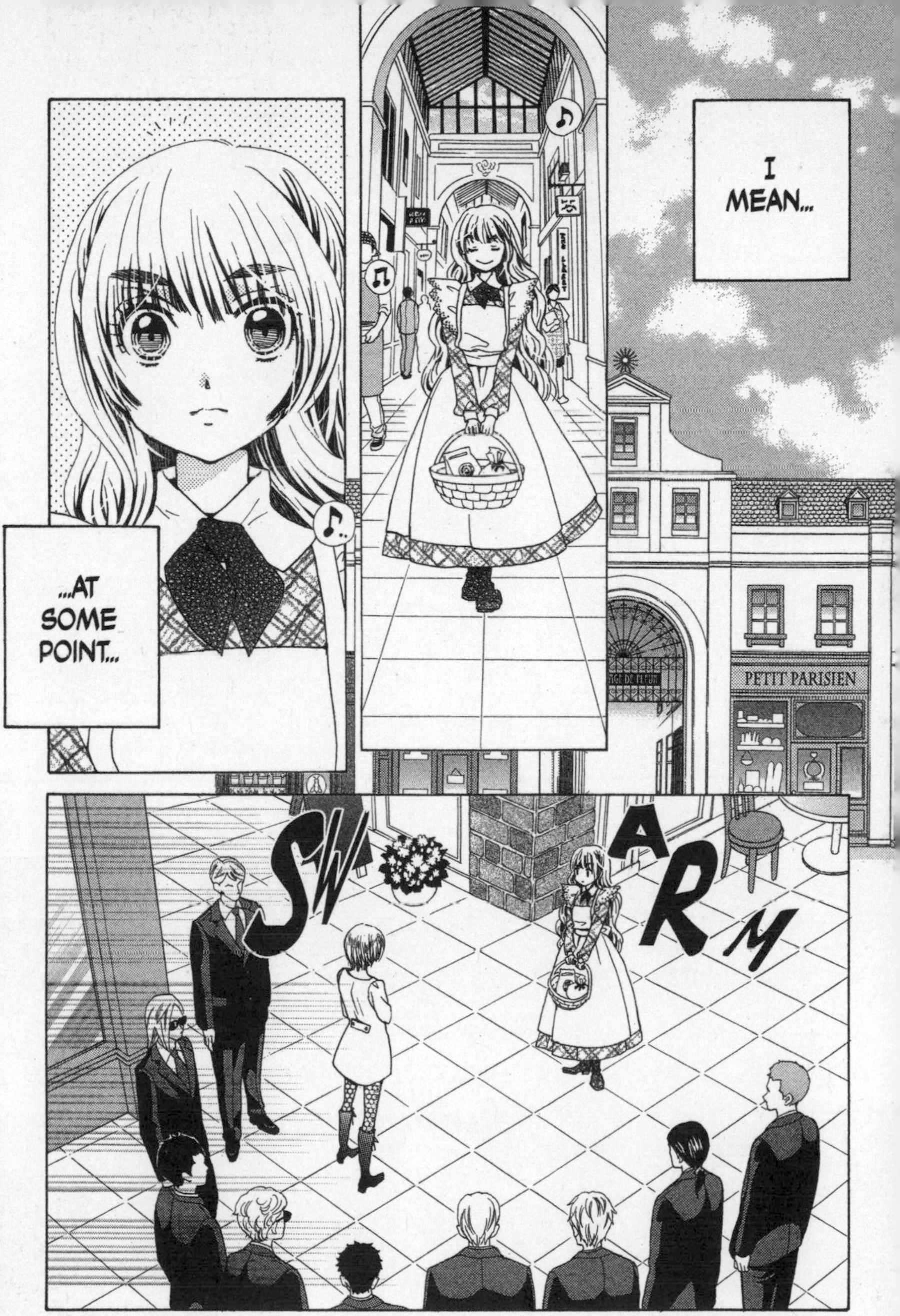

I MEAN...
PETIT PARISIEN
...AT SOME POINT...
SWARM

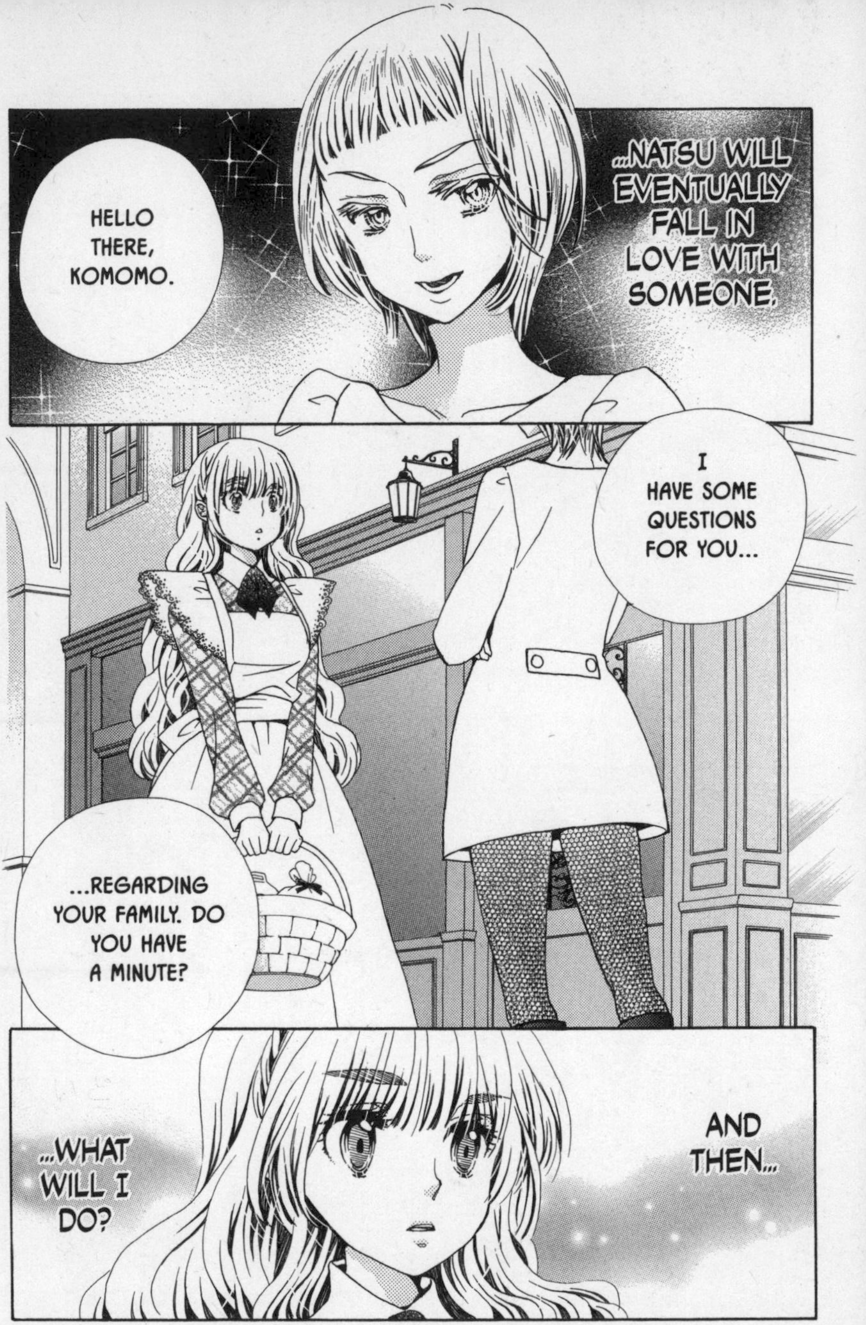
...NATSU WILL EVENTUALLY FALL IN LOVE WITH SOMEONE.
HELLO THERE, KOMOMO.
I HAVE SOME QUESTIONS FOR YOU...
...REGARDING YOUR FAMILY. DO YOU HAVE A MINUTE?
AND THEN...
...WHAT WILL I DO?

CHAPTER 20

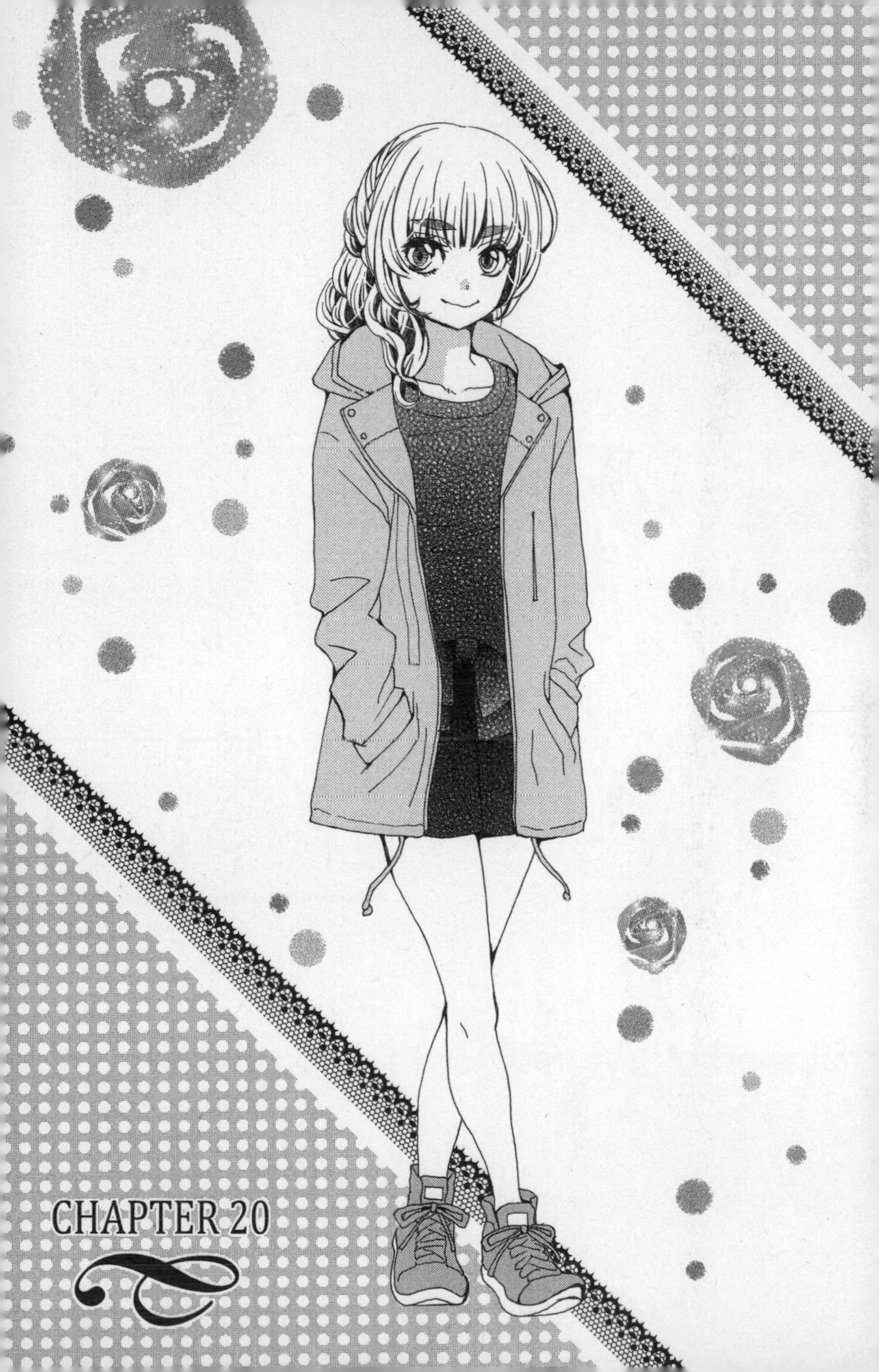

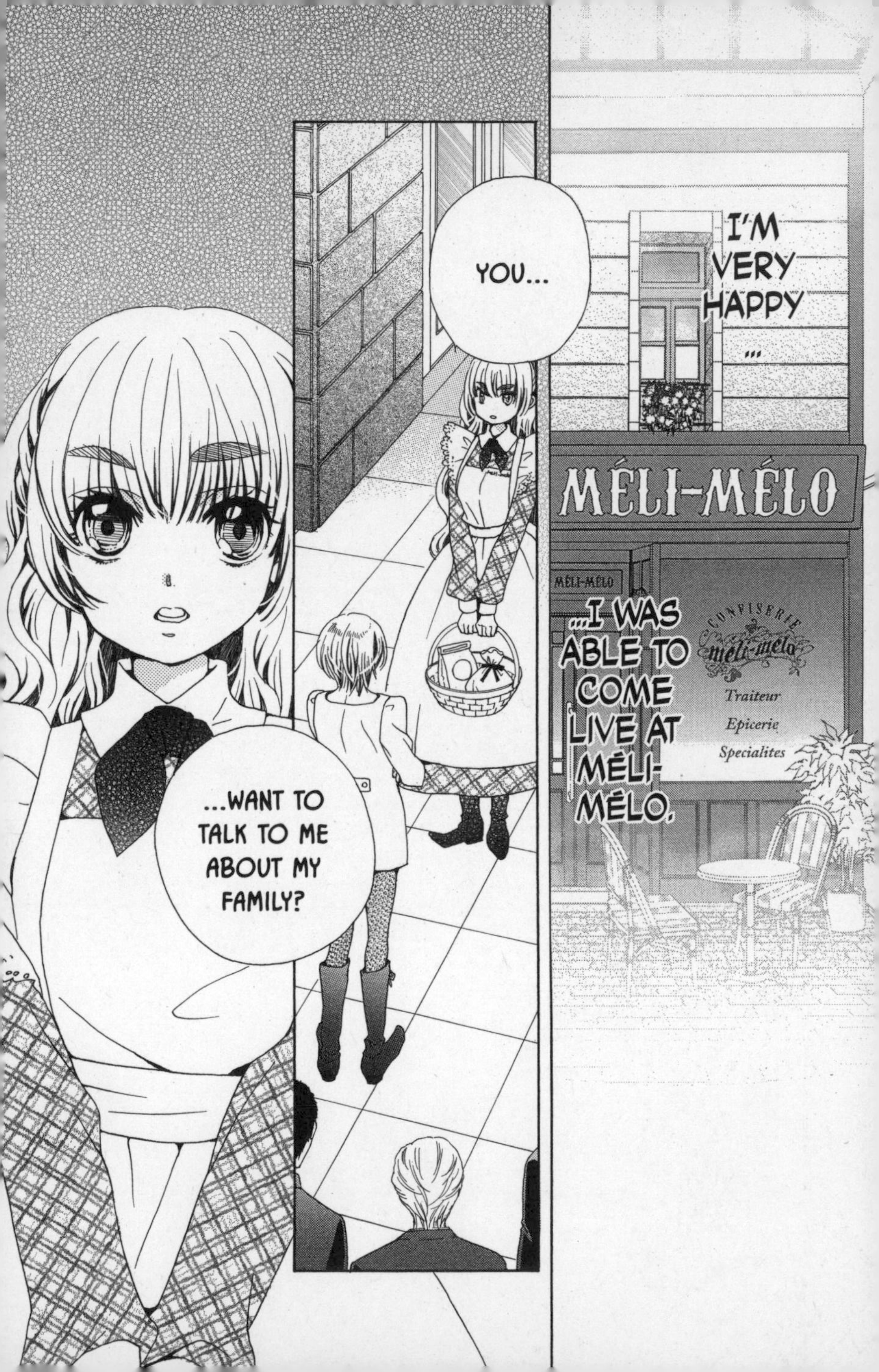
I'M VERY HAPPY ...
MÉLI-MÉLO
MÉLI-MÉLO
CONFISERIE méli-mélo
Traiteur
Epicerie
Specialites
...I WAS ABLE TO COME LIVE AT MÉLI-MÉLO.
YOU...
...WANT TO TALK TO ME ABOUT MY FAMILY?

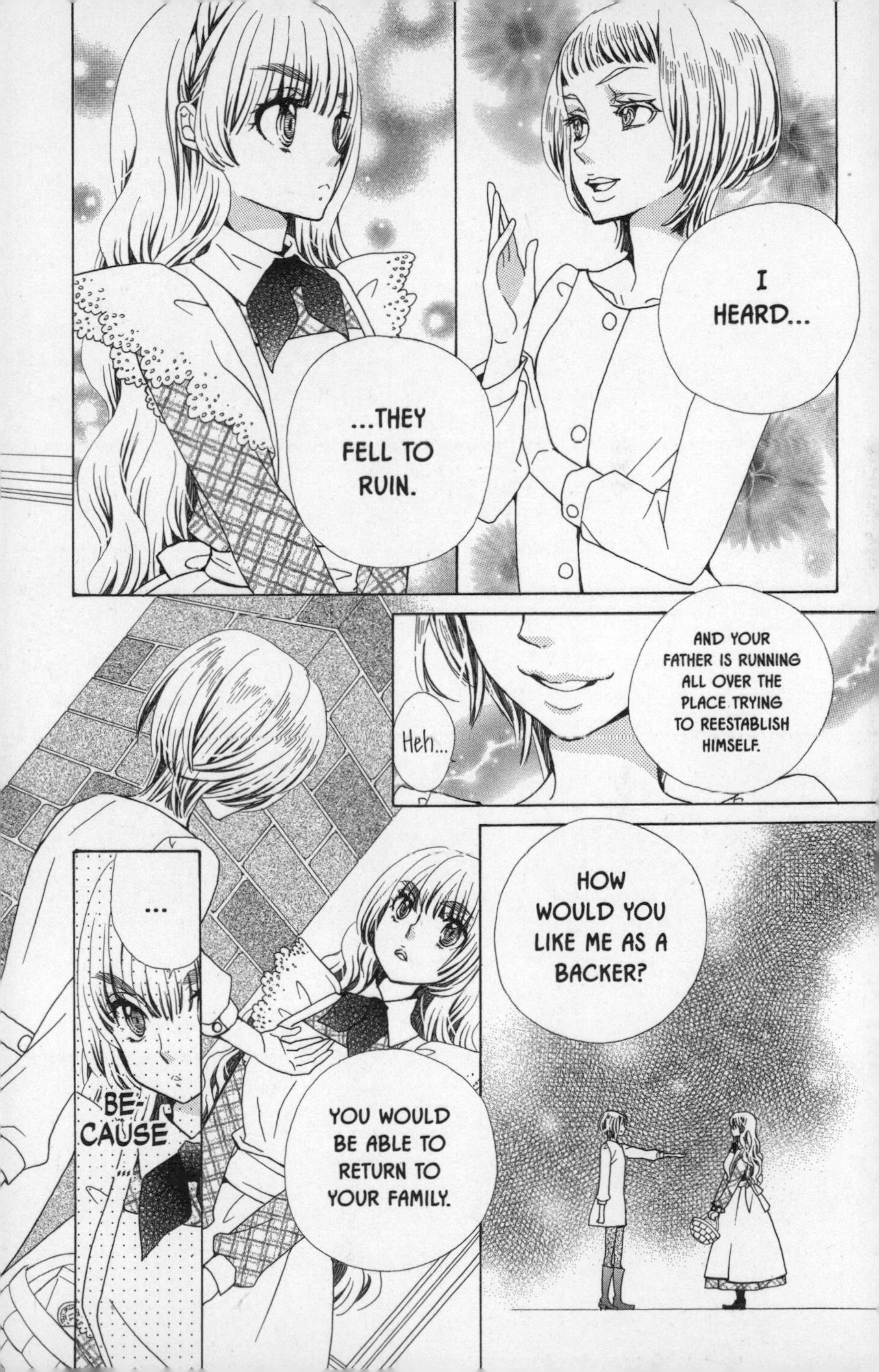
I HEARD...
...THEY FELL TO RUIN.
AND YOUR FATHER IS RUNNING ALL OVER THE PLACE TRYING TO REESTABLISH HIMSELF.
Heh...
HOW WOULD YOU LIKE ME AS A BACKER?
YOU WOULD BE ABLE TO RETURN TO YOUR FAMILY.
...
BE-CAUSE

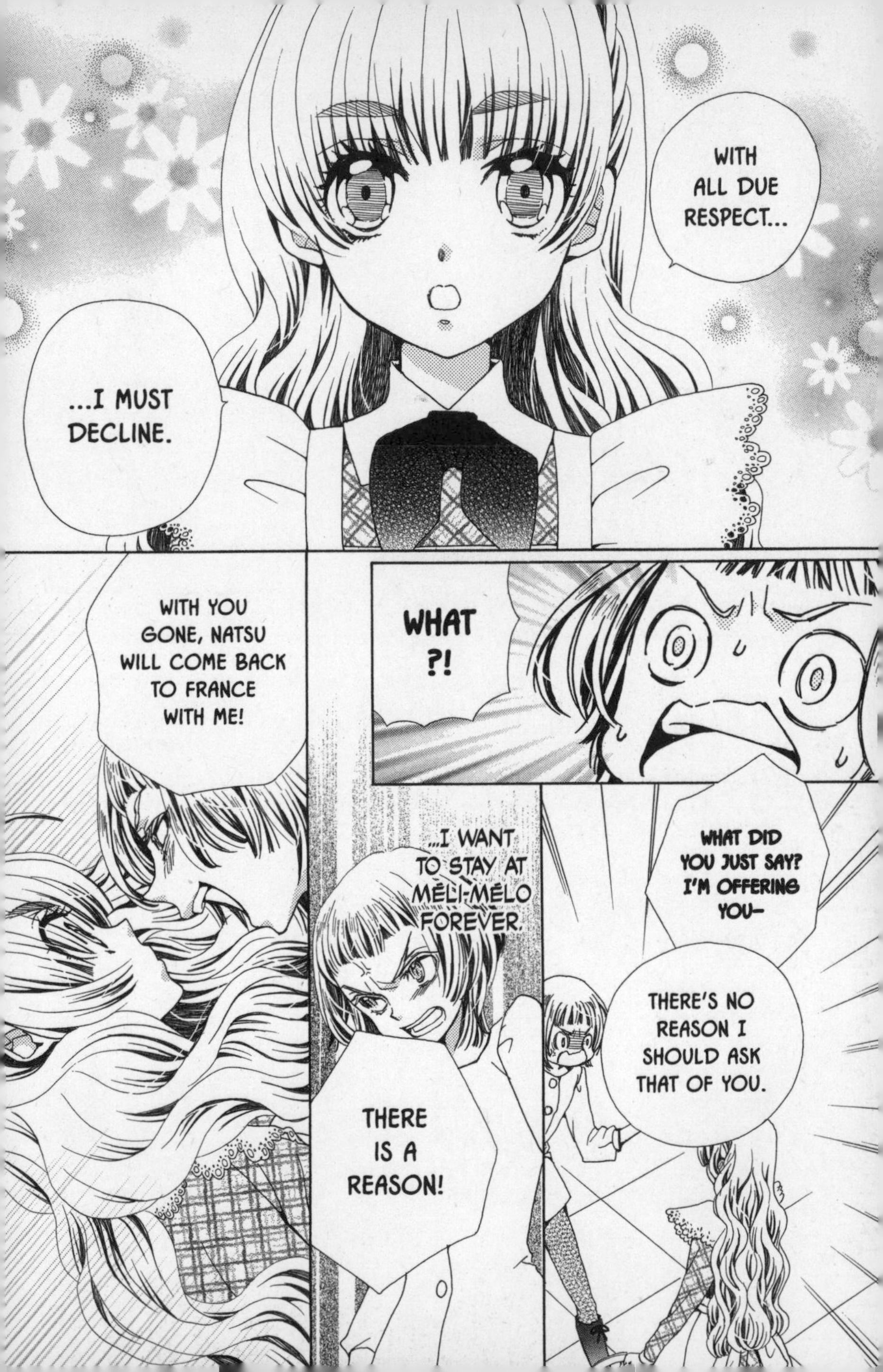
WITH ALL DUE RESPECT...
...I MUST DECLINE.
WHAT ?!
WHAT DID YOU JUST SAY? I'M OFFERING YOU–
THERE'S NO REASON I SHOULD ASK THAT OF YOU.
...I WANT TO STAY AT MÉLI-MÉLO FOREVER.
THERE IS A REASON!
WITH YOU GONE, NATSU WILL COME BACK TO FRANCE WITH ME!

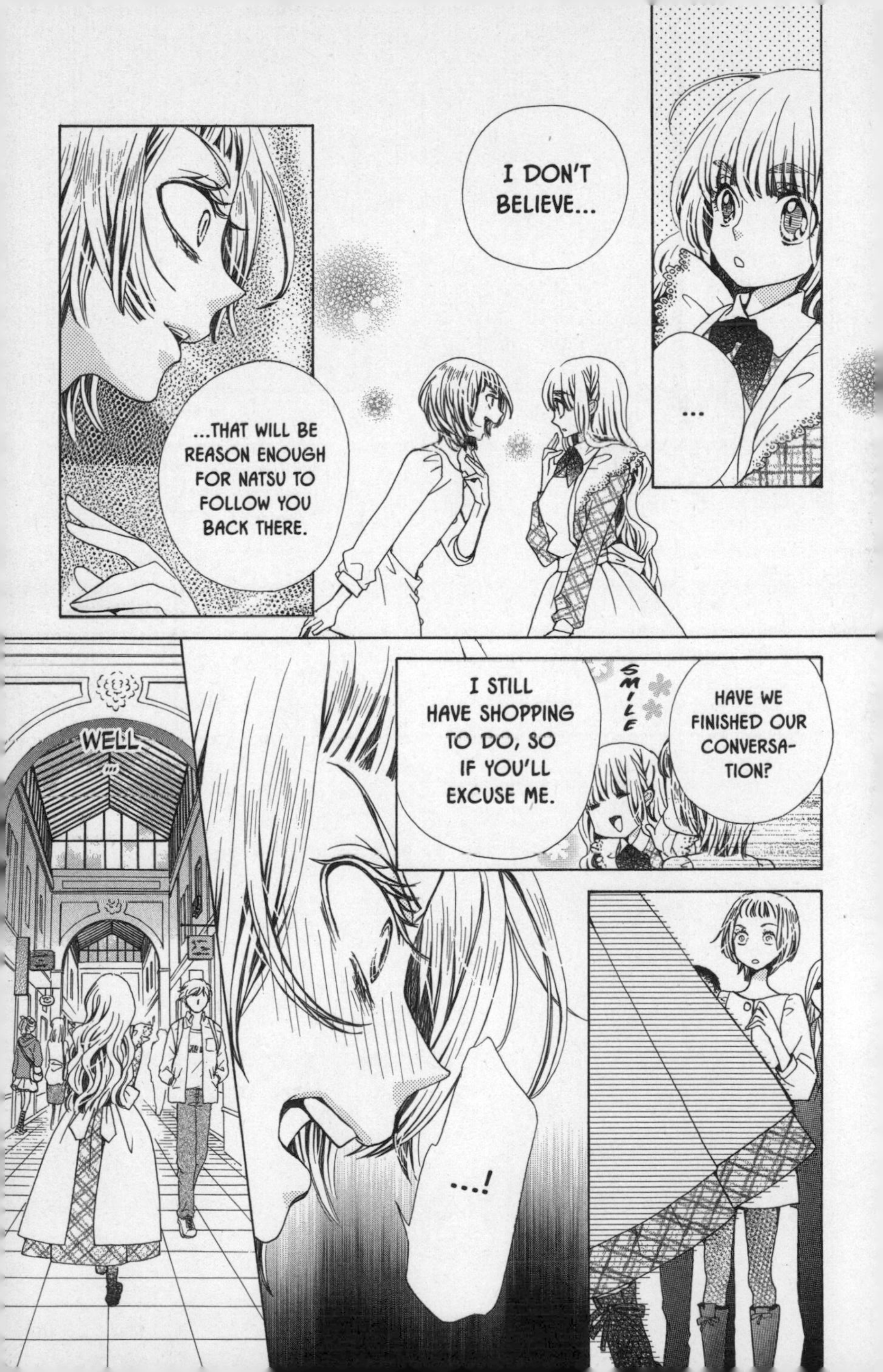
...
I DON'T BELIEVE...
...THAT WILL BE REASON ENOUGH FOR NATSU TO FOLLOW YOU BACK THERE.
HAVE WE FINISHED OUR CONVERSA-TION?
SMILE
I STILL HAVE SHOPPING TO DO, SO IF YOU'LL EXCUSE ME.
...!
WELL...

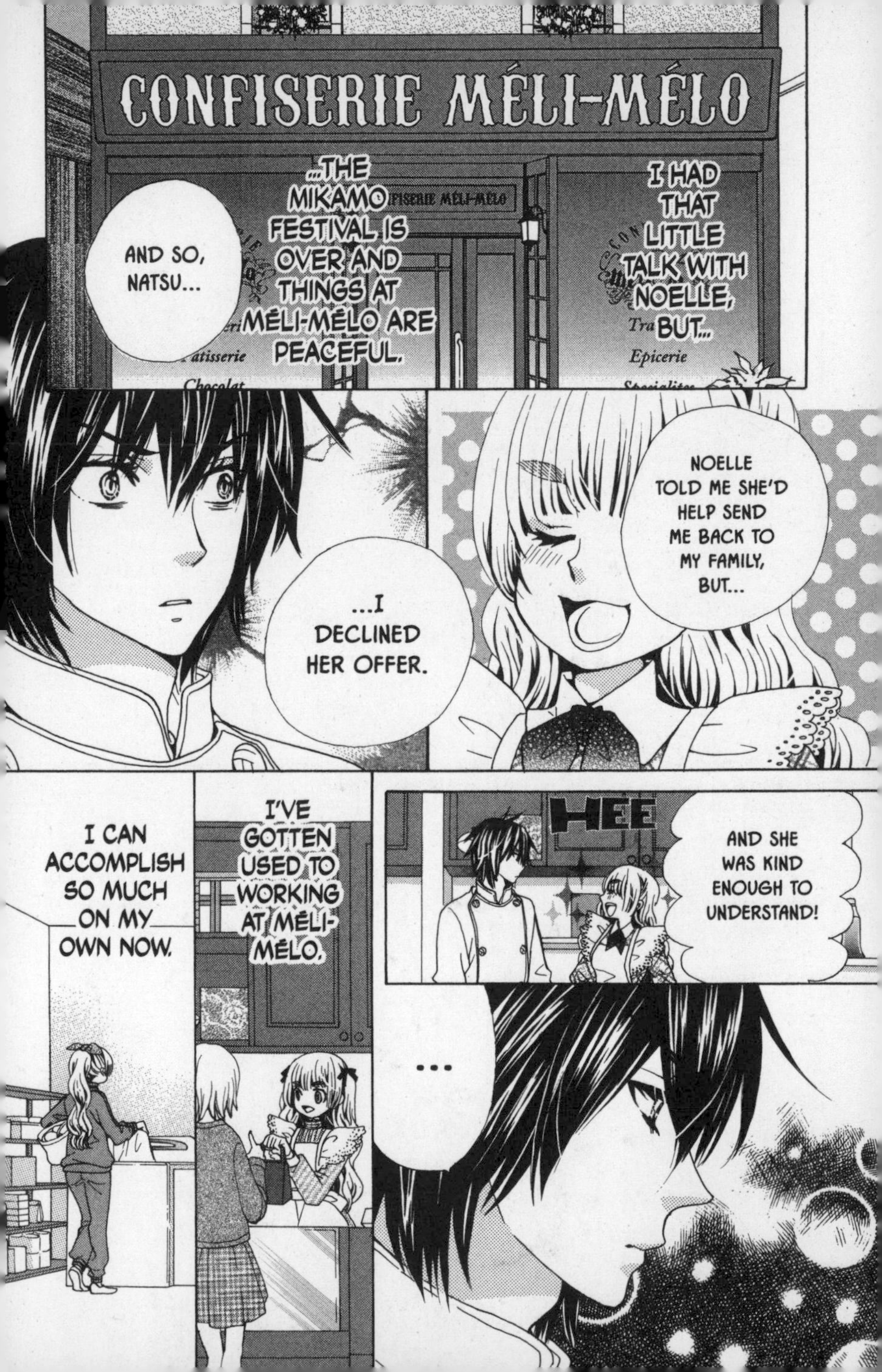
CONFISERIE MÉLI-MÉLO
I HAD THAT LITTLE TALK WITH NOELLE, BUT...
...THE MIKAMO FESTIVAL IS OVER AND THINGS AT MÉLI-MÉLO ARE PEACEFUL.
AND SO, NATSU...
NOELLE TOLD ME SHE'D HELP SEND ME BACK TO MY FAMILY, BUT...
...I DECLINED HER OFFER.
HEE
AND SHE WAS KIND ENOUGH TO UNDERSTAND!
...
I'VE GOTTEN USED TO WORKING AT MÉLI-MÉLO.
I CAN ACCOMPLISH SO MUCH ON MY OWN NOW.

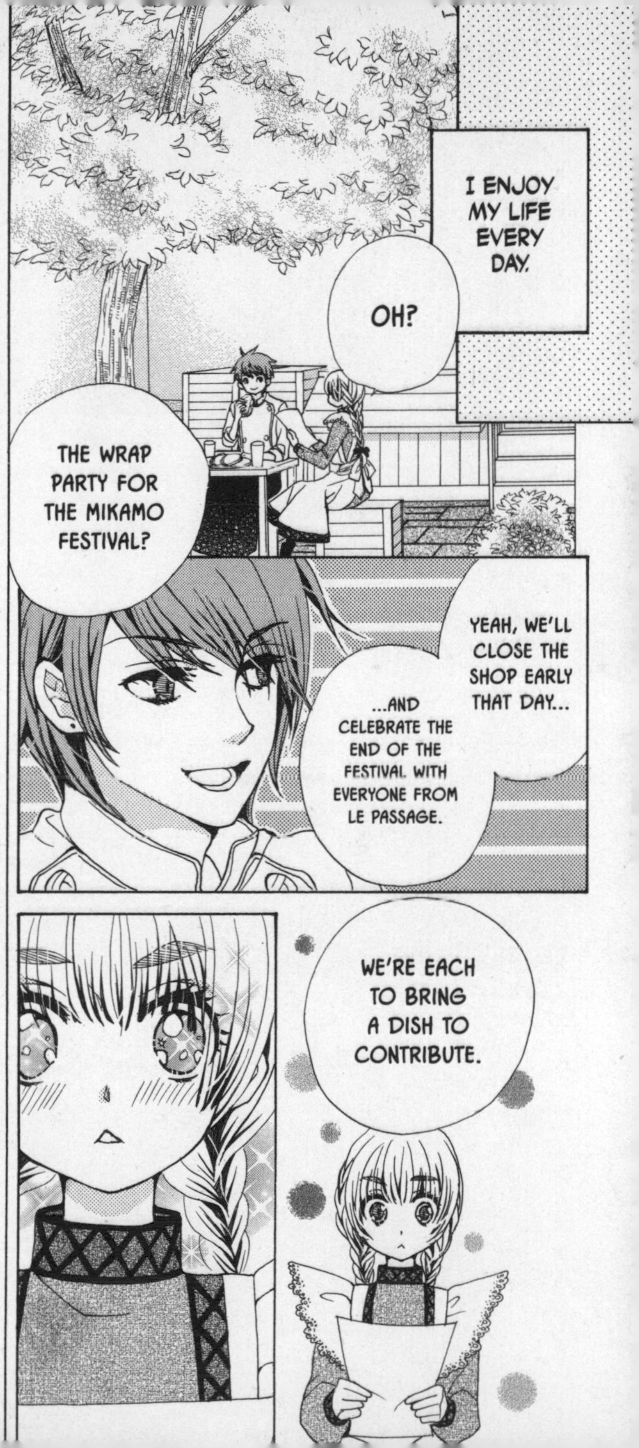
I ENJOY MY LIFE EVERY DAY.
OH?
THE WRAP PARTY FOR THE MIKAMO FESTIVAL?
YEAH, WE'LL CLOSE THE SHOP EARLY THAT DAY...
...AND CELEBRATE THE END OF THE FESTIVAL WITH EVERYONE FROM LE PASSAGE.
WE'RE EACH TO BRING A DISH TO CONTRIBUTE.

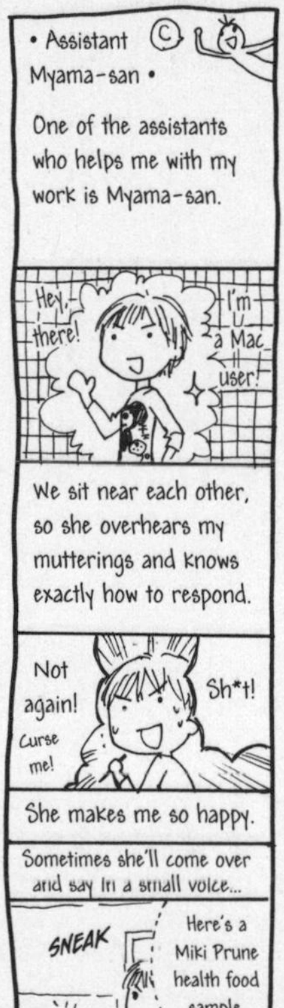
• Assistant Myama-san •
One of the assistants who helps me with my work is Myama-san.
Hey, there!
I'm a Mac user!
We sit near each other, so she overhears my mutterings and knows exactly how to respond.
Not again!
Curse me!
Sh*t!
She makes me so happy.
Sometimes she'll come over and say in a small voice...
SNEAK
Here's a Miki Prune health food sample.
CHOCOLATE
...while actually leaving a chocolate on my desk. (Miki Prunes would never taste that great.)
Yum!
She's a funny gal.
I'm so happy.

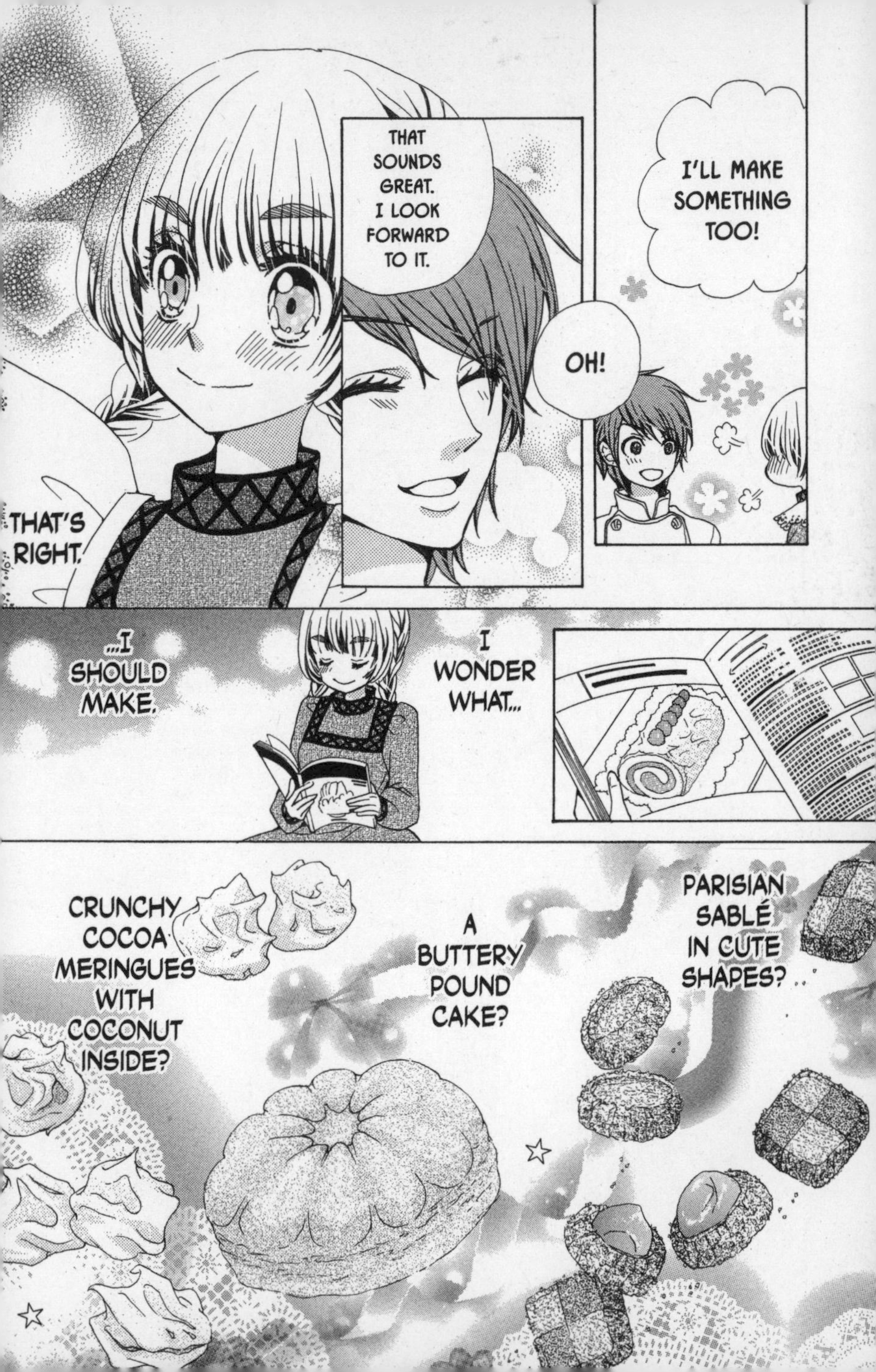
I'LL MAKE SOMETHING TOO!
OH!
THAT SOUNDS GREAT. I LOOK FORWARD TO IT.
THAT'S RIGHT.
I WONDER WHAT...
...I SHOULD MAKE.
PARISIAN SABLÉ IN CUTE SHAPES?
A BUTTERY POUND CAKE?
CRUNCHY COCOA MERINGUES WITH COCONUT INSIDE?

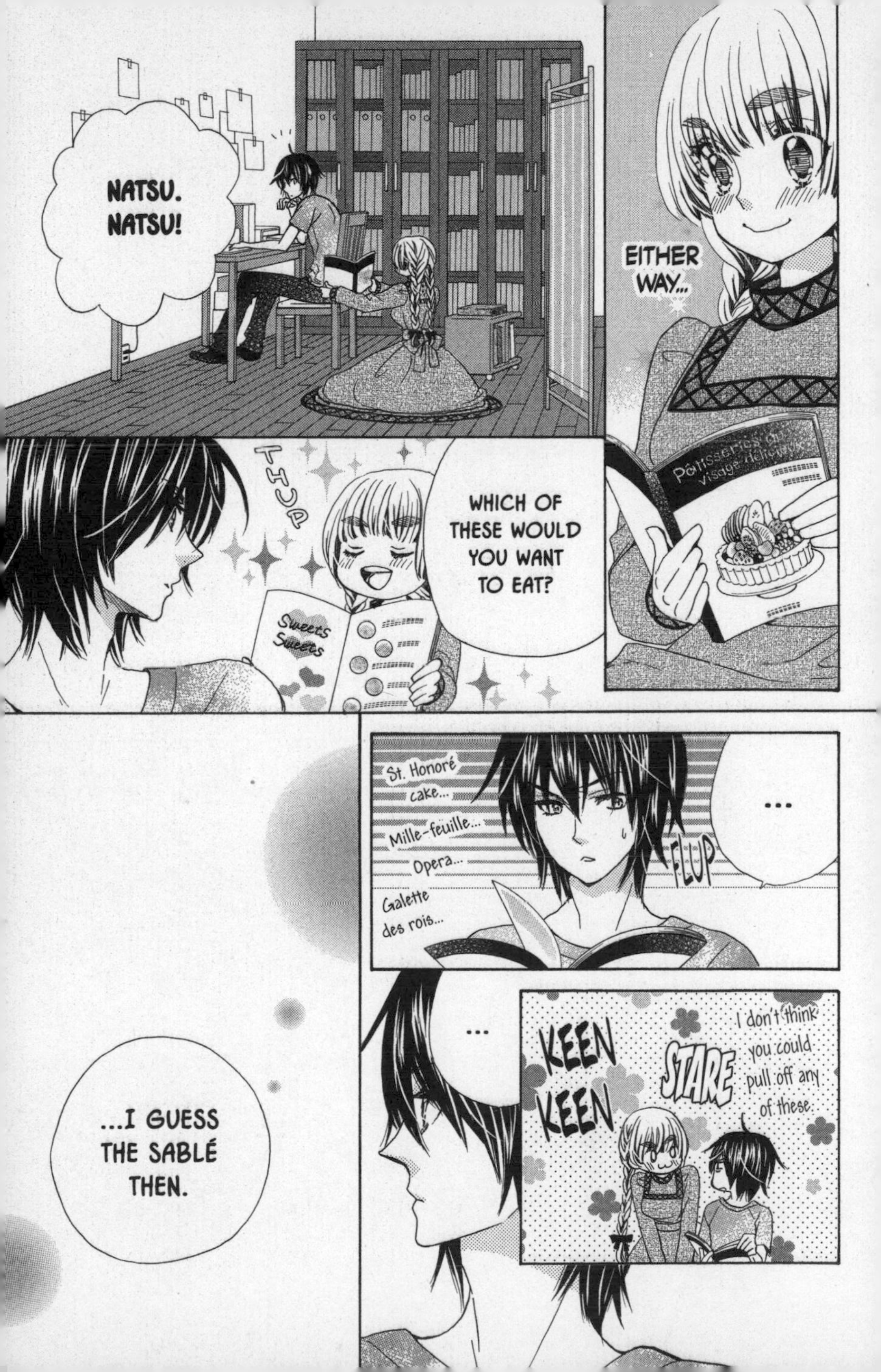
EITHER WAY...
NATSU.
NATSU!
THUP
WHICH OF THESE WOULD YOU WANT TO EAT?
Sweets Sweets
...
FLUP
St. Honoré cake...
Mille-feuille...
Opera...
Galette des rois...
I don't think you could pull off any of these.
STARE
KEEN KEEN
...
...I GUESS THE SABLÉ THEN.

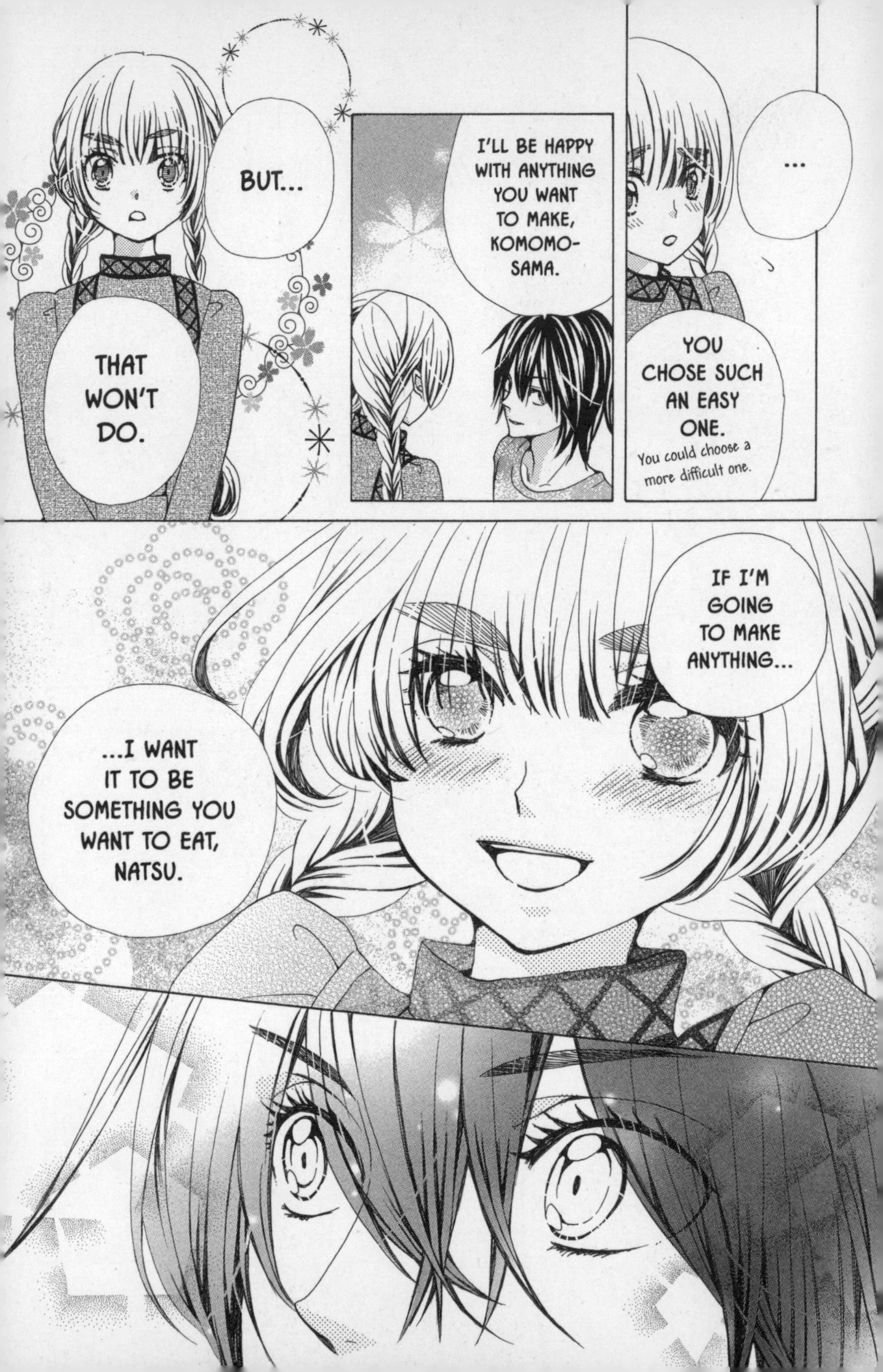
...
YOU CHOSE SUCH AN EASY ONE.
You could choose a more difficult one.
I'LL BE HAPPY WITH ANYTHING YOU WANT TO MAKE, KOMOMO-SAMA.
BUT...
THAT WON'T DO.
IF I'M GOING TO MAKE ANYTHING...
...I WANT IT TO BE SOMETHING YOU WANT TO EAT, NATSU.

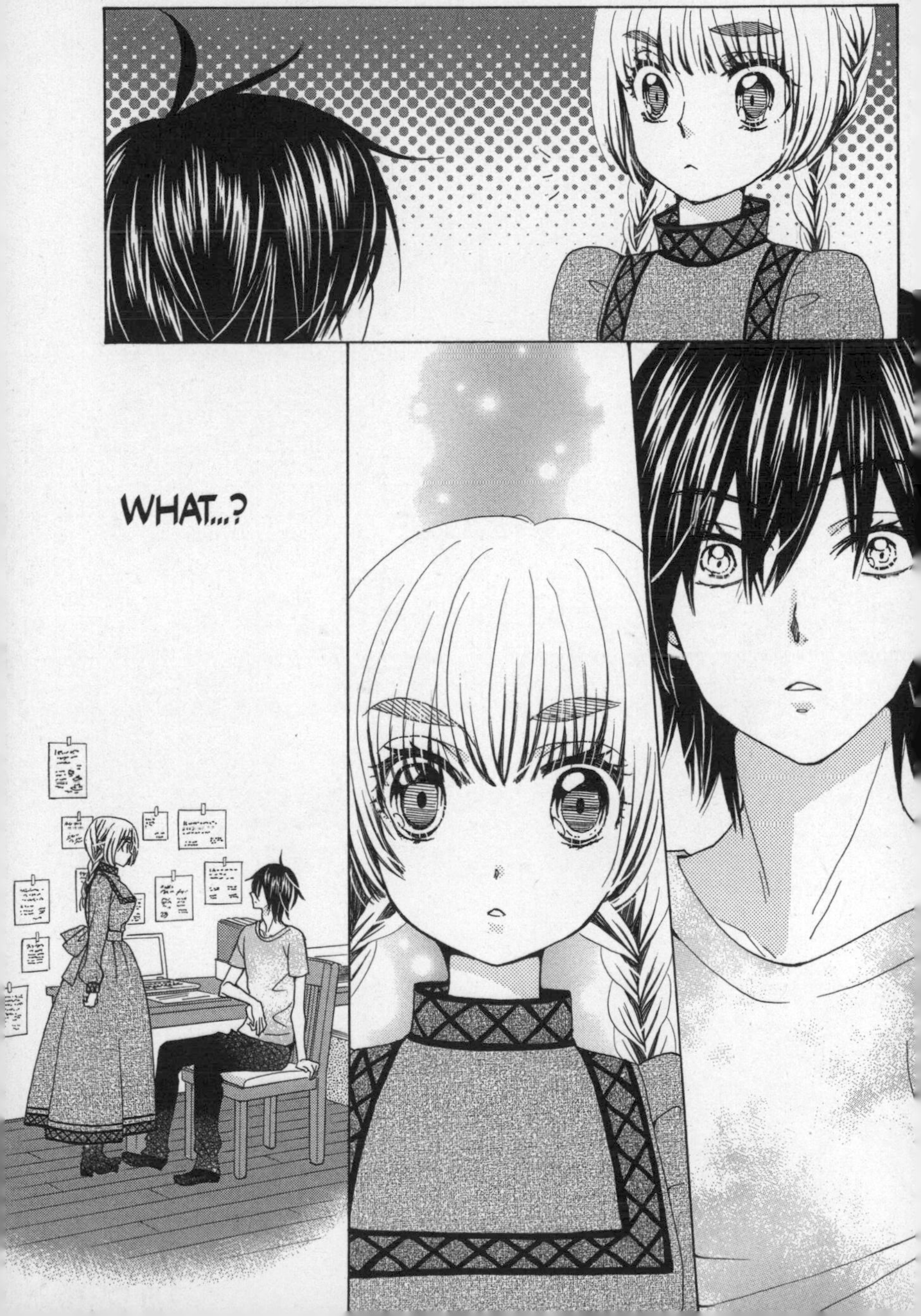
WHAT...?

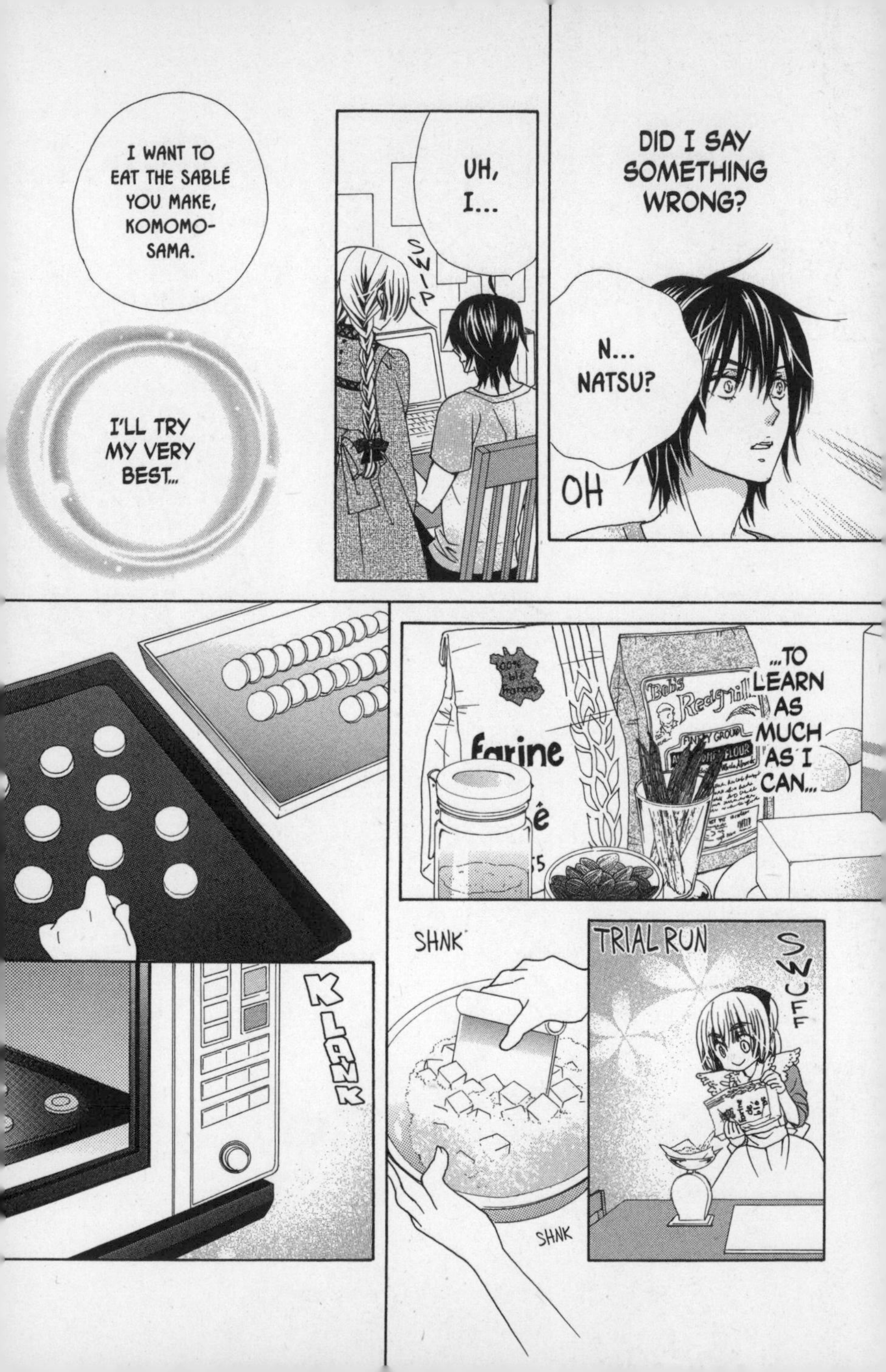

DID I SAY SOMETHING WRONG?
N... NATSU?
OH
UH, I...
SWIP
I WANT TO EAT THE SABLÉ YOU MAKE, KOMOMO-SAMA.
I'LL TRY MY VERY BEST...
...TO LEARN AS MUCH AS I CAN...
farine
Bob's Red Mill
TRIAL RUN
SWUFF
SHNK
SHNK
KLANK

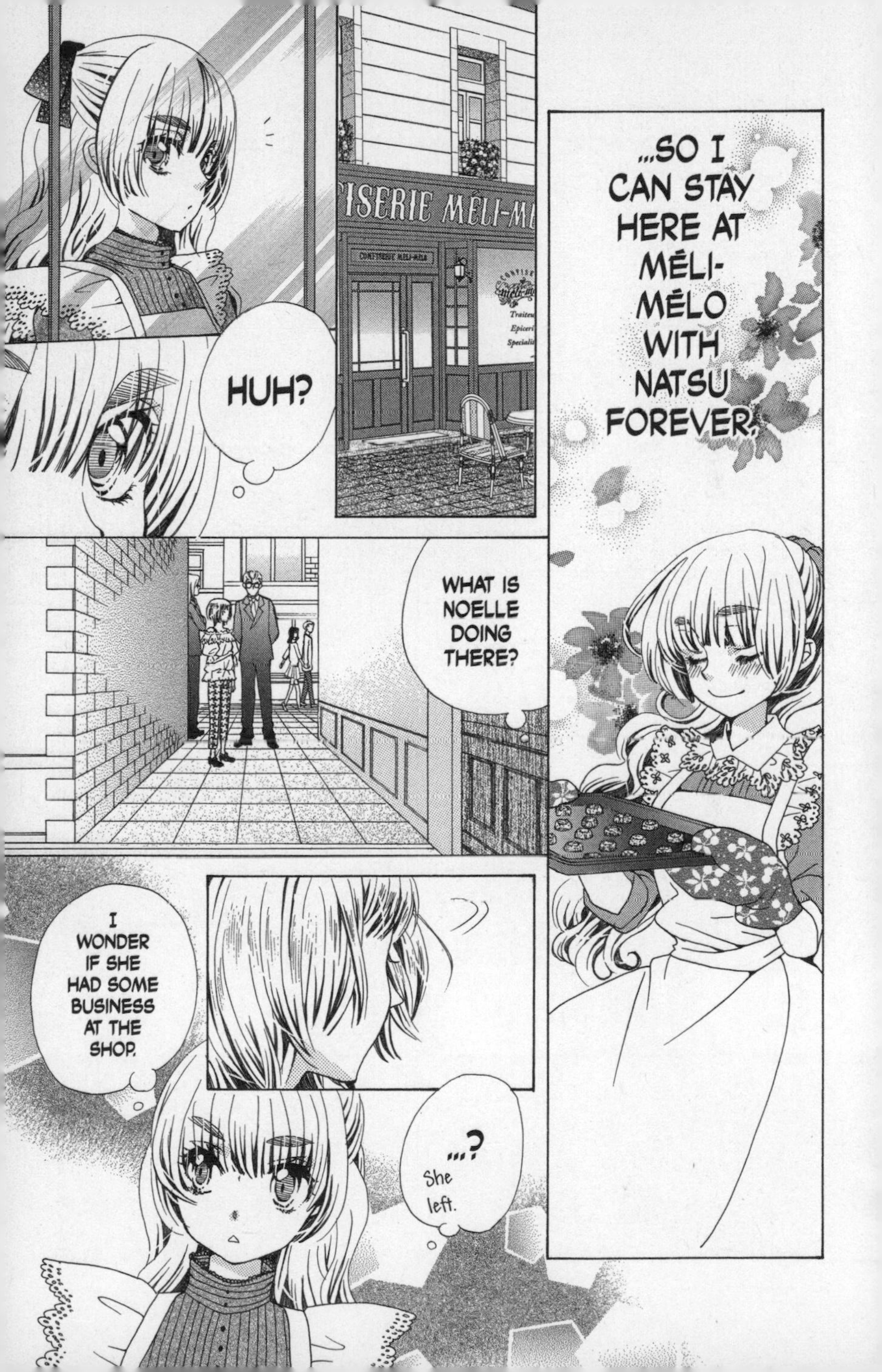
...SO I CAN STAY HERE AT MÉLI-MÉLO WITH NATSU FOREVER.
HUH?
WHAT IS NOELLE DOING THERE?
I WONDER IF SHE HAD SOME BUSINESS AT THE SHOP.
...?
She left.

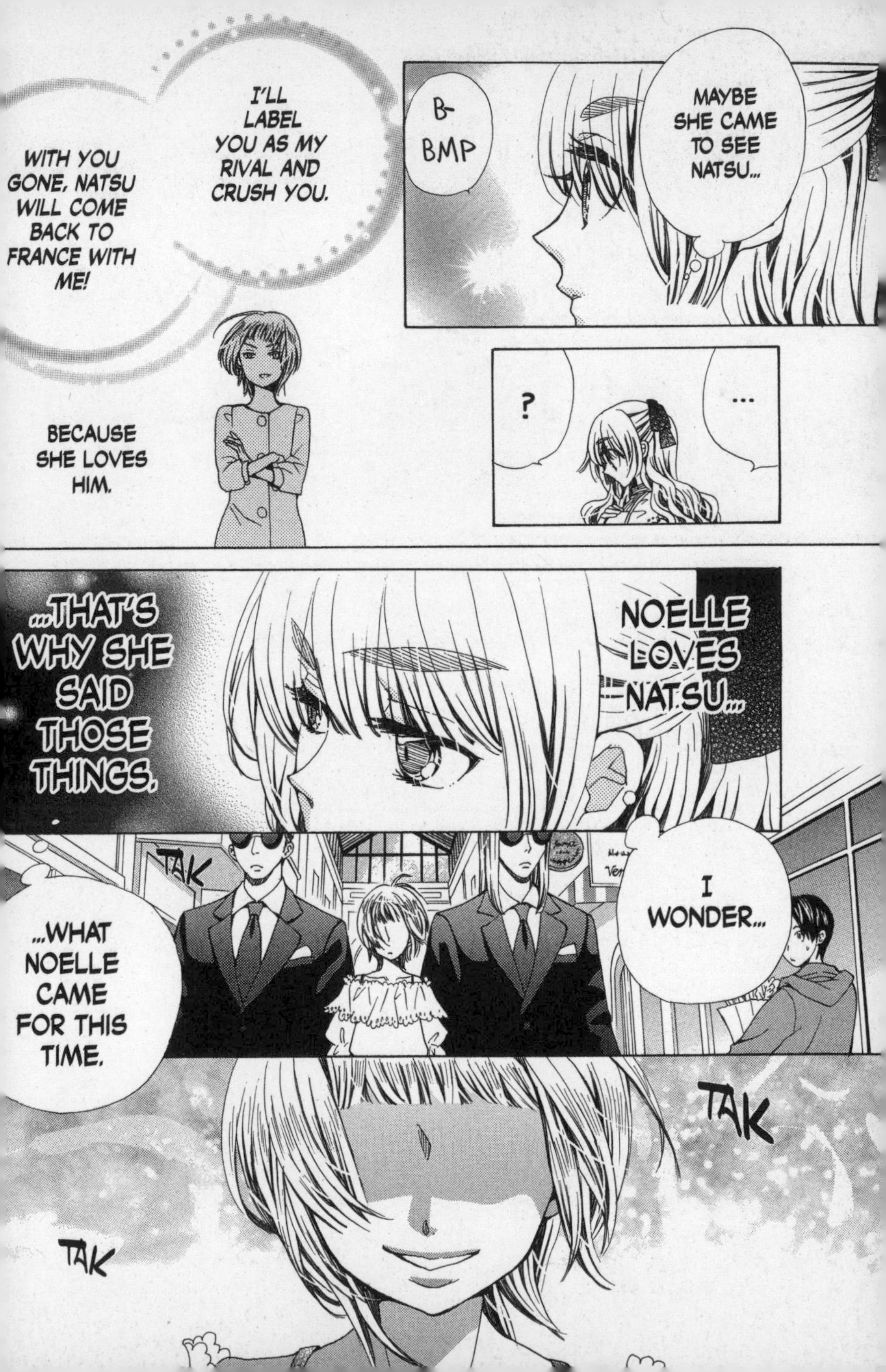
MAYBE SHE CAME TO SEE NATSU...
B-BMP
...
?
I'LL LABEL YOU AS MY RIVAL AND CRUSH YOU.
WITH YOU GONE, NATSU WILL COME BACK TO FRANCE WITH ME!
BECAUSE SHE LOVES HIM.
NOELLE LOVES NATSU...
...THAT'S WHY SHE SAID THOSE THINGS.
I WONDER...
TAK
...WHAT NOELLE CAME FOR THIS TIME.
TAK
TAK

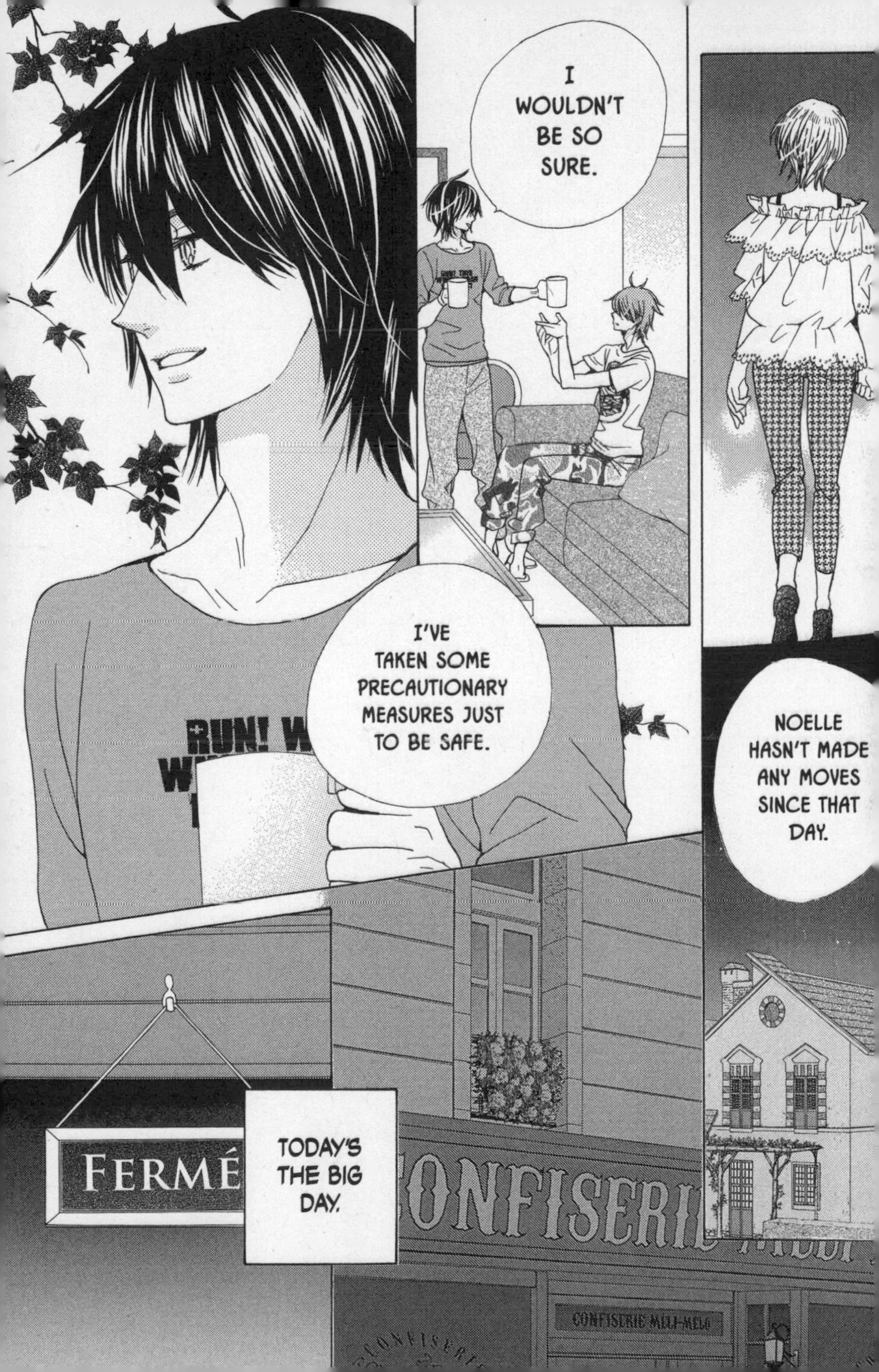
NOELLE HASN'T MADE ANY MOVES SINCE THAT DAY.
I WOULDN'T BE SO SURE.
I'VE TAKEN SOME PRECAUTIONARY MEASURES JUST TO BE SAFE.
CONFISERIE MELI-MELO
CONFISERIE
TODAY'S THE BIG DAY.
FERMÉ

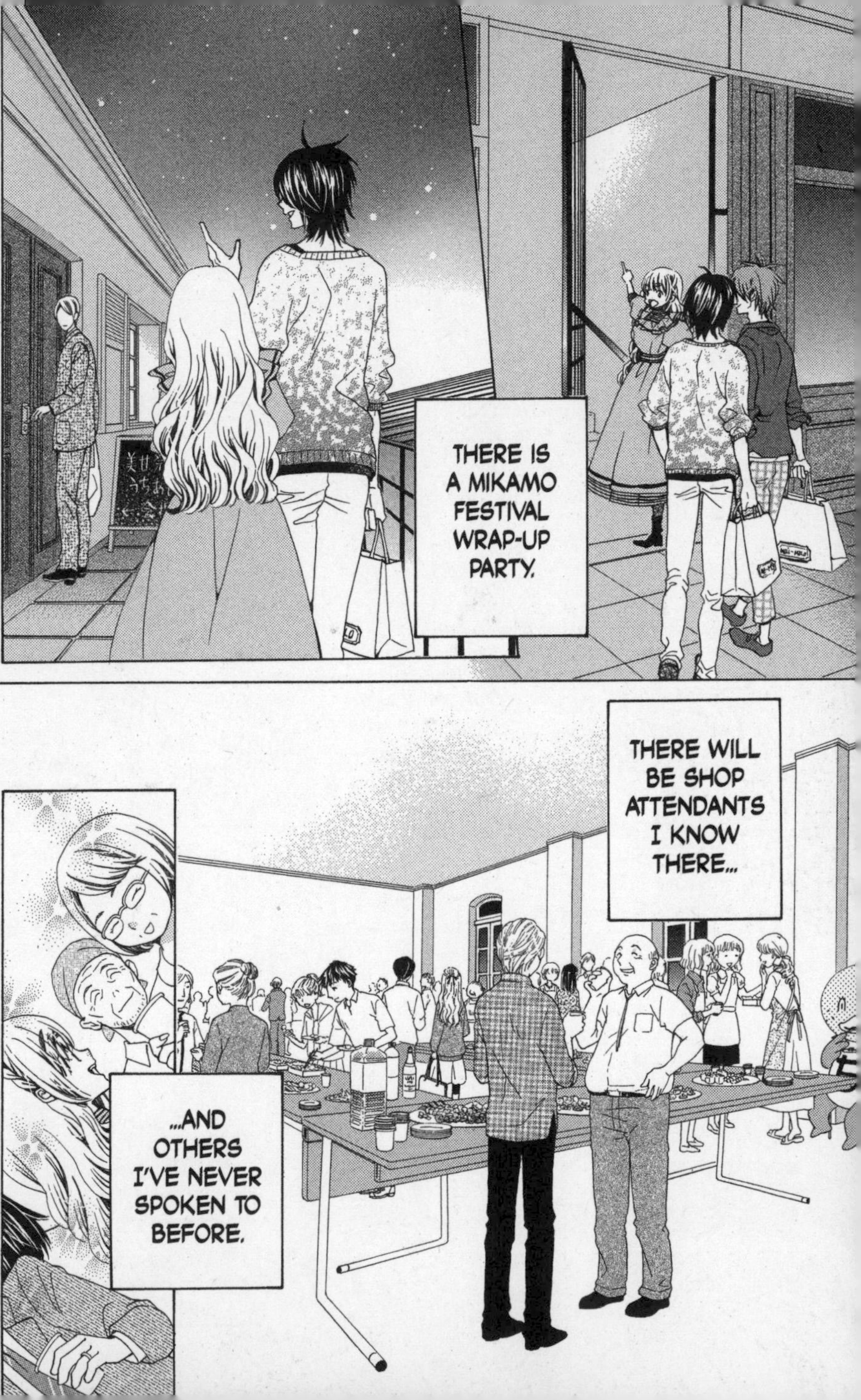
THERE IS A MIKAMO FESTIVAL WRAP-UP PARTY.
THERE WILL BE SHOP ATTENDANTS I KNOW THERE...
...AND OTHERS I'VE NEVER SPOKEN TO BEFORE.

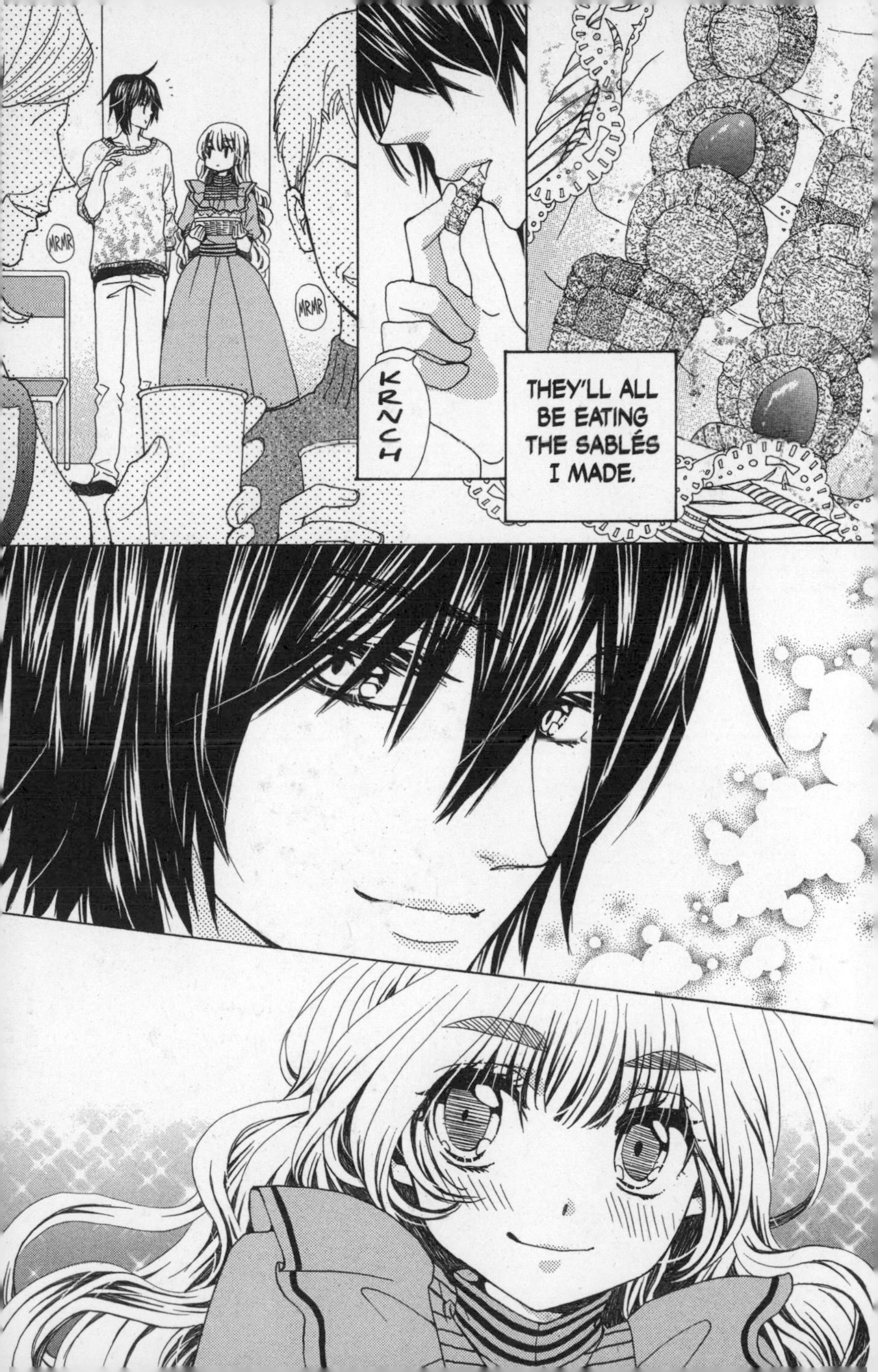
THEY'LL ALL BE EATING THE SABLÉS I MADE.
KRNCH
MRMR
MRMR

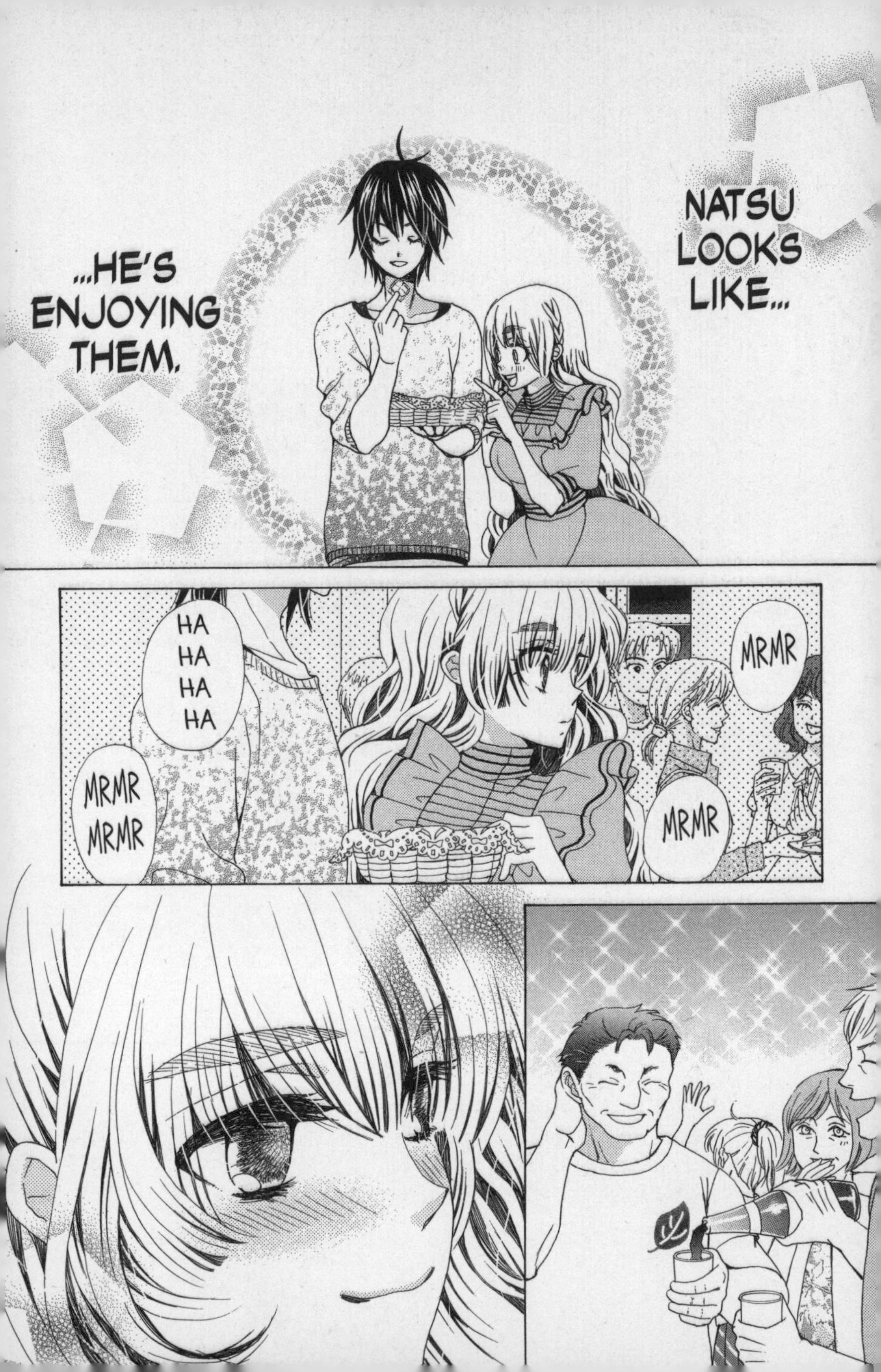
NATSU LOOKS LIKE...
...HE'S ENJOYING THEM.
MRMR
MRMR
HA HA HA HA
MRMR MRMR

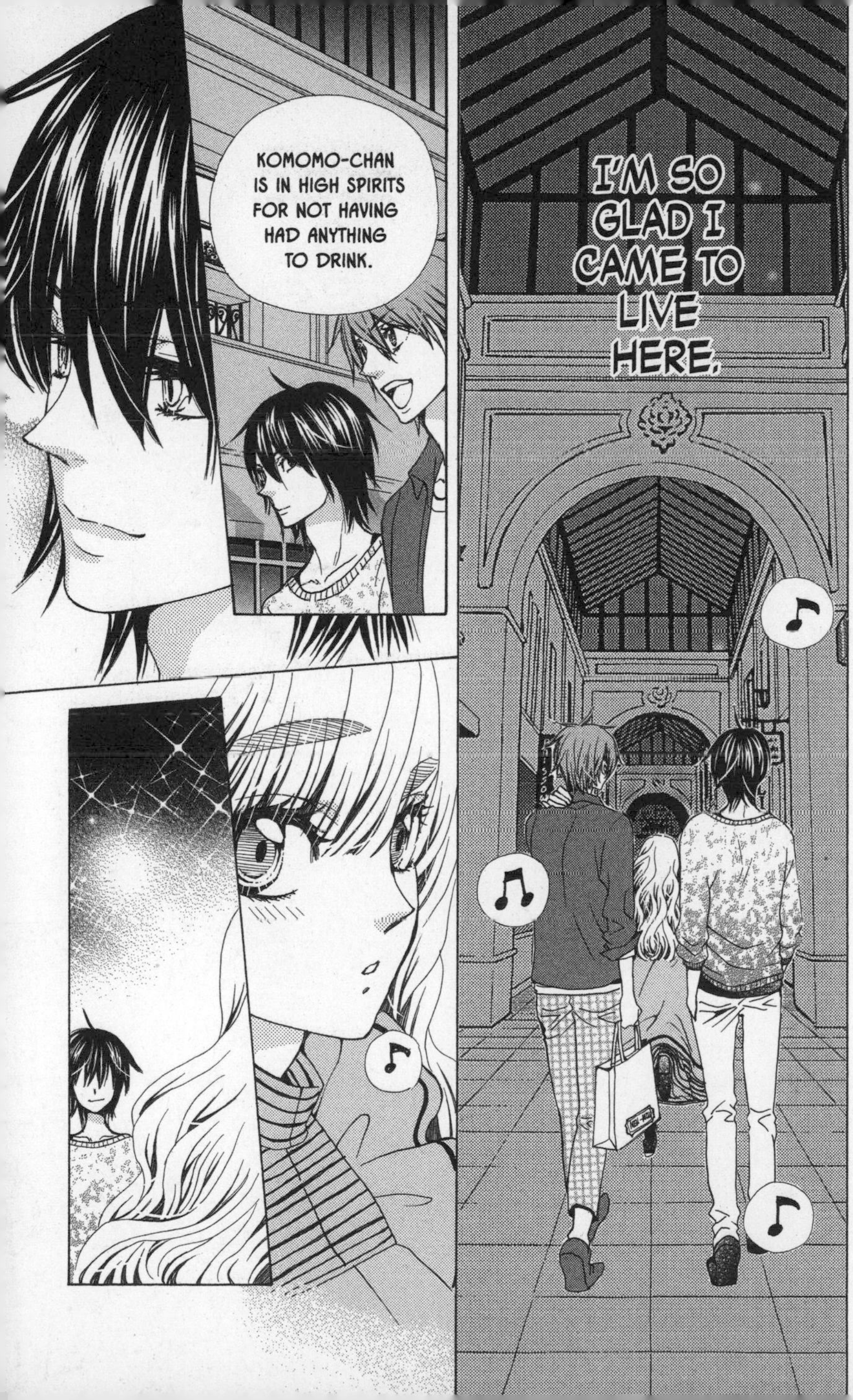
I'M SO GLAD I CAME TO LIVE HERE.
♪
♫
♪
KOMOMO-CHAN IS IN HIGH SPIRITS FOR NOT HAVING HAD ANYTHING TO DRINK.
♪

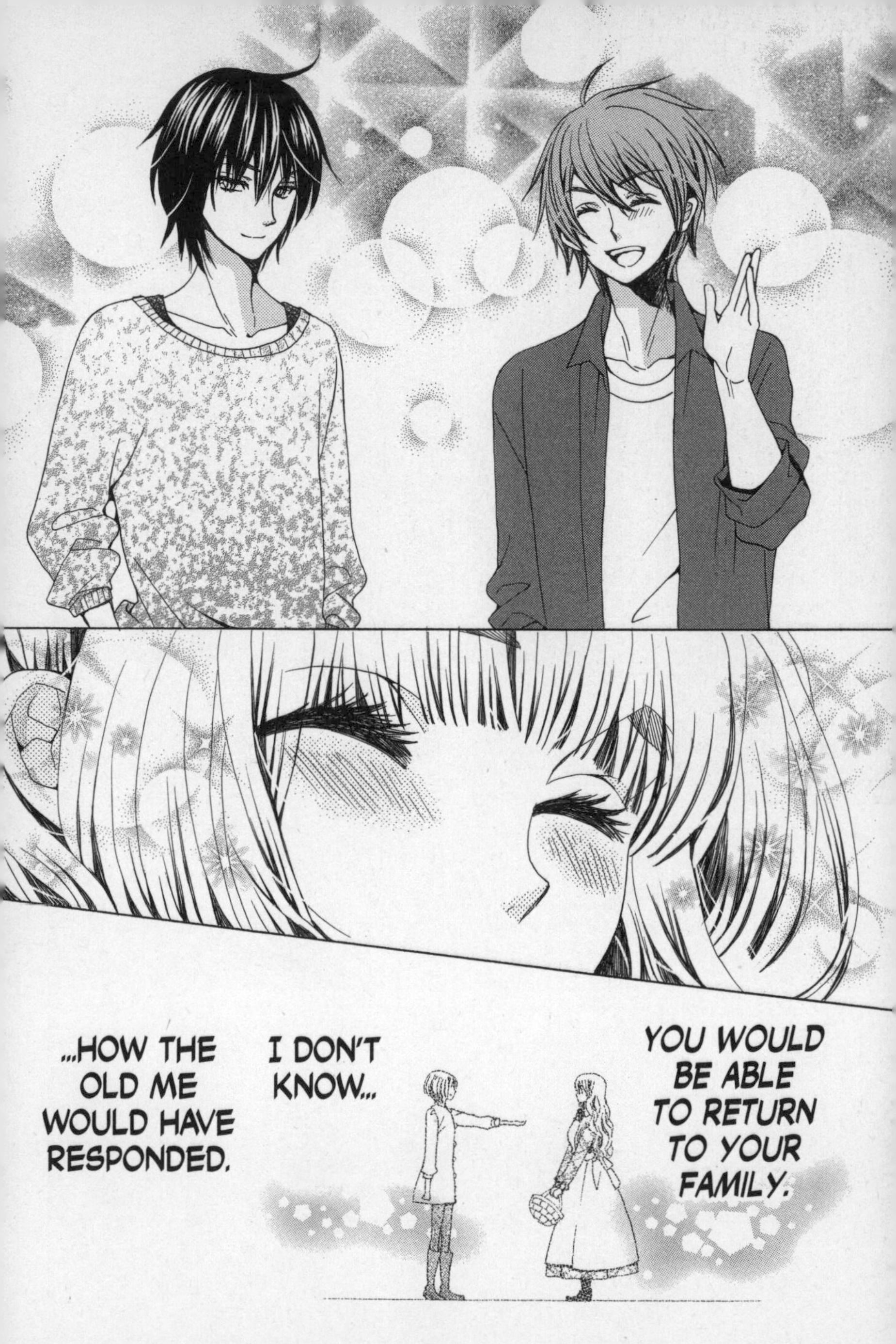
YOU WOULD BE ABLE TO RETURN TO YOUR FAMILY.
I DON'T KNOW...
...HOW THE OLD ME WOULD HAVE RESPONDED.

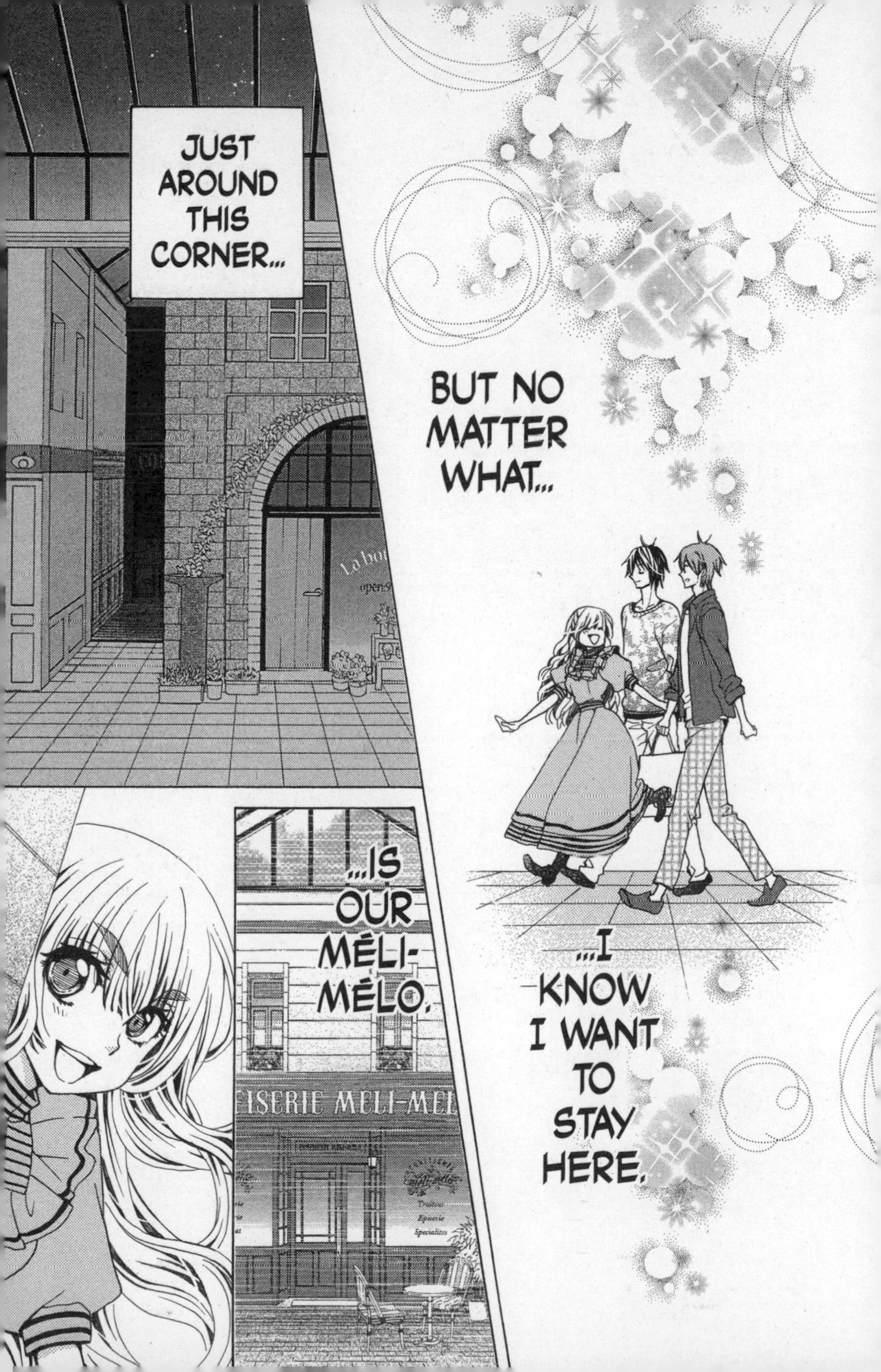
BUT NO MATTER WHAT...
...I KNOW I WANT TO STAY HERE.
JUST AROUND THIS CORNER...
...IS OUR MÉLI-MÉLO.

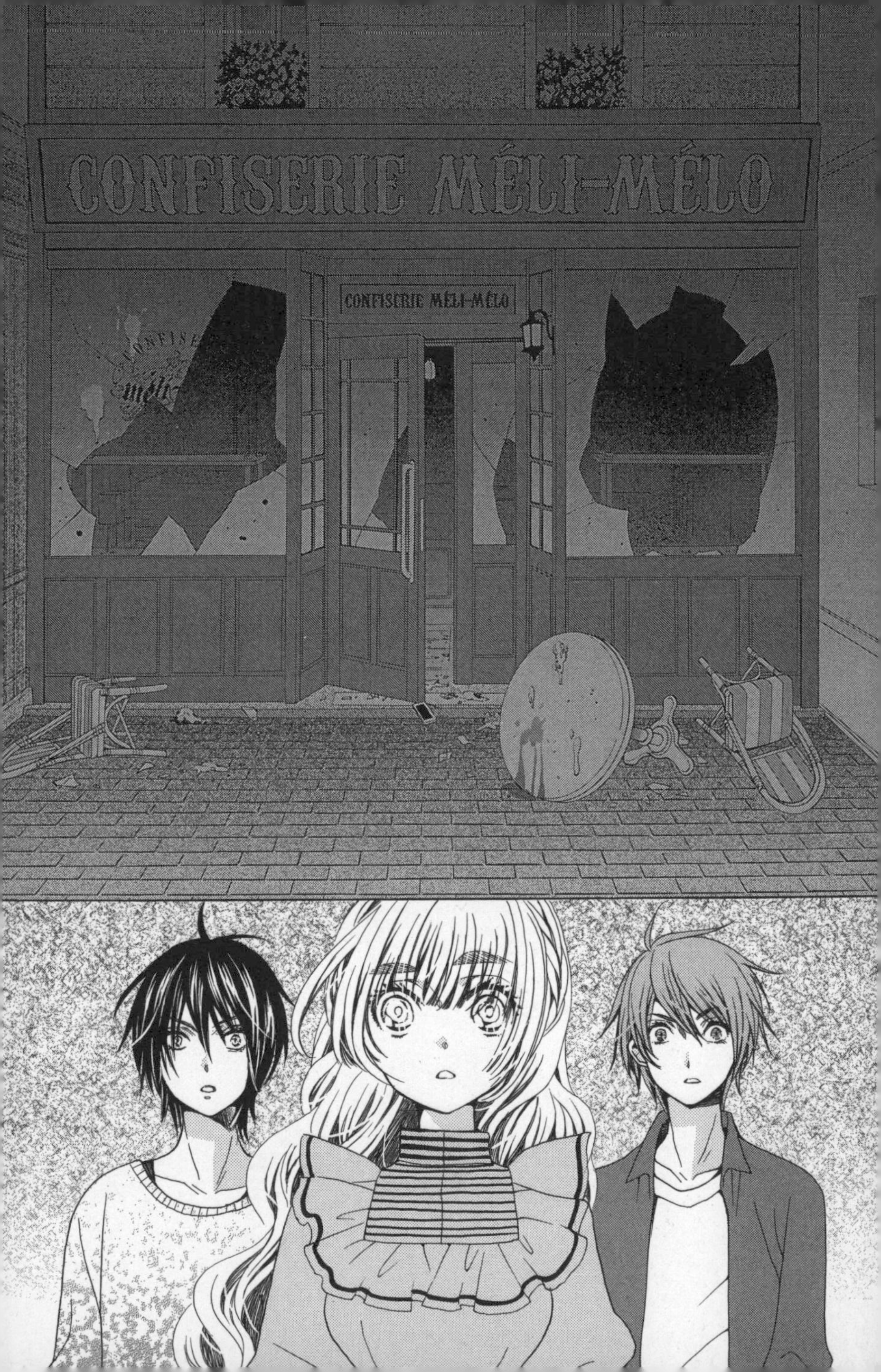
CONFISERIE MÉLI-MÉLO
CONFISERIE MÉLI-MÉLO

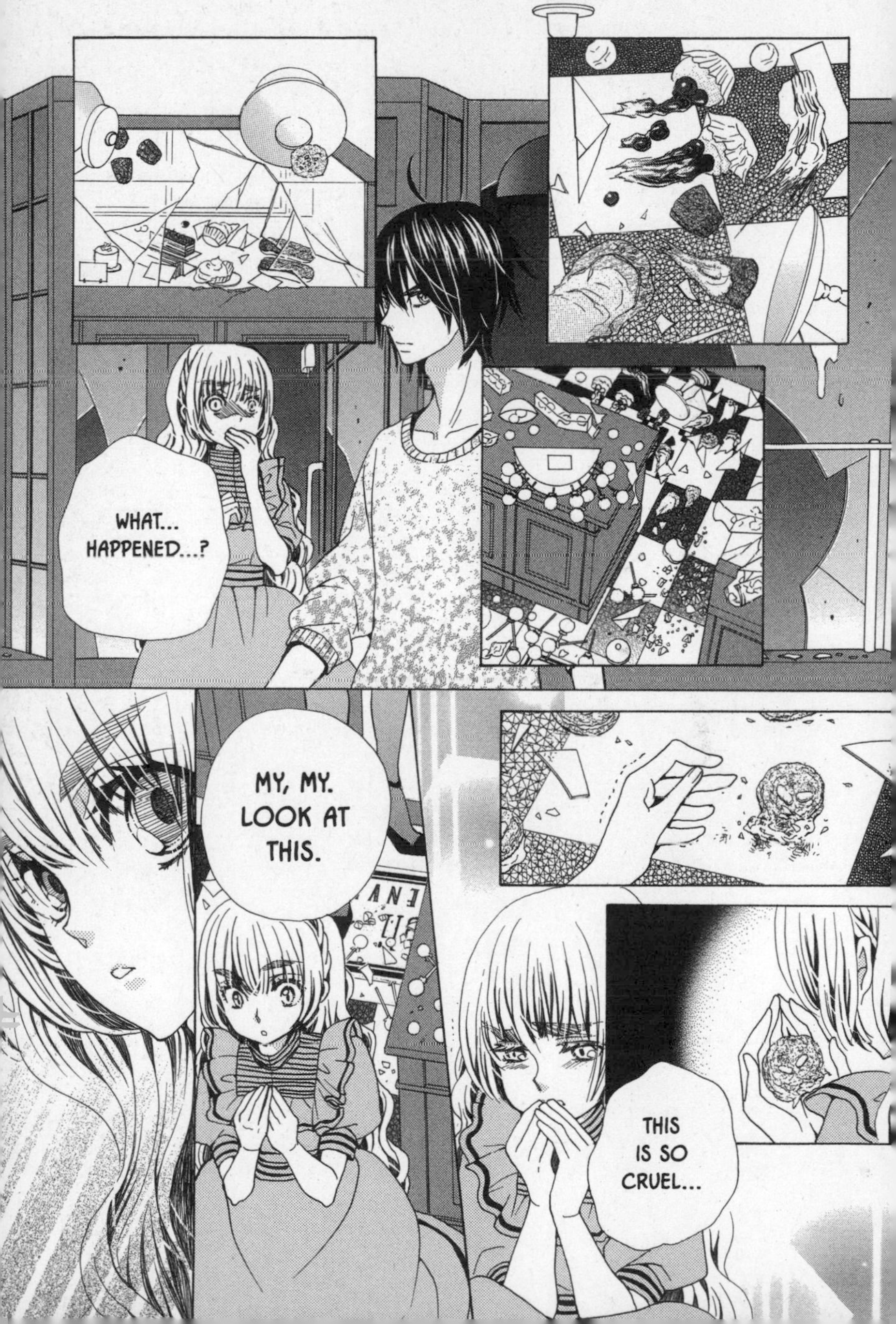
WHAT... HAPPENED...?
THIS IS SO CRUEL...
MY, MY. LOOK AT THIS.

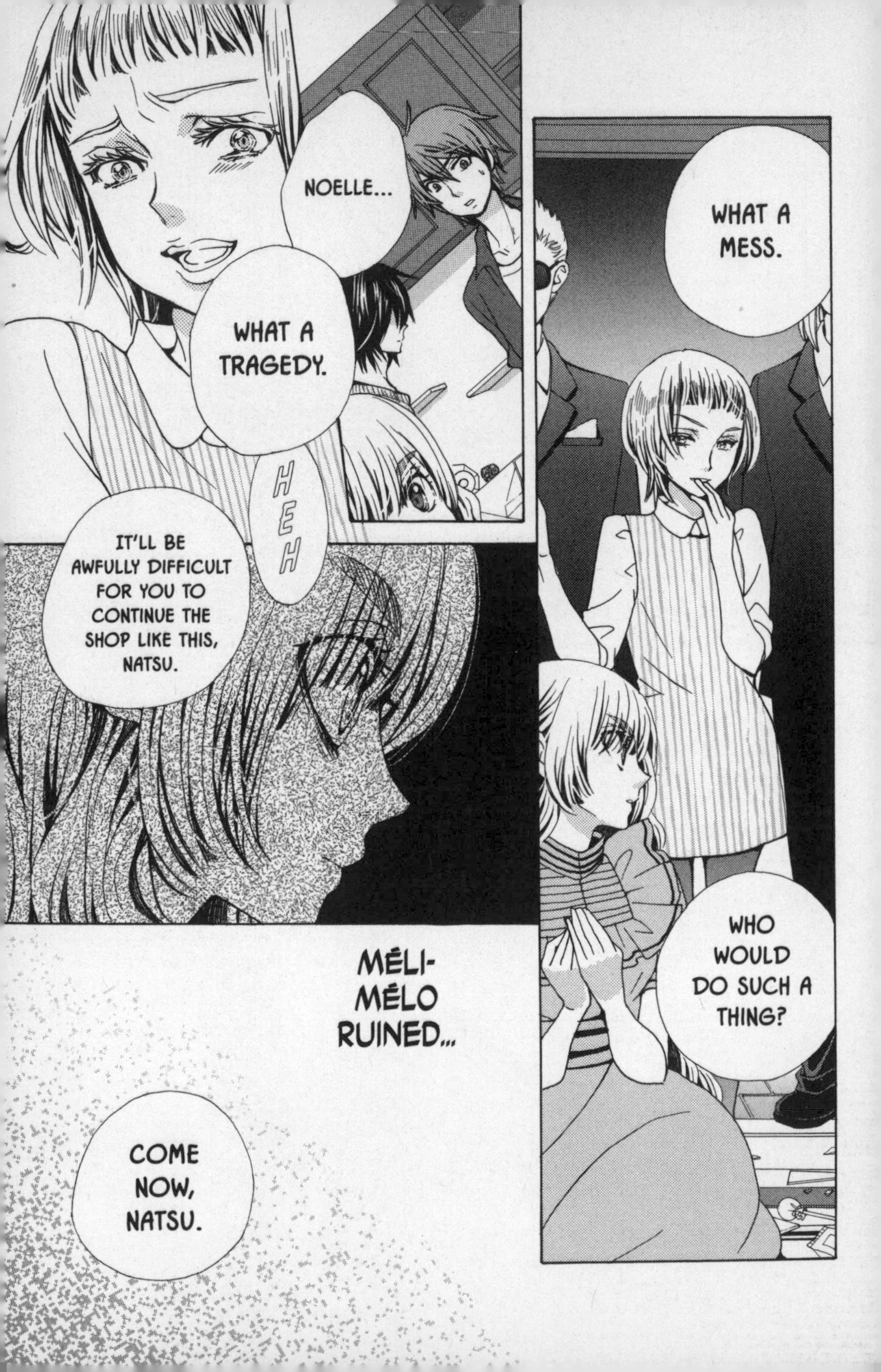
WHAT A MESS.
WHO WOULD DO SUCH A THING?
NOELLE...
WHAT A TRAGEDY.
HEH HEH
IT'LL BE AWFULLY DIFFICULT FOR YOU TO CONTINUE THE SHOP LIKE THIS, NATSU.
MÉLI-MÉLO RUINED...
COME NOW, NATSU.

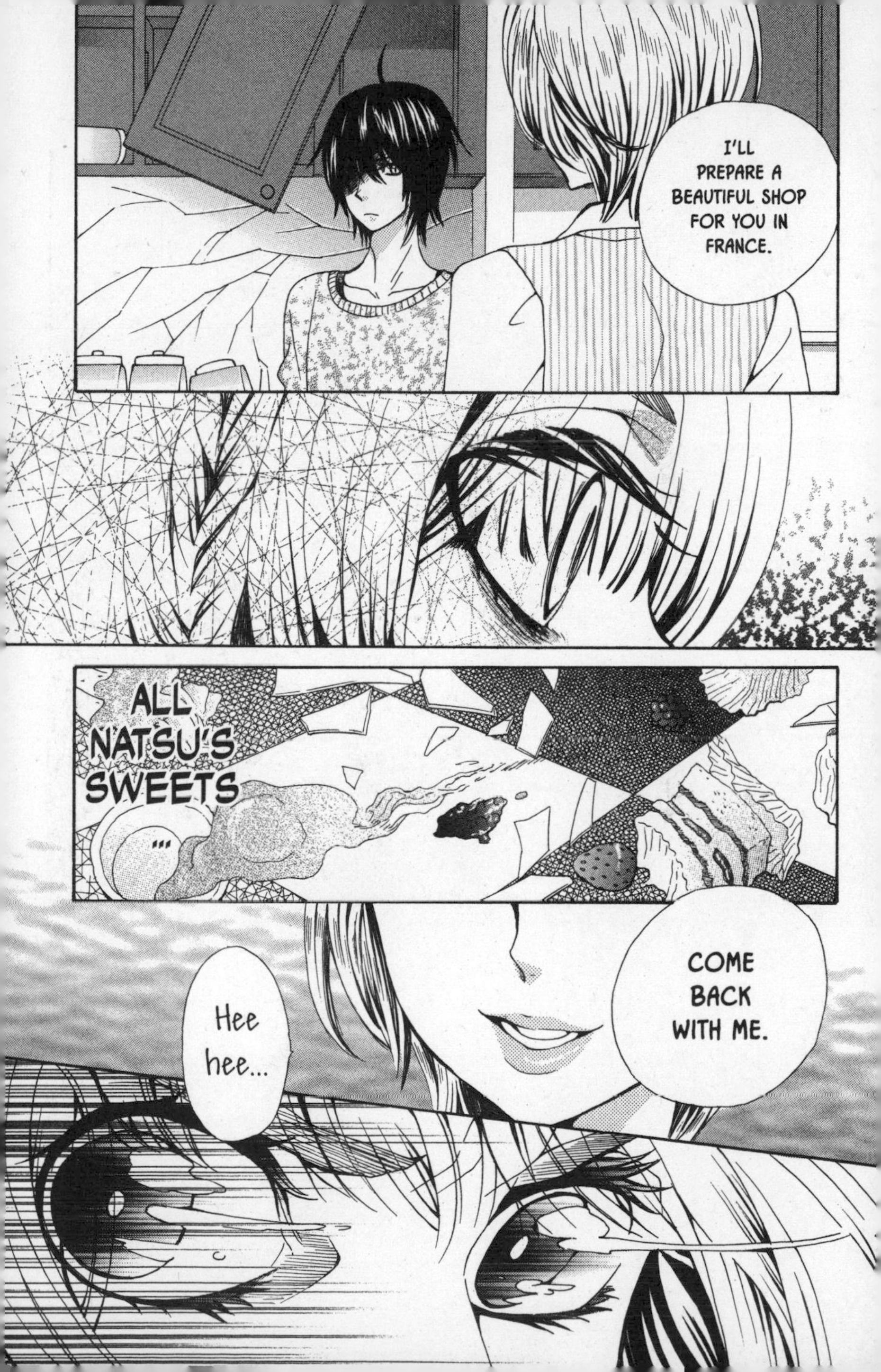
I'LL PREPARE A BEAUTIFUL SHOP FOR YOU IN FRANCE.
ALL NATSU'S SWEETS
...
COME BACK WITH ME.
Hee hee...

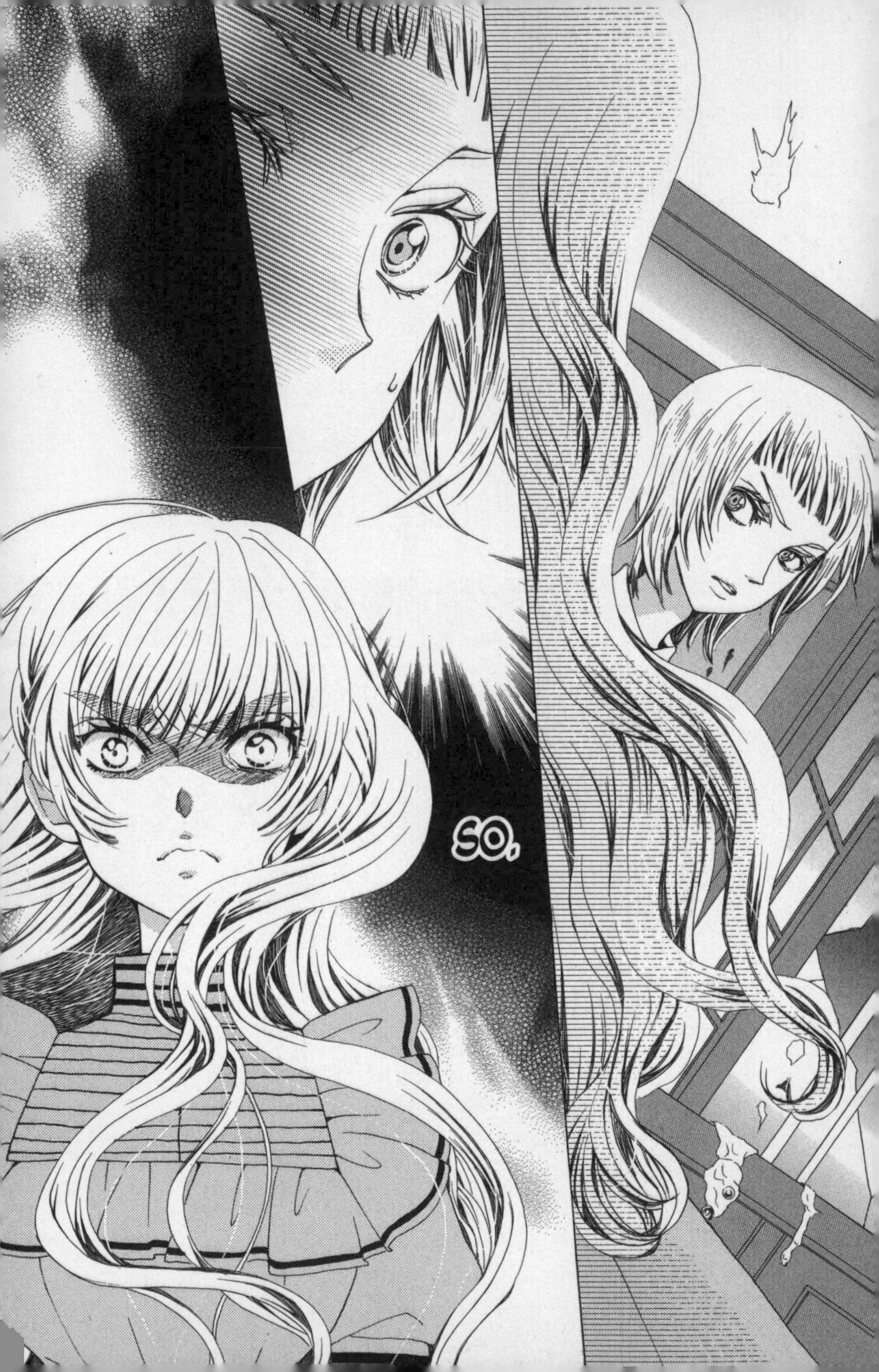
SO,

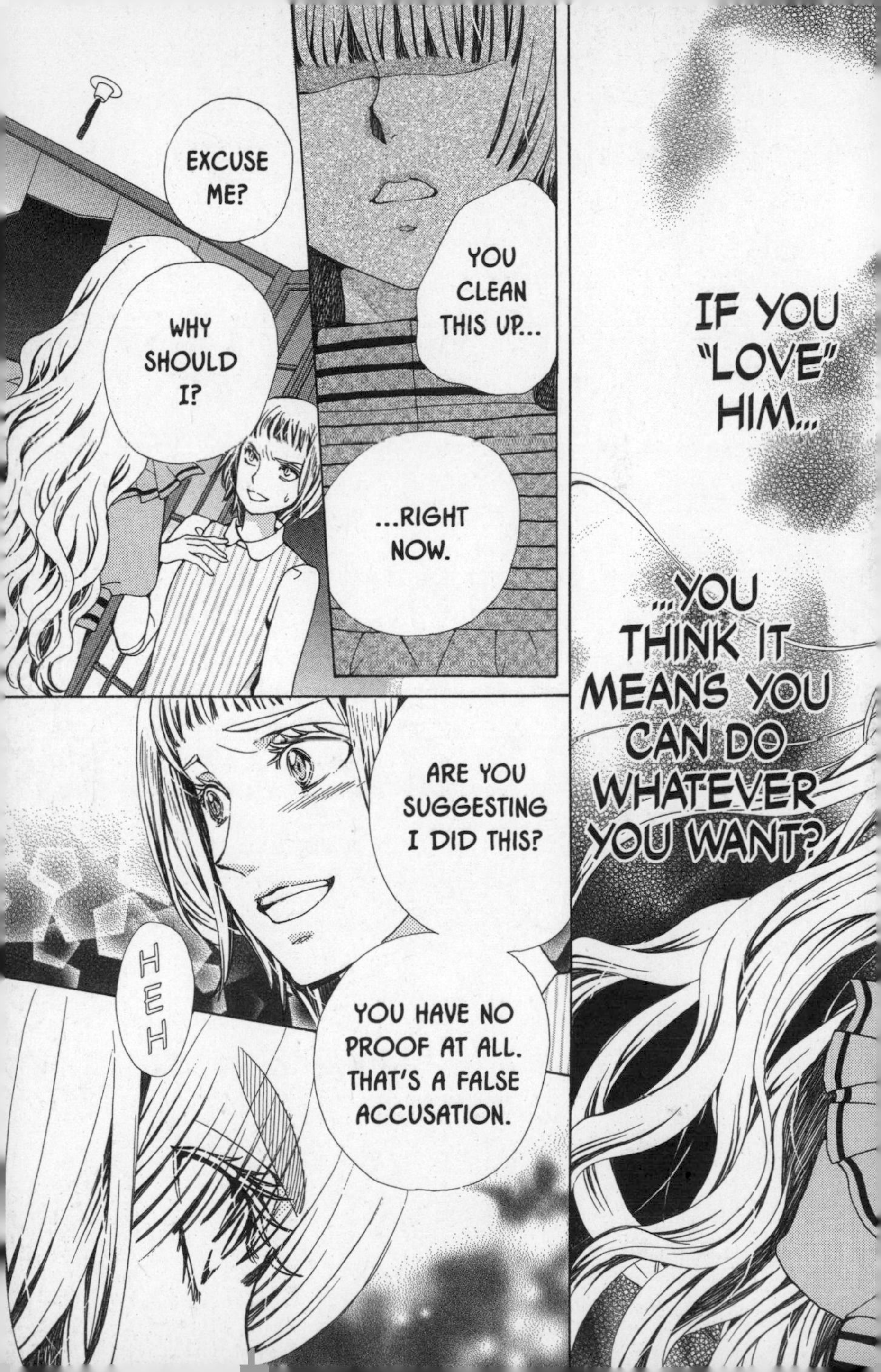
IF YOU "LOVE" HIM...
...YOU THINK IT MEANS YOU CAN DO WHATEVER YOU WANT?
YOU CLEAN THIS UP...
...RIGHT NOW.
EXCUSE ME?
WHY SHOULD I?
ARE YOU SUGGESTING I DID THIS?
HEH
YOU HAVE NO PROOF AT ALL. THAT'S A FALSE ACCUSATION.

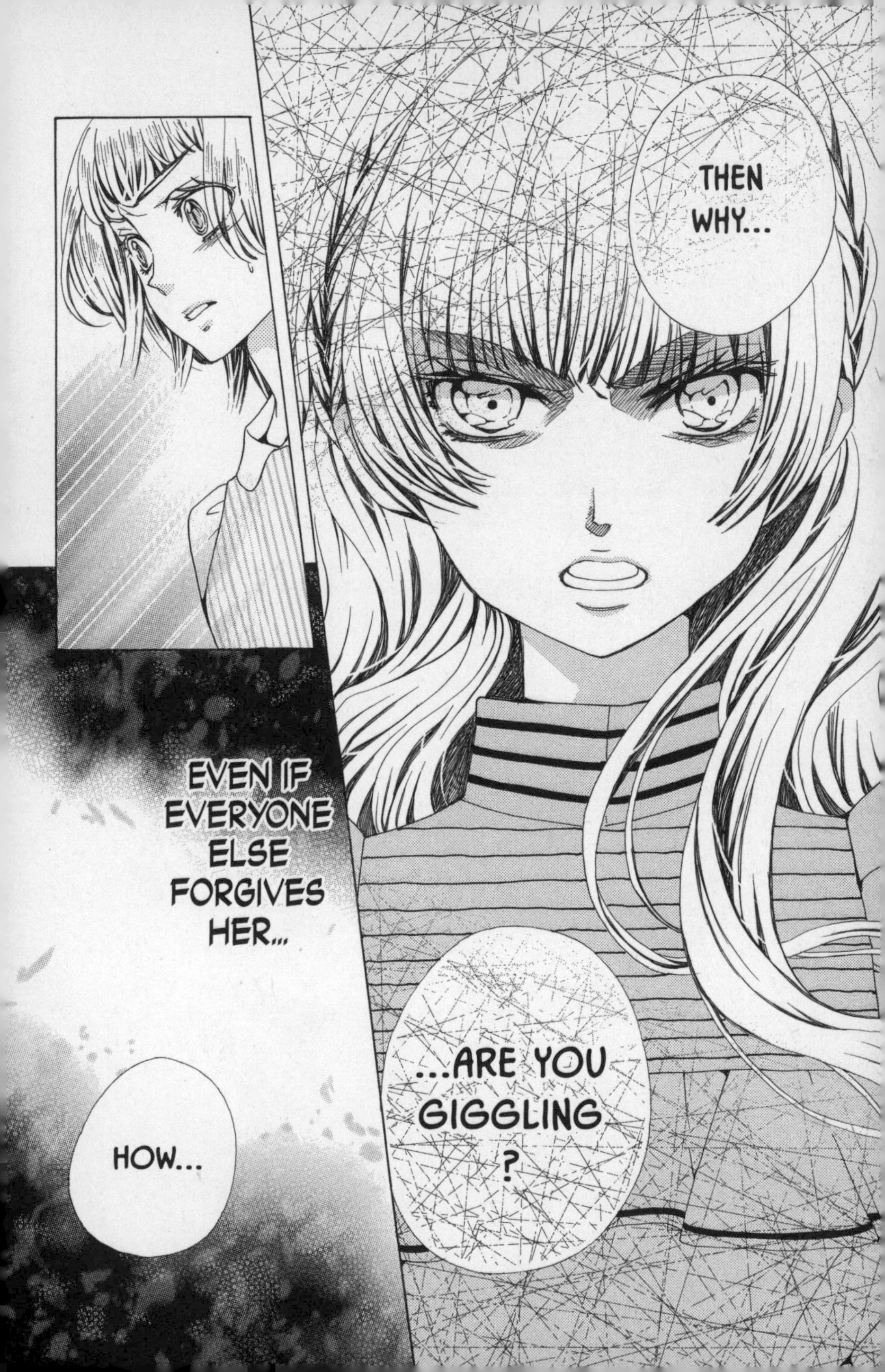
THEN WHY...
...ARE YOU GIGGLING?
EVEN IF EVERYONE ELSE FORGIVES HER...
HOW...

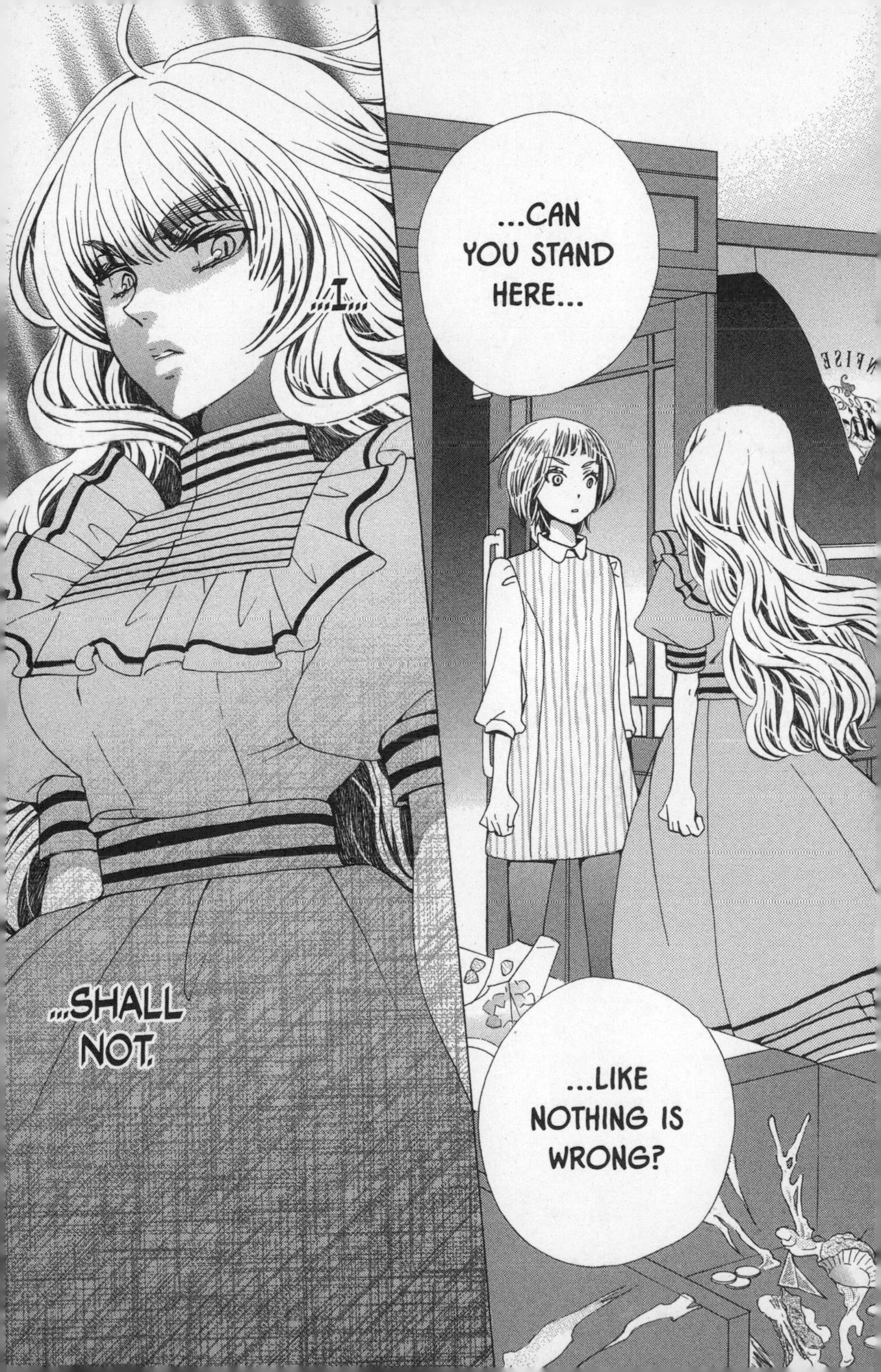
...CAN YOU STAND HERE...
...LIKE NOTHING IS WRONG?
...I...
...SHALL NOT.

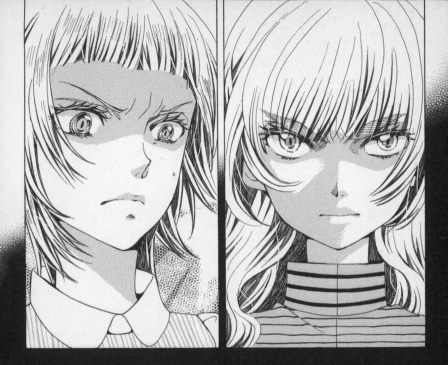

...I HAVE NEVER FELT SO ENRAGED.

IN ALL MY LIFE...

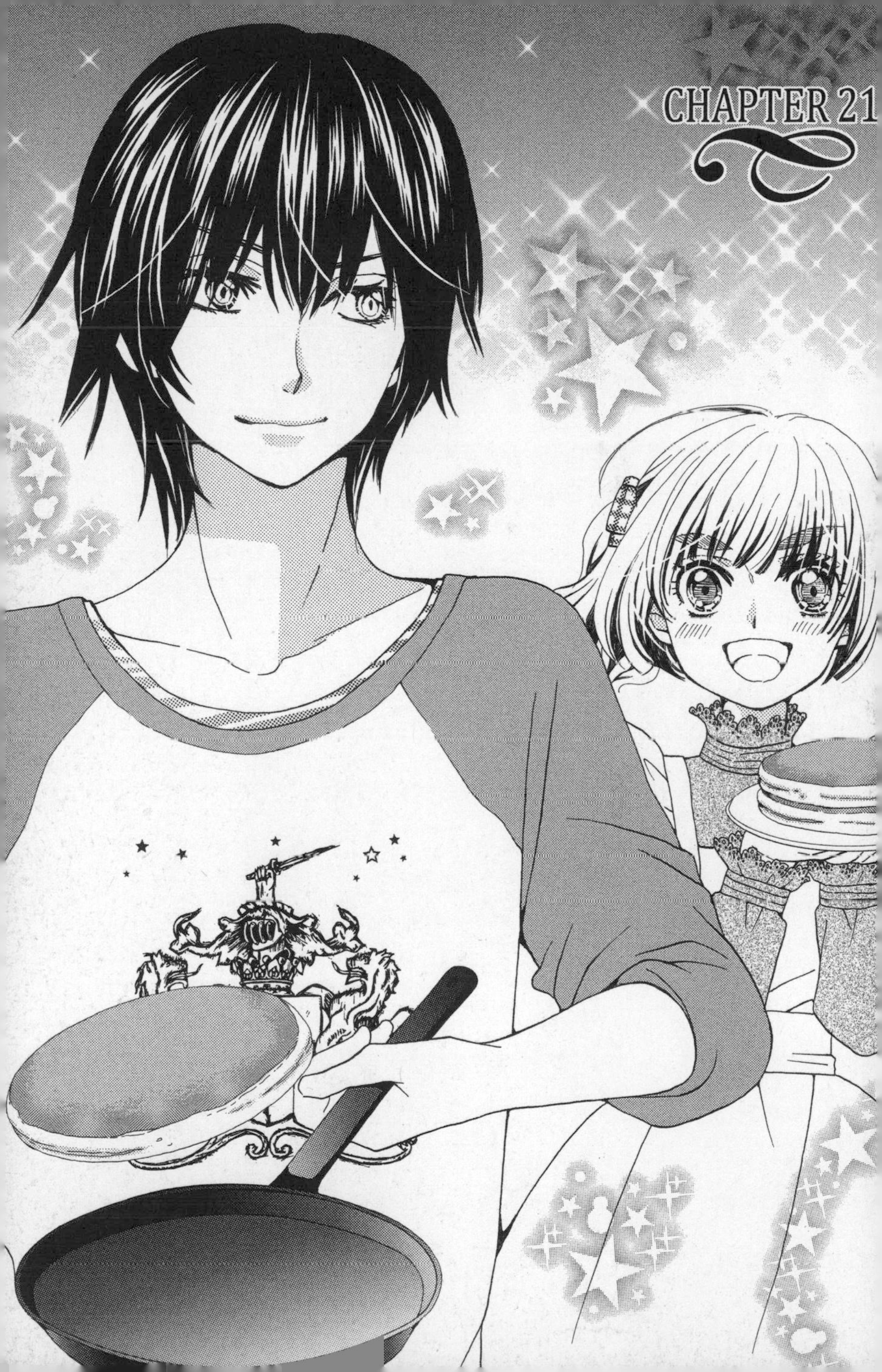
CHAPTER 21

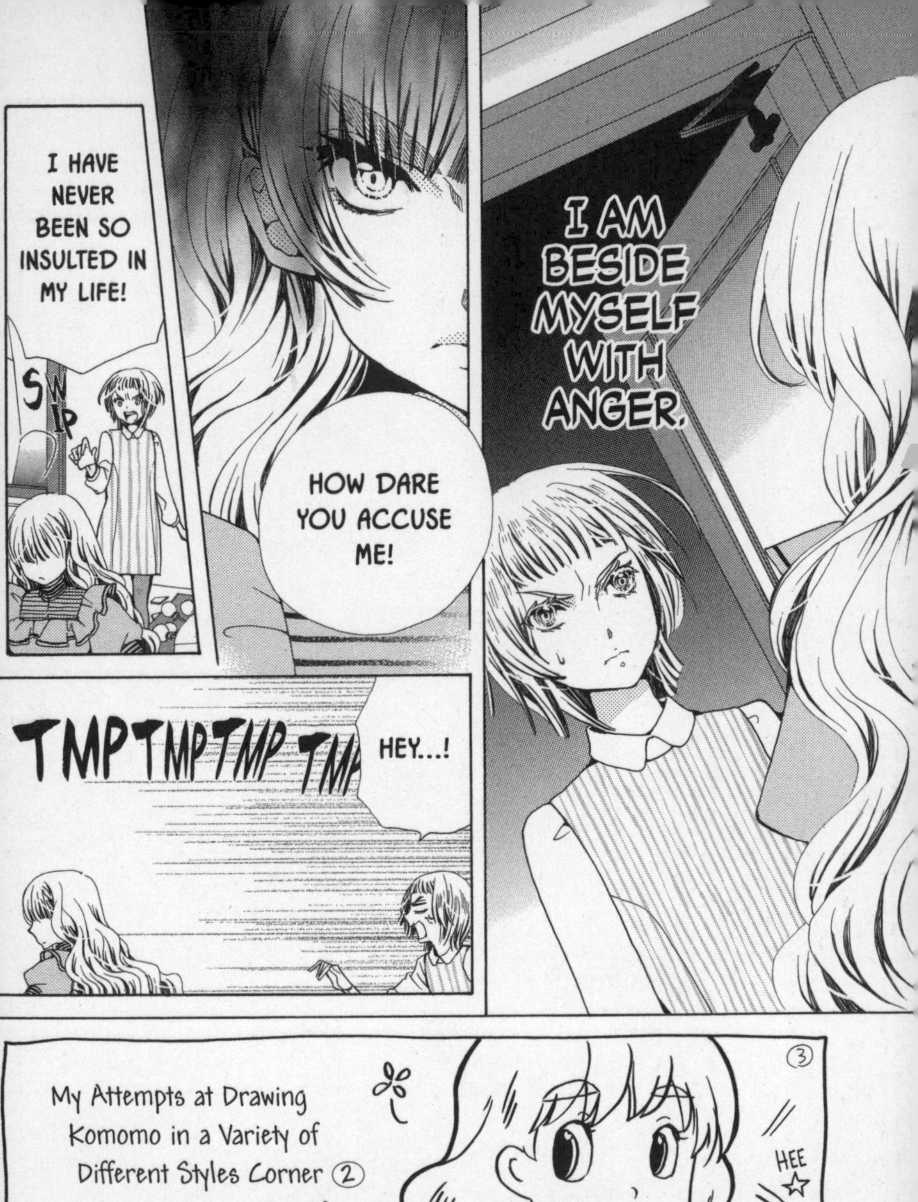
I AM BESIDE MYSELF WITH ANGER.
HOW DARE YOU ACCUSE ME!
I HAVE NEVER BEEN SO INSULTED IN MY LIFE!
SWIP
HEY...!
TMPTMPTMP TMP

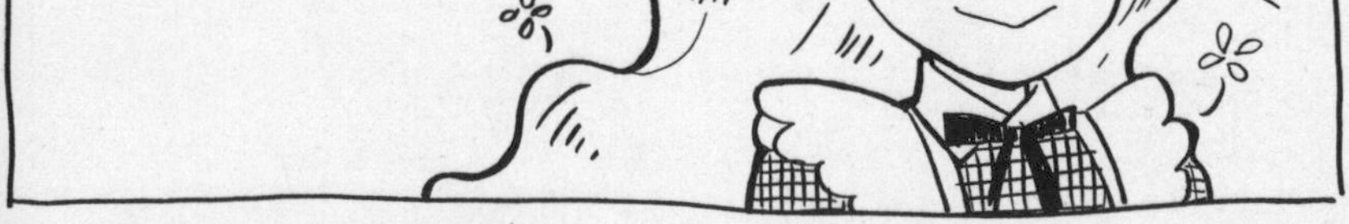
③
My Attempts at Drawing Komomo in a Variety of Different Styles Corner ②
HEE ☆

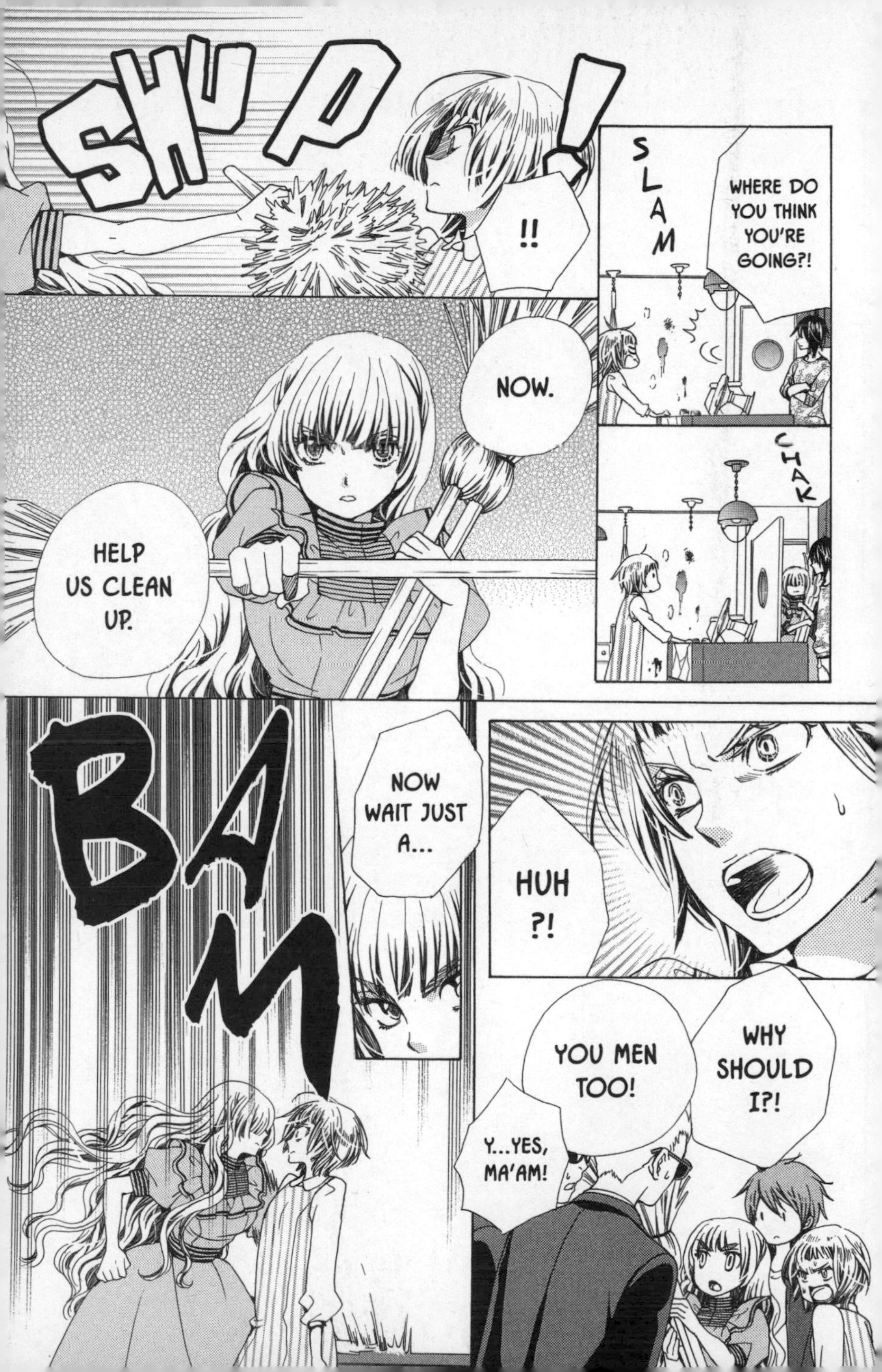
SLAM
WHERE DO YOU THINK YOU'RE GOING?!
CHAK
SHUP!
!!
NOW.
HELP US CLEAN UP.
HUH?!
NOW WAIT JUST A...
BAM
WHY SHOULD I?!
YOU MEN TOO!
Y...YES, MA'AM!

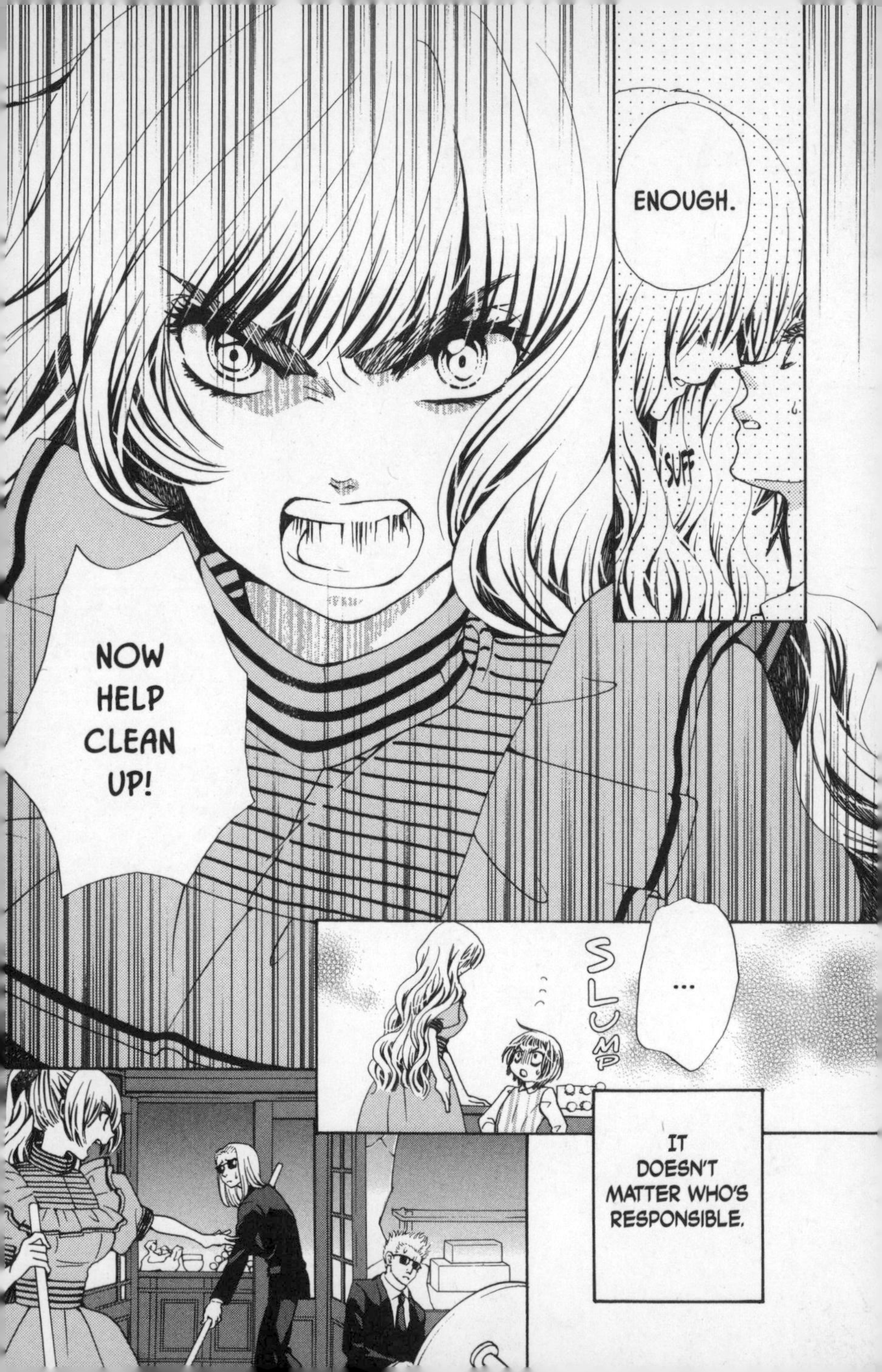
ENOUGH.
SUFF
NOW HELP CLEAN UP!
...
SLUMP
IT DOESN'T MATTER WHO'S RESPONSIBLE.

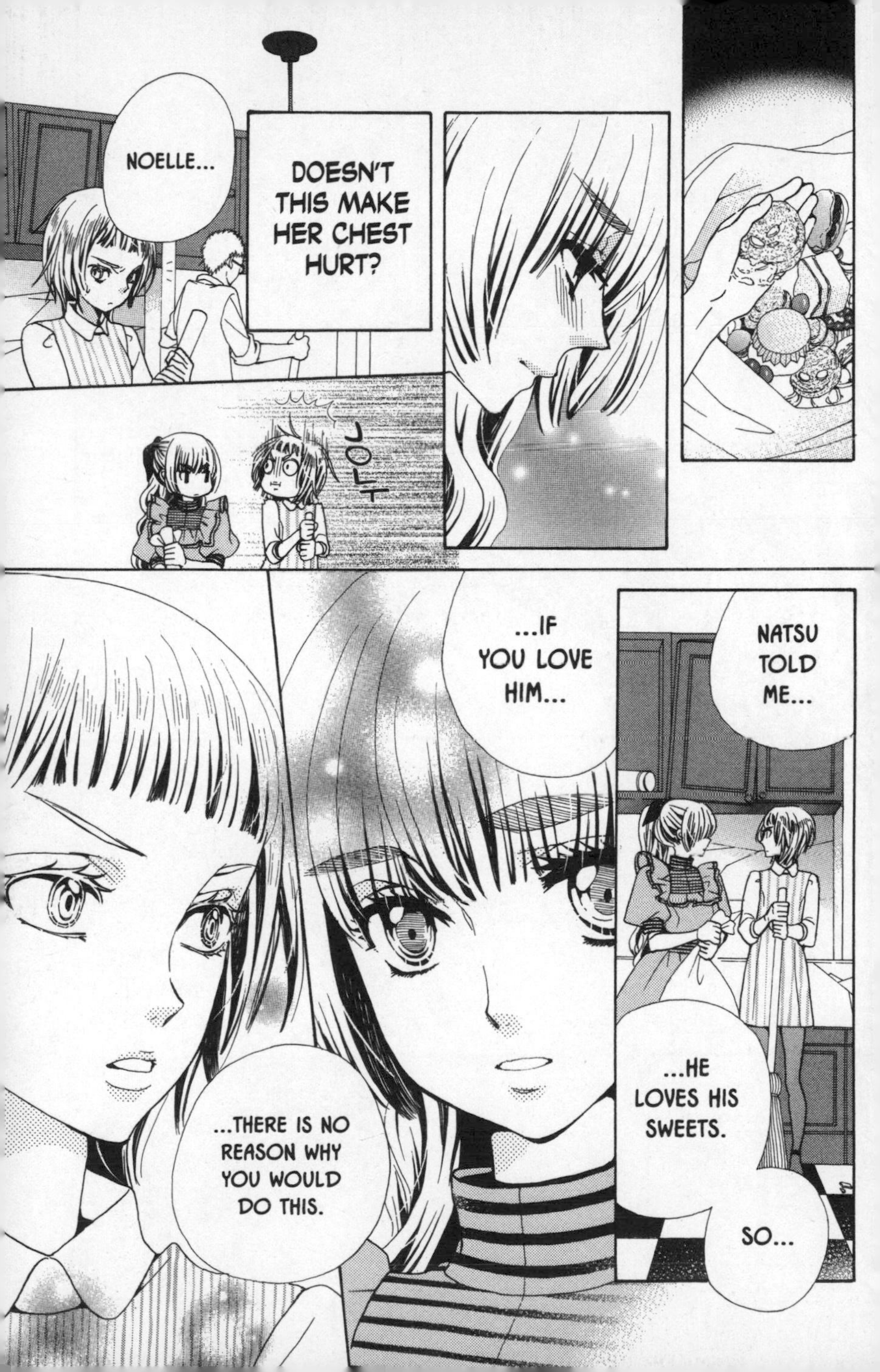
DOESN'T THIS MAKE HER CHEST HURT?
NOELLE...
JOLT
NATSU TOLD ME...
...HE LOVES HIS SWEETS.
SO...
...IF YOU LOVE HIM...
...THERE IS NO REASON WHY YOU WOULD DO THIS.

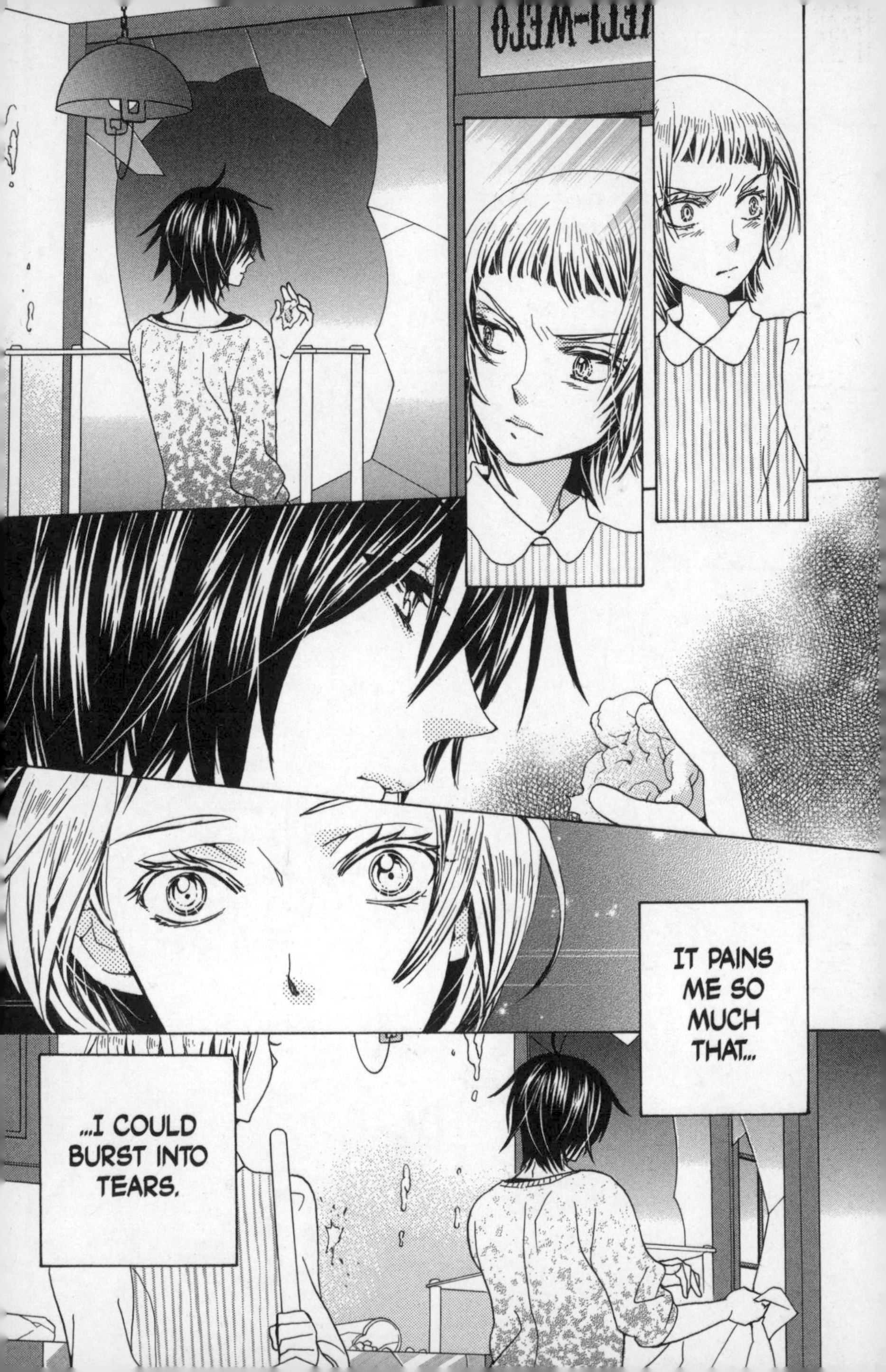
IT PAINS ME SO MUCH THAT...
...I COULD BURST INTO TEARS.

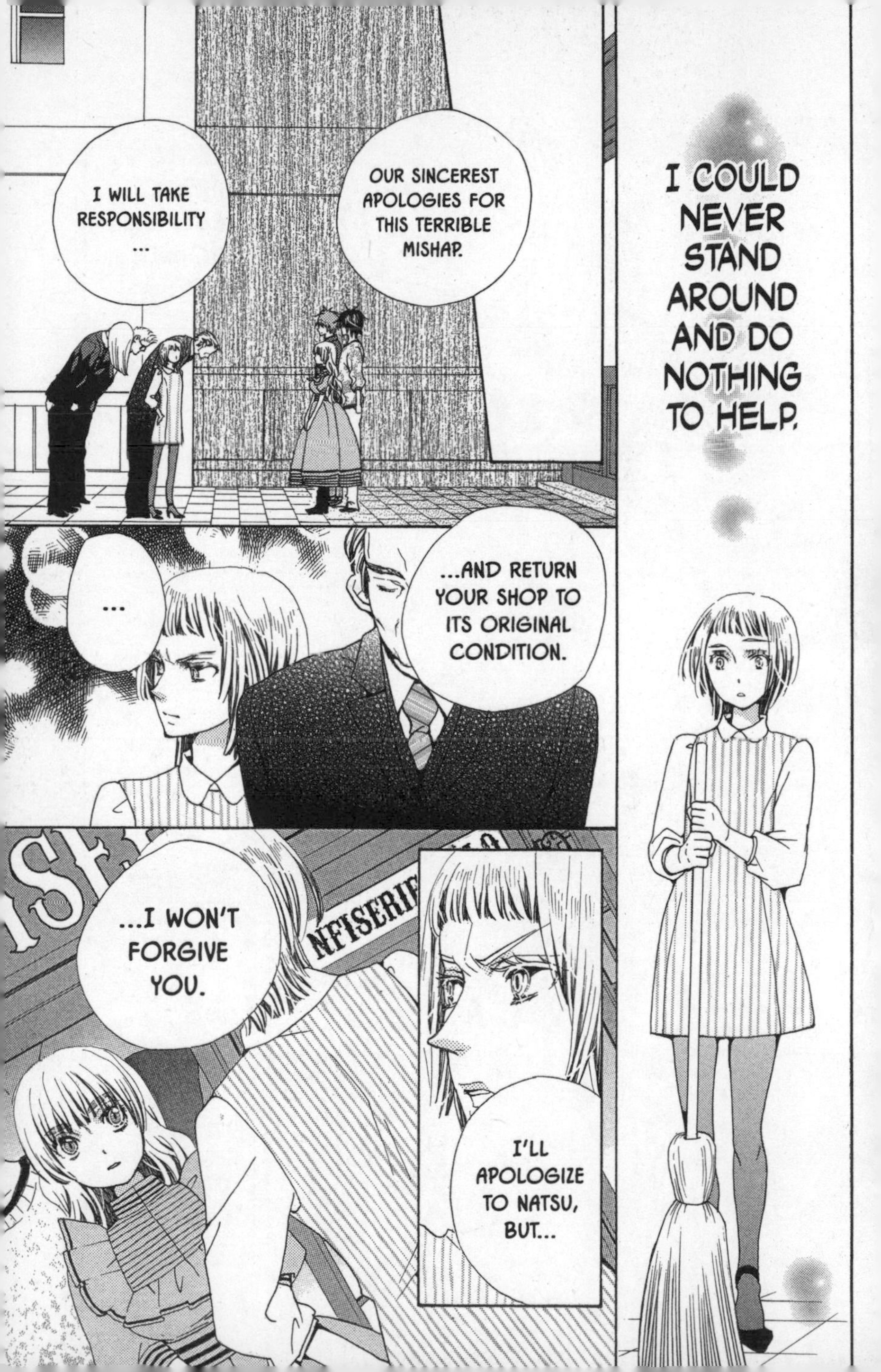
I COULD NEVER STAND AROUND AND DO NOTHING TO HELP.
OUR SINCEREST APOLOGIES FOR THIS TERRIBLE MISHAP.
I WILL TAKE RESPONSIBILITY ...
...AND RETURN YOUR SHOP TO ITS ORIGINAL CONDITION.
...
I'LL APOLOGIZE TO NATSU, BUT...
...I WON'T FORGIVE YOU.

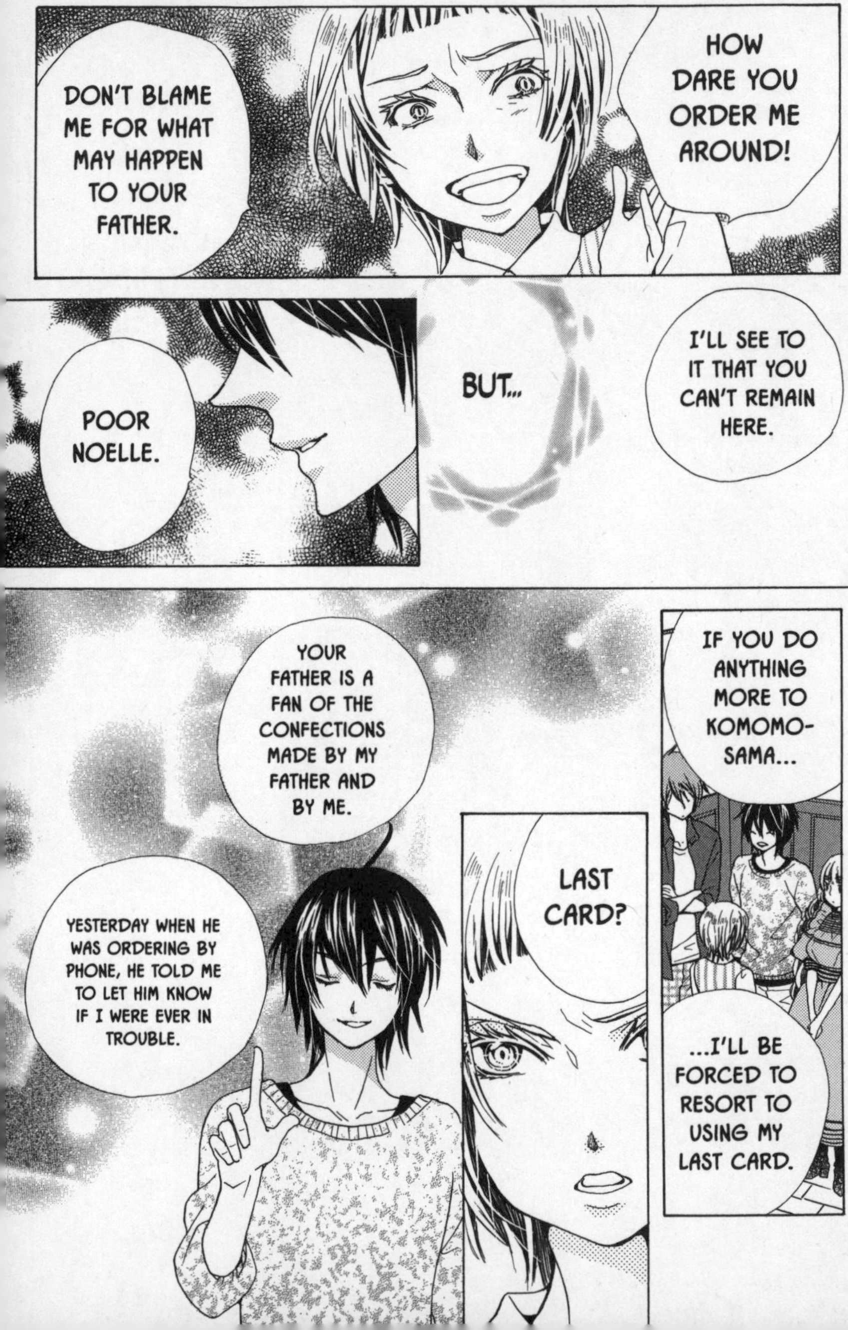
HOW DARE YOU ORDER ME AROUND!
DON'T BLAME ME FOR WHAT MAY HAPPEN TO YOUR FATHER.
I'LL SEE TO IT THAT YOU CAN'T REMAIN HERE.
BUT...
POOR NOELLE.
IF YOU DO ANYTHING MORE TO KOMOMO-SAMA...
...I'LL BE FORCED TO RESORT TO USING MY LAST CARD.
LAST CARD?
YOUR FATHER IS A FAN OF THE CONFECTIONS MADE BY MY FATHER AND BY ME.
YESTERDAY WHEN HE WAS ORDERING BY PHONE, HE TOLD ME TO LET HIM KNOW IF I WERE EVER IN TROUBLE.

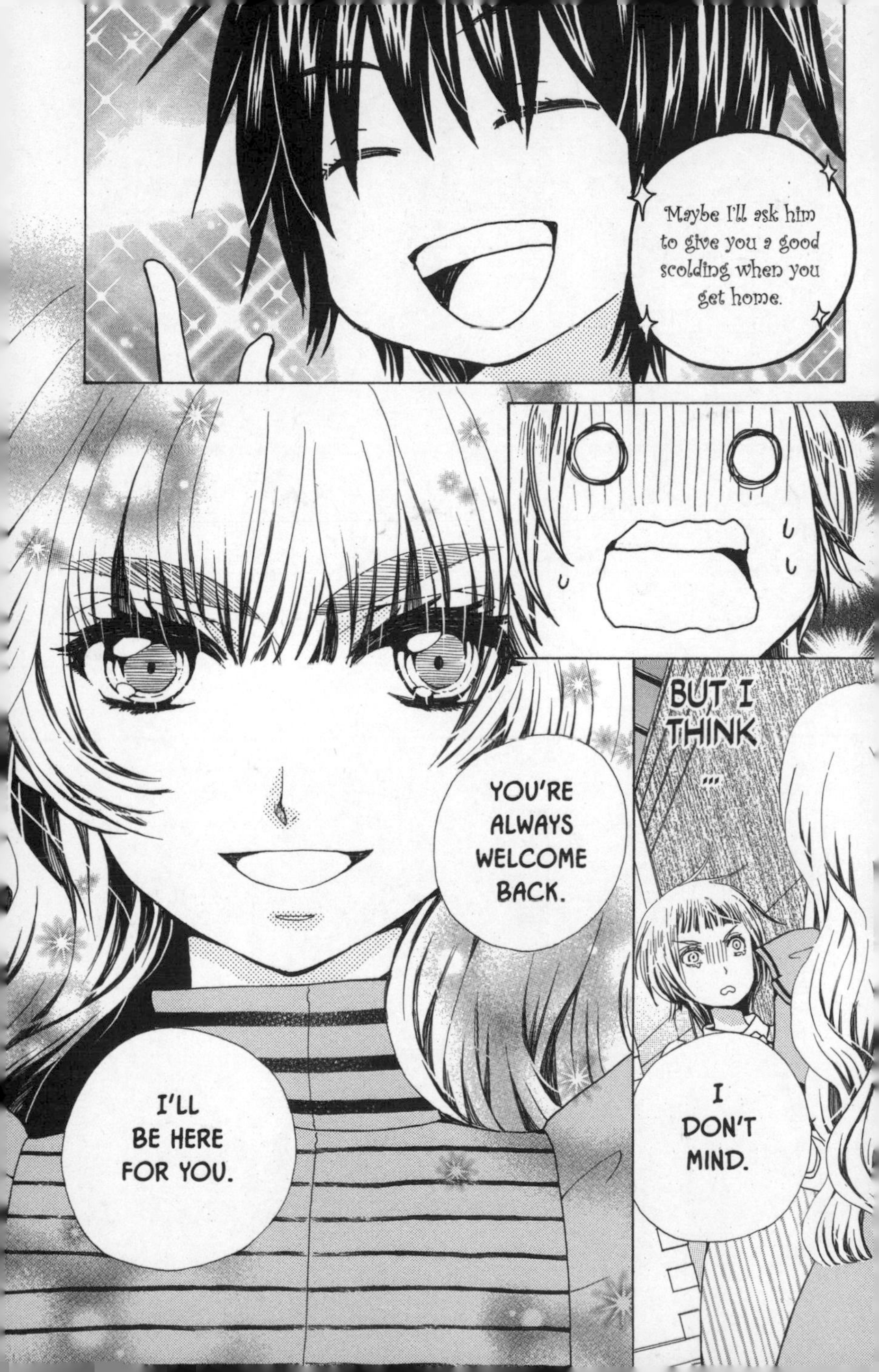
Maybe I'll ask him to give you a good scolding when you get home.
BUT I THINK ...
I DON'T MIND.
YOU'RE ALWAYS WELCOME BACK.
I'LL BE HERE FOR YOU.

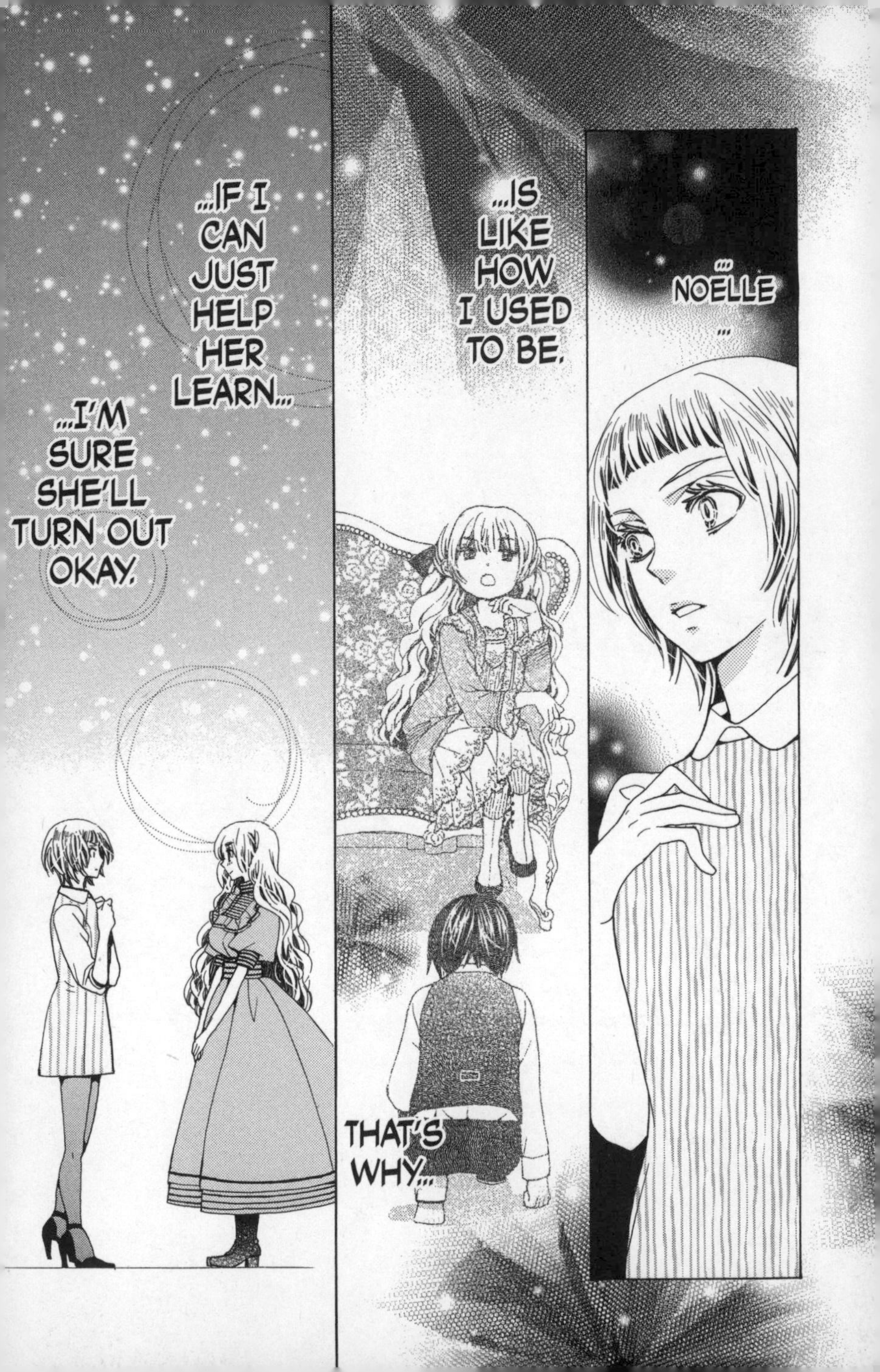
...NOELLE...
...IS LIKE HOW I USED TO BE.
THAT'S WHY...
...IF I CAN JUST HELP HER LEARN...
...I'M SURE SHE'LL TURN OUT OKAY.

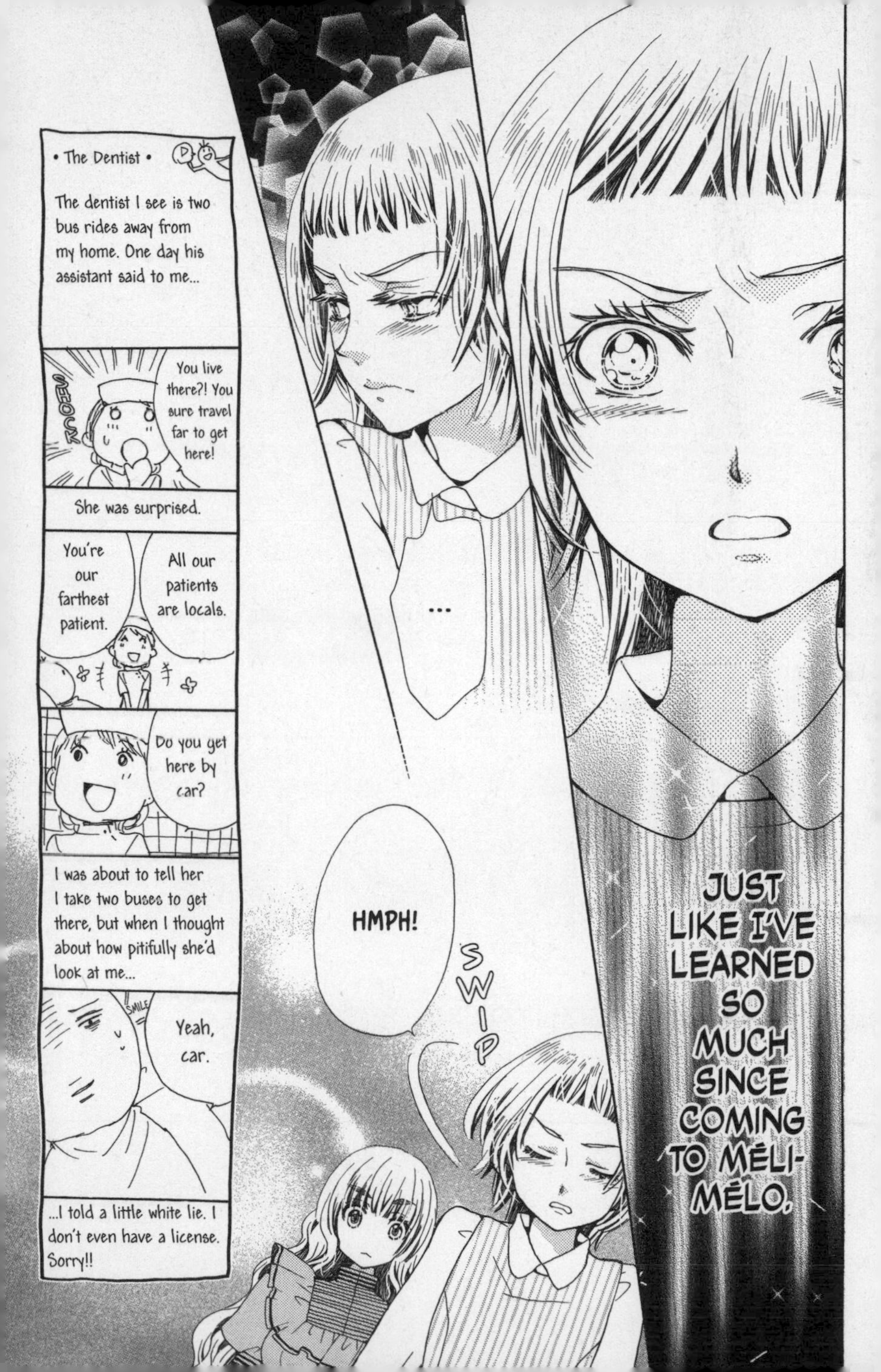
JUST LIKE I'VE LEARNED SO MUCH SINCE COMING TO MÉLI-MÉLO.
...
HMPH!
SWIP
• The Dentist •
The dentist I see is two bus rides away from my home. One day his assistant said to me...
SHOCK
You live there?! You sure travel far to get here!
She was surprised.
All our patients are locals.
You're our farthest patient.
Do you get here by car?
I was about to tell her I take two buses to get there, but when I thought about how pitifully she'd look at me...
SMILE
Yeah, car.
...I told a little white lie. I don't even have a license. Sorry!!

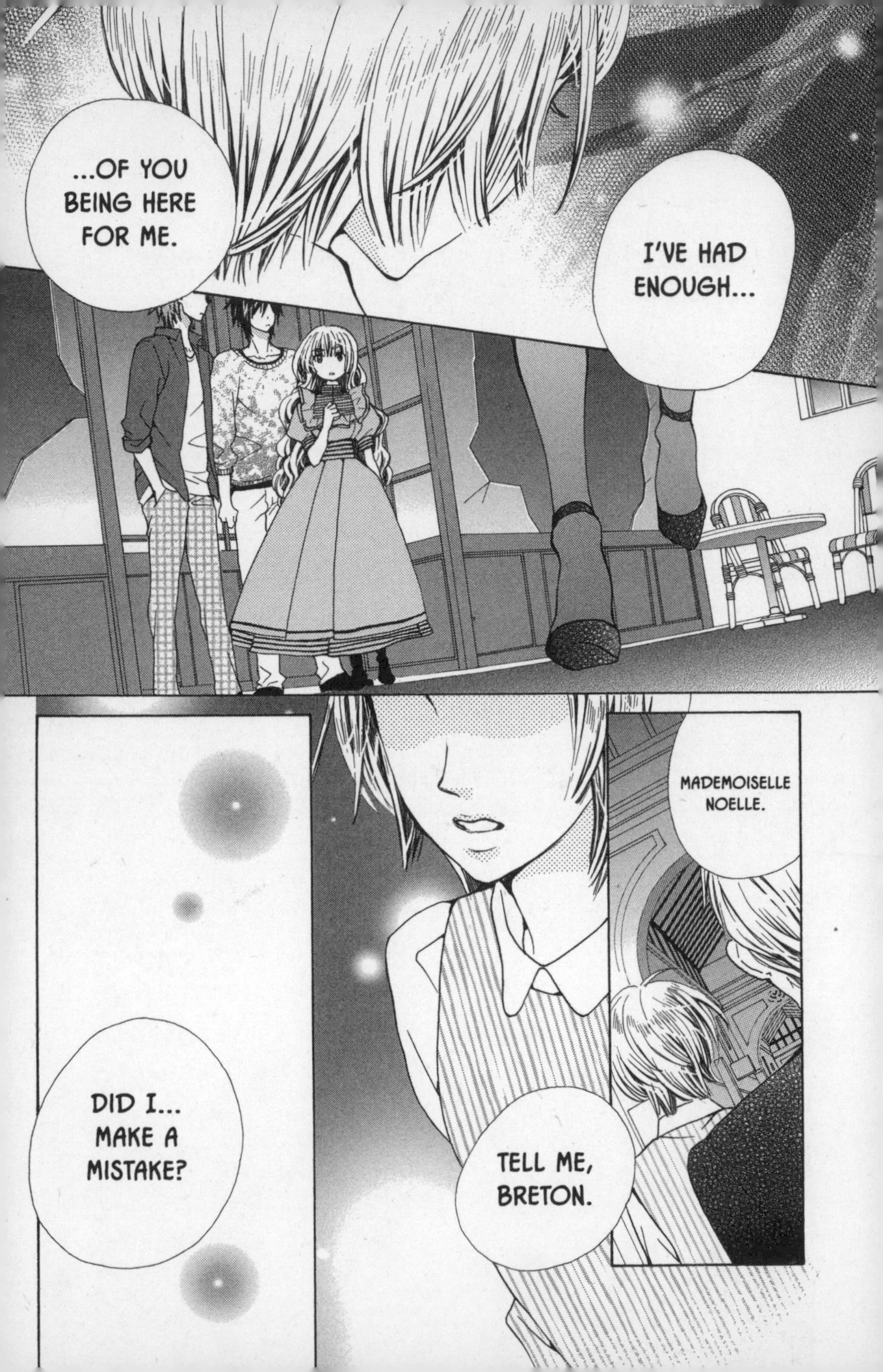
I'VE HAD ENOUGH...
...OF YOU BEING HERE FOR ME.
MADEMOISELLE NOELLE.
TELL ME, BRETON.
DID I... MAKE A MISTAKE?

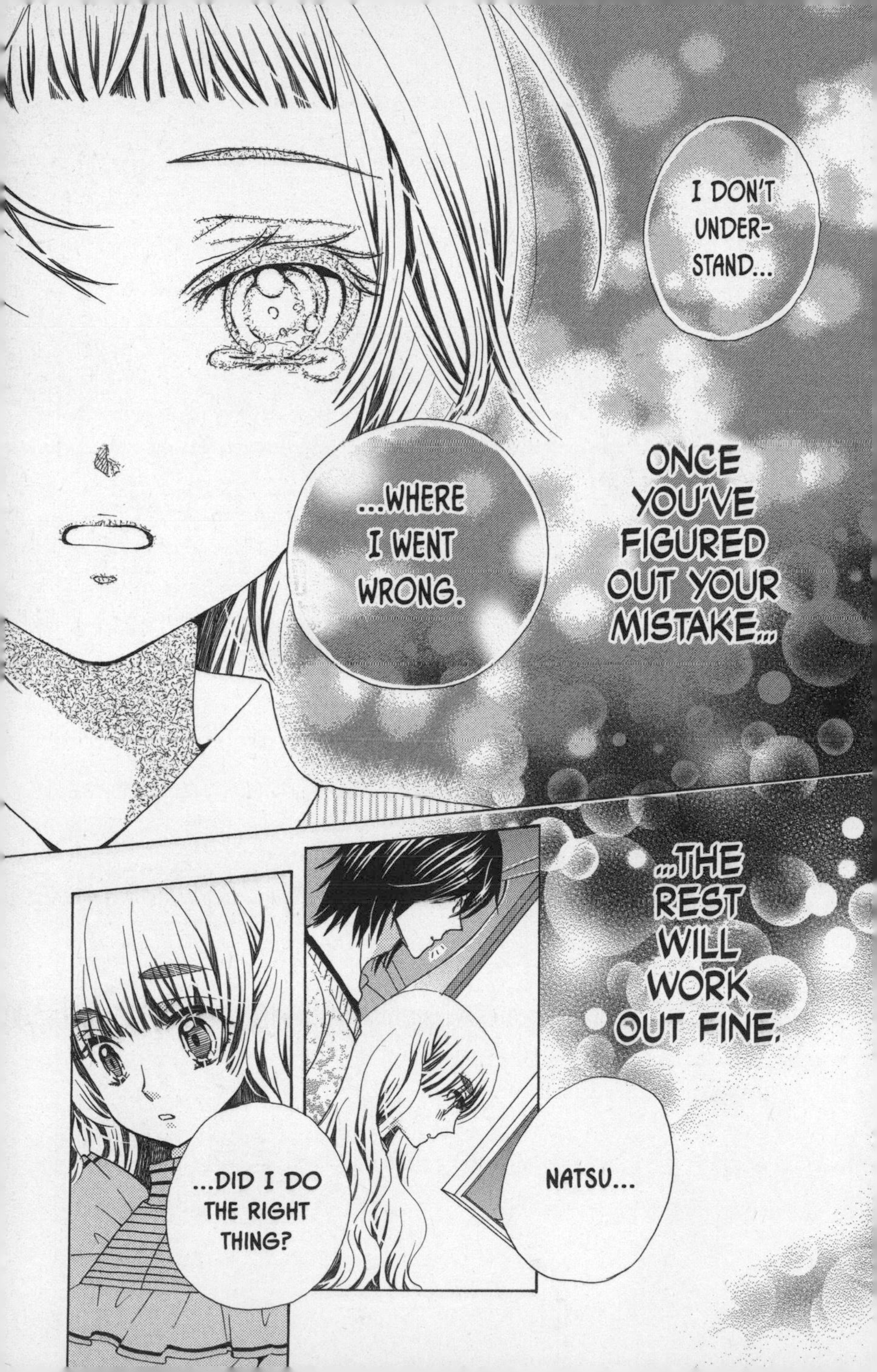
I DON'T UNDER-STAND...
...WHERE I WENT WRONG.
ONCE YOU'VE FIGURED OUT YOUR MISTAKE...
...THE REST WILL WORK OUT FINE.
NATSU...
...DID I DO THE RIGHT THING?

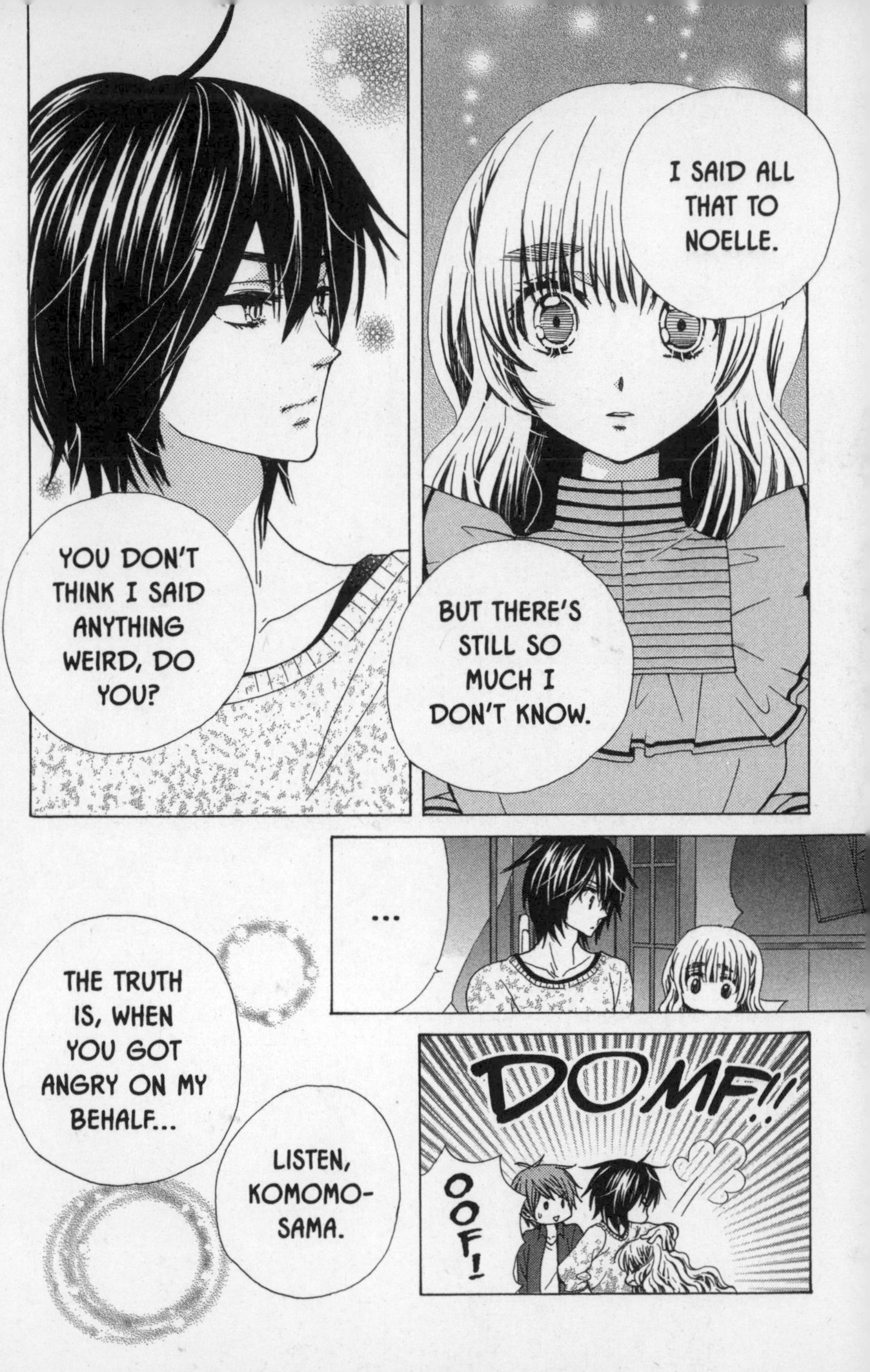
I SAID ALL THAT TO NOELLE.
BUT THERE'S STILL SO MUCH I DON'T KNOW.
YOU DON'T THINK I SAID ANYTHING WEIRD, DO YOU?
...
THE TRUTH IS, WHEN YOU GOT ANGRY ON MY BEHALF...
LISTEN, KOMOMO-SAMA.
DOMF!!
OOF!

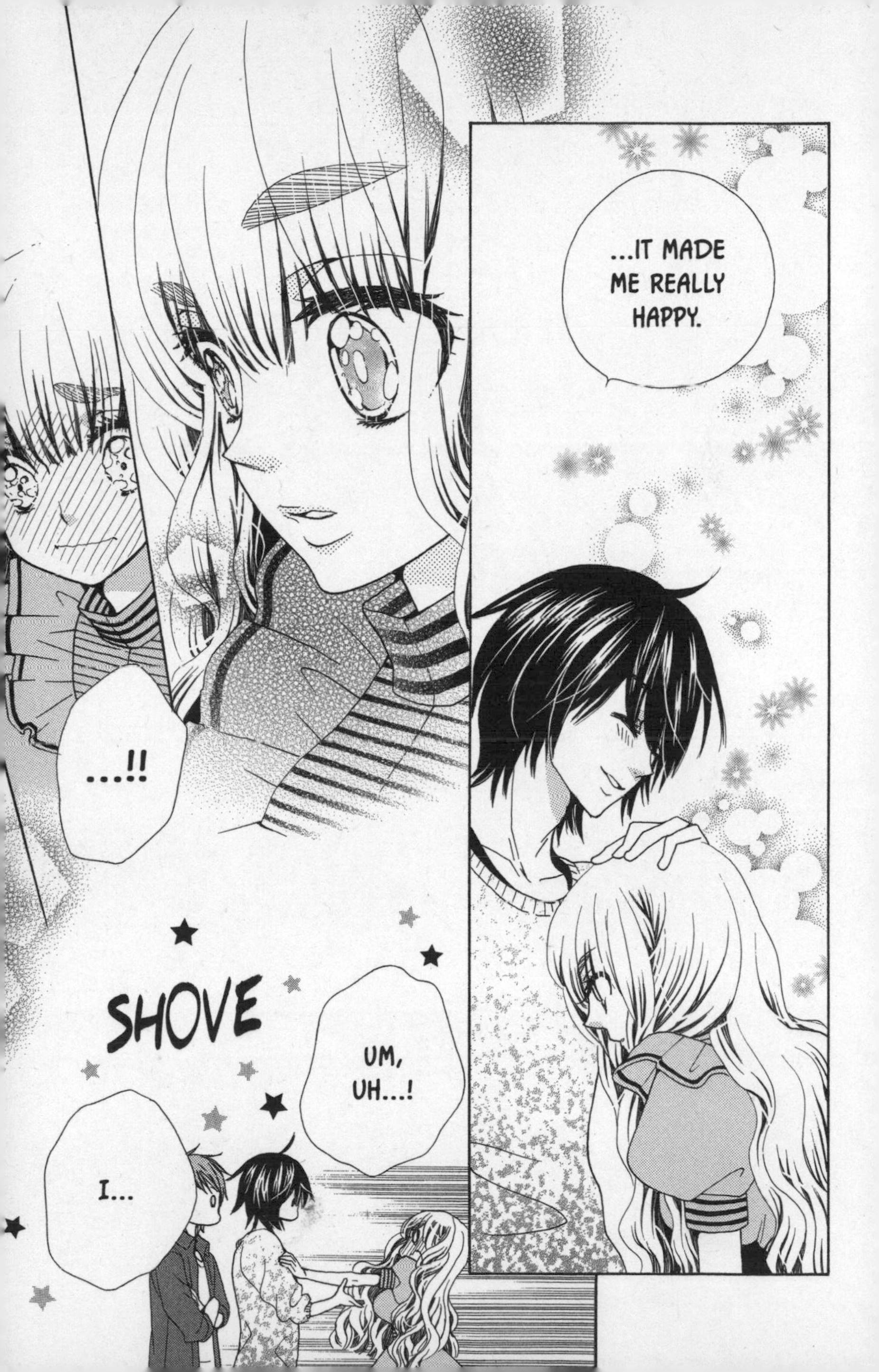
...IT MADE ME REALLY HAPPY.
...!!
UM, UH...!
SHOVE
I...

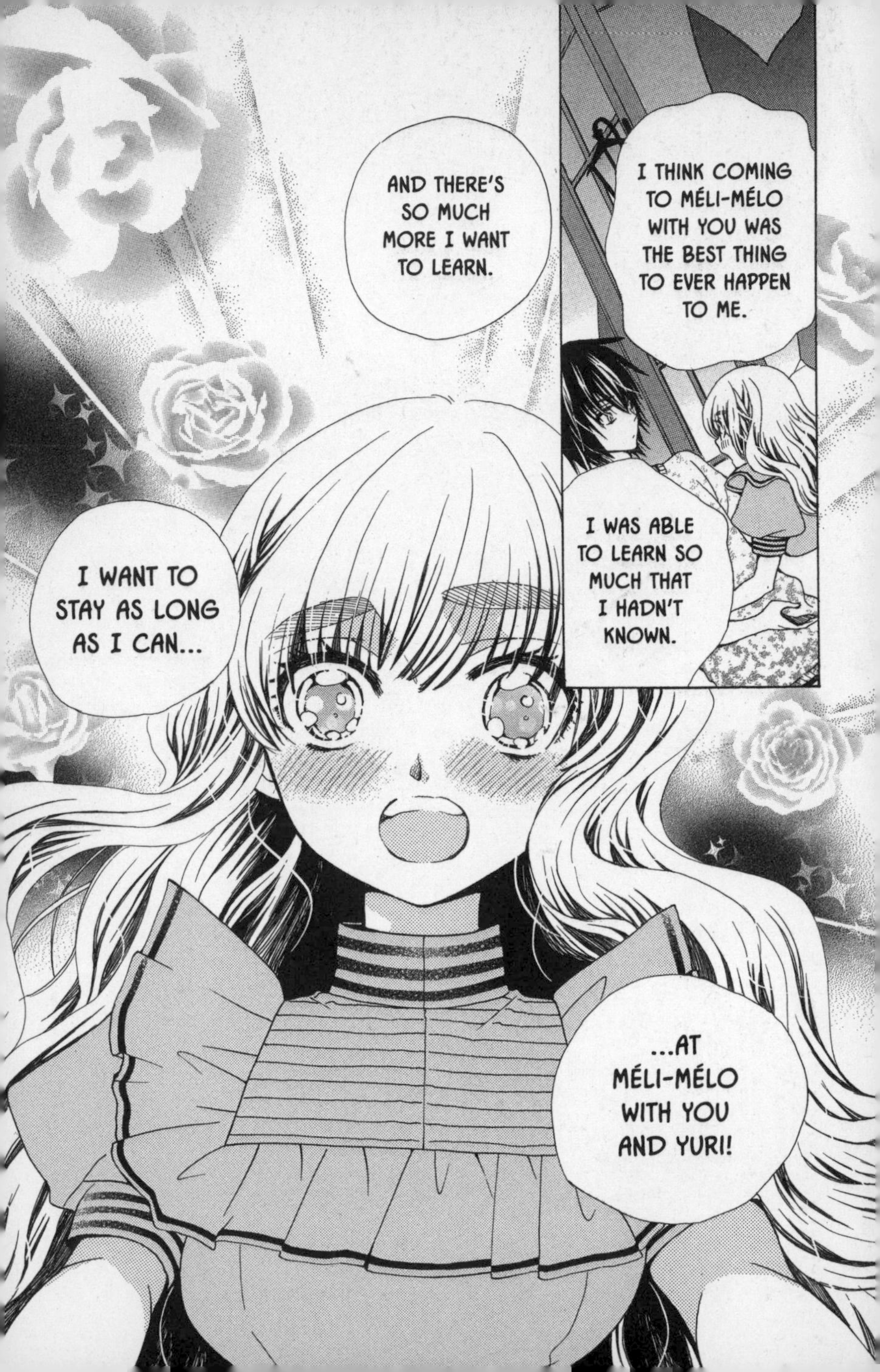
I THINK COMING TO MÉLI-MÉLO WITH YOU WAS THE BEST THING TO EVER HAPPEN TO ME.
I WAS ABLE TO LEARN SO MUCH THAT I HADN'T KNOWN.
AND THERE'S SO MUCH MORE I WANT TO LEARN.
I WANT TO STAY AS LONG AS I CAN...
...AT MÉLI-MÉLO WITH YOU AND YURI!

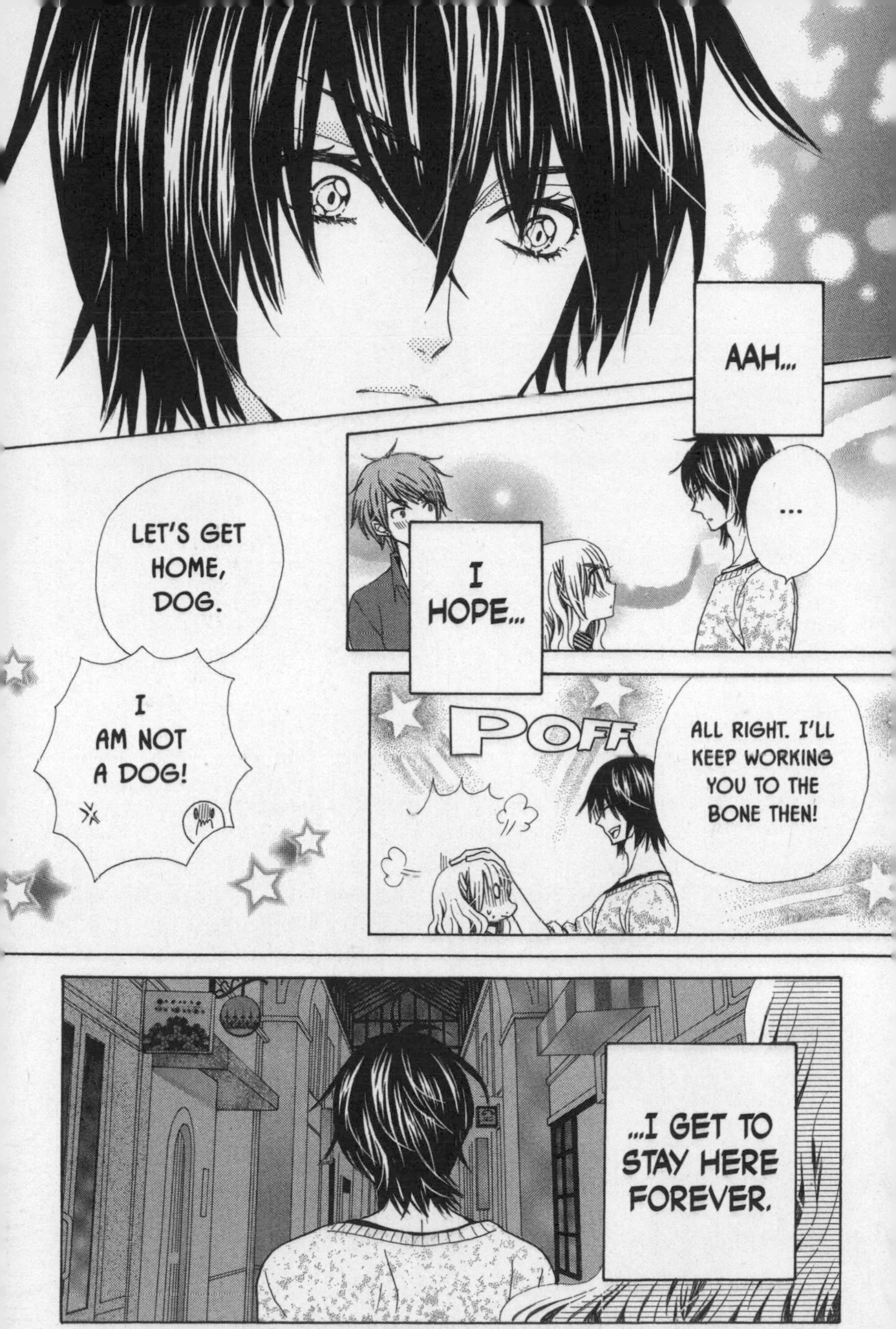
AAH...
...
I HOPE...
LET'S GET HOME, DOG.
ALL RIGHT. I'LL KEEP WORKING YOU TO THE BONE THEN!
POFF
I AM NOT A DOG!
...I GET TO STAY HERE FOREVER.

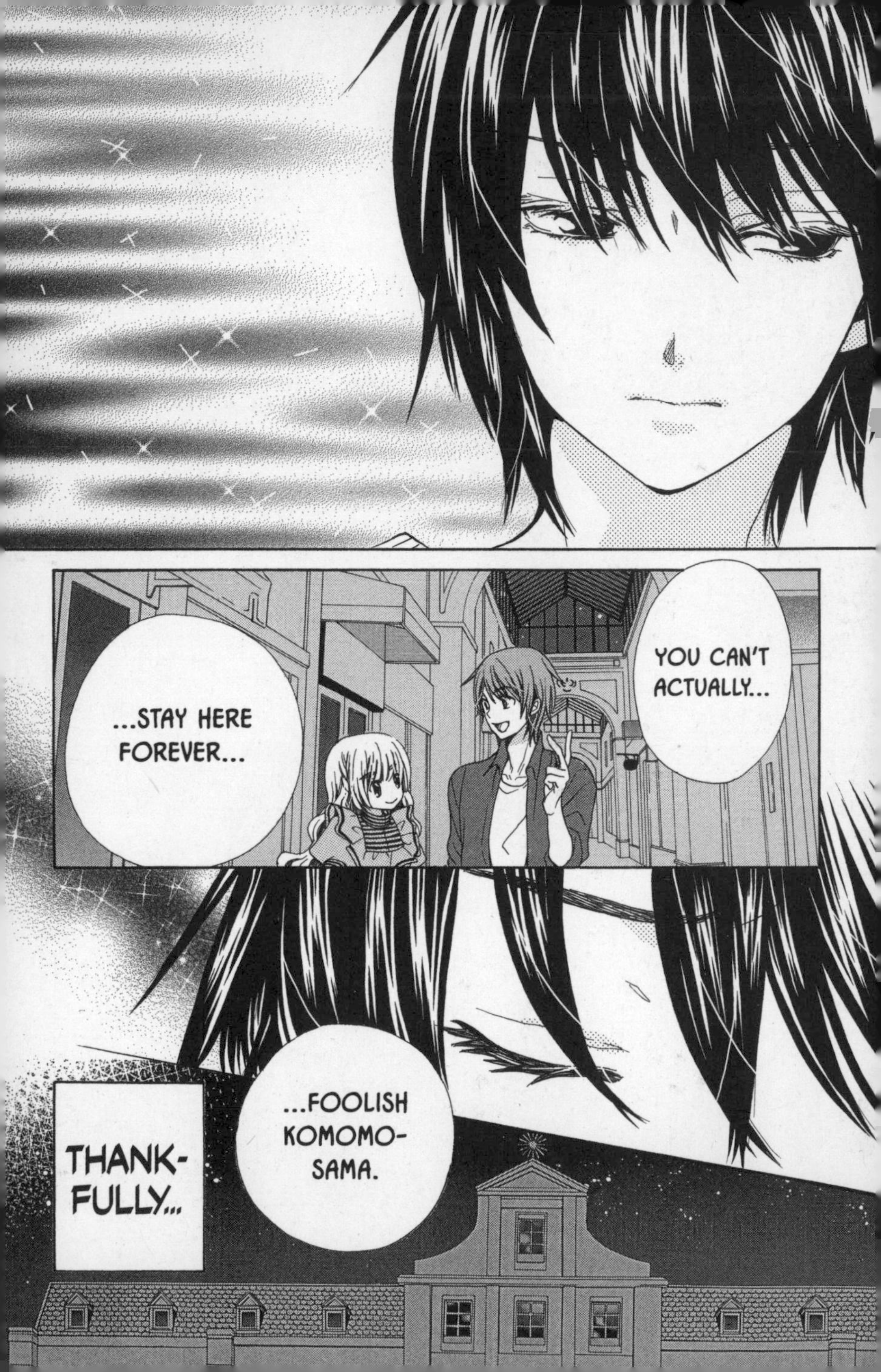
YOU CAN'T ACTUALLY...
...STAY HERE FOREVER...
...FOOLISH KOMOMO-SAMA.
THANK-FULLY...

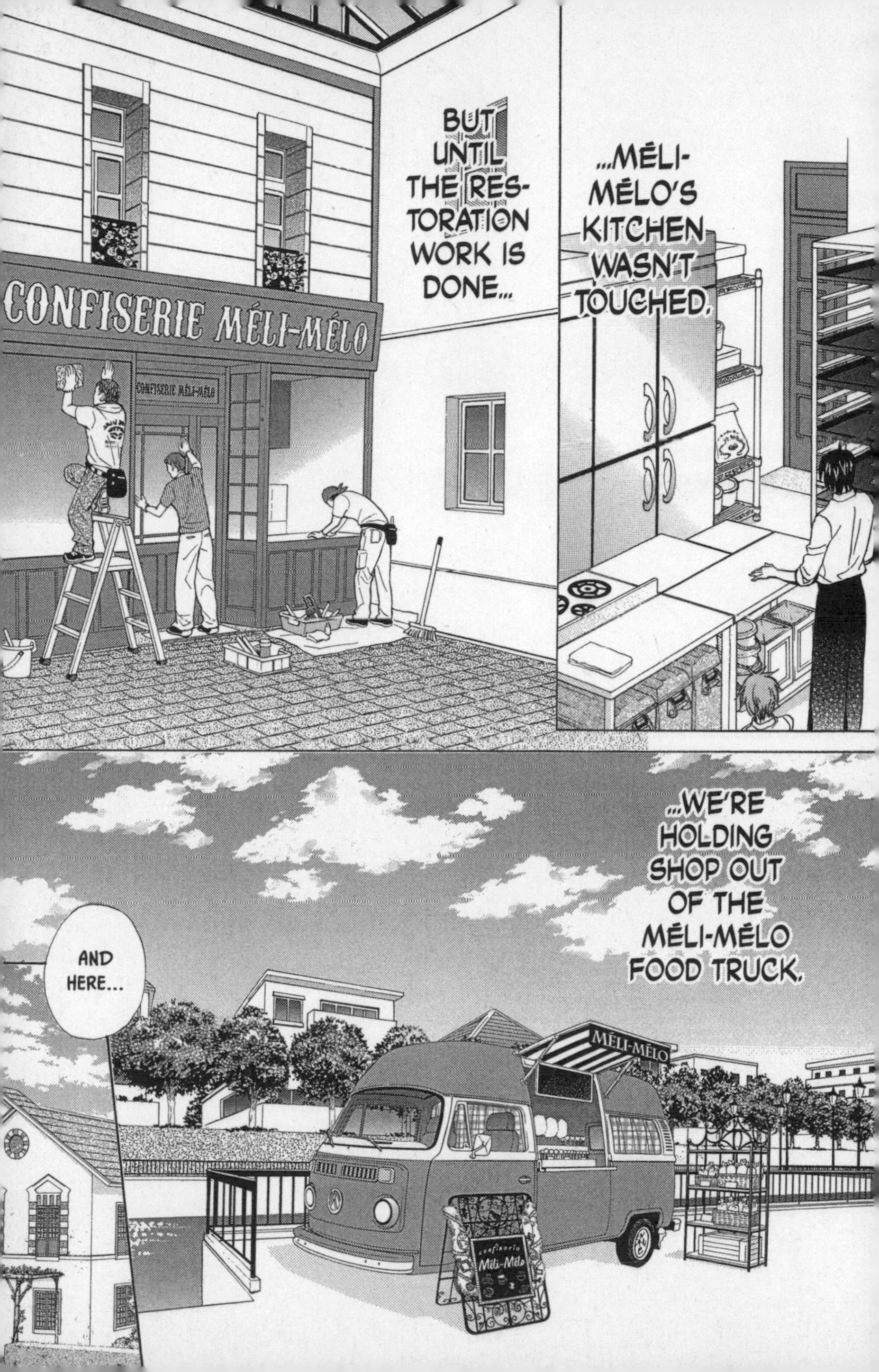
...MÉLI-MÉLO'S KITCHEN WASN'T TOUCHED.
CONFISERIE MÉLI-MÉLO
CONFISERIE MÉLI-MÉLO
BUT UNTIL THE RES-TORATION WORK IS DONE...
...WE'RE HOLDING SHOP OUT OF THE MÉLI-MÉLO FOOD TRUCK.
MÉLI-MÉLO
AND HERE...
confiserie Méli-Mélo

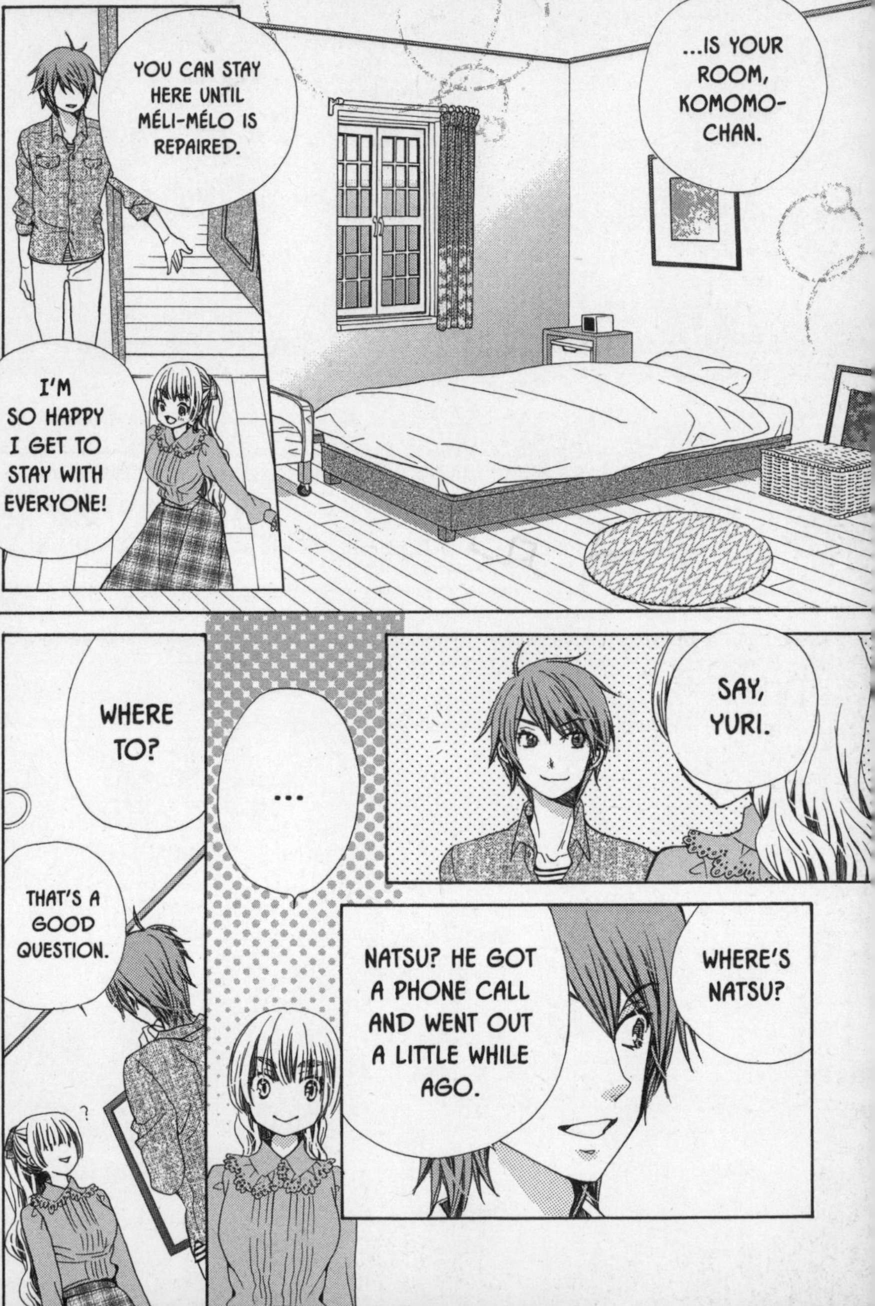
...IS YOUR ROOM, KOMOMO-CHAN.
YOU CAN STAY HERE UNTIL MÉLI-MÉLO IS REPAIRED.
I'M SO HAPPY I GET TO STAY WITH EVERYONE!
SAY, YURI.
WHERE'S NATSU?
NATSU? HE GOT A PHONE CALL AND WENT OUT A LITTLE WHILE AGO.
...
WHERE TO?
THAT'S A GOOD QUESTION.

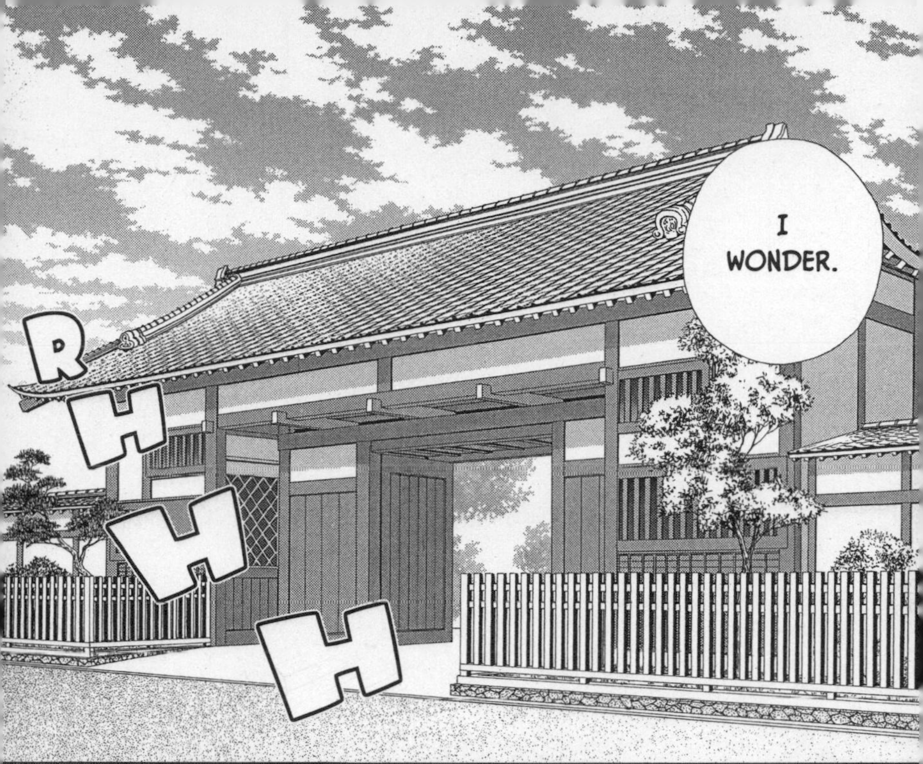
I WONDER.
RHHH
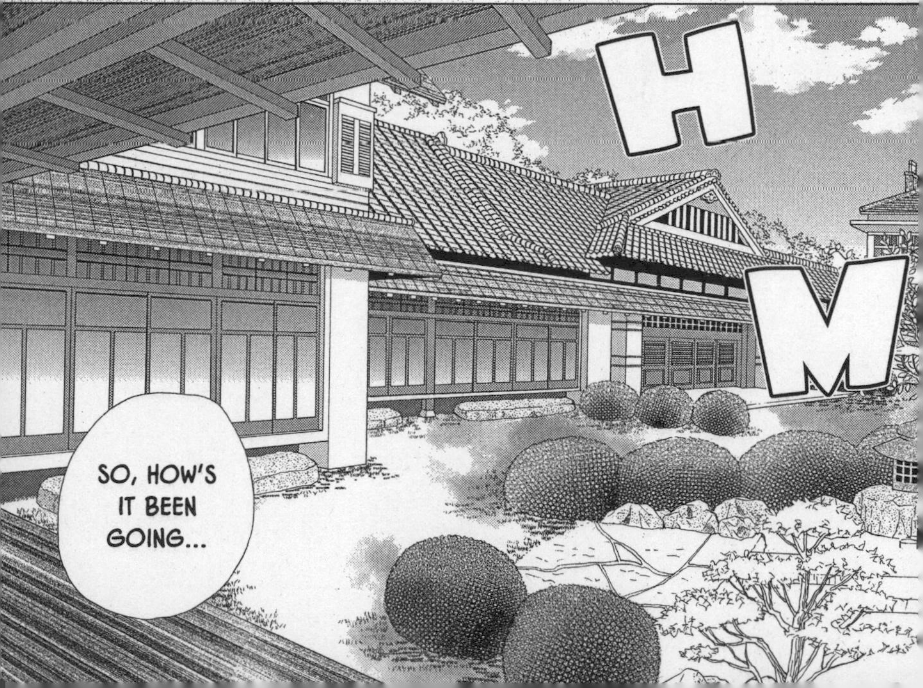
HM
SO, HOW'S IT BEEN GOING...

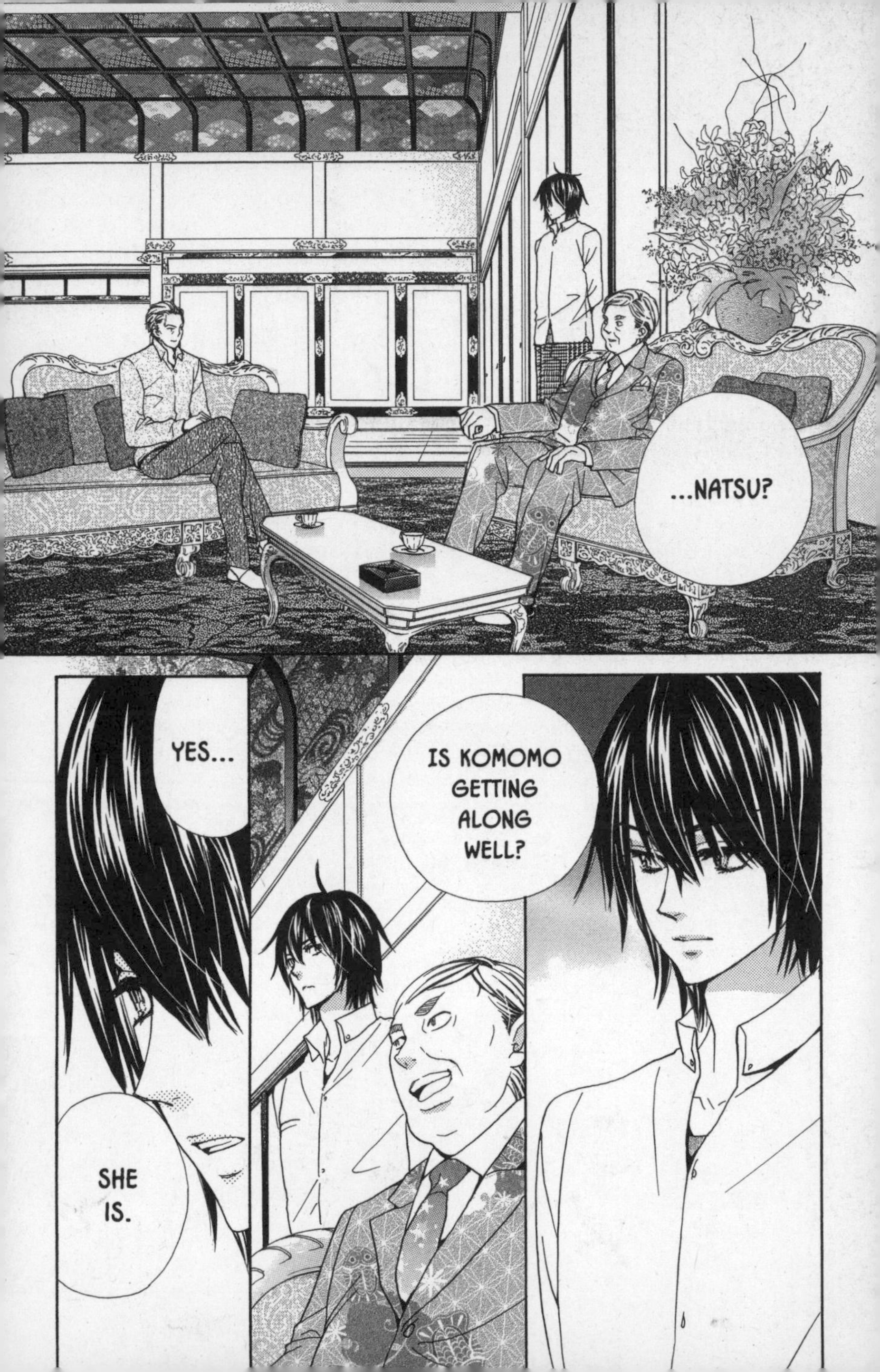
...NATSU?
IS KOMOMO GETTING ALONG WELL?
YES...
SHE IS.

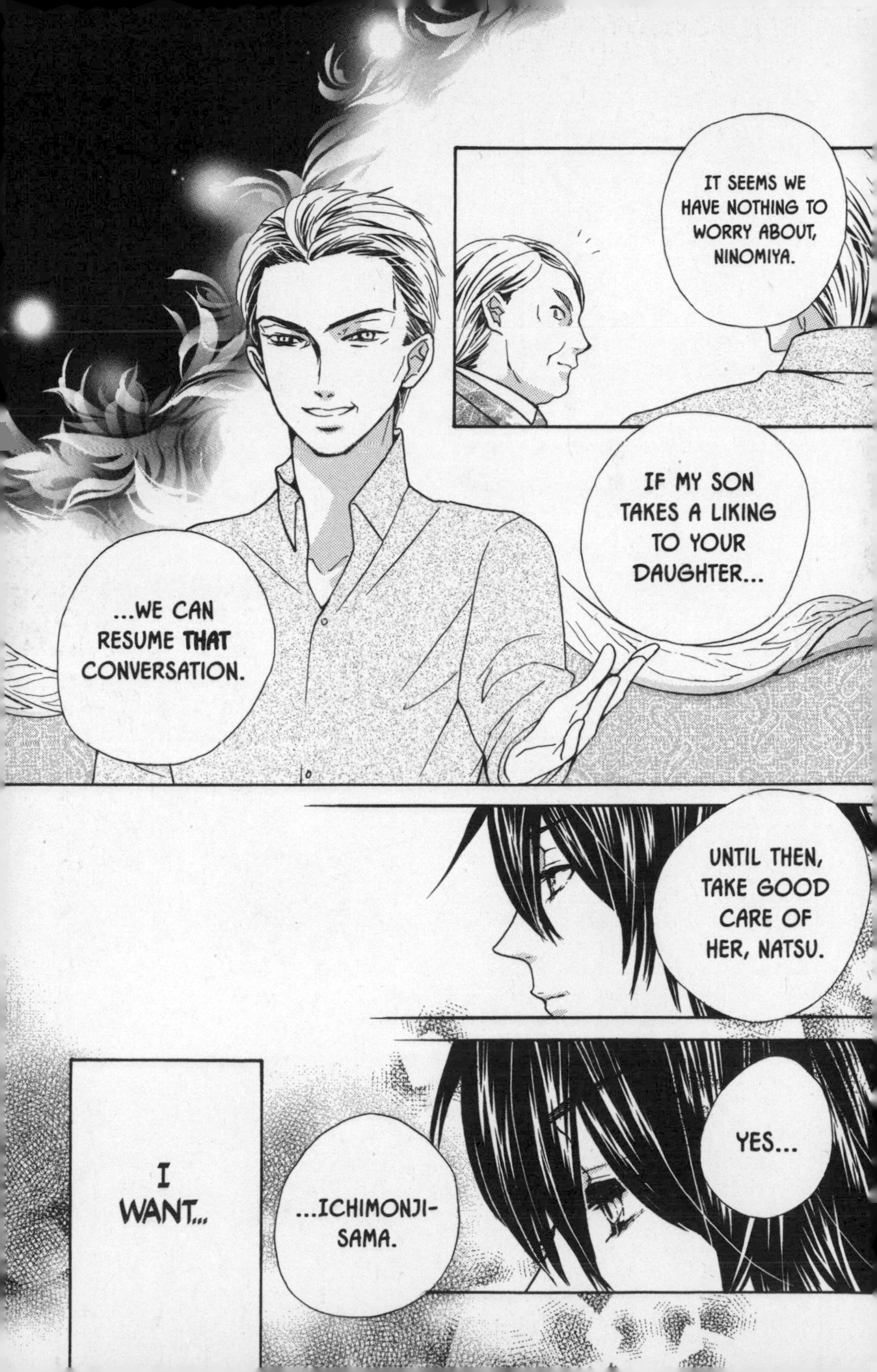
IT SEEMS WE HAVE NOTHING TO WORRY ABOUT, NINOMIYA.
IF MY SON TAKES A LIKING TO YOUR DAUGHTER...
...WE CAN RESUME **THAT** CONVERSATION.
UNTIL THEN, TAKE GOOD CARE OF HER, NATSU.
YES...
...ICHIMONJI-SAMA.
I WANT...

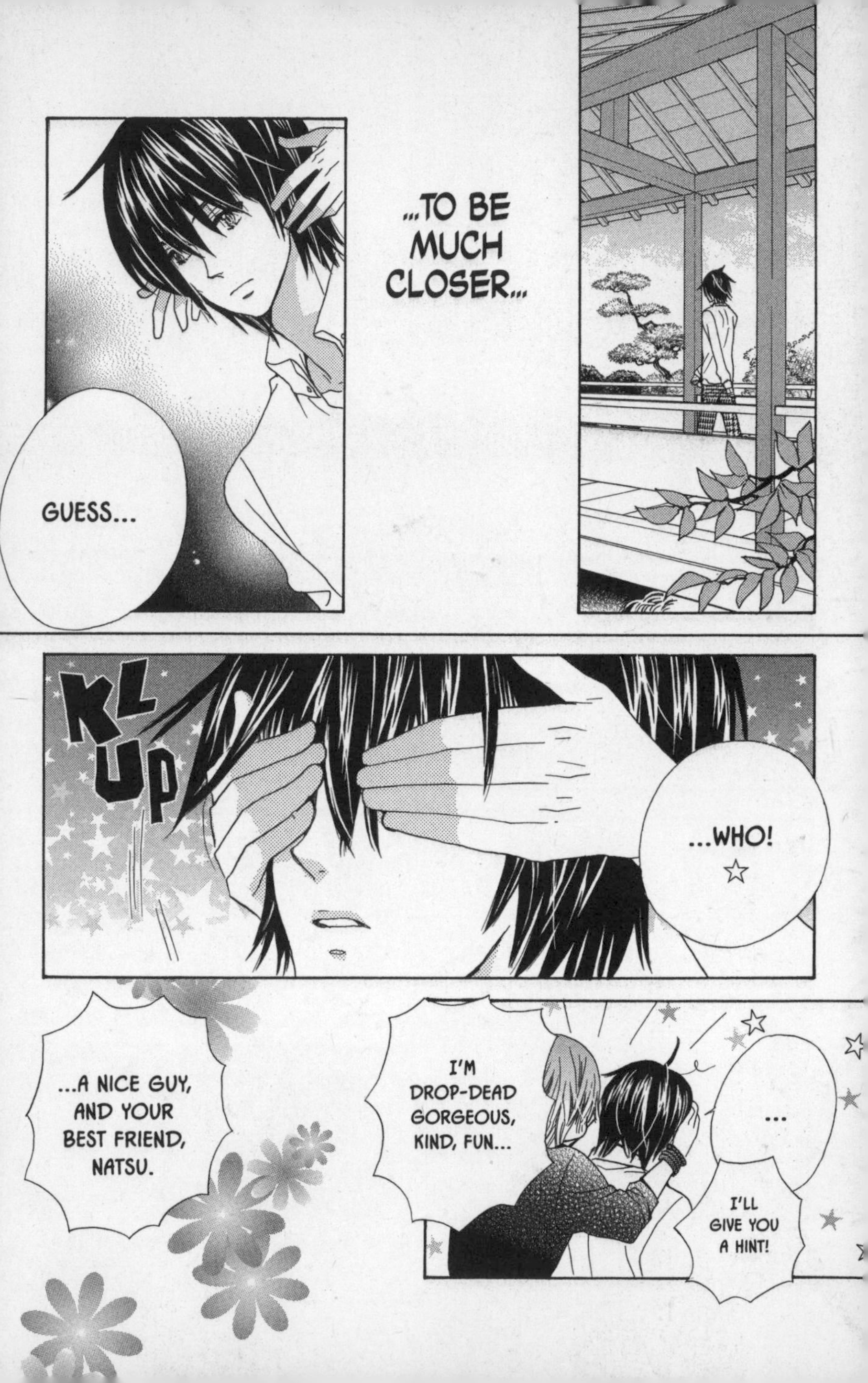
...TO BE MUCH CLOSER...
GUESS...
...WHO! ☆
KLUP
...
I'LL GIVE YOU A HINT!
I'M DROP-DEAD GORGEOUS, KIND, FUN...
...A NICE GUY, AND YOUR BEST FRIEND, NATSU.

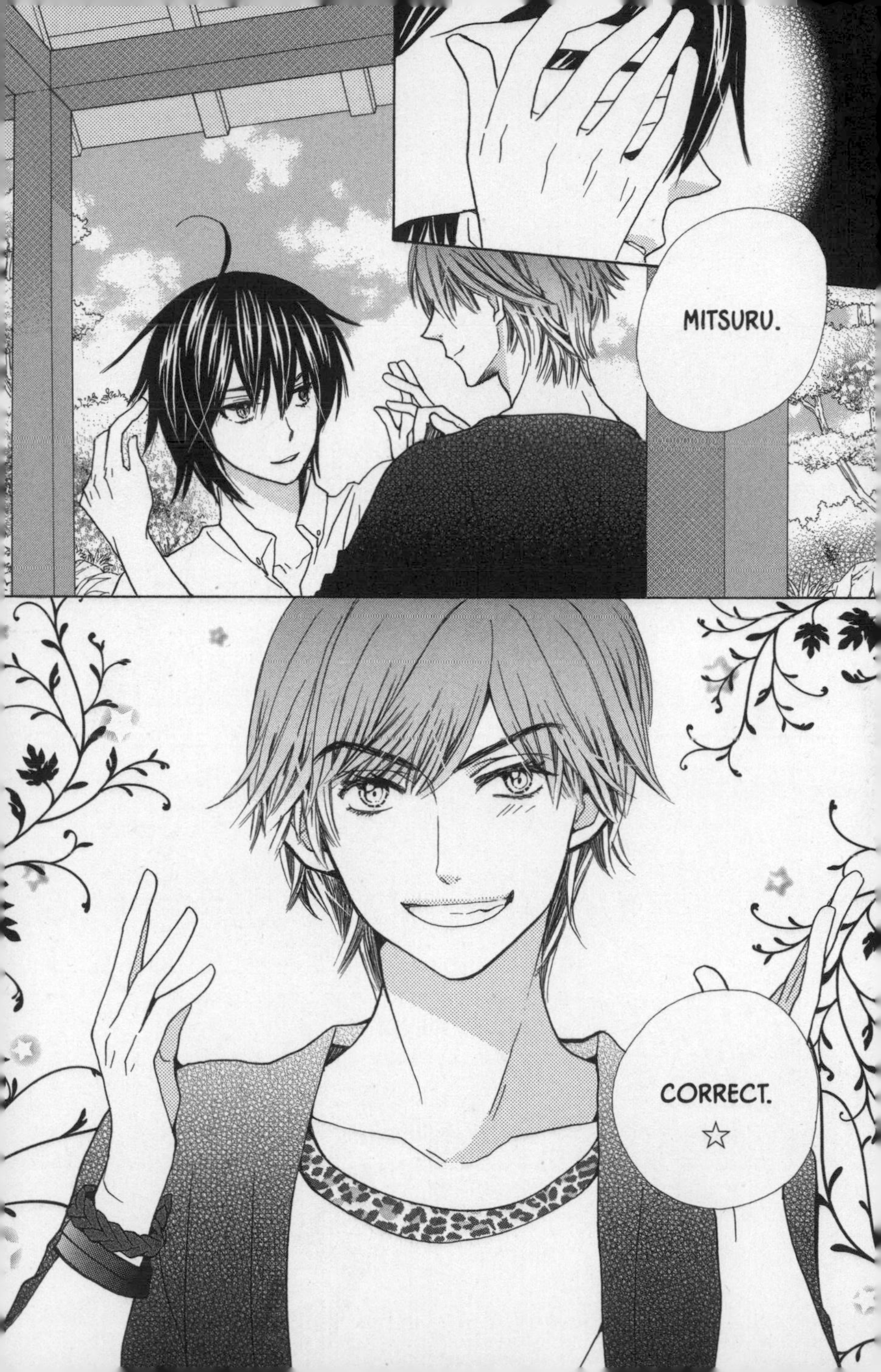
MITSURU.
CORRECT. ☆

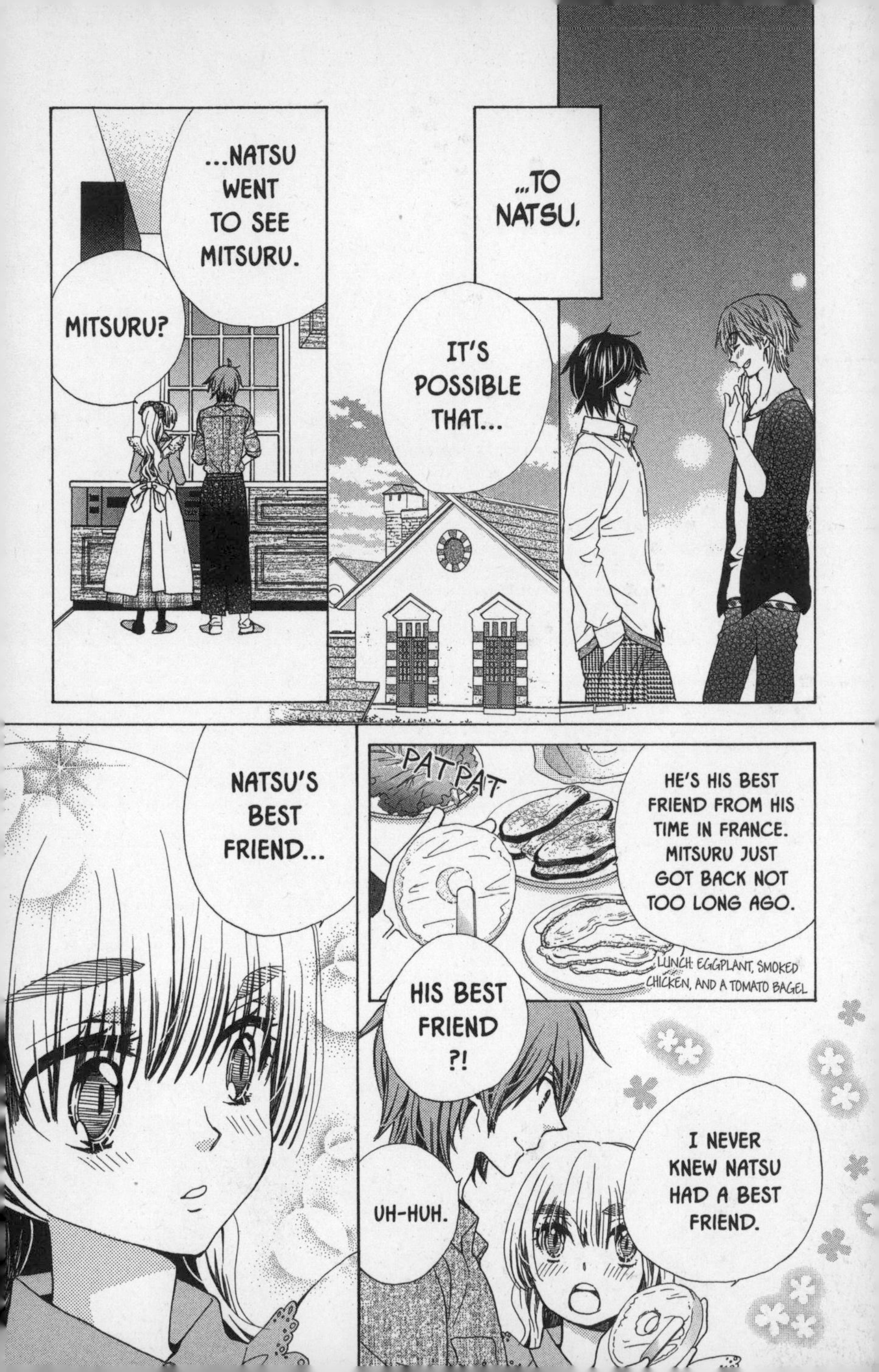
...TO NATSU.
IT'S POSSIBLE THAT...
...NATSU WENT TO SEE MITSURU.
MITSURU?
PAT PAT
HE'S HIS BEST FRIEND FROM HIS TIME IN FRANCE. MITSURU JUST GOT BACK NOT TOO LONG AGO.
LUNCH: EGGPLANT, SMOKED CHICKEN, AND A TOMATO BAGEL
HIS BEST FRIEND ?!
I NEVER KNEW NATSU HAD A BEST FRIEND.
UH-HUH.
NATSU'S BEST FRIEND...

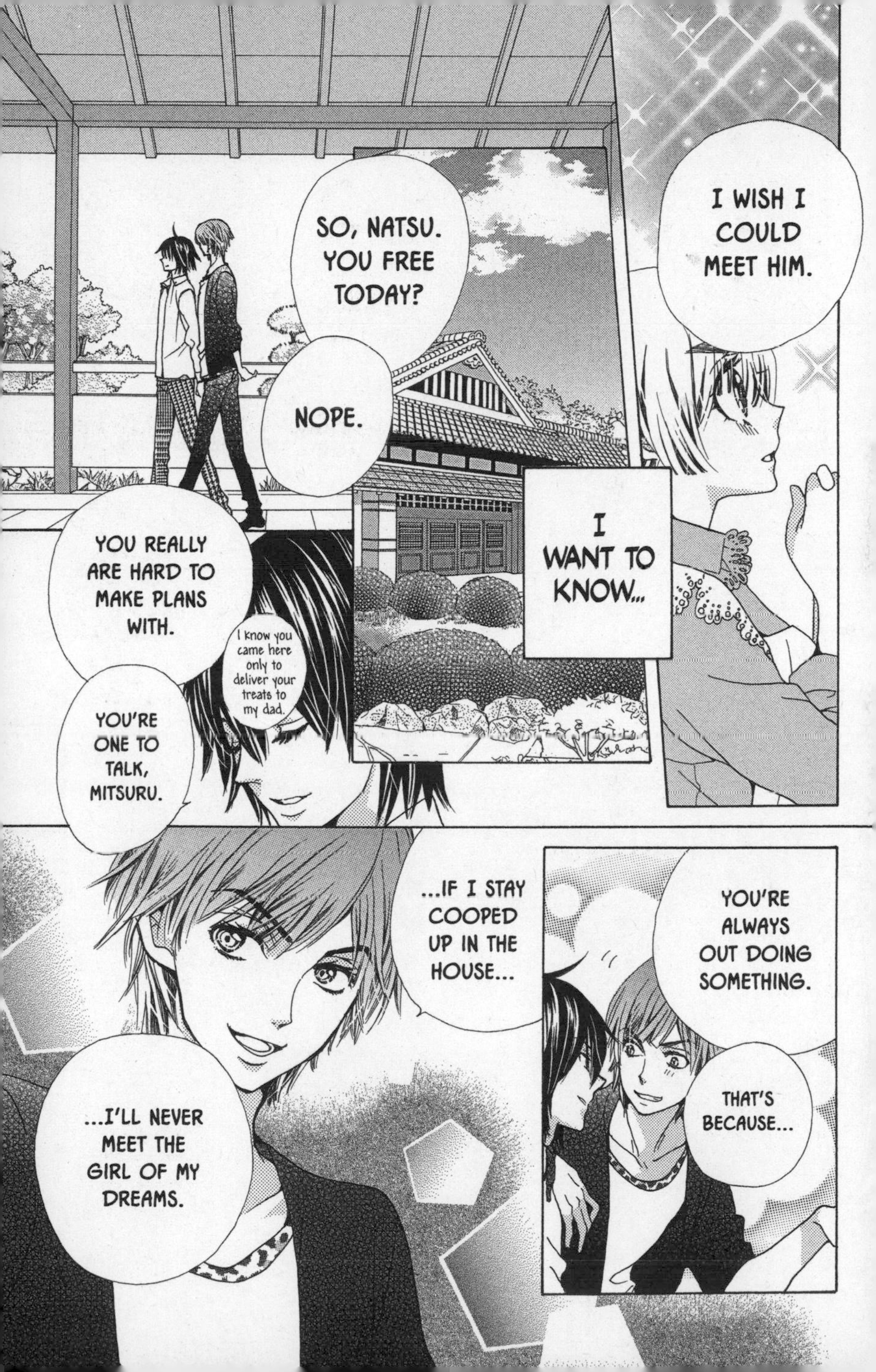
I WISH I COULD MEET HIM.
I WANT TO KNOW...
SO, NATSU. YOU FREE TODAY?
NOPE.
YOU REALLY ARE HARD TO MAKE PLANS WITH.
I know you came here only to deliver your treats to my dad.
YOU'RE ONE TO TALK, MITSURU.
YOU'RE ALWAYS OUT DOING SOMETHING.
THAT'S BECAUSE...
...IF I STAY COOPED UP IN THE HOUSE...
...I'LL NEVER MEET THE GIRL OF MY DREAMS.

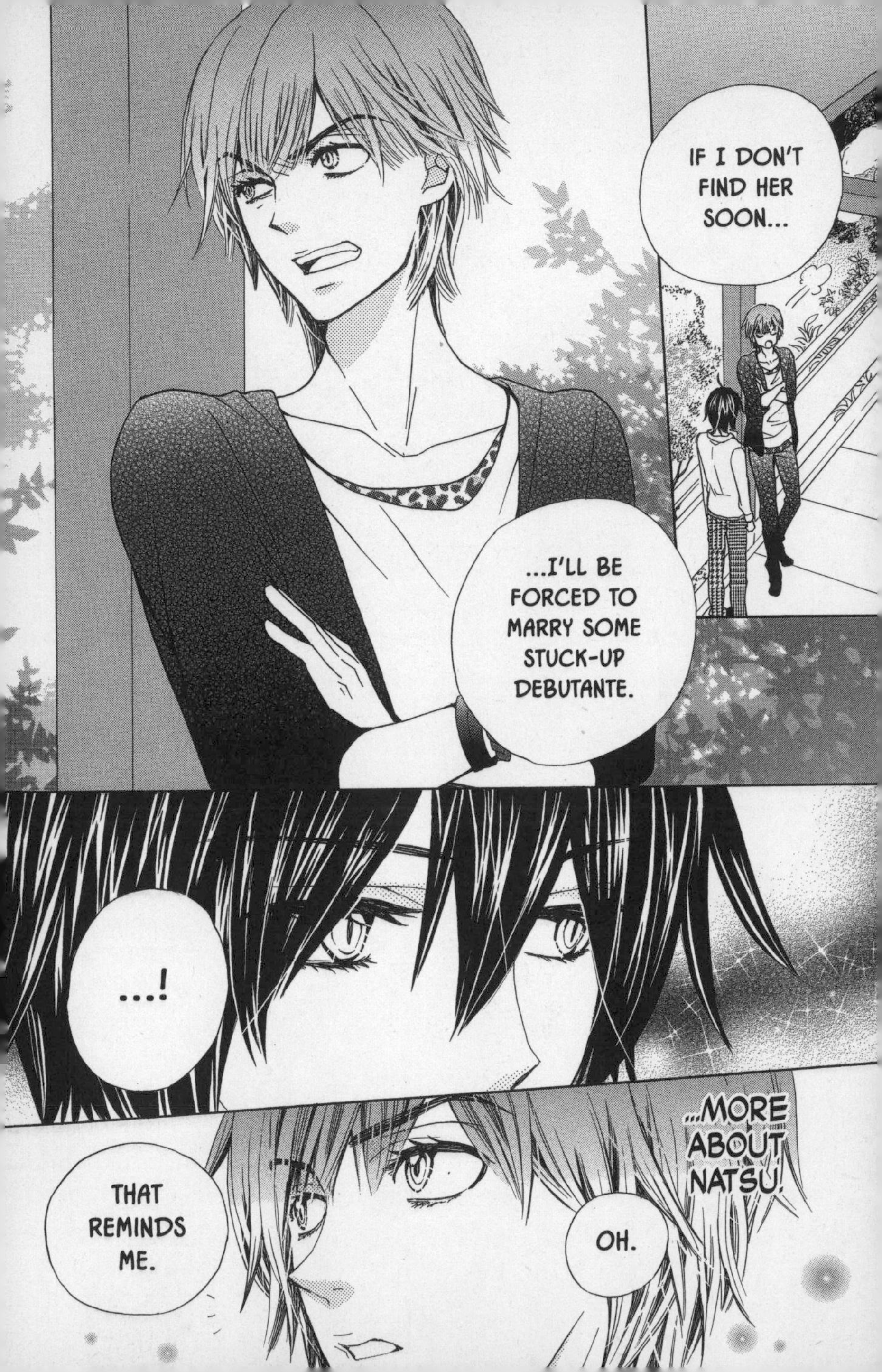
IF I DON'T FIND HER SOON...
...I'LL BE FORCED TO MARRY SOME STUCK-UP DEBUTANTE.
...!
...MORE ABOUT NATSU.
OH.
THAT REMINDS ME.

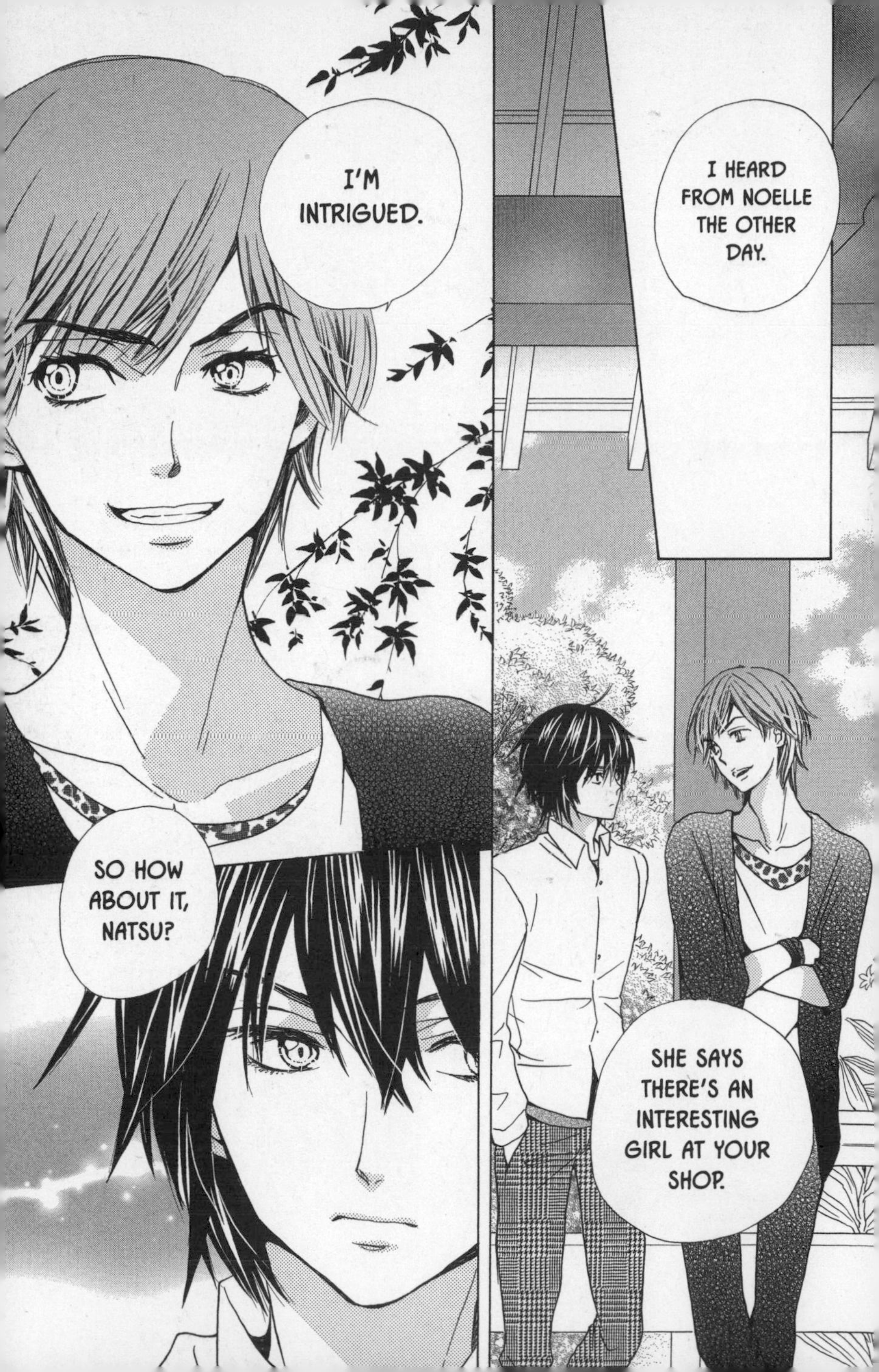
I HEARD FROM NOELLE THE OTHER DAY.
SHE SAYS THERE'S AN INTERESTING GIRL AT YOUR SHOP.
I'M INTRIGUED.
SO HOW ABOUT IT, NATSU?

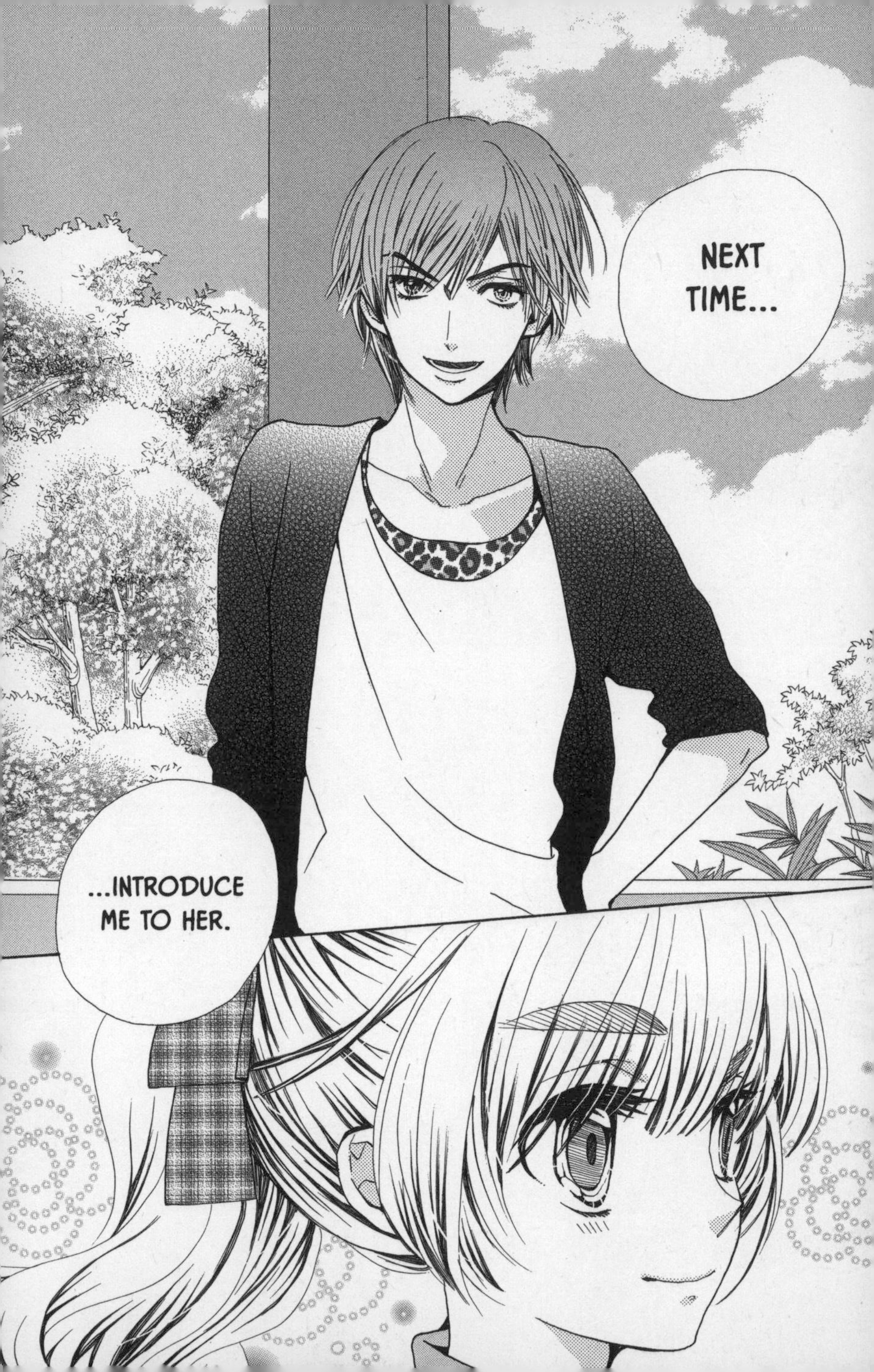
NEXT TIME...
...INTRODUCE ME TO HER.

CHAPTER 22

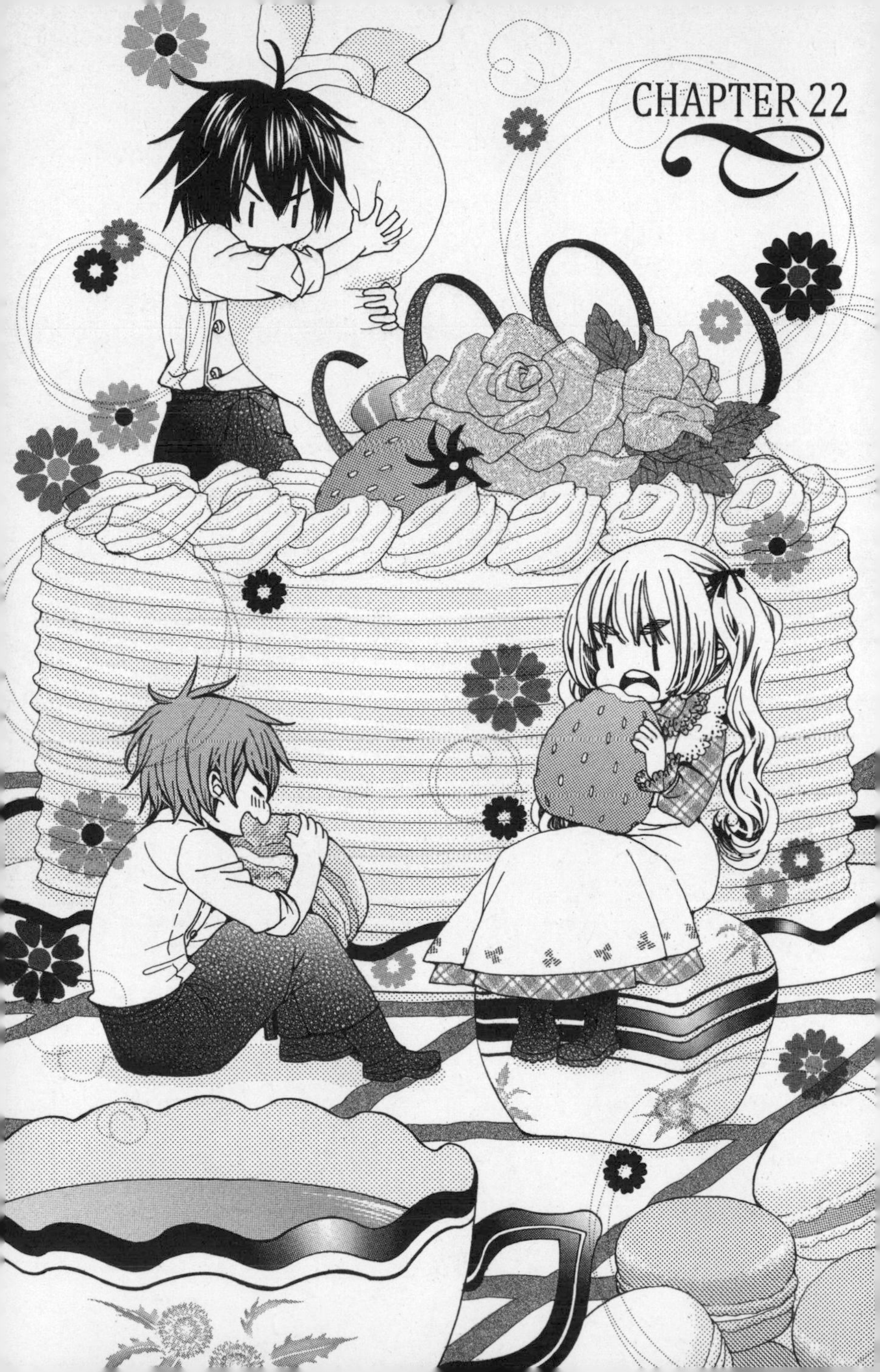

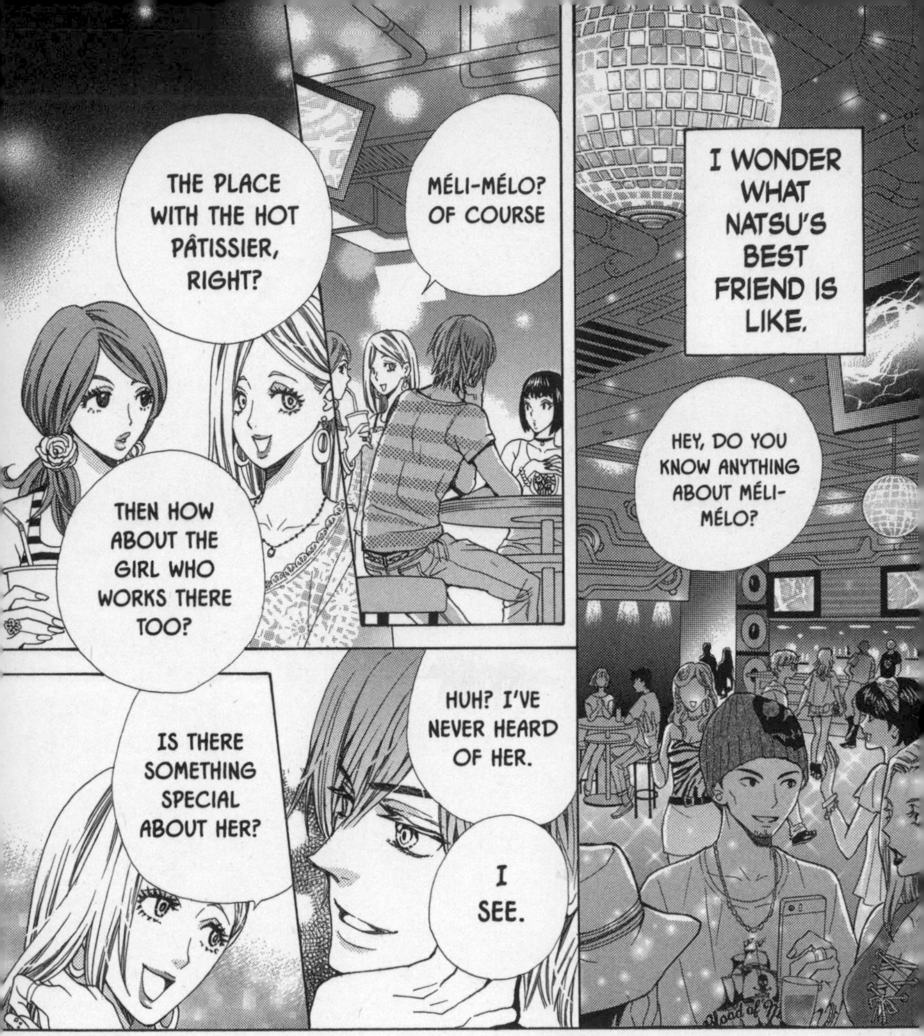
I WONDER WHAT NATSU'S BEST FRIEND IS LIKE.
HEY, DO YOU KNOW ANYTHING ABOUT MÉLI-MÉLO?
MÉLI-MÉLO? OF COURSE
THE PLACE WITH THE HOT PÂTISSIER, RIGHT?
THEN HOW ABOUT THE GIRL WHO WORKS THERE TOO?
HUH? I'VE NEVER HEARD OF HER.
IS THERE SOMETHING SPECIAL ABOUT HER?
I SEE.

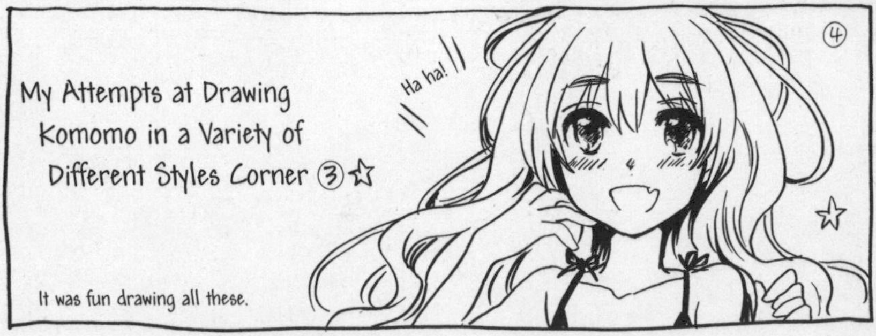
④
My Attempts at Drawing Komomo in a Variety of Different Styles Corner ③☆
Ha ha!
It was fun drawing all these.

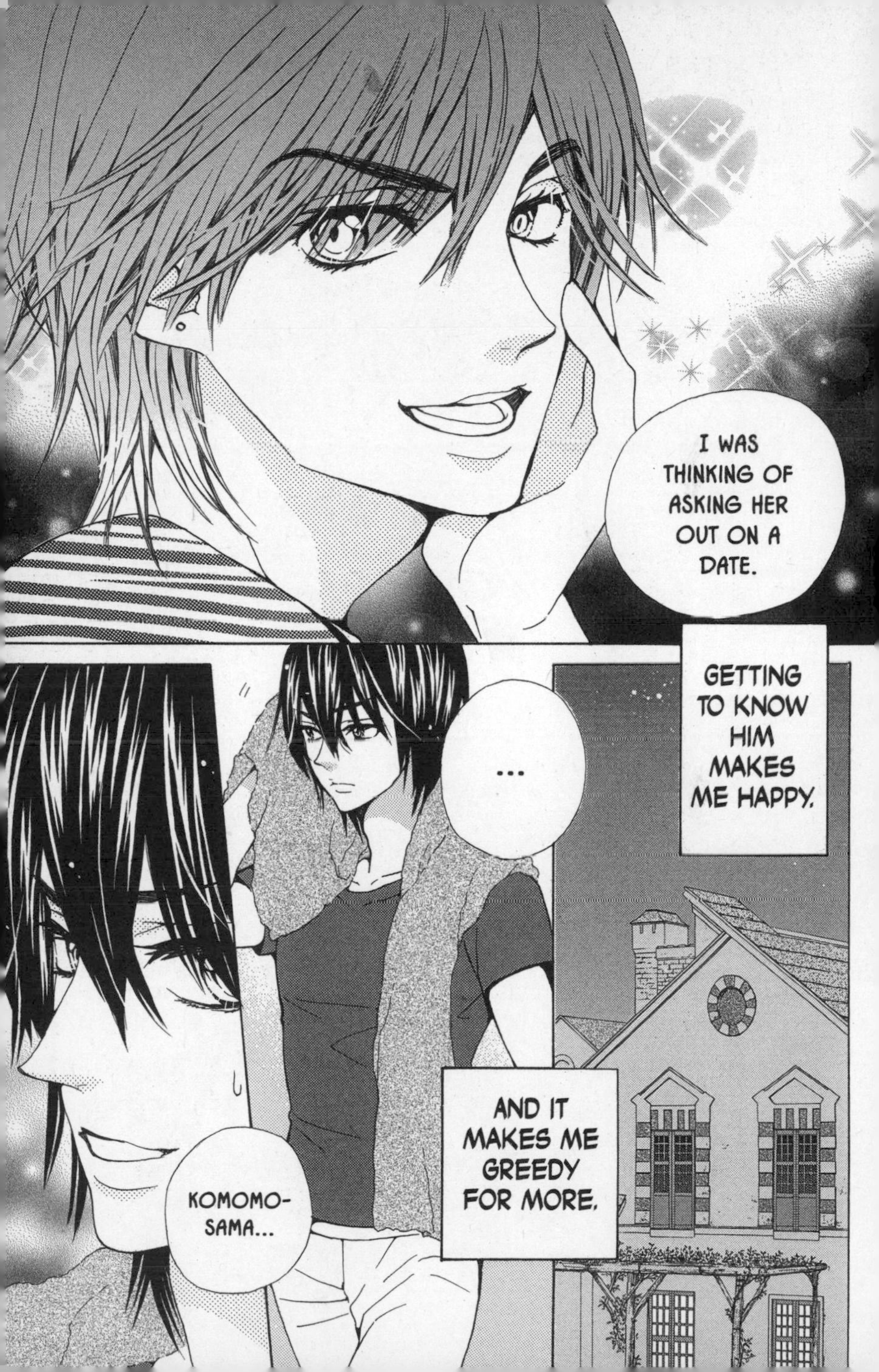
I WAS THINKING OF ASKING HER OUT ON A DATE.
GETTING TO KNOW HIM MAKES ME HAPPY.
AND IT MAKES ME GREEDY FOR MORE.
...
KOMOMO-SAMA...

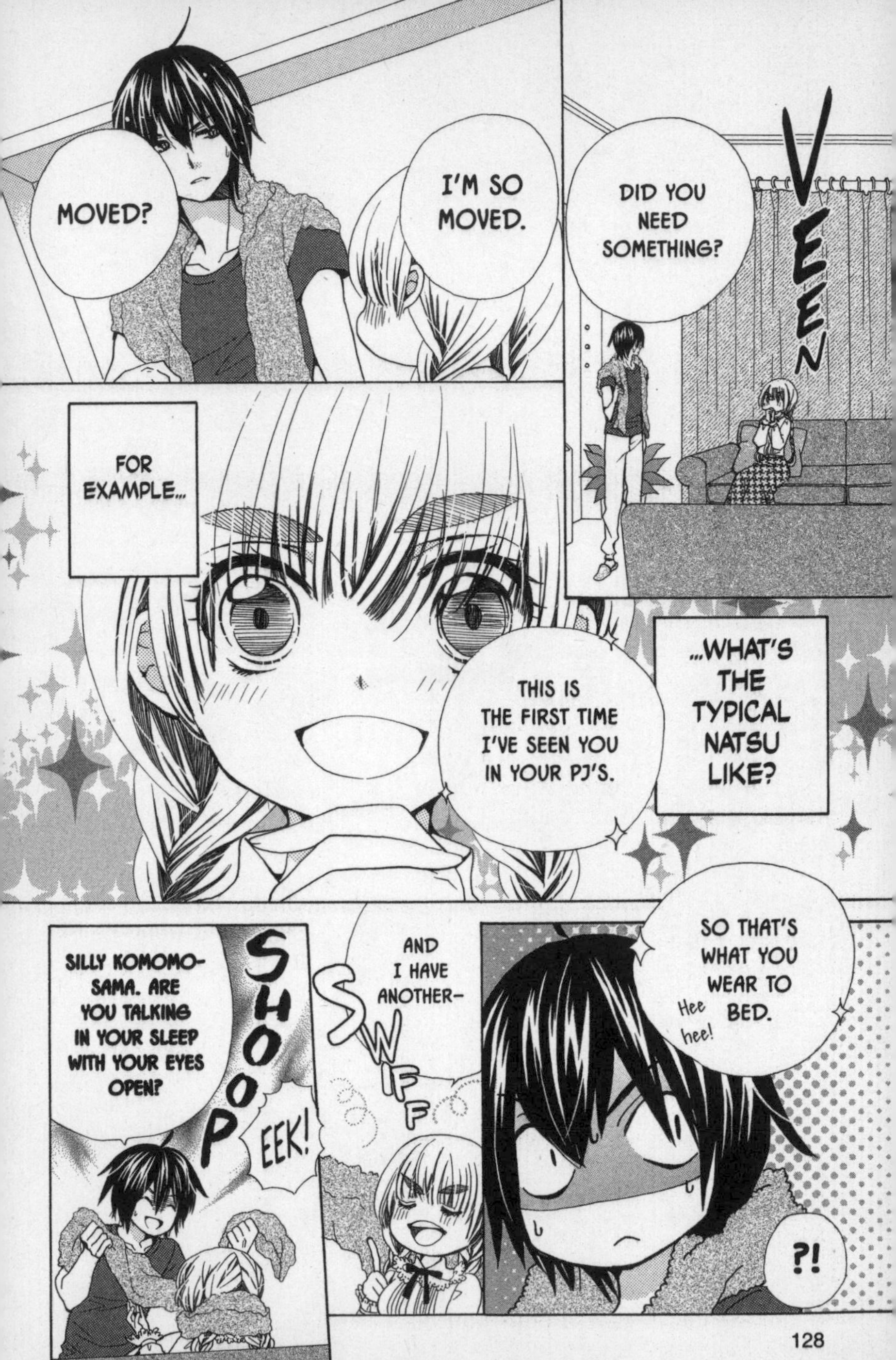
DID YOU NEED SOMETHING?
VEEN
I'M SO MOVED.
MOVED?
...WHAT'S THE TYPICAL NATSU LIKE?
FOR EXAMPLE...
THIS IS THE FIRST TIME I'VE SEEN YOU IN YOUR PJ'S.
SO THAT'S WHAT YOU WEAR TO BED.
Hee hee!
?!
AND I HAVE ANOTHER–
SWIFF
EEK!
SHOOOP
SILLY KOMOMO-SAMA. ARE YOU TALKING IN YOUR SLEEP WITH YOUR EYES OPEN?

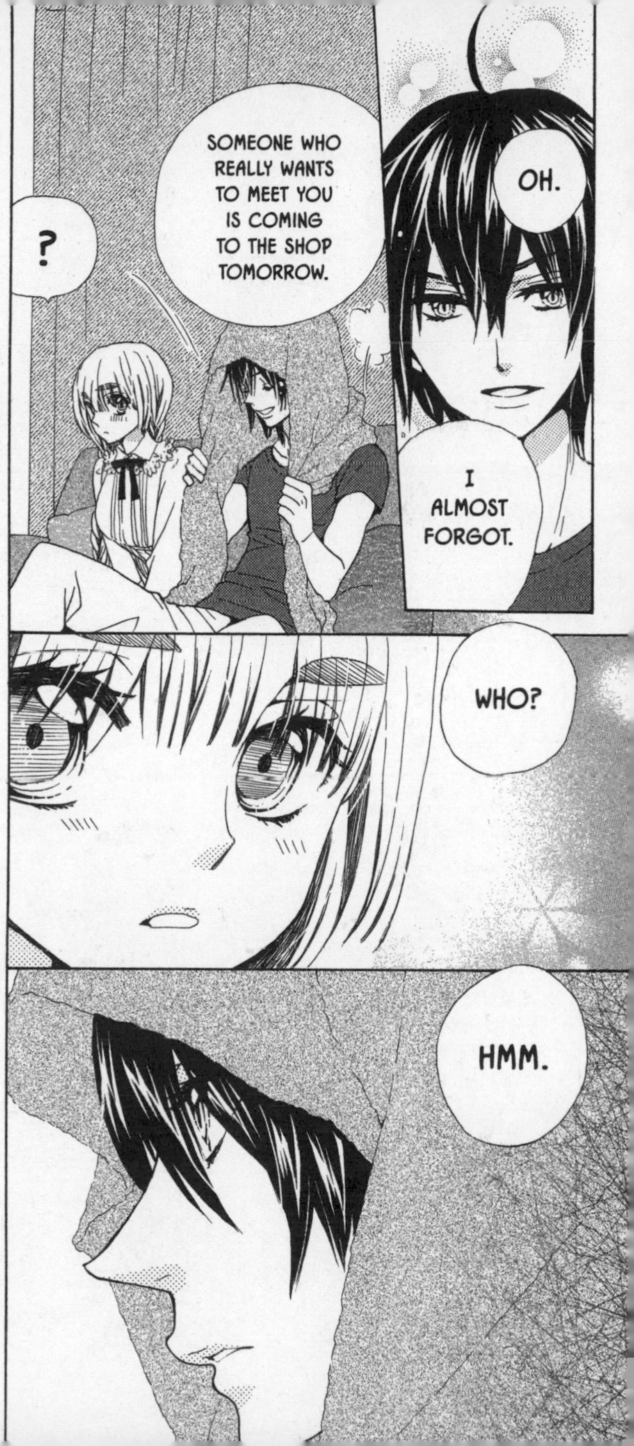
OH.
I ALMOST FORGOT.
SOMEONE WHO REALLY WANTS TO MEET YOU IS COMING TO THE SHOP TOMORROW.
?
WHO?
HMM.

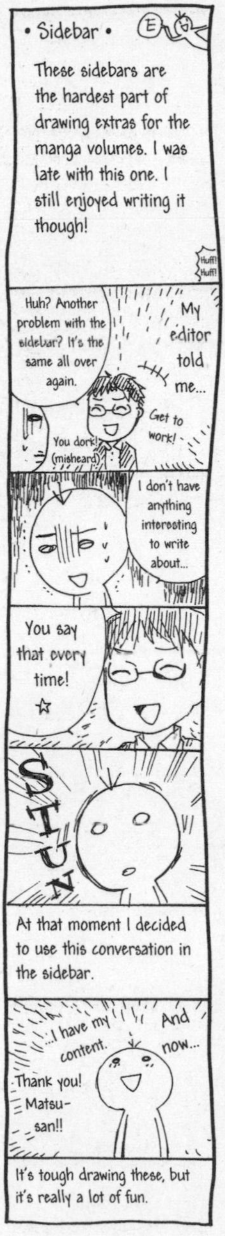
• Sidebar •
These sidebars are the hardest part of drawing extras for the manga volumes. I was late with this one. I still enjoyed writing it though!
Huff! Huff!
My editor told me...
Huh? Another problem with the sidebar? It's the same all over again.
Get to work!
You dork! (misheard)
I don't have anything interesting to write about...
You say that every time! ☆
STUN
At that moment I decided to use this conversation in the sidebar.
And now...
...I have my content.
Thank you! Matsu-san!!
It's tough drawing these, but it's really a lot of fun.

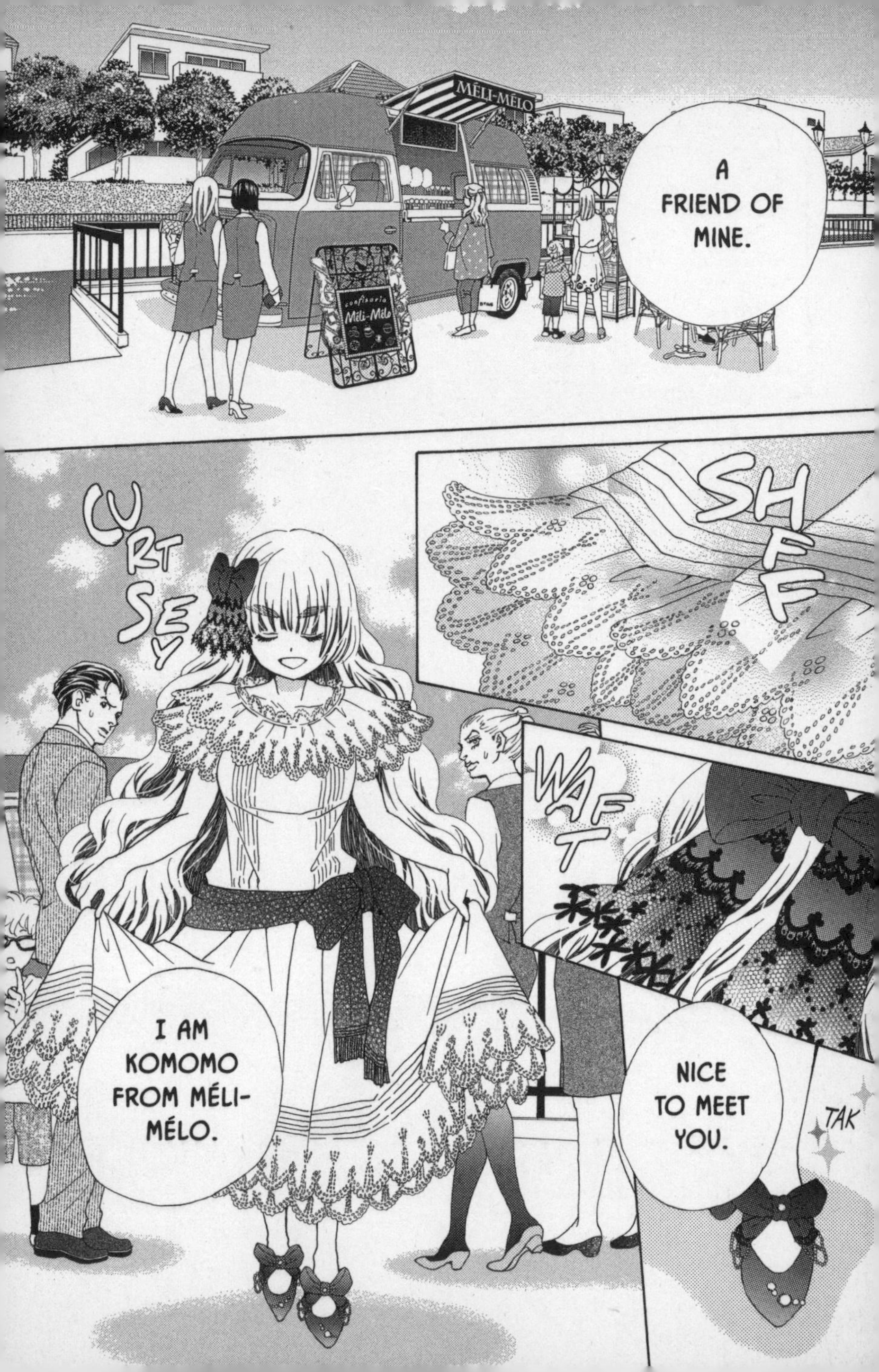
MÉLI-MÉLO
confiserie
Méli-Mélo
A FRIEND OF MINE.
SHFF
WAFT
NICE TO MEET YOU.
TAK
CURTSEY
I AM KOMOMO FROM MÉLI-MÉLO.

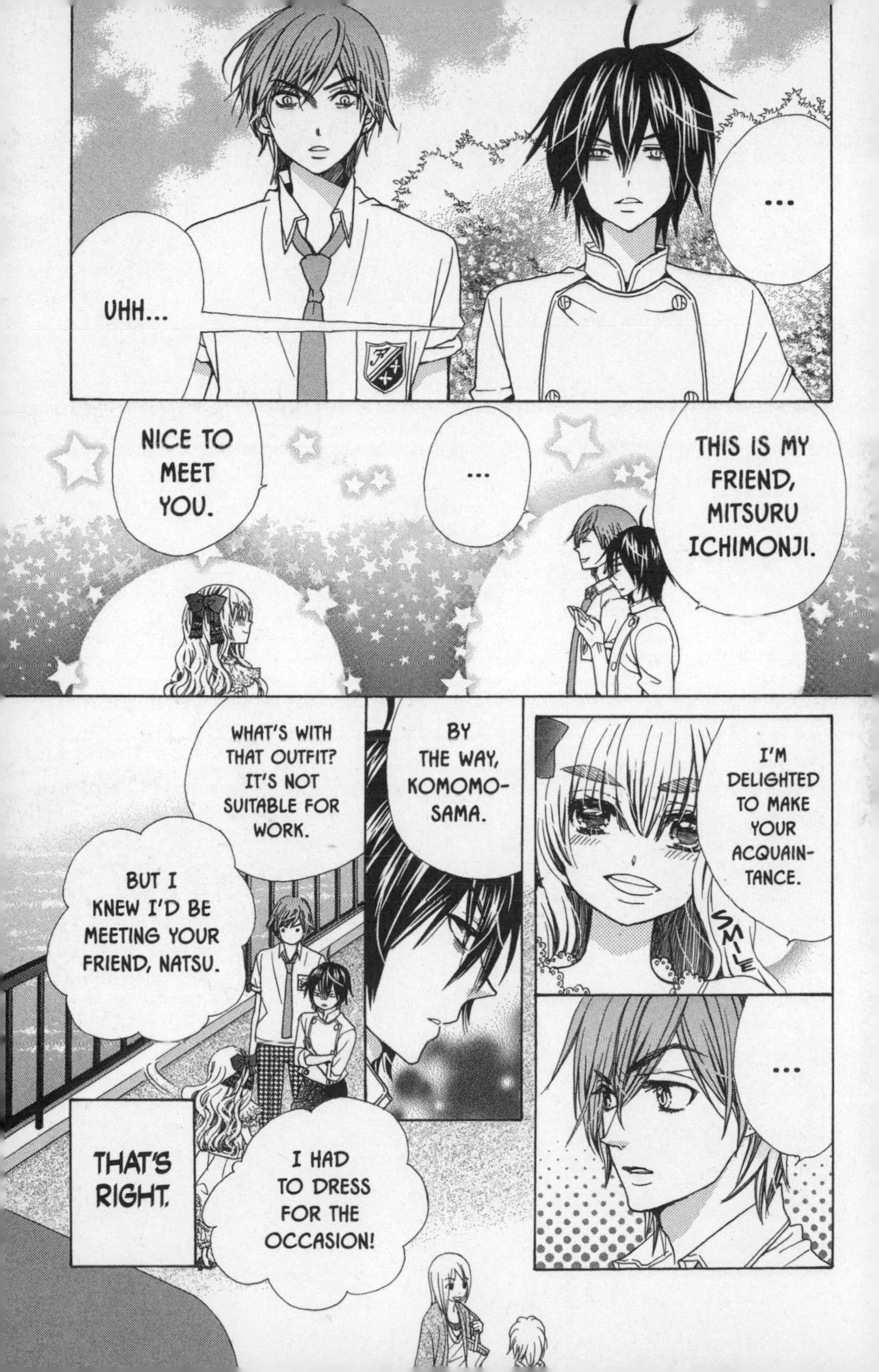
...
UHH...
THIS IS MY FRIEND, MITSURU ICHIMONJI.
...
NICE TO MEET YOU.
I'M DELIGHTED TO MAKE YOUR ACQUAINTANCE.
SMILE
...
BY THE WAY, KOMOMO-SAMA.
WHAT'S WITH THAT OUTFIT? IT'S NOT SUITABLE FOR WORK.
BUT I KNEW I'D BE MEETING YOUR FRIEND, NATSU.
I HAD TO DRESS FOR THE OCCASION!
THAT'S RIGHT.

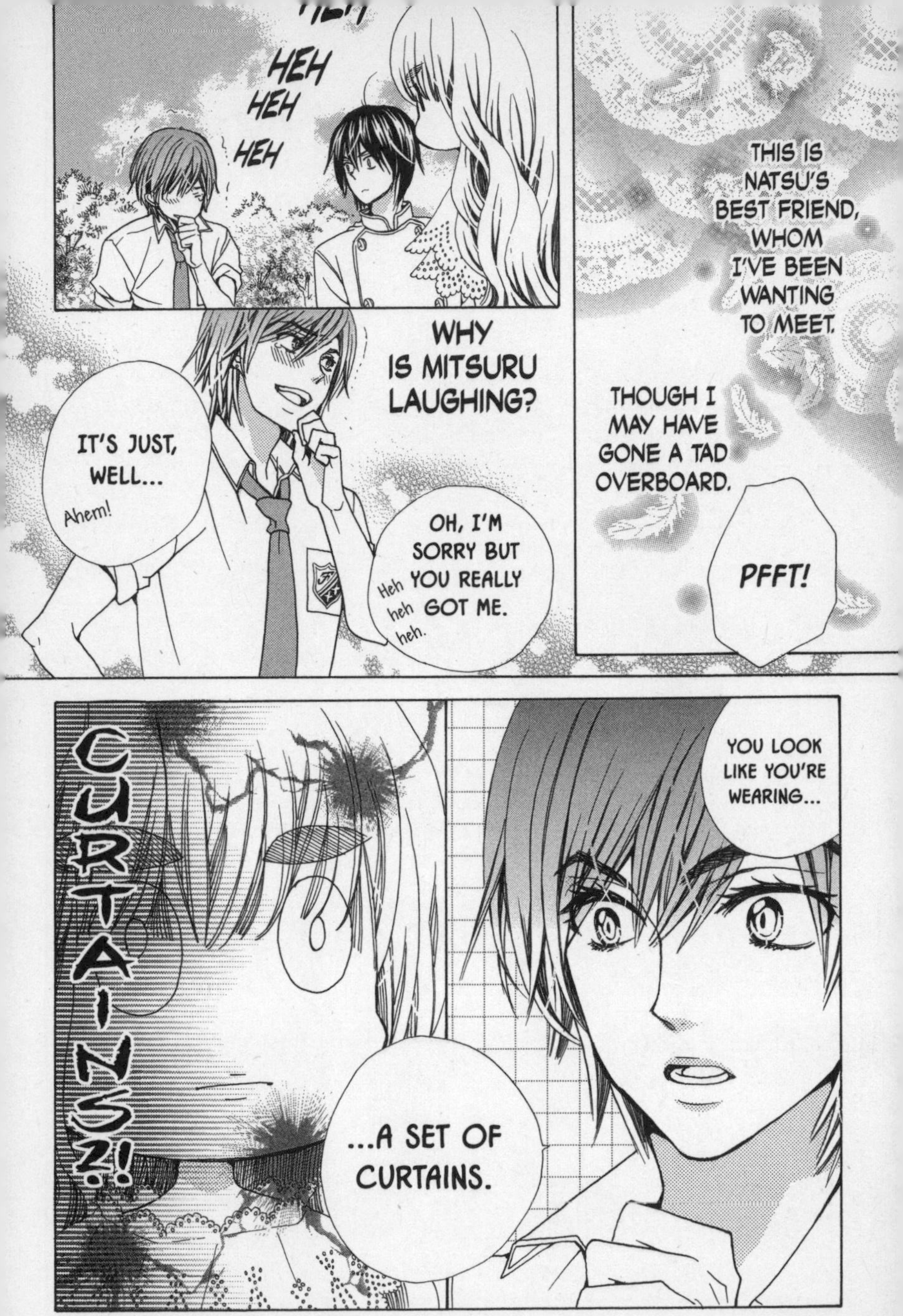
THIS IS NATSU'S BEST FRIEND, WHOM I'VE BEEN WANTING TO MEET.
THOUGH I MAY HAVE GONE A TAD OVERBOARD.
PFFT!
HEH HEH HEH
WHY IS MITSURU LAUGHING?
OH, I'M SORRY BUT YOU REALLY GOT ME.
Heh heh heh.
IT'S JUST, WELL...
Ahem!
YOU LOOK LIKE YOU'RE WEARING...
...A SET OF CURTAINS.
CURTAINS?!

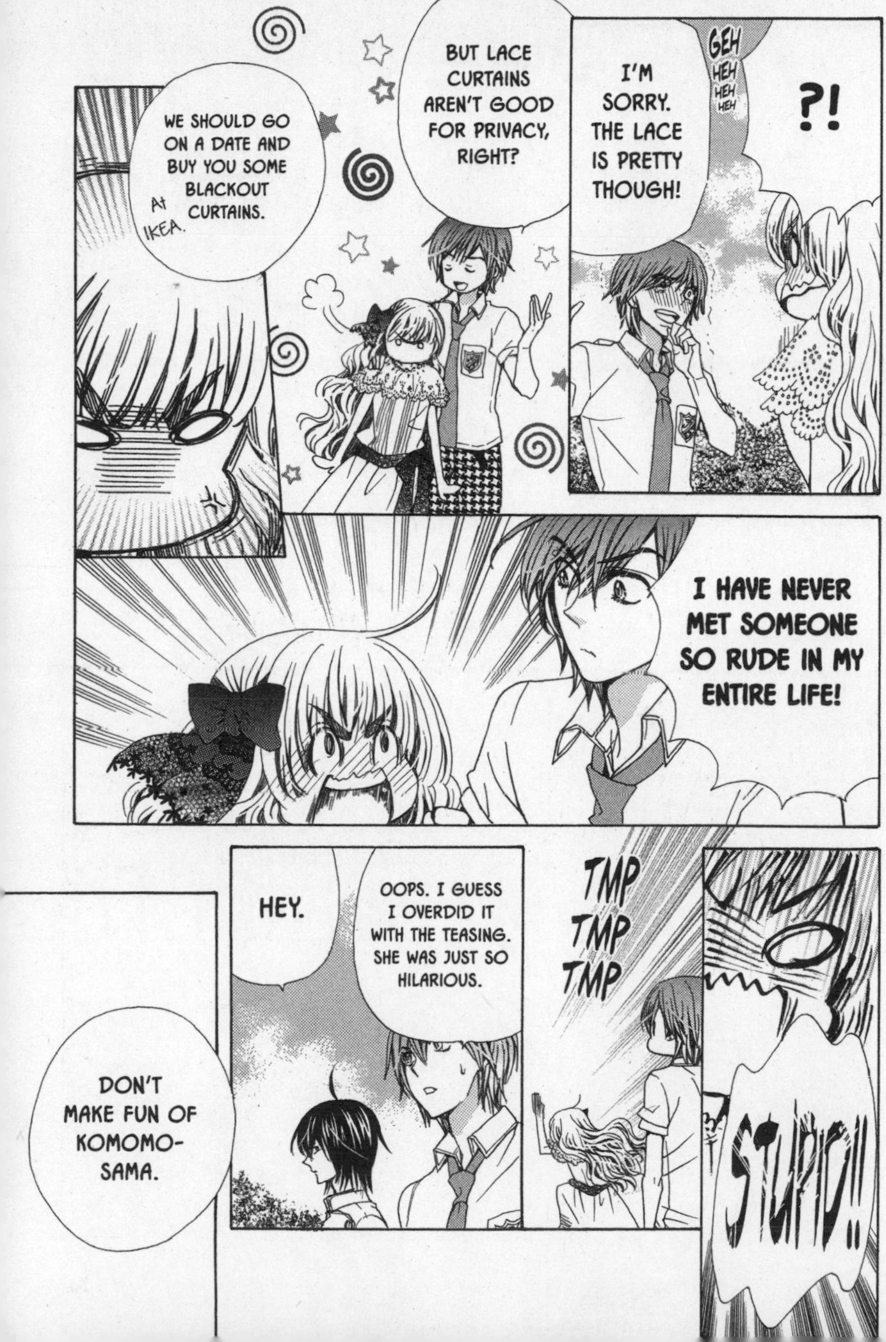
?!
GEH HEH HEH HEH
I'M SORRY. THE LACE IS PRETTY THOUGH!
BUT LACE CURTAINS AREN'T GOOD FOR PRIVACY, RIGHT?
WE SHOULD GO ON A DATE AND BUY YOU SOME BLACKOUT CURTAINS.
At IKEA.
I HAVE NEVER MET SOMEONE SO RUDE IN MY ENTIRE LIFE!
STUPID!!
TMP TMP TMP
OOPS. I GUESS I OVERDID IT WITH THE TEASING. SHE WAS JUST SO HILARIOUS.
HEY.
DON'T MAKE FUN OF KOMOMO-SAMA.

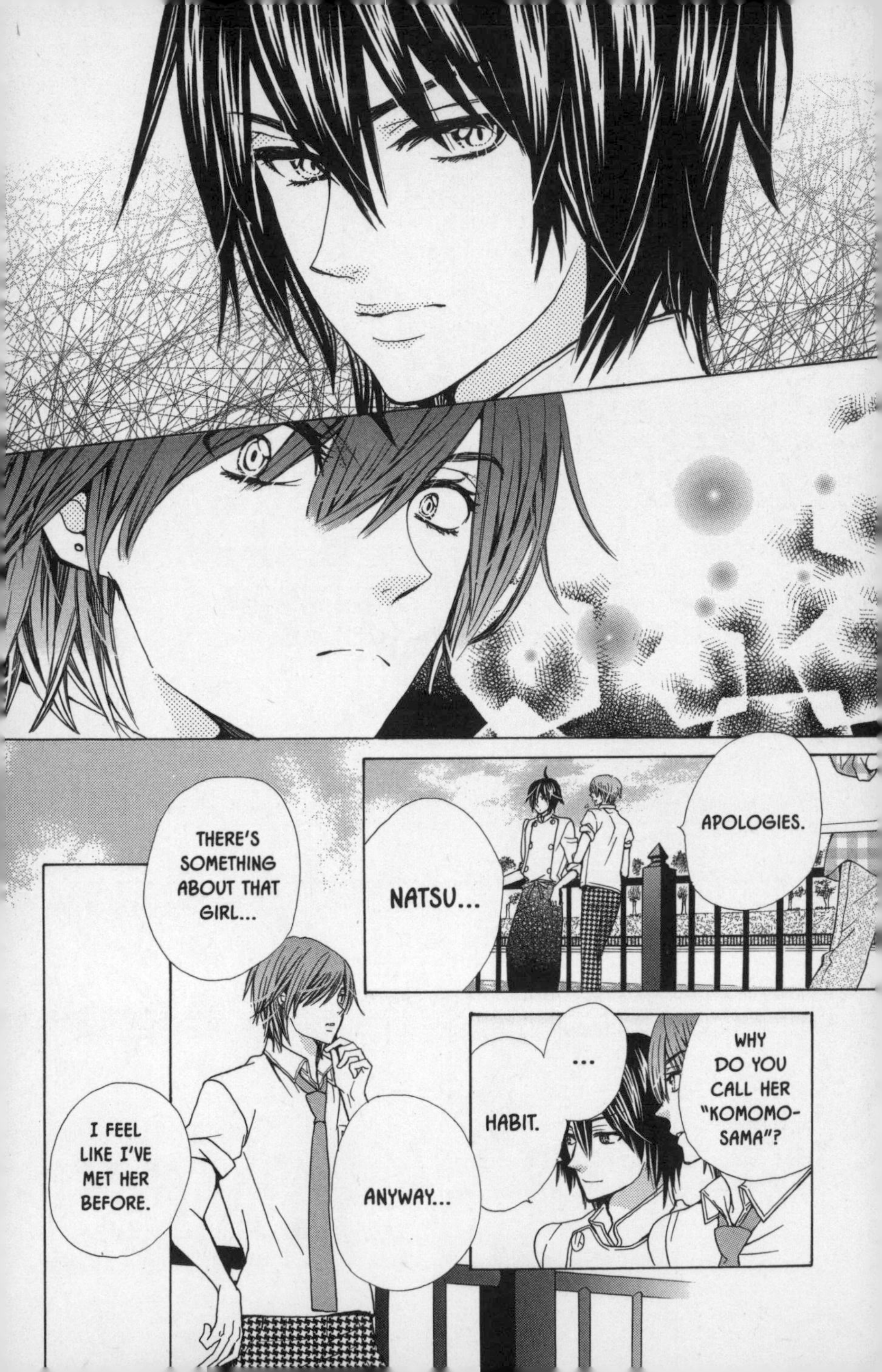
APOLOGIES.
NATSU...
WHY DO YOU CALL HER "KOMOMO-SAMA"?
...
HABIT.
ANYWAY...
THERE'S SOMETHING ABOUT THAT GIRL...
I FEEL LIKE I'VE MET HER BEFORE.

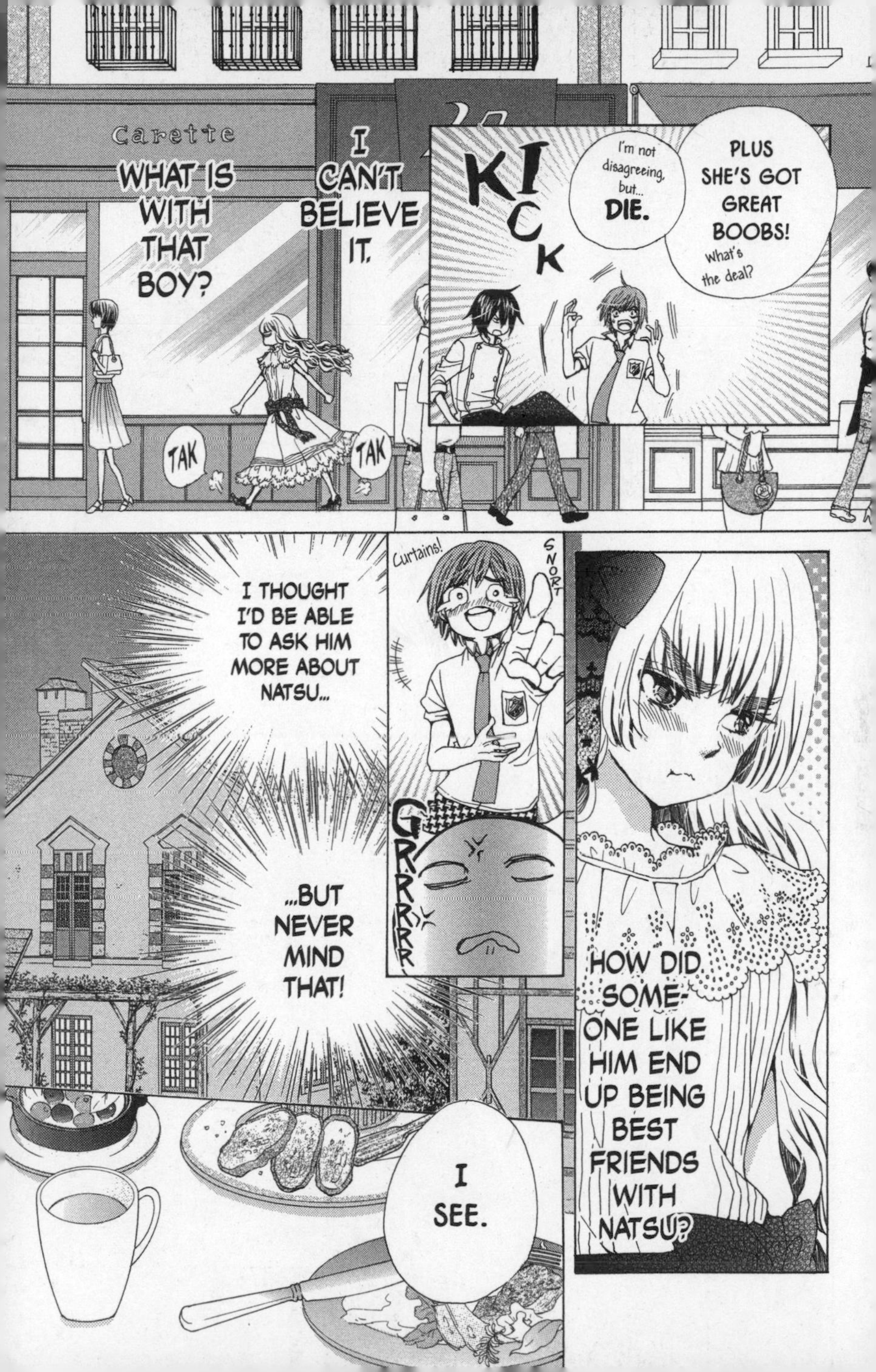
PLUS SHE'S GOT GREAT BOOBS!
what's the deal?
I'm not disagreeing, but... DIE.
KICK
I CAN'T BELIEVE IT.
WHAT IS WITH THAT BOY?
Carette
TAK
TAK
HOW DID SOME-ONE LIKE HIM END UP BEING BEST FRIENDS WITH NATSU?
SNORT
Curtains!
GRRRRR
I THOUGHT I'D BE ABLE TO ASK HIM MORE ABOUT NATSU...
...BUT NEVER MIND THAT!
I SEE.

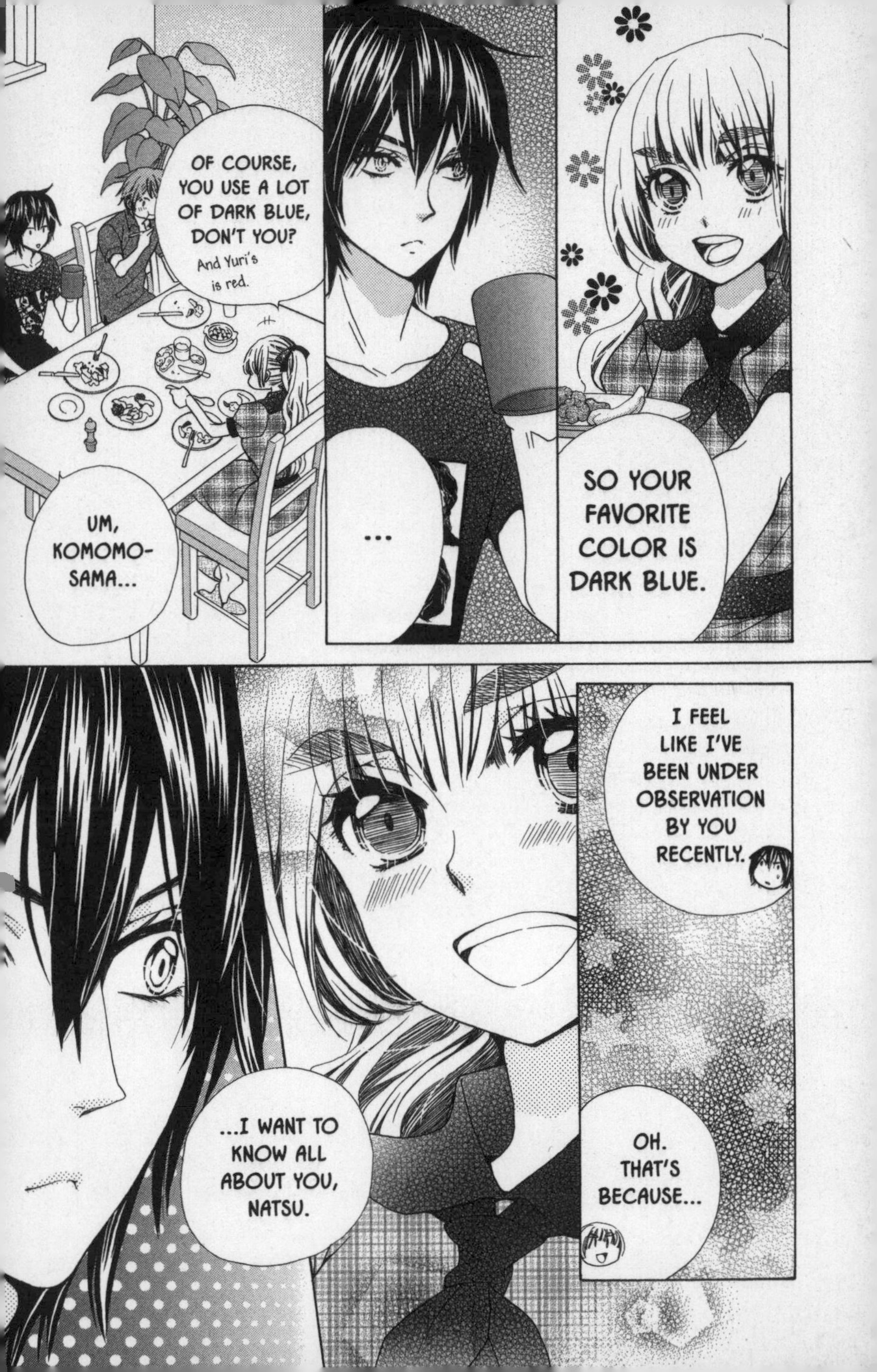
SO YOUR FAVORITE COLOR IS DARK BLUE.
...
OF COURSE, YOU USE A LOT OF DARK BLUE, DON'T YOU?
And Yuri's is red.
UM, KOMOMO-SAMA...
I FEEL LIKE I'VE BEEN UNDER OBSERVATION BY YOU RECENTLY.
OH. THAT'S BECAUSE...
...I WANT TO KNOW ALL ABOUT YOU, NATSU.

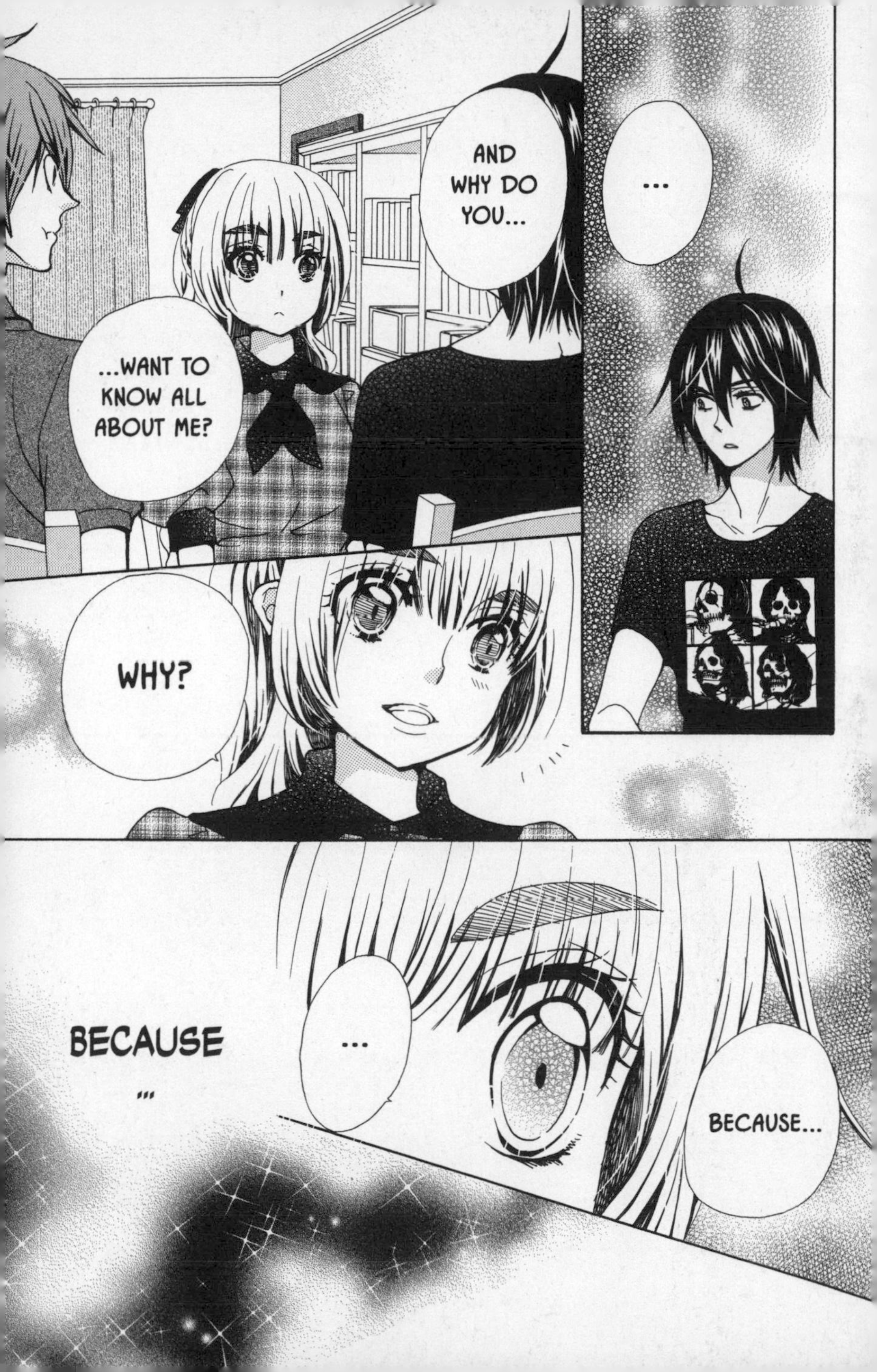
...
AND WHY DO YOU...
...WANT TO KNOW ALL ABOUT ME?
WHY?
BECAUSE...
...
BECAUSE
...

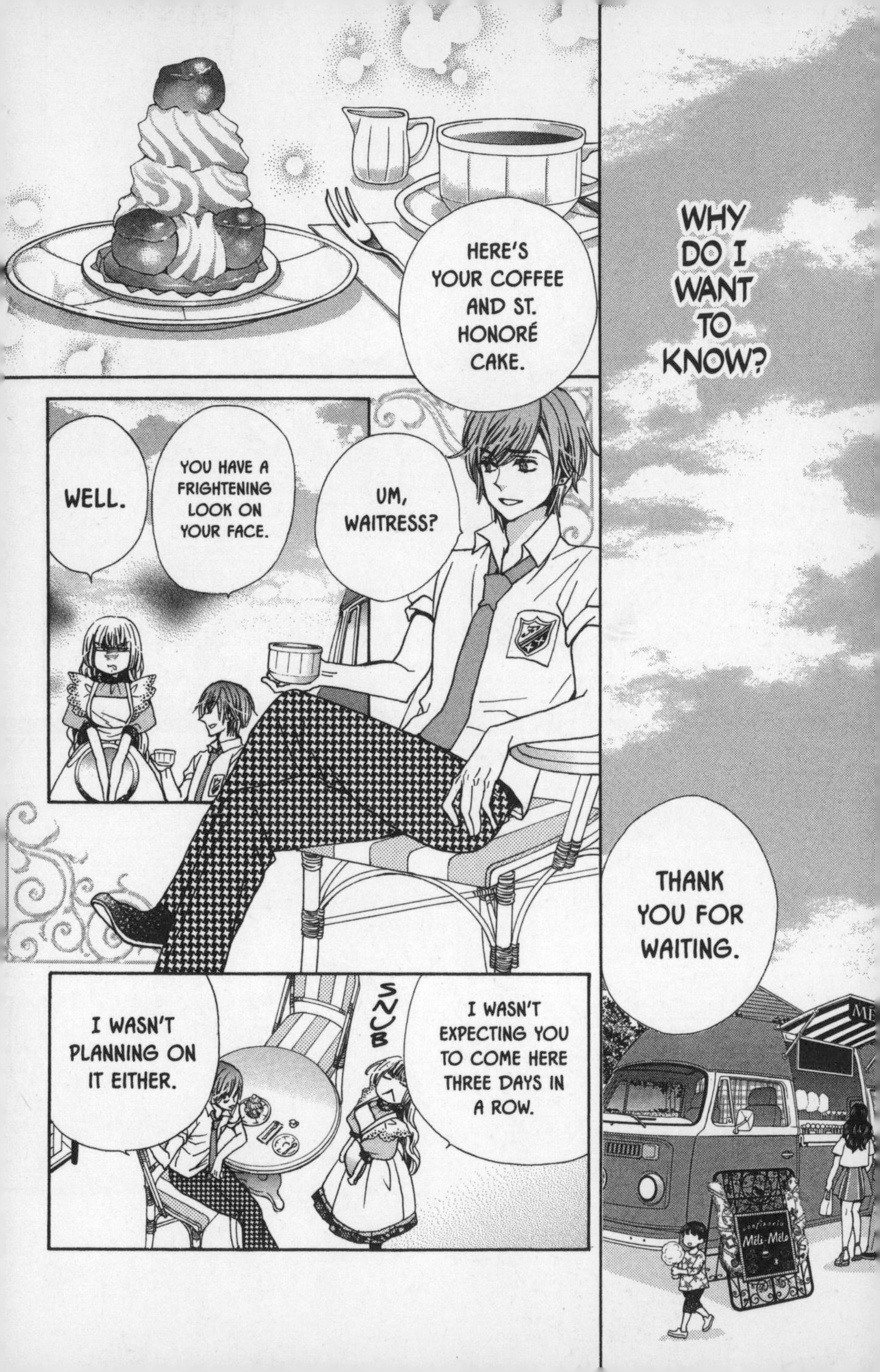
WHY DO I WANT TO KNOW?
THANK YOU FOR WAITING.
Méli-Mélo
HERE'S YOUR COFFEE AND ST. HONORÉ CAKE.
UM, WAITRESS?
YOU HAVE A FRIGHTENING LOOK ON YOUR FACE.
WELL.
I WASN'T EXPECTING YOU TO COME HERE THREE DAYS IN A ROW.
SNUB
I WASN'T PLANNING ON IT EITHER.

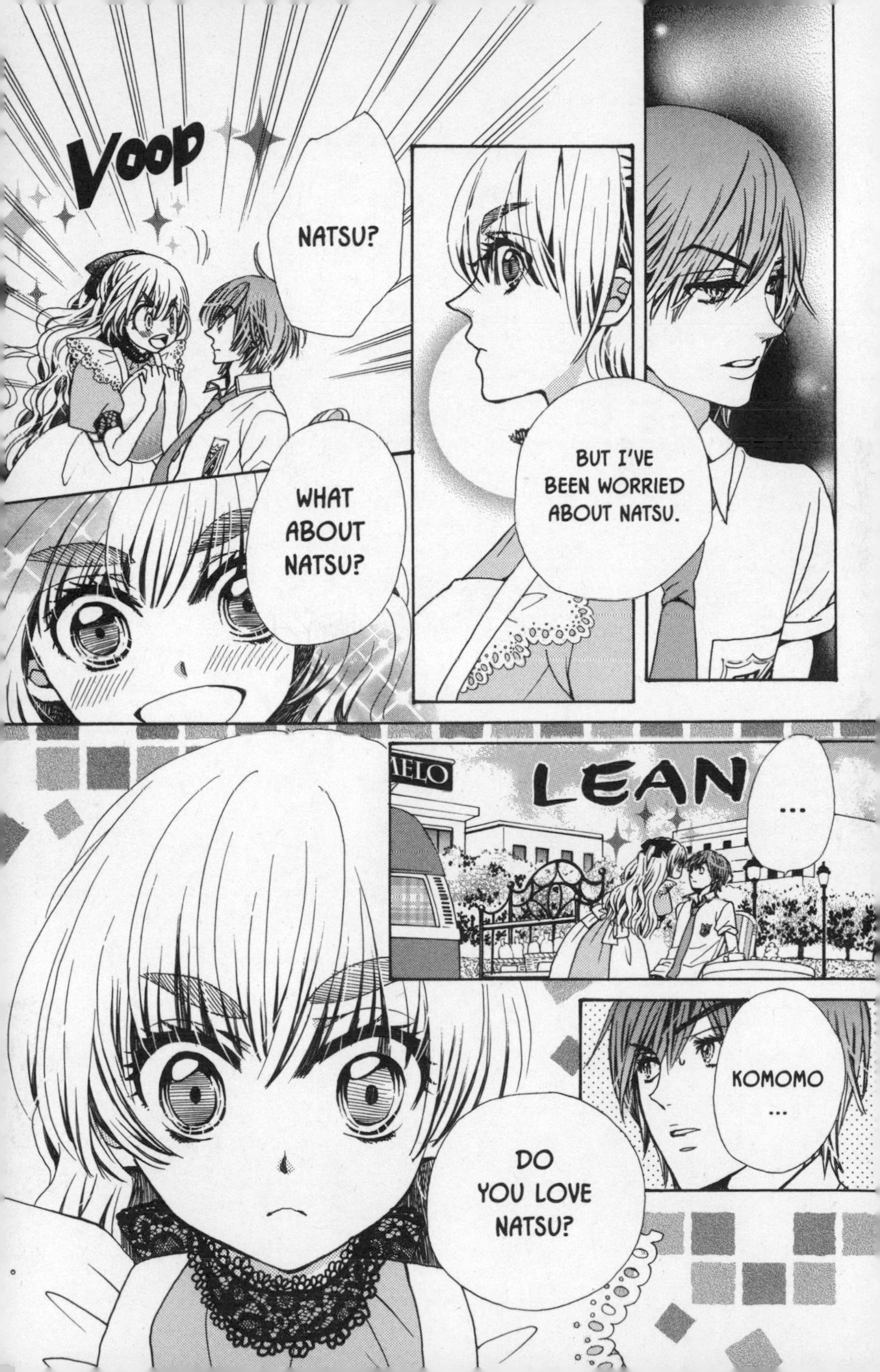
BUT I'VE BEEN WORRIED ABOUT NATSU.
VOOP
NATSU?
WHAT ABOUT NATSU?
MELO
LEAN
...
KOMOMO ...
DO YOU LOVE NATSU?

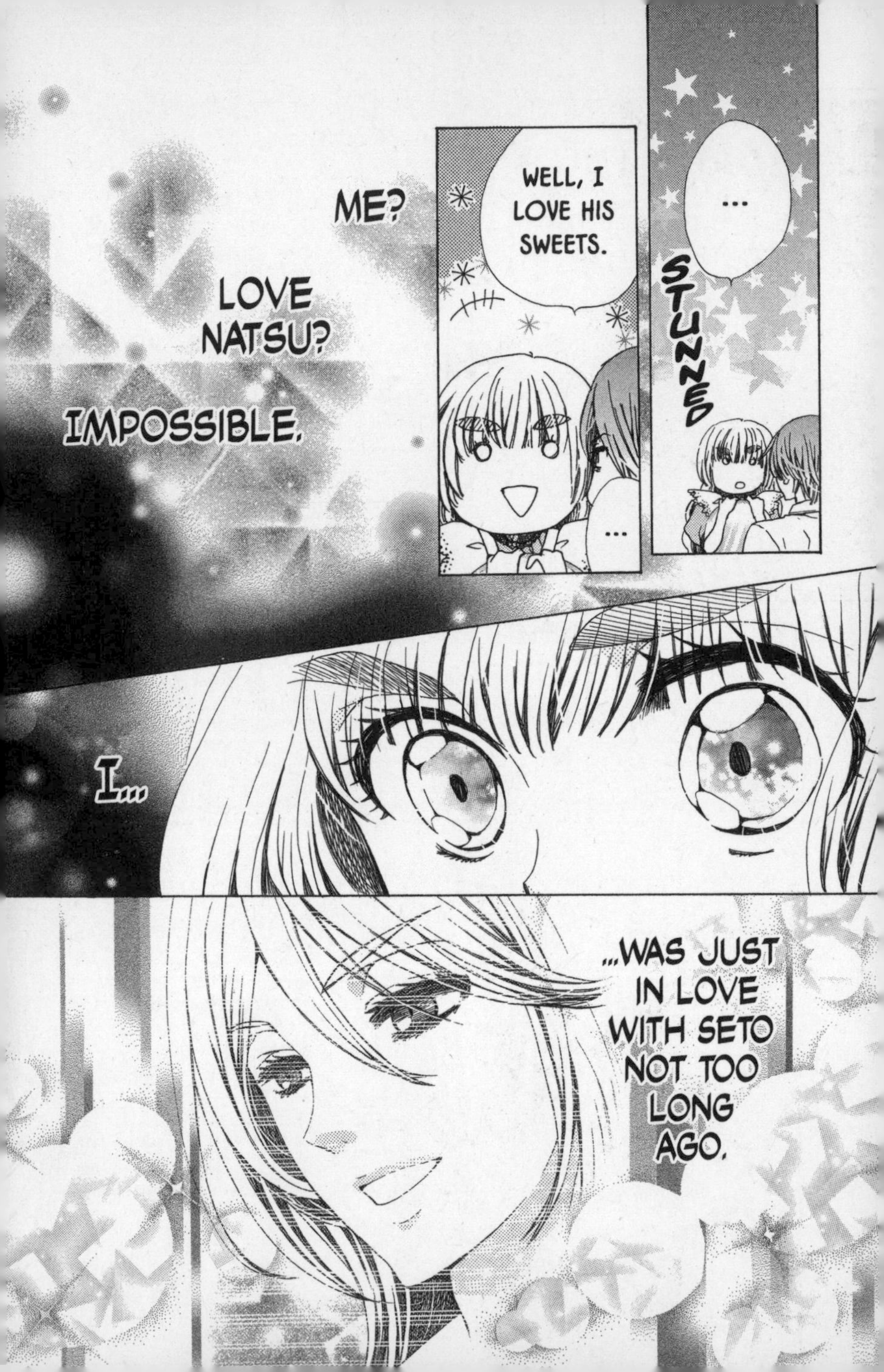
...
STUNNED
WELL, I LOVE HIS SWEETS.
...
ME?
LOVE NATSU?
IMPOSSIBLE.
I...
...WAS JUST IN LOVE WITH SETO NOT TOO LONG AGO.

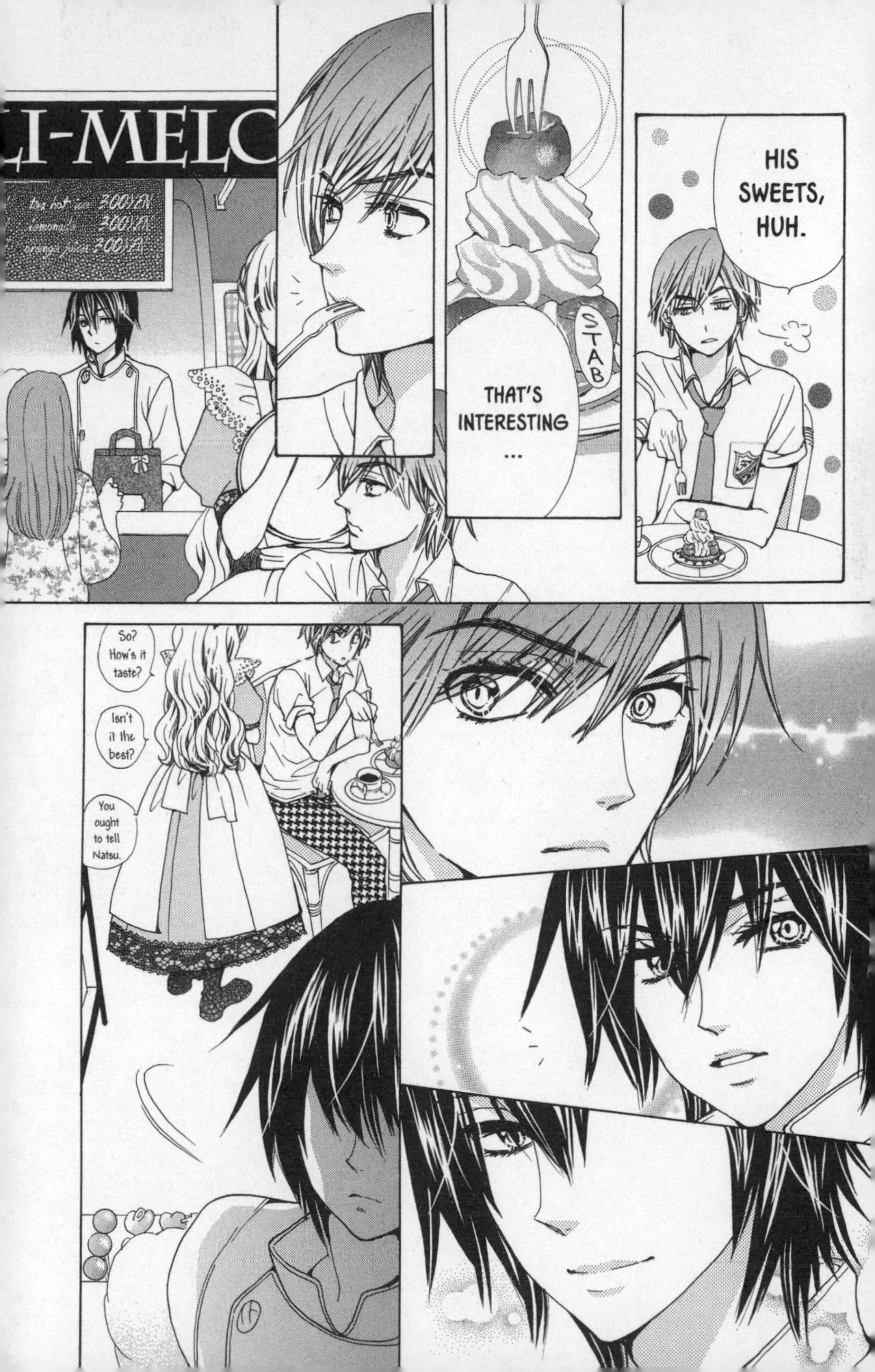
HIS SWEETS, HUH.
STAB
THAT'S INTERESTING ...
LI-MELO
So? How's it taste?
Isn't it the best?
You ought to tell Natsu.

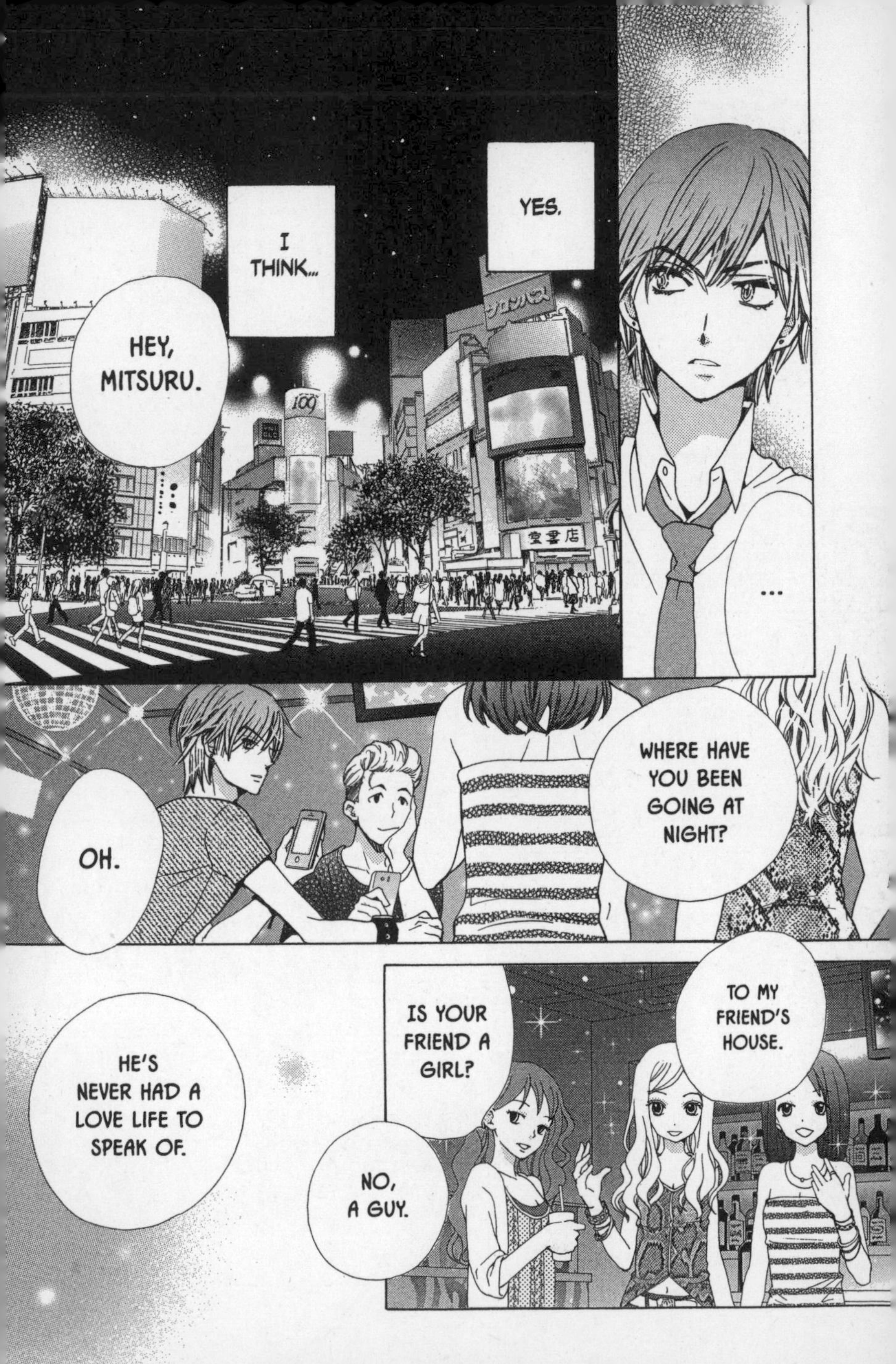
...
YES.
I THINK...
HEY, MITSURU.
WHERE HAVE YOU BEEN GOING AT NIGHT?
OH.
TO MY FRIEND'S HOUSE.
IS YOUR FRIEND A GIRL?
NO, A GUY.
HE'S NEVER HAD A LOVE LIFE TO SPEAK OF.

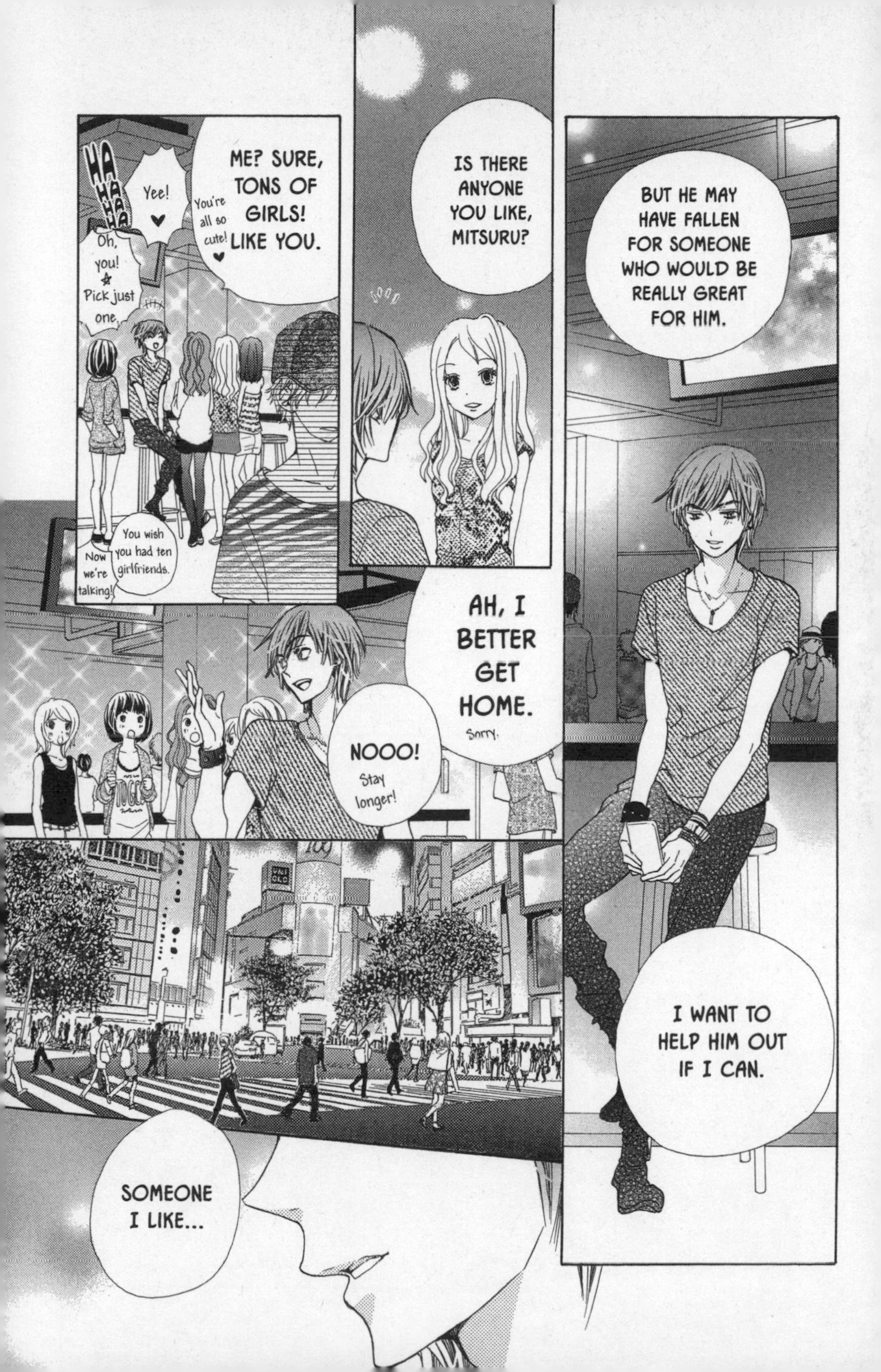
BUT HE MAY HAVE FALLEN FOR SOMEONE WHO WOULD BE REALLY GREAT FOR HIM.
I WANT TO HELP HIM OUT IF I CAN.
IS THERE ANYONE YOU LIKE, MITSURU?
ME? SURE, TONS OF GIRLS! LIKE YOU.
You're all so cute! ♥
HAHAHAHA
Yee! ♥
Oh, you! ☆ Pick just one.
You wish you had ten girlfriends.
Now we're talking!
AH, I BETTER GET HOME.
Sorry.
NOOO!
Stay longer!
SOMEONE I LIKE...

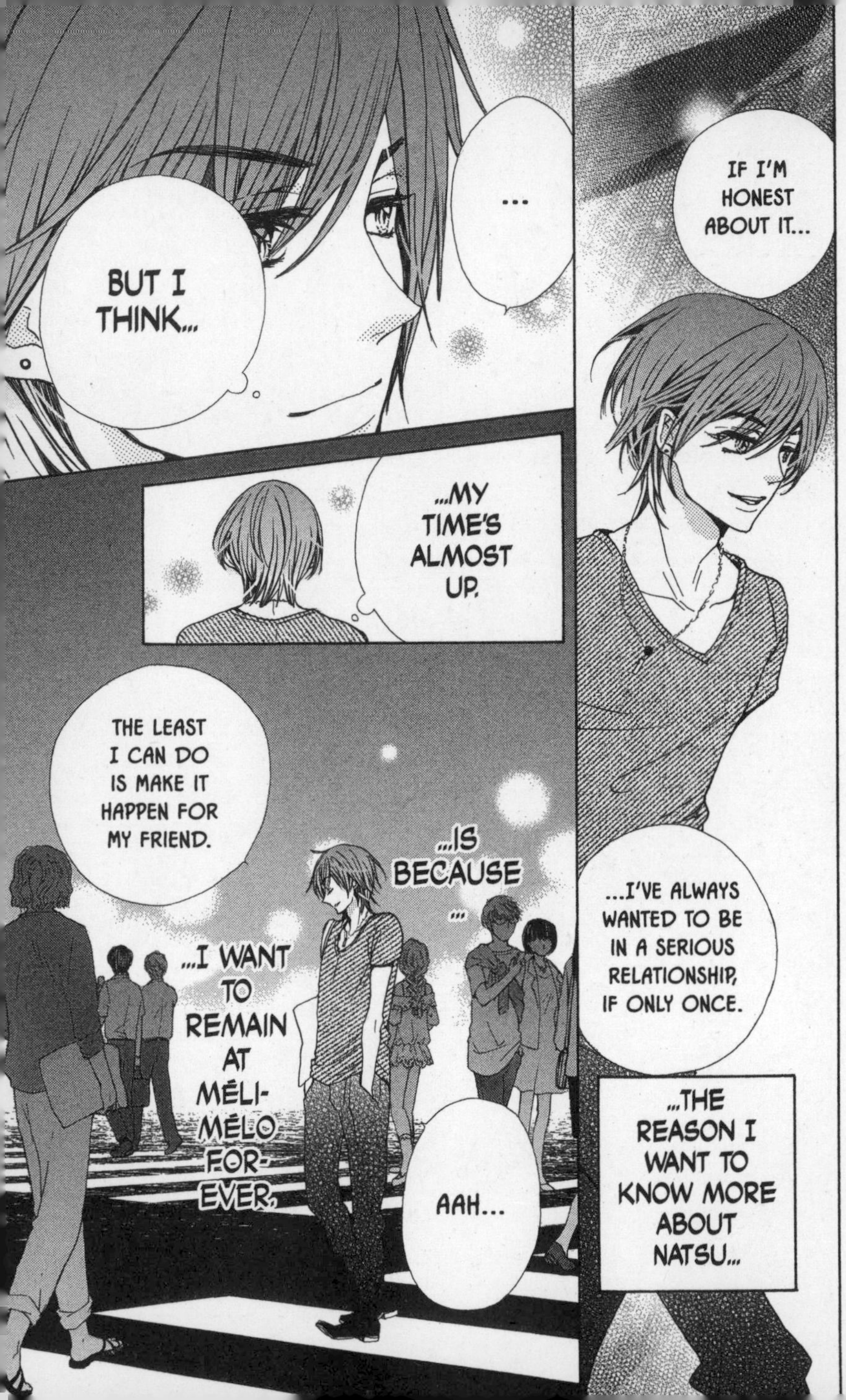
IF I'M HONEST ABOUT IT...
...I'VE ALWAYS WANTED TO BE IN A SERIOUS RELATIONSHIP, IF ONLY ONCE.
...THE REASON I WANT TO KNOW MORE ABOUT NATSU...
...
BUT I THINK...
...MY TIME'S ALMOST UP.
AAH...
...IS BECAUSE ...
THE LEAST I CAN DO IS MAKE IT HAPPEN FOR MY FRIEND.
...I WANT TO REMAIN AT MÉLI-MÉLO FOR-EVER,

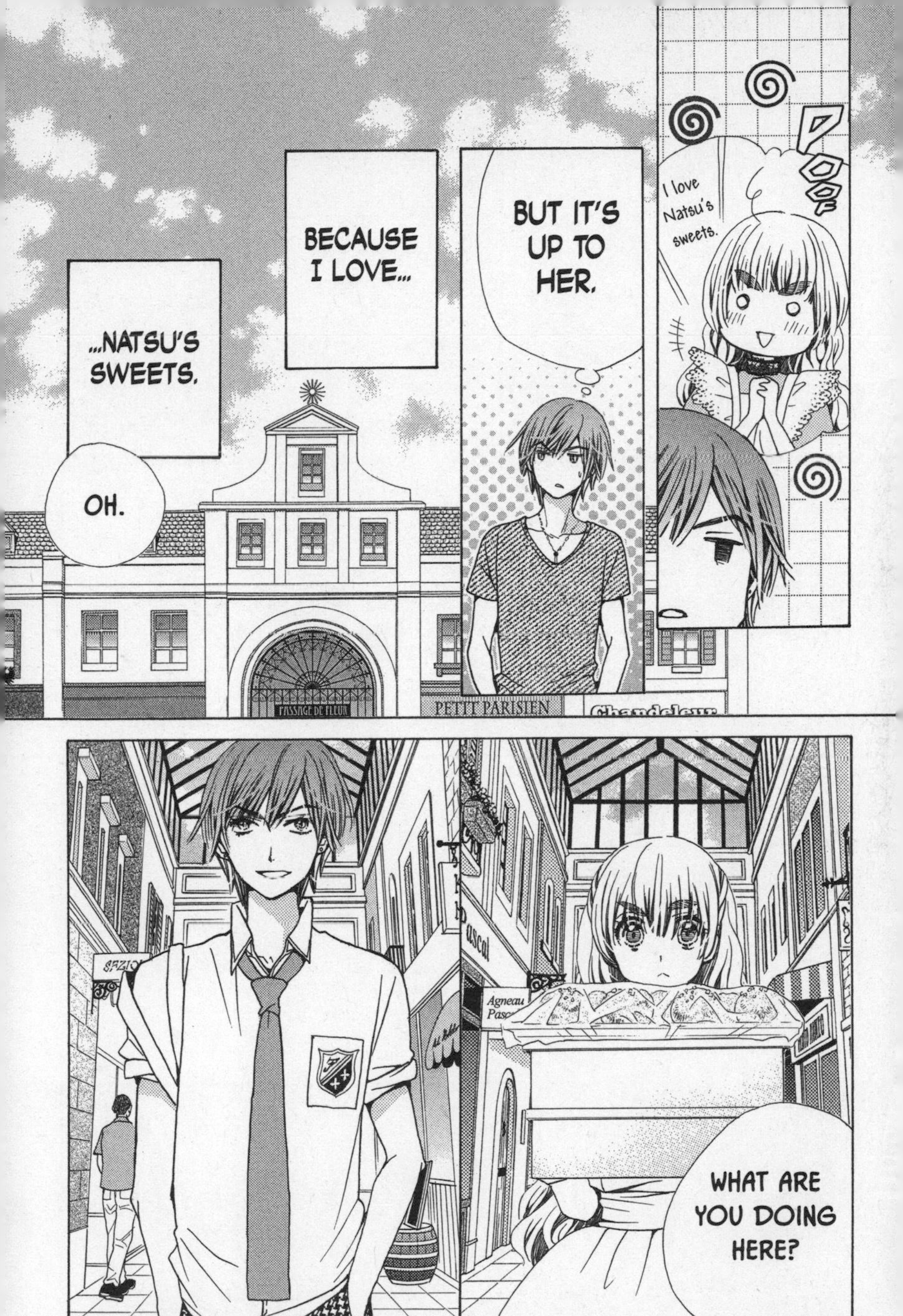
I love Natsu's sweets.
BUT IT'S UP TO HER.
BECAUSE I LOVE...
...NATSU'S SWEETS.
OH.
PASSAGE DE FLEUR
PETIT PARISIEN
WHAT ARE YOU DOING HERE?

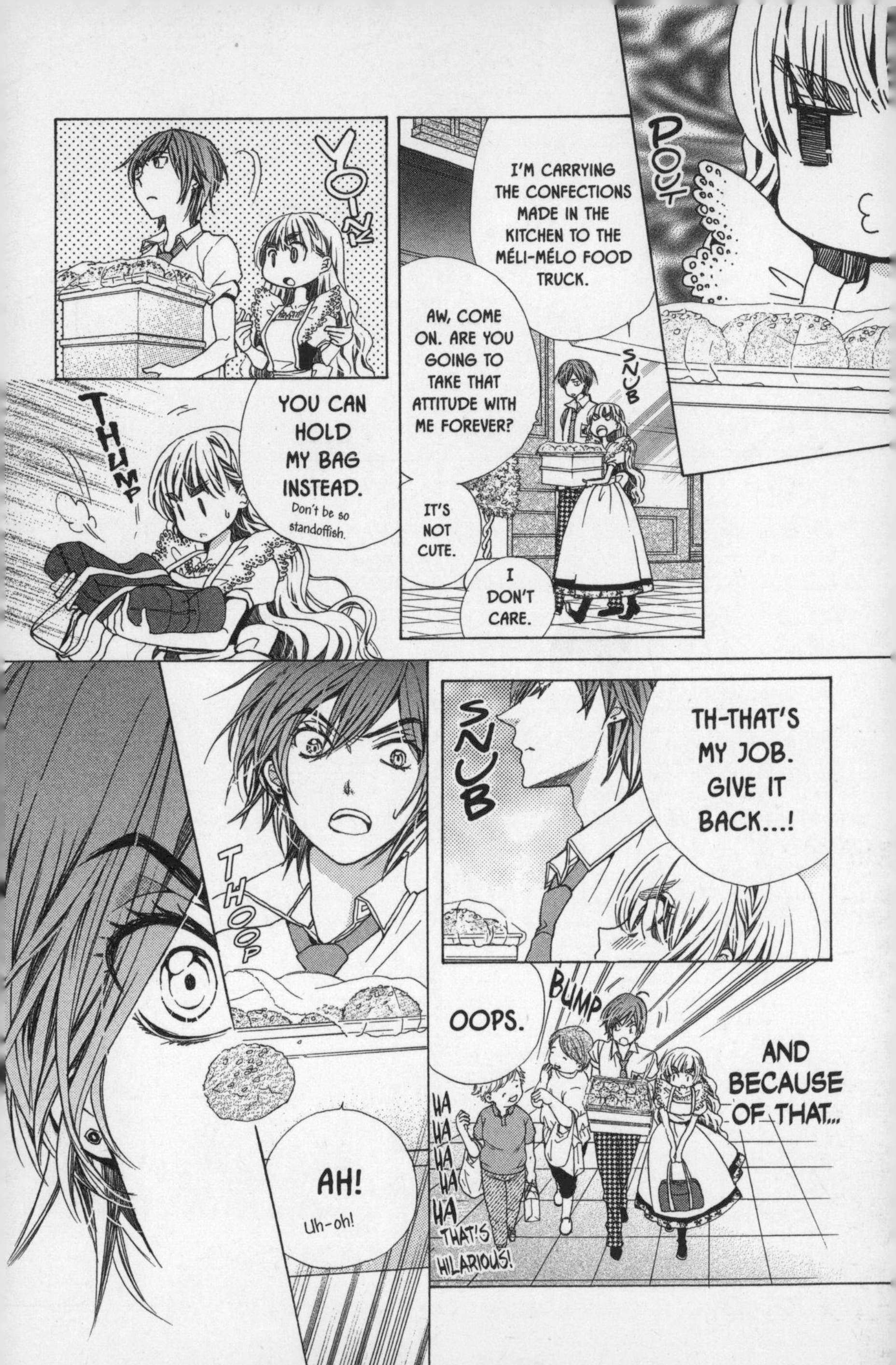
POUT
I'M CARRYING THE CONFECTIONS MADE IN THE KITCHEN TO THE MÉLI-MÉLO FOOD TRUCK.
AW, COME ON. ARE YOU GOING TO TAKE THAT ATTITUDE WITH ME FOREVER?
SNUB
IT'S NOT CUTE.
I DON'T CARE.
YOINK
THUMP
YOU CAN HOLD MY BAG INSTEAD.
Don't be so standoffish.
SNUB
TH-THAT'S MY JOB. GIVE IT BACK...!
BUMP
OOPS.
AND BECAUSE OF THAT...
HA HA HA HA HA HA
THAT'S HILARIOUS!
THOOP
AH!
Uh-oh!

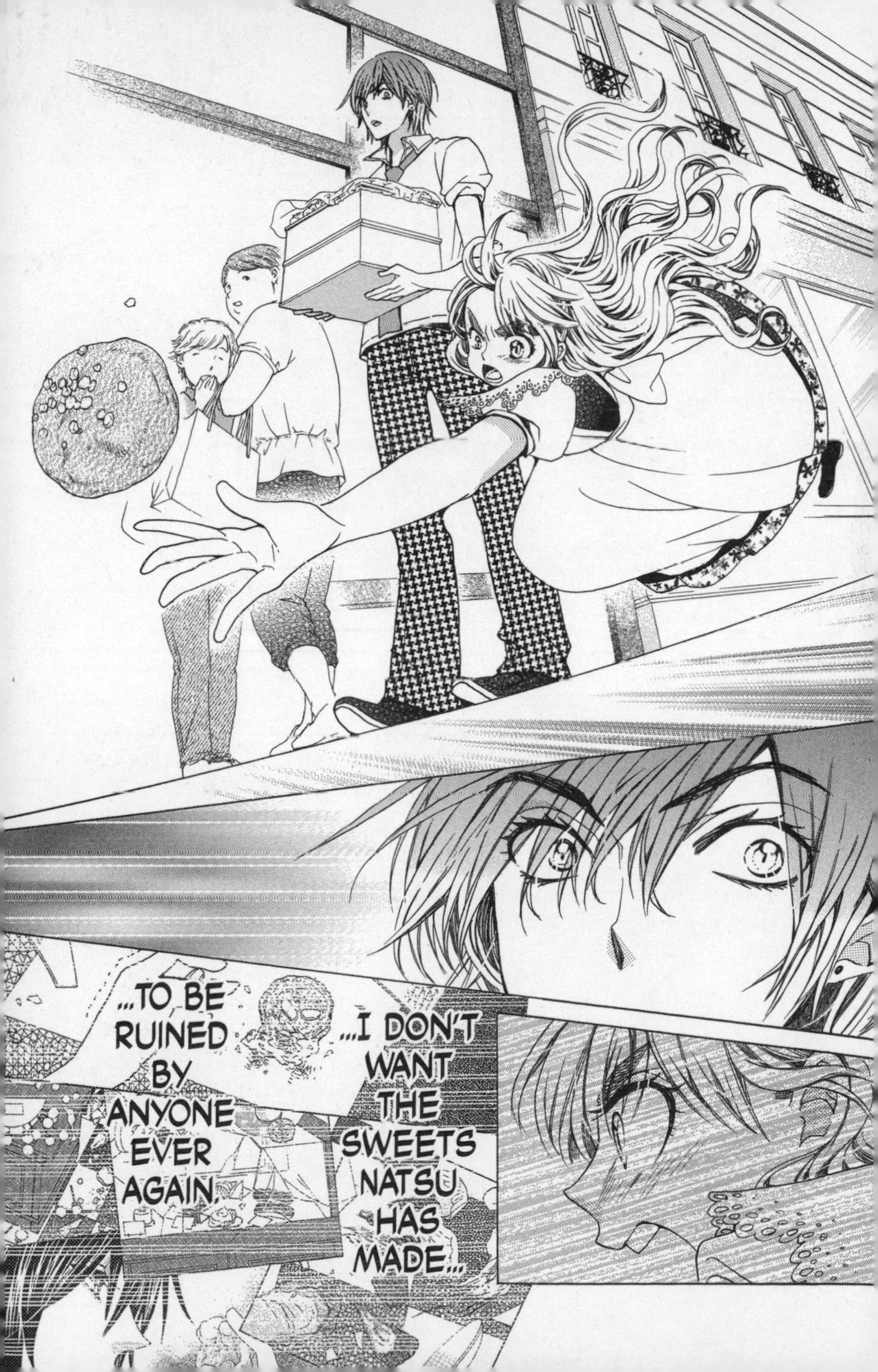
...I DON'T WANT THE SWEETS NATSU HAS MADE...
...TO BE RUINED BY ANYONE EVER AGAIN.

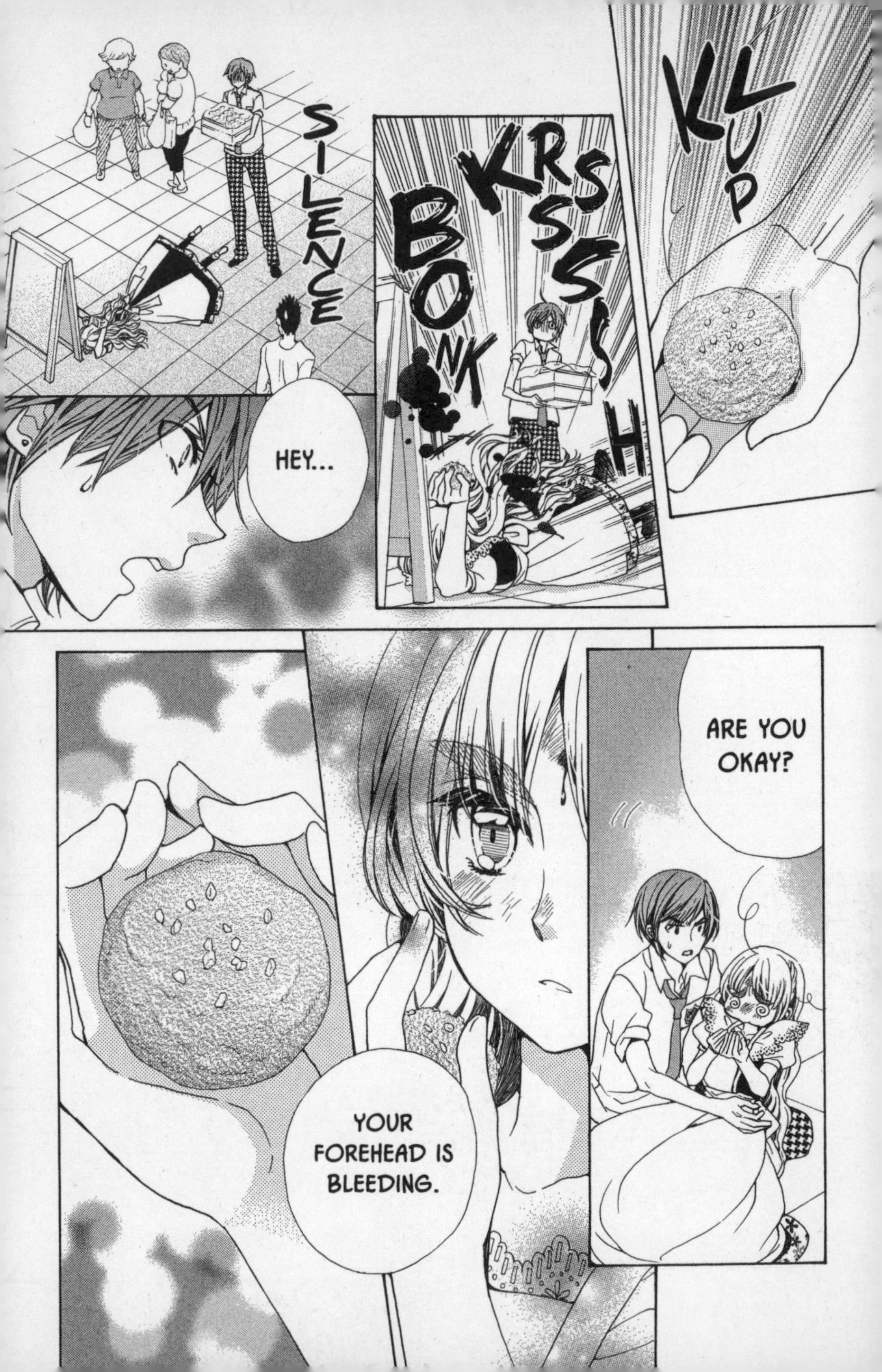
KLLUP
KRSSSH
BONK
SILENCE
HEY...
ARE YOU OKAY?
YOUR FOREHEAD IS BLEEDING.

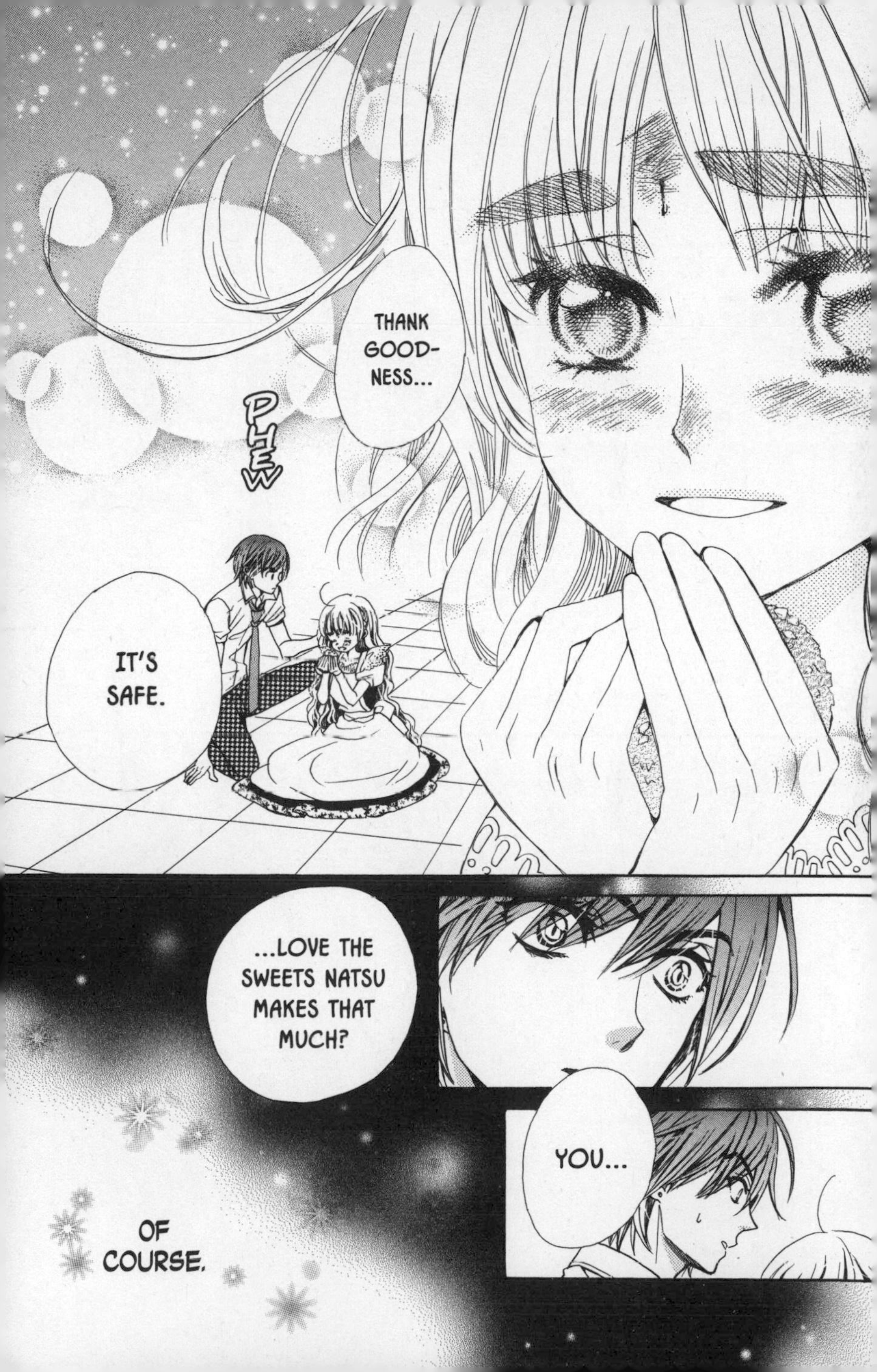
THANK GOODNESS...
PHEW
IT'S SAFE.
YOU...
...LOVE THE SWEETS NATSU MAKES THAT MUCH?
OF COURSE.

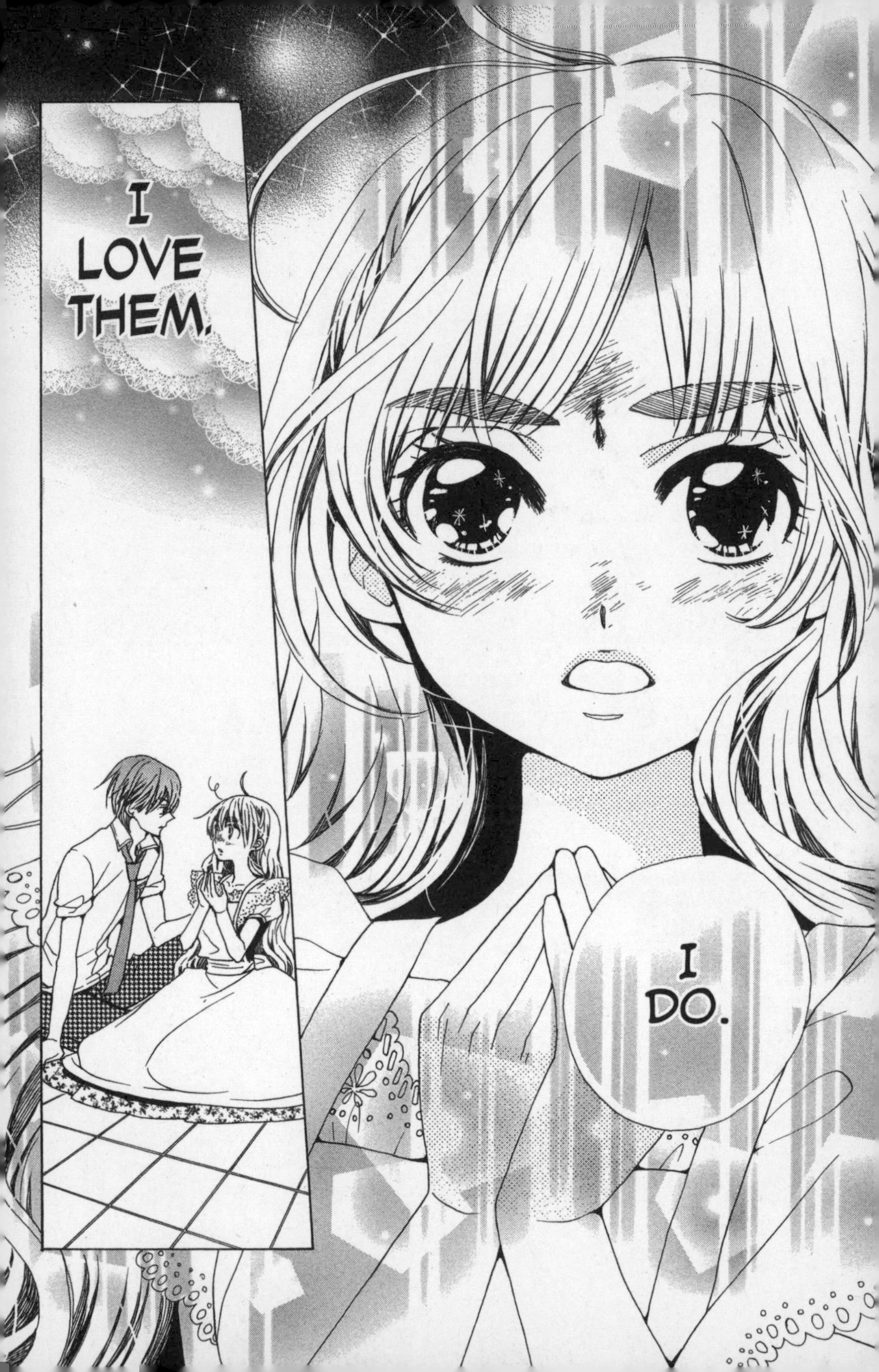
I LOVE THEM.
I DO.

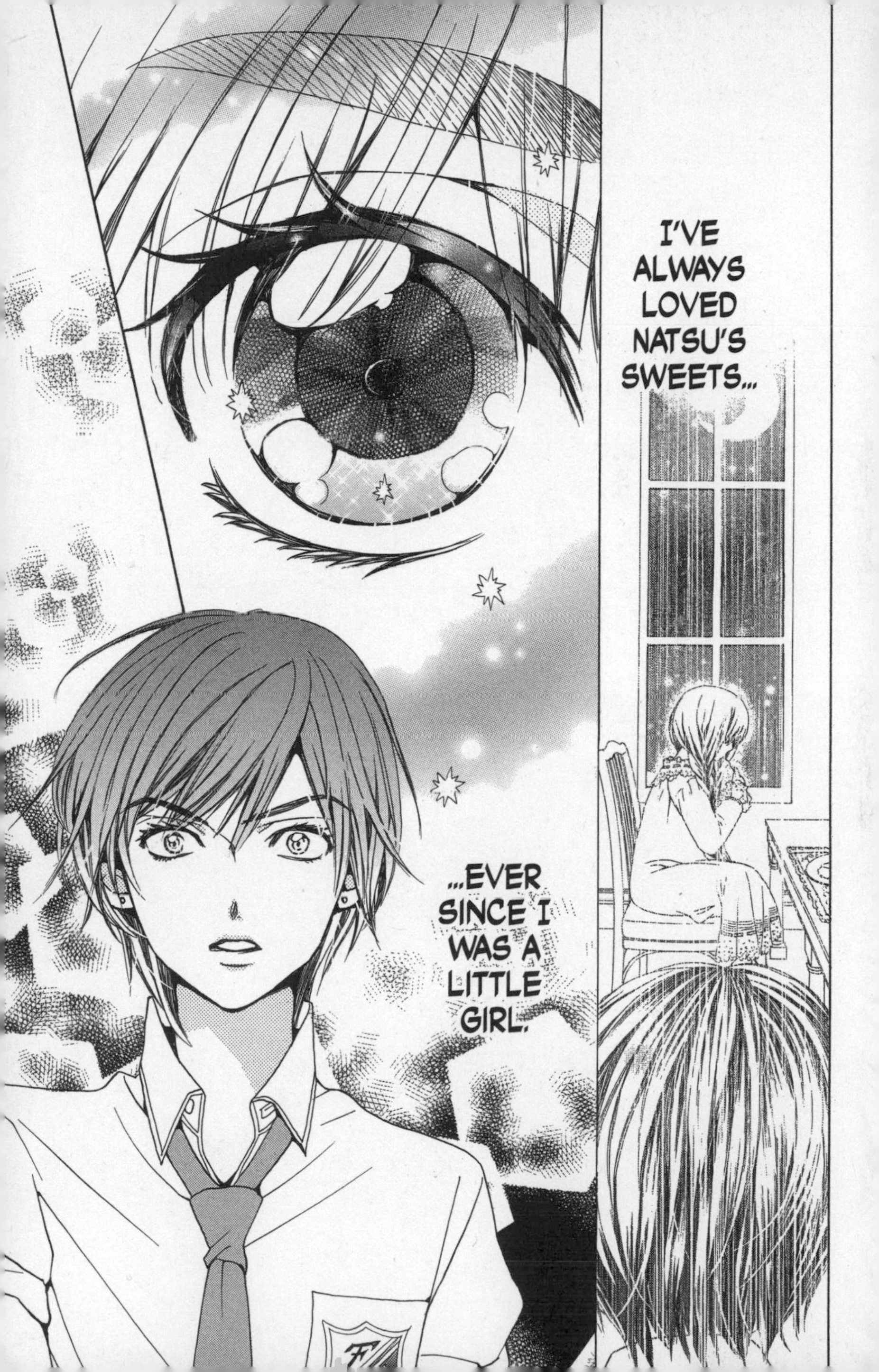
I'VE ALWAYS LOVED NATSU'S SWEETS...
...EVER SINCE I WAS A LITTLE GIRL.

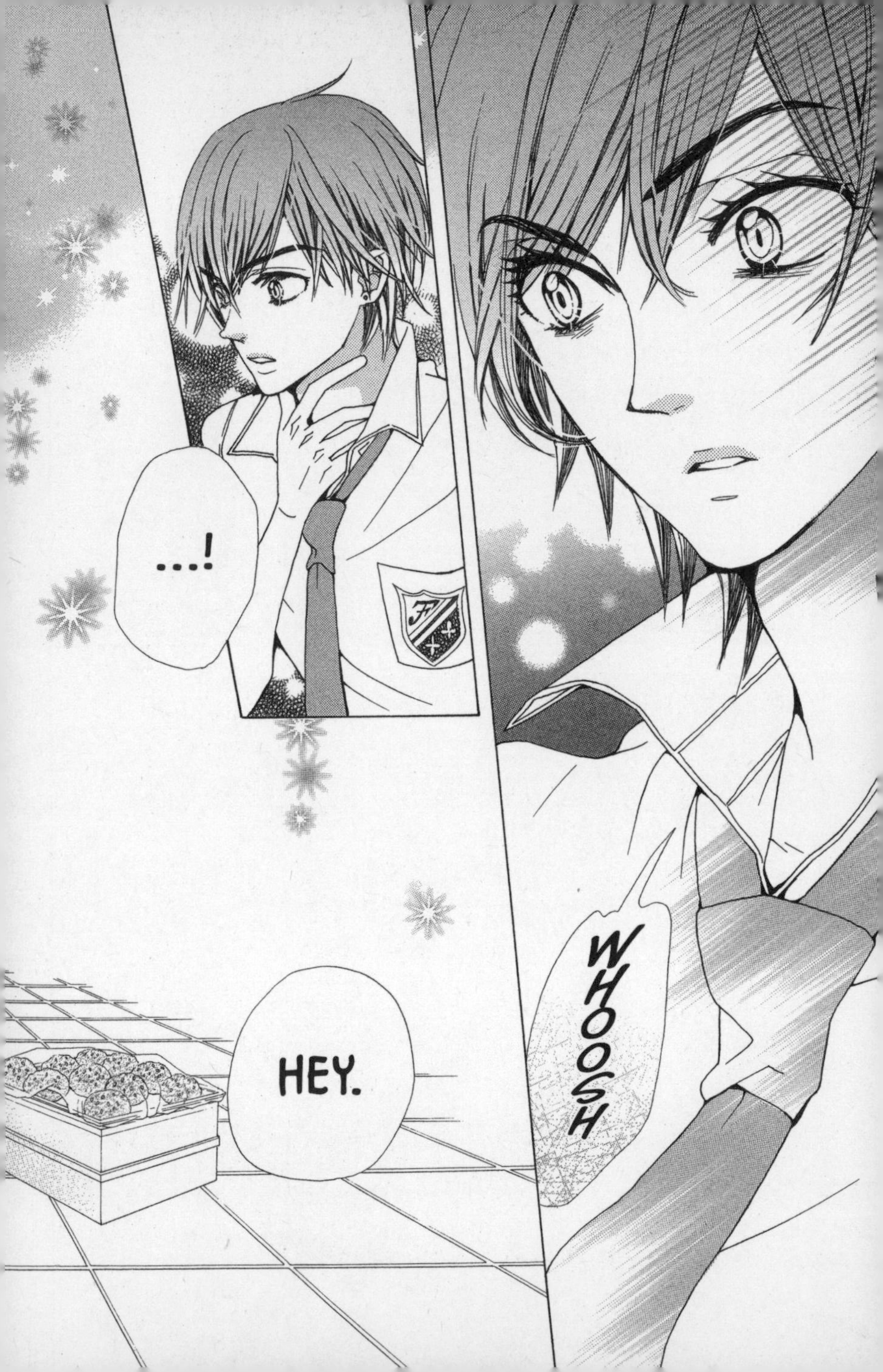
WHOOOSH
...!
HEY.

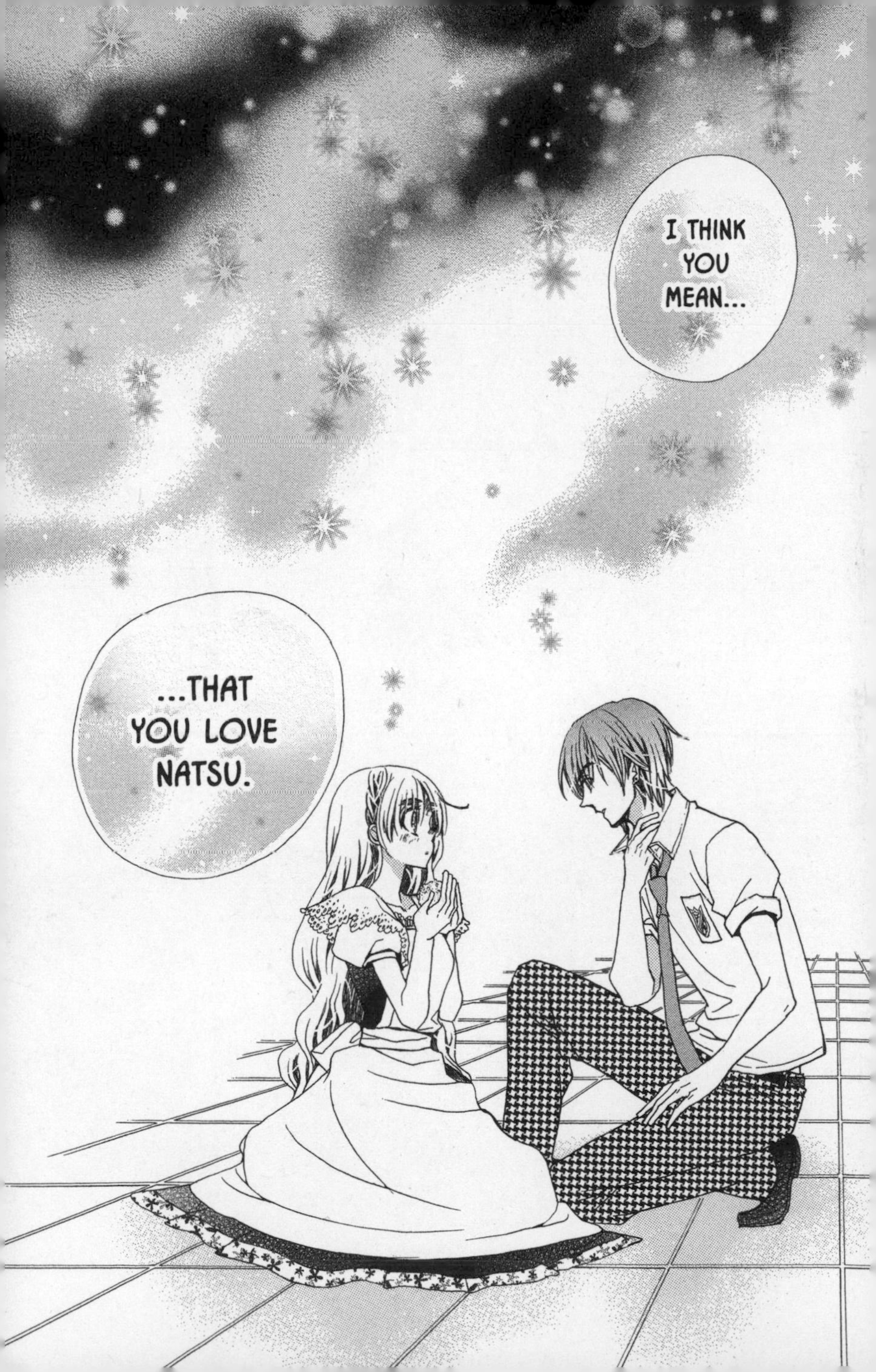
I THINK YOU MEAN...
...THAT YOU LOVE NATSU.

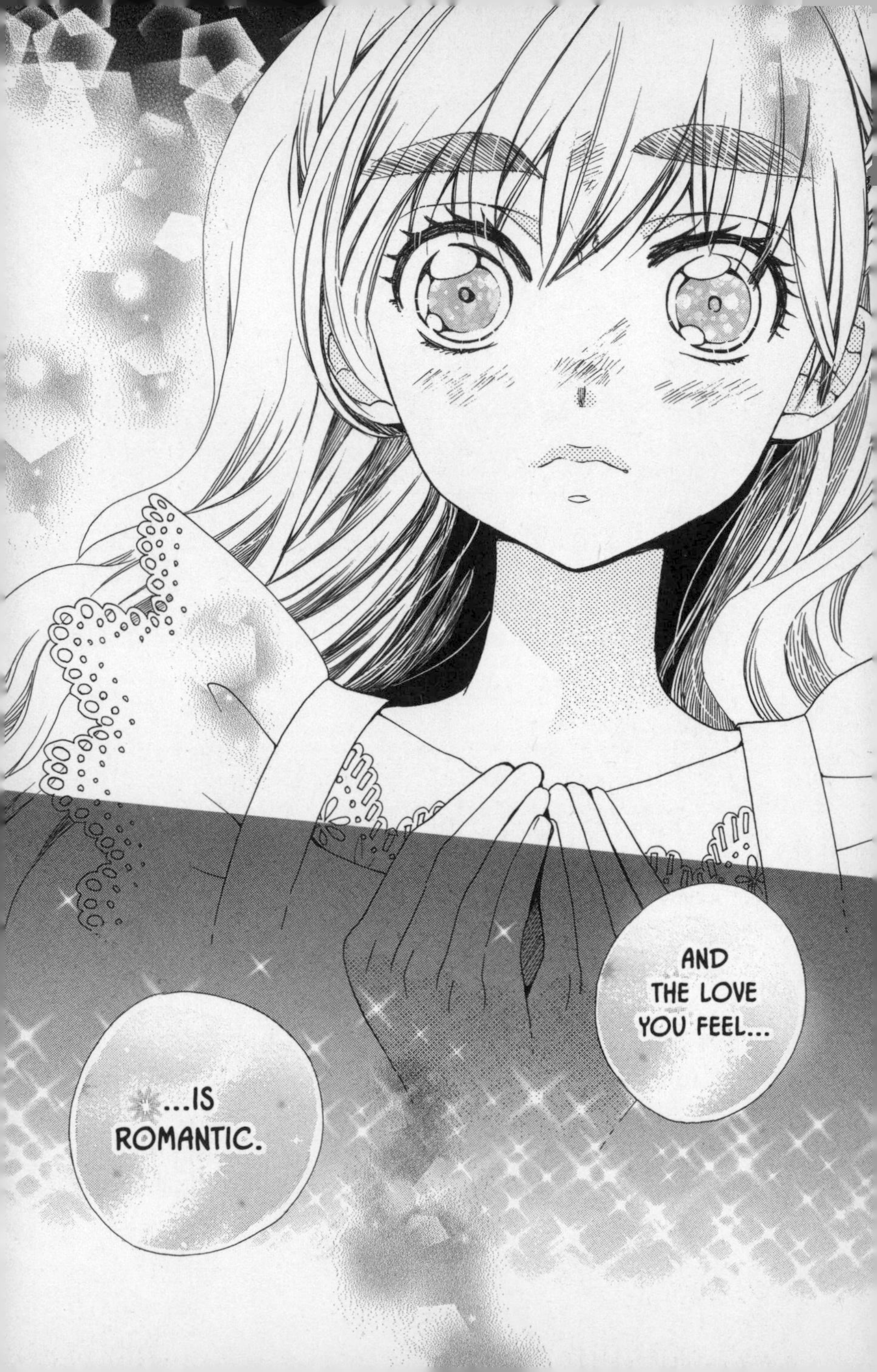
AND THE LOVE YOU FEEL...
...IS ROMANTIC.

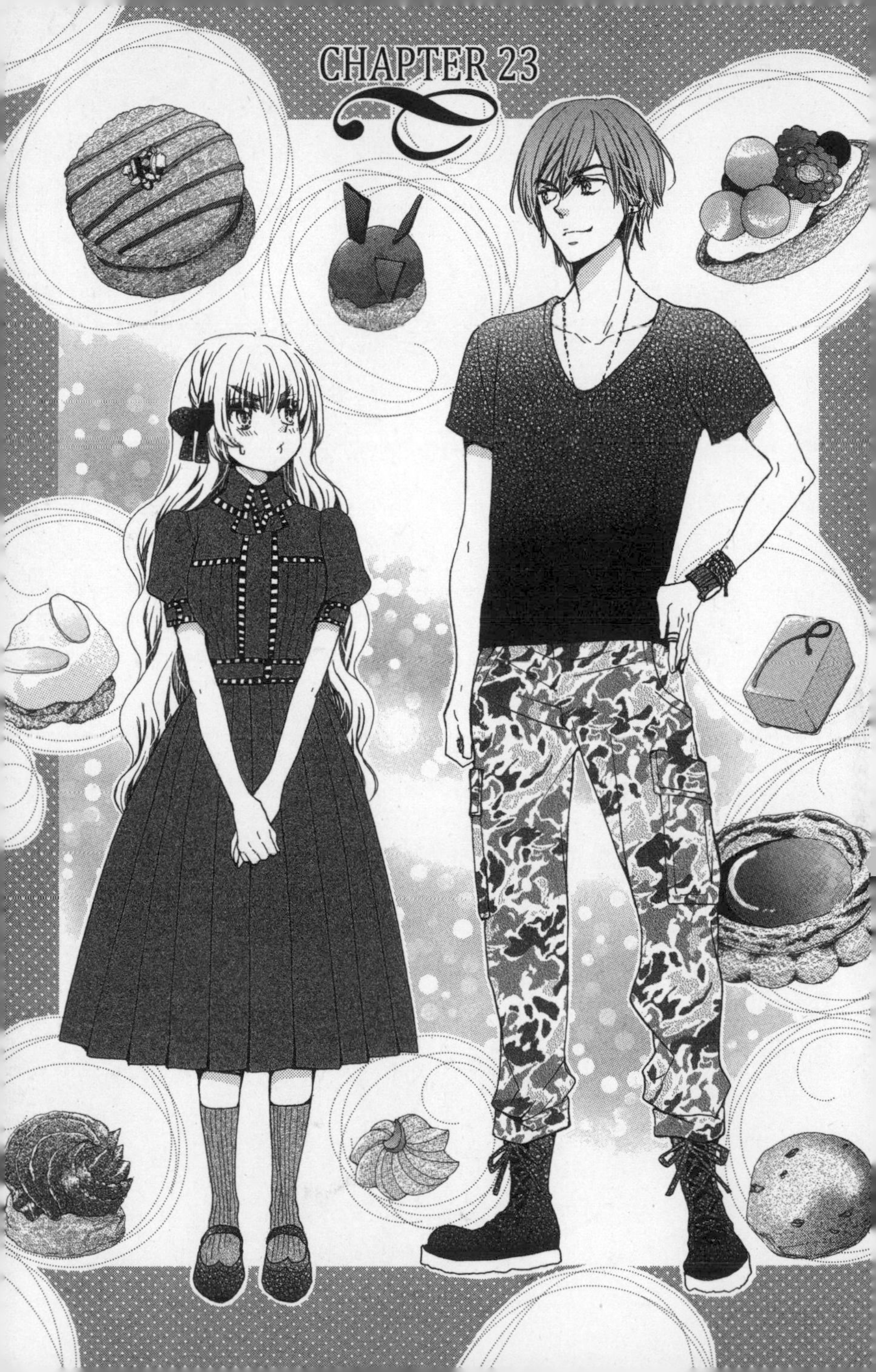
CHAPTER 23

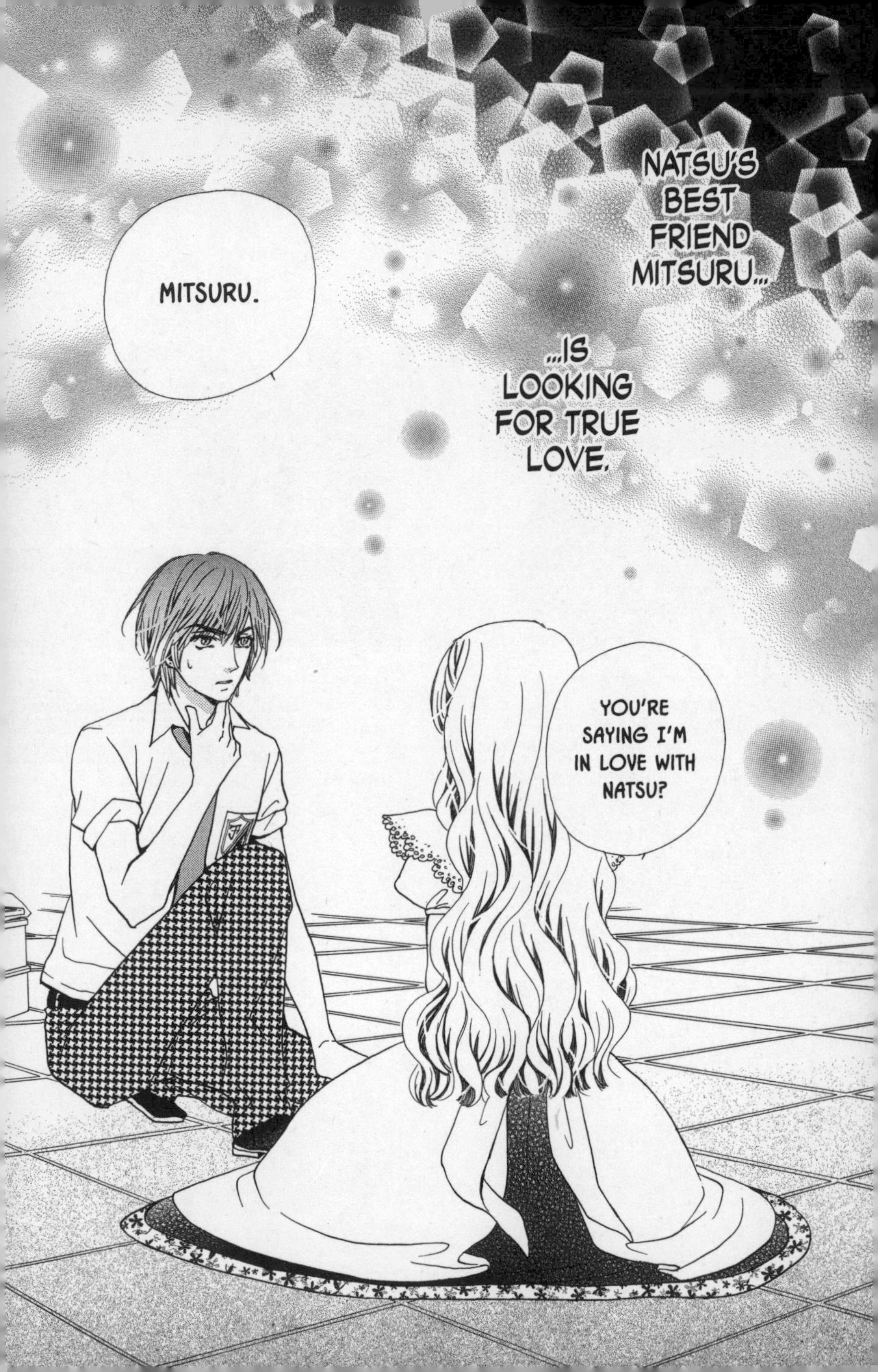
NATSU'S BEST FRIEND MITSURU...
...IS LOOKING FOR TRUE LOVE.
MITSURU.
YOU'RE SAYING I'M IN LOVE WITH NATSU?

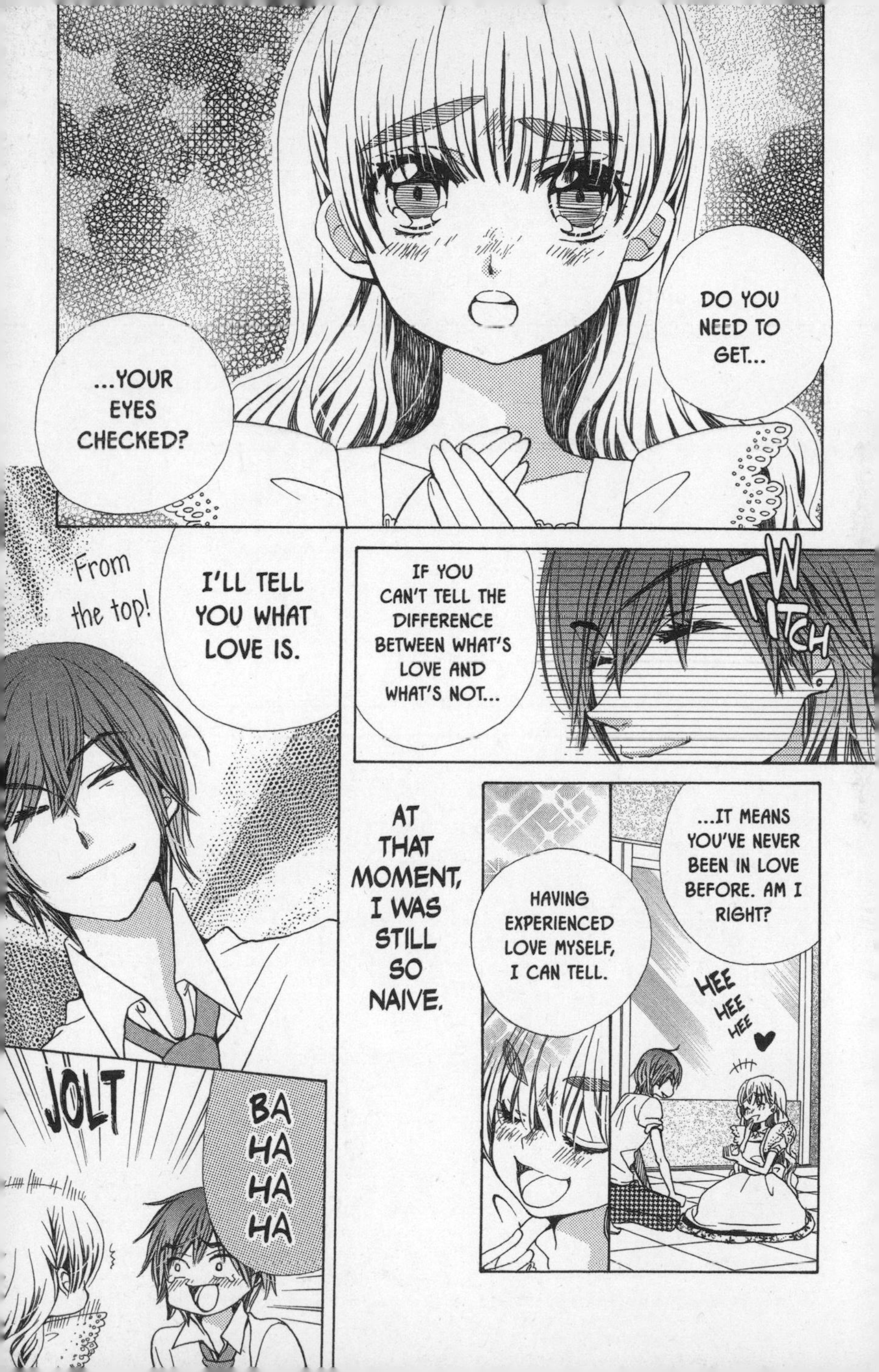
DO YOU NEED TO GET...
...YOUR EYES CHECKED?
TWITCH
IF YOU CAN'T TELL THE DIFFERENCE BETWEEN WHAT'S LOVE AND WHAT'S NOT...
...IT MEANS YOU'VE NEVER BEEN IN LOVE BEFORE. AM I RIGHT?
HAVING EXPERIENCED LOVE MYSELF, I CAN TELL.
HEE HEE HEE
AT THAT MOMENT, I WAS STILL SO NAIVE.
I'LL TELL YOU WHAT LOVE IS.
From the top!
BA HA HA HA HA
JOLT

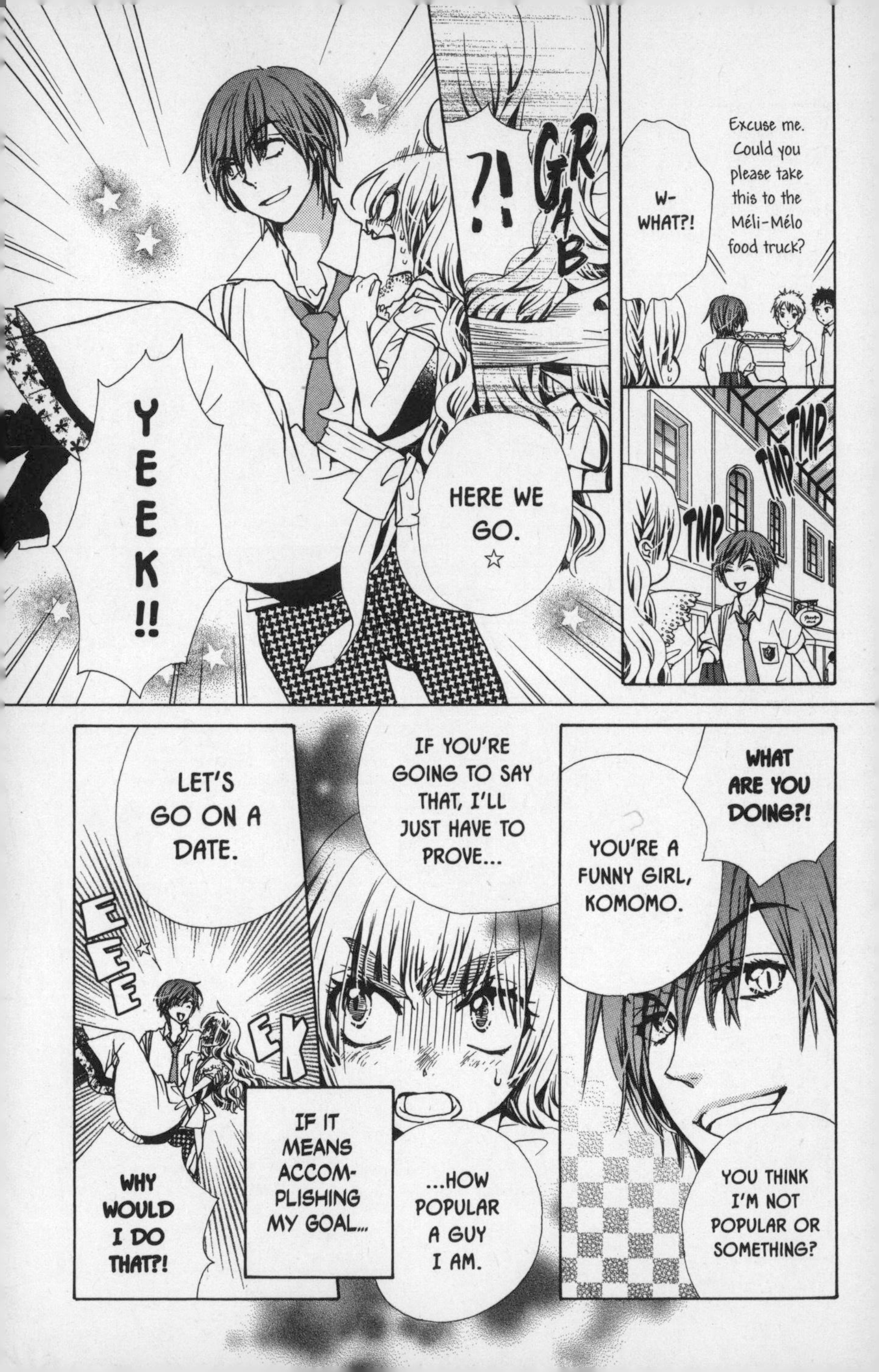
Excuse me. Could you please take this to the Méli-Mélo food truck?
W-WHAT?!
TMP TMP TMP
GRAB
?!
HERE WE GO. ☆
YEEK!!
WHAT ARE YOU DOING?!
YOU'RE A FUNNY GIRL, KOMOMO.
YOU THINK I'M NOT POPULAR OR SOMETHING?
IF YOU'RE GOING TO SAY THAT, I'LL JUST HAVE TO PROVE...
...HOW POPULAR A GUY I AM.
LET'S GO ON A DATE.
EEEEK
IF IT MEANS ACCOM-PLISHING MY GOAL...
WHY WOULD I DO THAT?!

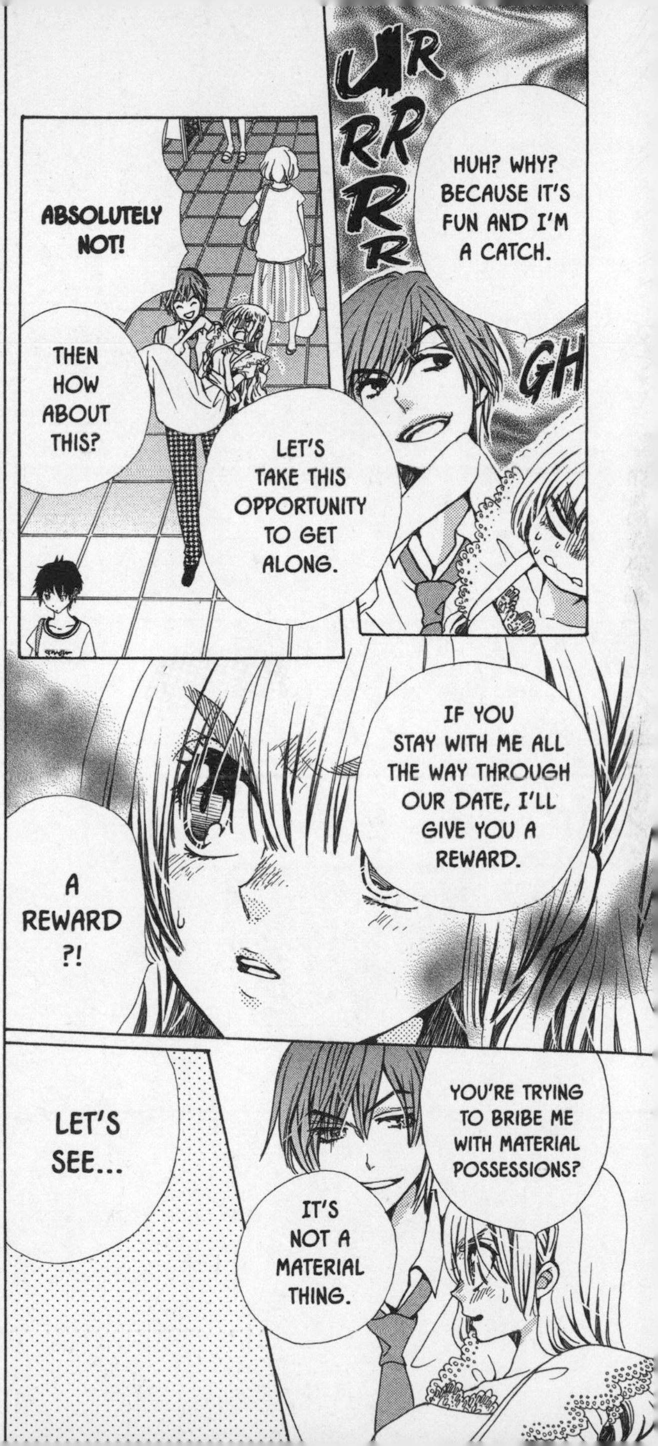
URRRRR
HUH? WHY? BECAUSE IT'S FUN AND I'M A CATCH.
GH
ABSOLUTELY NOT!
THEN HOW ABOUT THIS?
LET'S TAKE THIS OPPORTUNITY TO GET ALONG.
IF YOU STAY WITH ME ALL THE WAY THROUGH OUR DATE, I'LL GIVE YOU A REWARD.
A REWARD?!
YOU'RE TRYING TO BRIBE ME WITH MATERIAL POSSESSIONS?
IT'S NOT A MATERIAL THING.
LET'S SEE...

• Various •

We've arrived at the final sidbar. Thank you so much for sticking with me through the whole thing!

...the fireworks I bought in July. I still haven't used...

I just remembered that Matsu-san told me, "You say that every year!" This won't do.

This time I had the pleasure and honor of Kamio Sensei drawing the crowds for me!! What do I do? She's an angel! How can I ever repay you? I'll do anything.

I'll help out somehow. (by Kamio Sensei)

An angel!

Thank you so much!!

Now I want to thank everyone who has read this far, all my assistants who always help me out, my editors, Kosaka-sama for helping me collect reference materials and everyone from Tsujicho Cooking School. Thanks also to Blondir-sama, my friends, Kamio Sensei and my family. ♥ Thank you so much! ♥

With all my love.

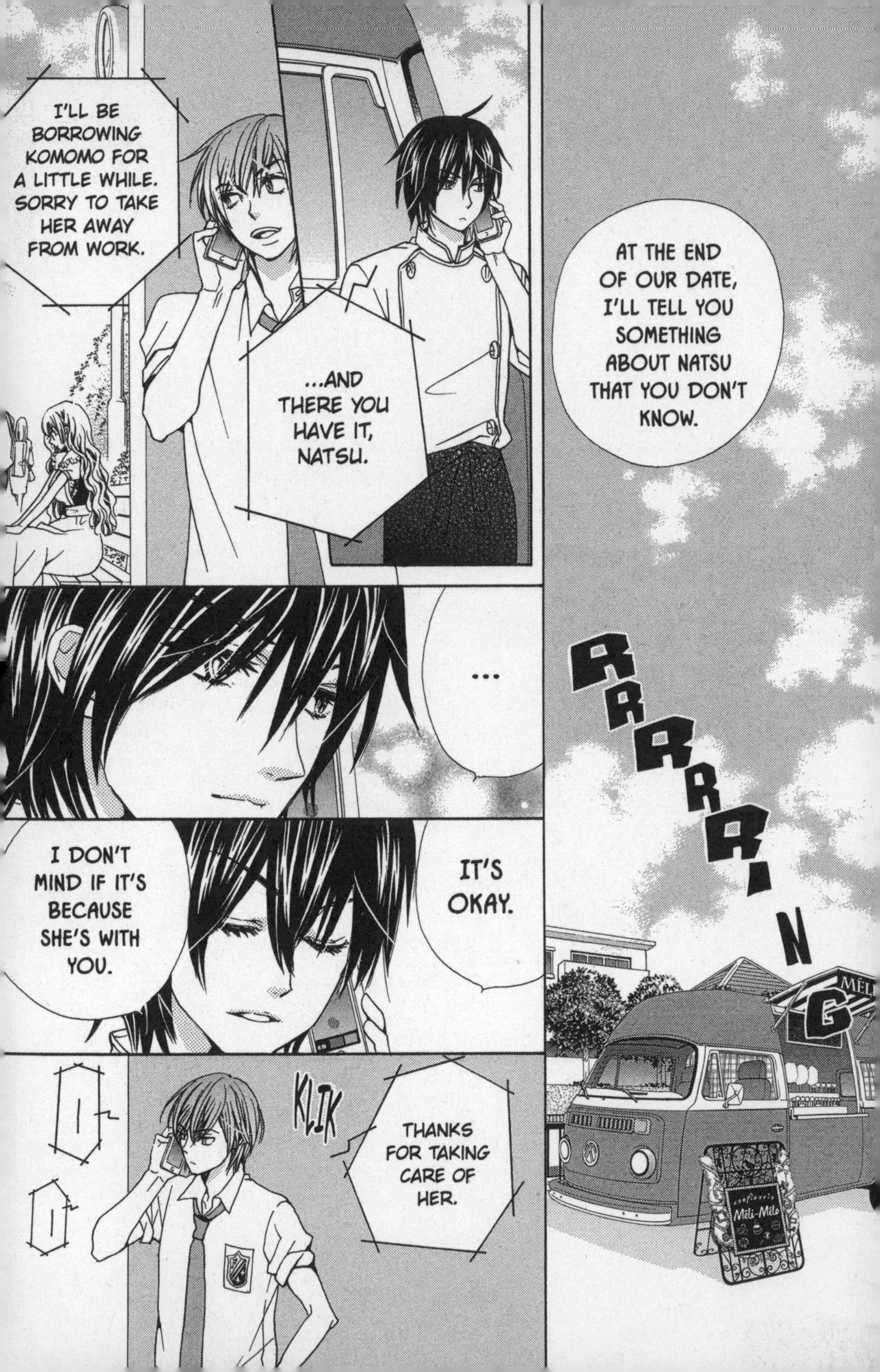
AT THE END OF OUR DATE, I'LL TELL YOU SOMETHING ABOUT NATSU THAT YOU DON'T KNOW.
RRRRRING
I'LL BE BORROWING KOMOMO FOR A LITTLE WHILE. SORRY TO TAKE HER AWAY FROM WORK.
...AND THERE YOU HAVE IT, NATSU.
...
IT'S OKAY.
I DON'T MIND IF IT'S BECAUSE SHE'S WITH YOU.
KLIK
THANKS FOR TAKING CARE OF HER.

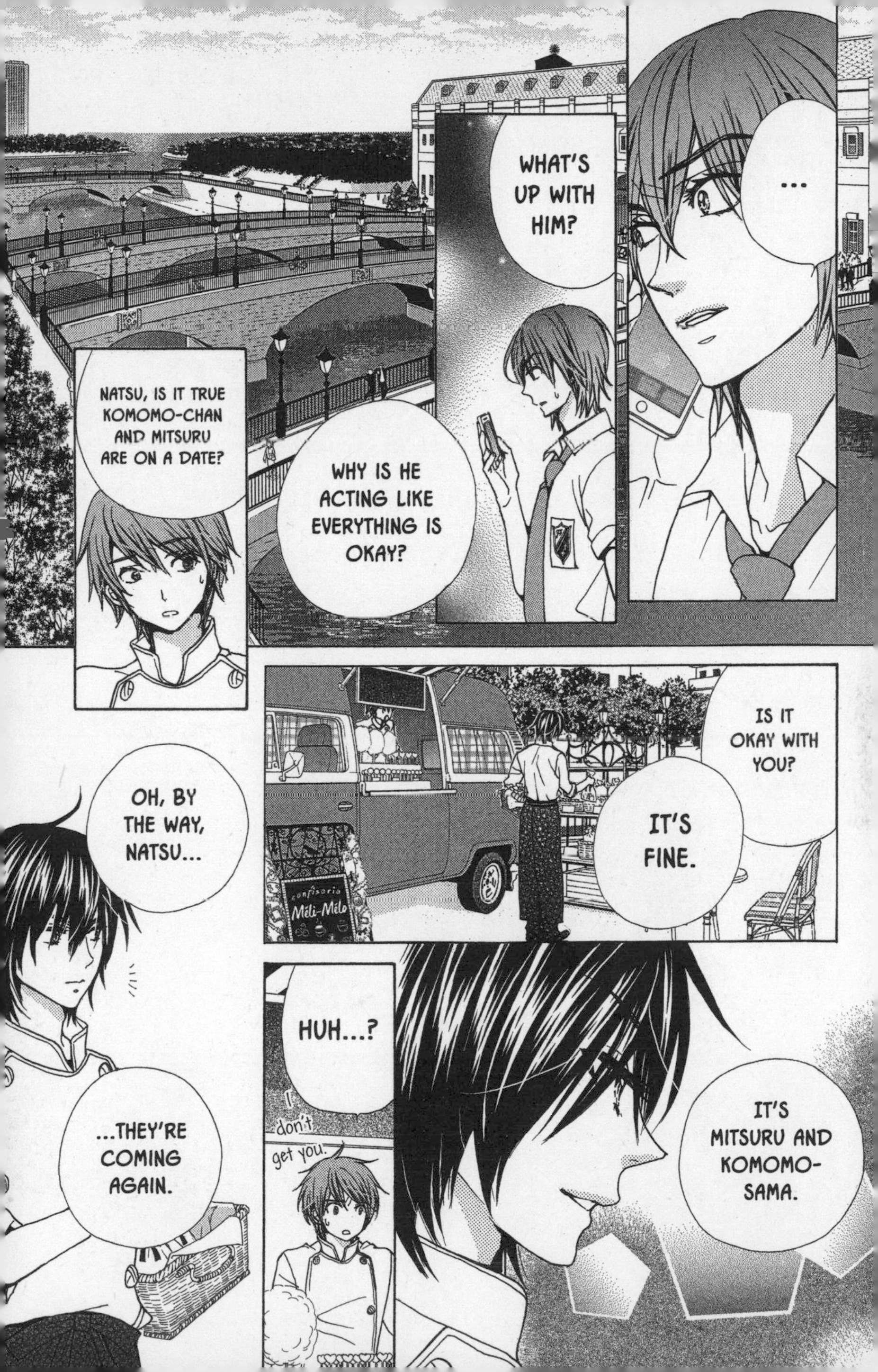
...
WHAT'S UP WITH HIM?
WHY IS HE ACTING LIKE EVERYTHING IS OKAY?
NATSU, IS IT TRUE KOMOMO-CHAN AND MITSURU ARE ON A DATE?
IS IT OKAY WITH YOU?
IT'S FINE.
confiserie Méli-Mélo
IT'S MITSURU AND KOMOMO-SAMA.
HUH...?
I don't get you.
OH, BY THE WAY, NATSU...
...THEY'RE COMING AGAIN.

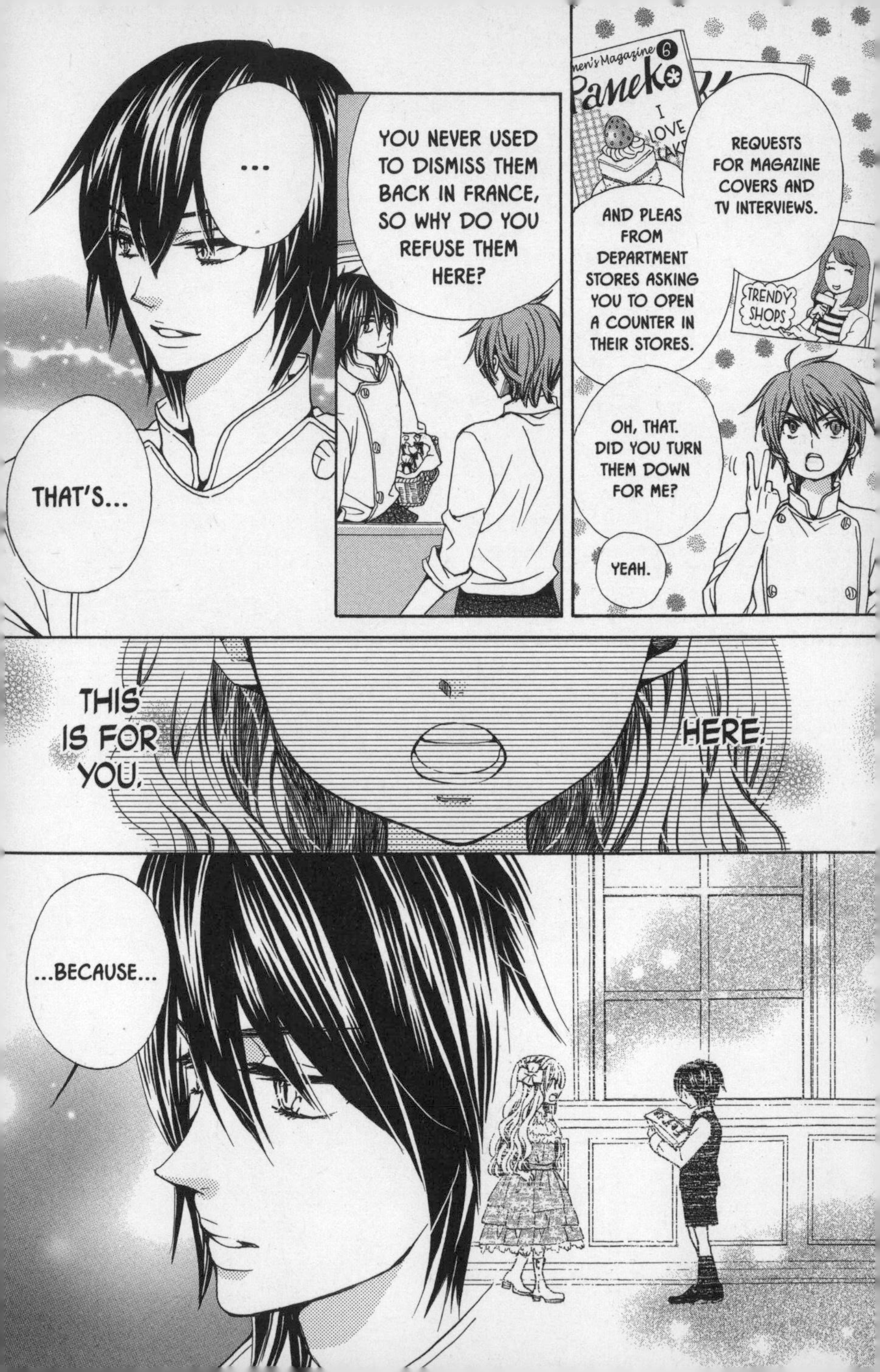
Paneko
I LOVE
REQUESTS FOR MAGAZINE COVERS AND TV INTERVIEWS.
AND PLEAS FROM DEPARTMENT STORES ASKING YOU TO OPEN A COUNTER IN THEIR STORES.
TRENDY SHOPS
OH, THAT. DID YOU TURN THEM DOWN FOR ME?
YEAH.
YOU NEVER USED TO DISMISS THEM BACK IN FRANCE, SO WHY DO YOU REFUSE THEM HERE?
...
THAT'S...
HERE.
THIS IS FOR YOU.
...BECAUSE...

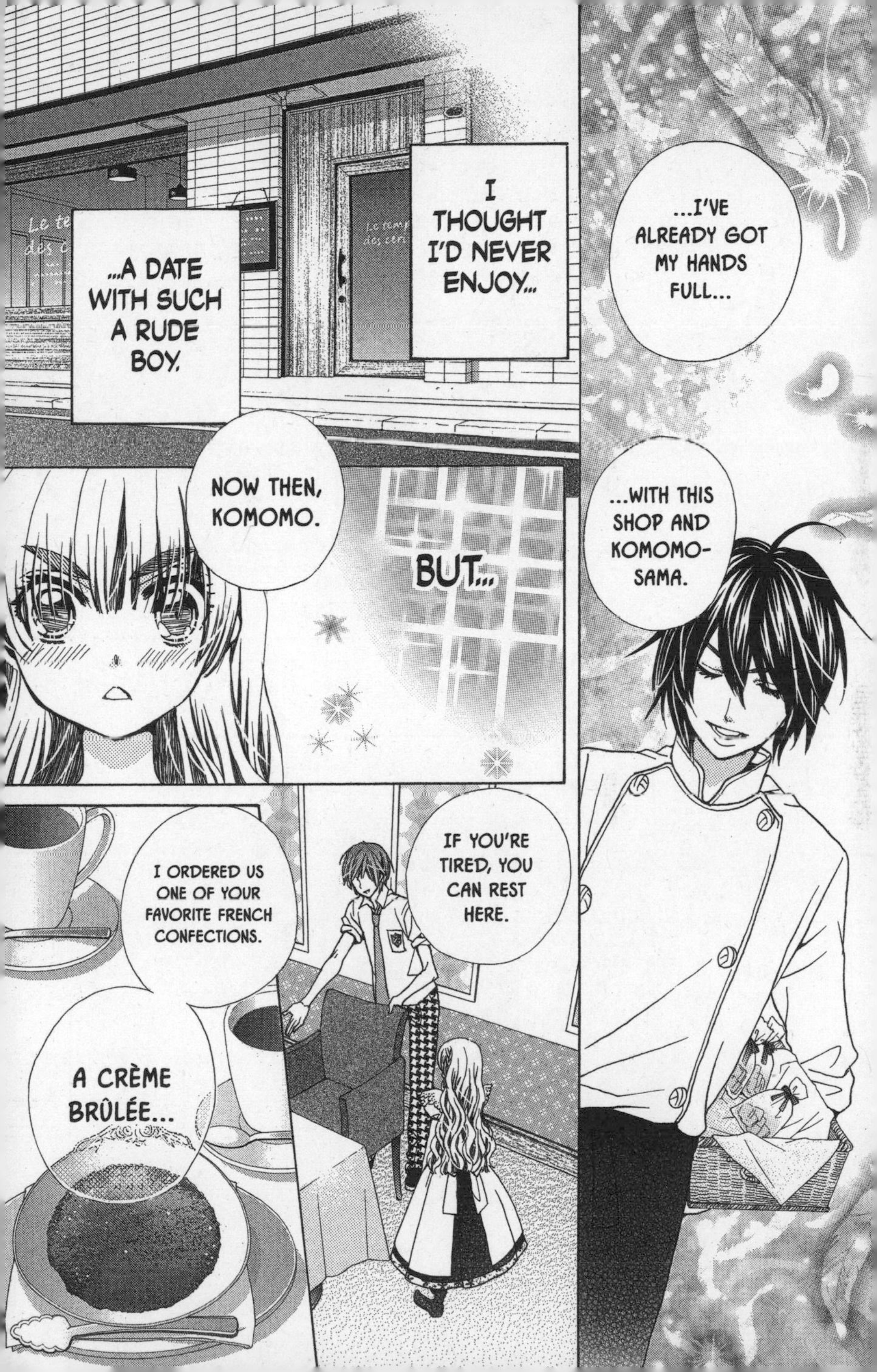
...I'VE ALREADY GOT MY HANDS FULL...
...WITH THIS SHOP AND KOMOMO-SAMA.
I THOUGHT I'D NEVER ENJOY...
...A DATE WITH SUCH A RUDE BOY.
BUT...
NOW THEN, KOMOMO.
IF YOU'RE TIRED, YOU CAN REST HERE.
I ORDERED US ONE OF YOUR FAVORITE FRENCH CONFECTIONS.
A CRÈME BRÛLÉE...

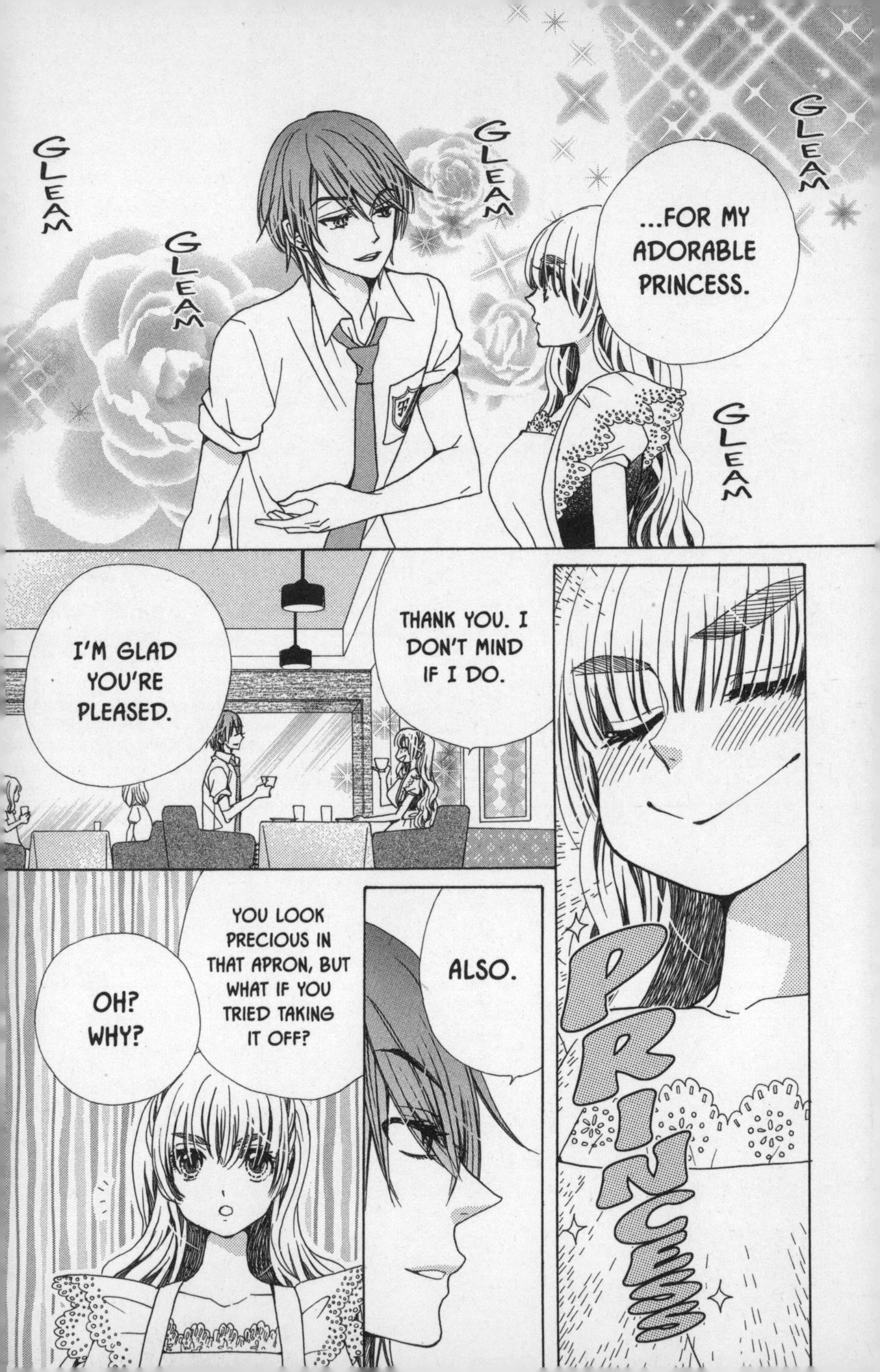
GLEAM
...FOR MY ADORABLE PRINCESS.
GLEAM
GLEAM
GLEAM
GLEAM
PRINCESS
THANK YOU. I DON'T MIND IF I DO.
I'M GLAD YOU'RE PLEASED.
ALSO.
YOU LOOK PRECIOUS IN THAT APRON, BUT WHAT IF YOU TRIED TAKING IT OFF?
OH? WHY?

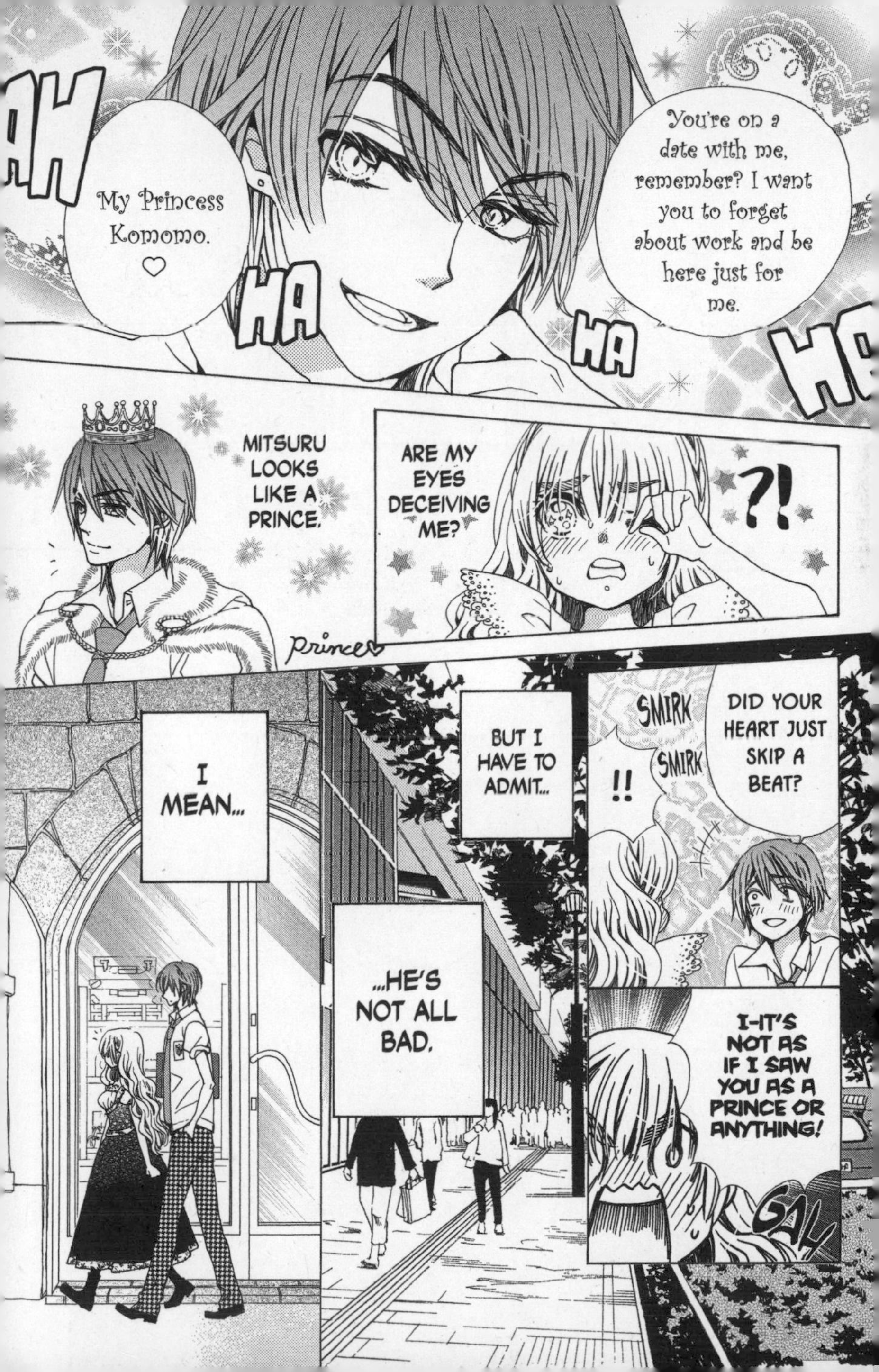
HA
You're on a date with me, remember? I want you to forget about work and be here just for me.
HA
HA
My Princess Komomo. ♡
AH
?!
ARE MY EYES DECEIVING ME?
MITSURU LOOKS LIKE A PRINCE.
Prince♡
DID YOUR HEART JUST SKIP A BEAT?
SMIRK
SMIRK
!!
I-IT'S NOT AS IF I SAW YOU AS A PRINCE OR ANYTHING!
BUT I HAVE TO ADMIT...
...HE'S NOT ALL BAD.
I MEAN...

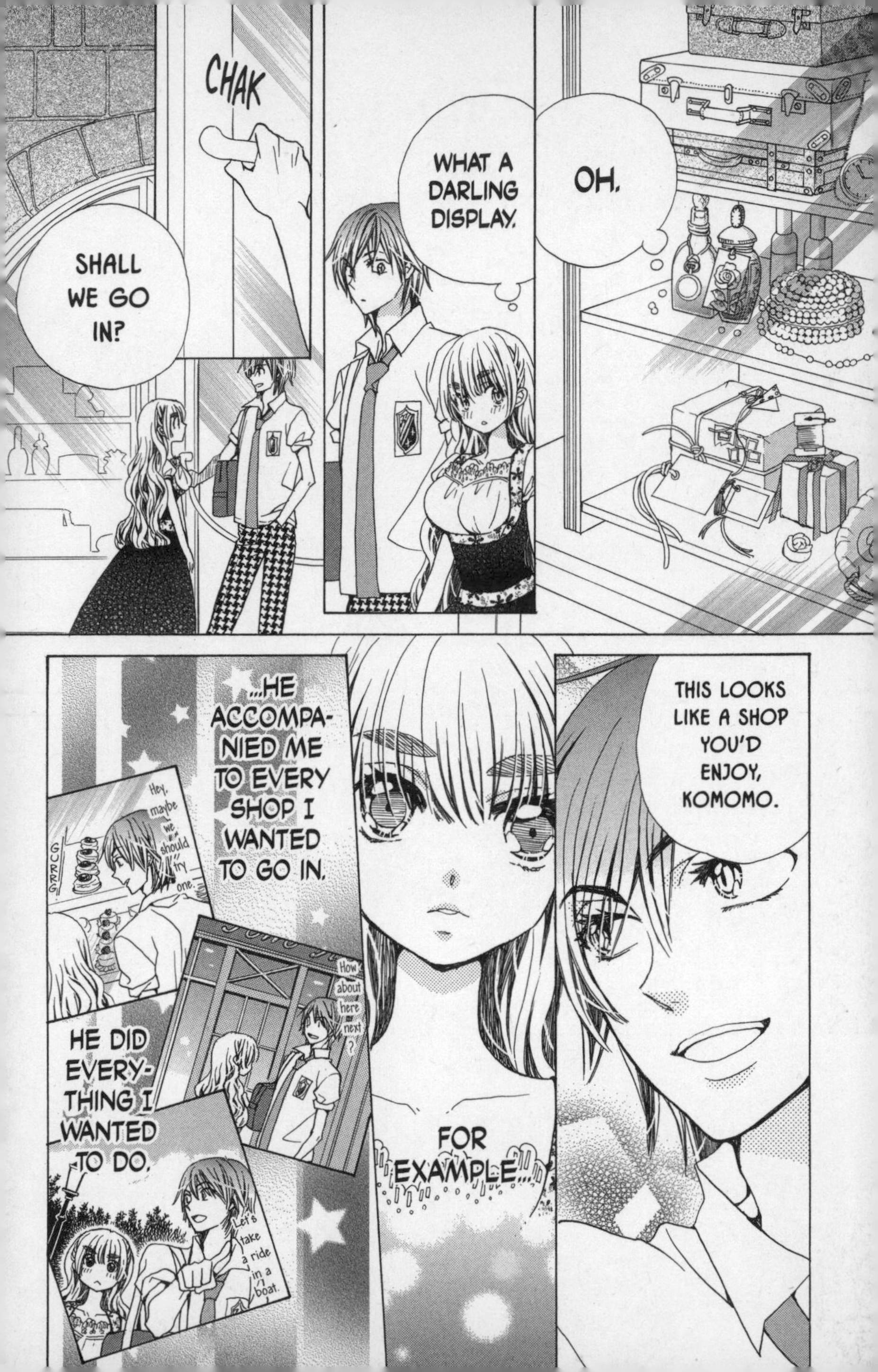
OH.
WHAT A DARLING DISPLAY.
CHAK
SHALL WE GO IN?
THIS LOOKS LIKE A SHOP YOU'D ENJOY, KOMOMO.
FOR EXAMPLE...
...HE ACCOMPA-NIED ME TO EVERY SHOP I WANTED TO GO IN.
Hey, maybe we should try one.
GURRG
How about here next?
HE DID EVERY-THING I WANTED TO DO.
Let's take a ride in a boat.

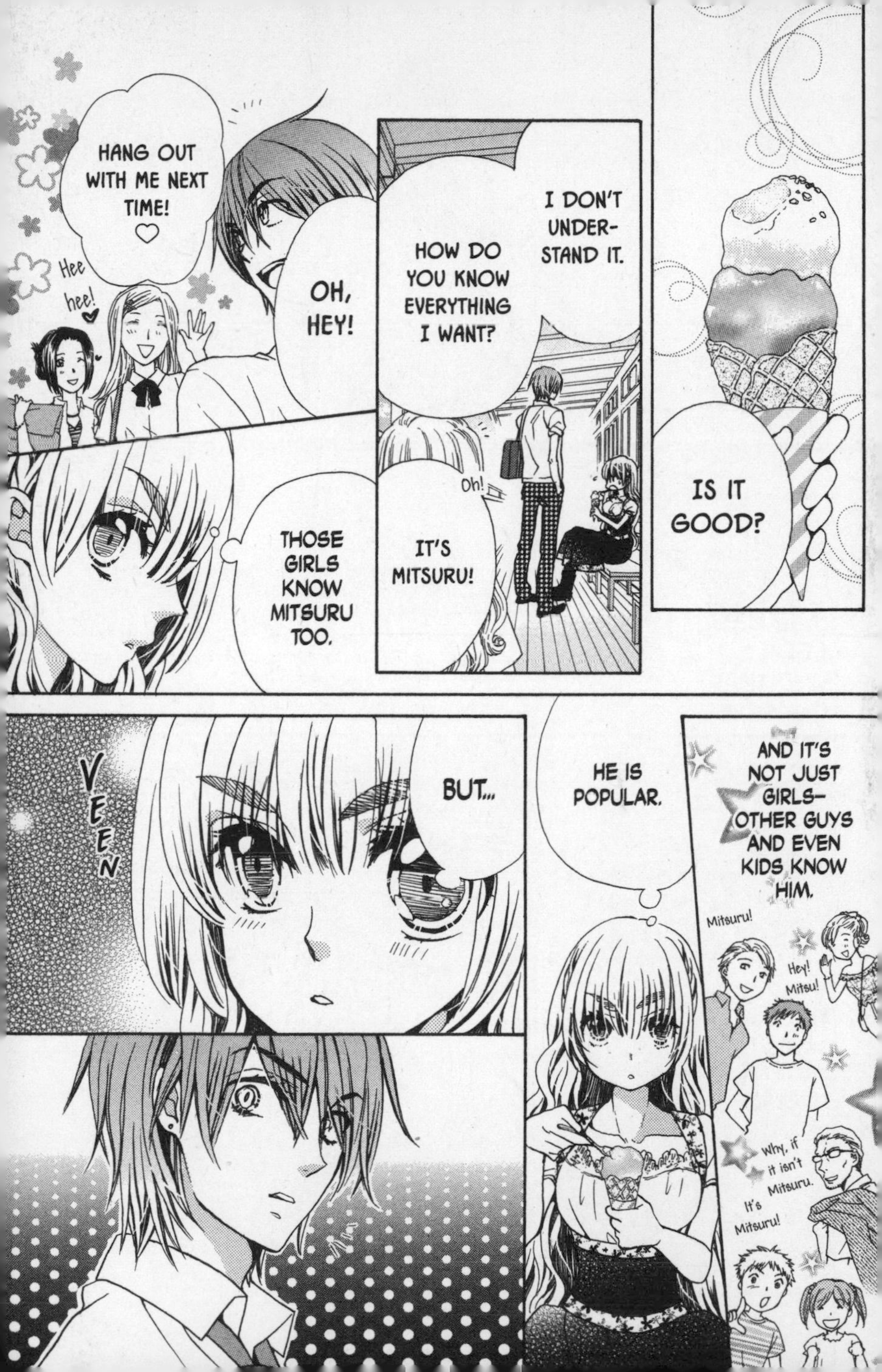

IS IT GOOD?
I DON'T UNDER-STAND IT.
HOW DO YOU KNOW EVERYTHING I WANT?
Oh!
IT'S MITSURU!
OH, HEY!
HANG OUT WITH ME NEXT TIME! ♡
Hee hee! ♥
THOSE GIRLS KNOW MITSURU TOO.
AND IT'S NOT JUST GIRLS— OTHER GUYS AND EVEN KIDS KNOW HIM.
Mitsuru!
Hey! Mitsu!
Why, if it isn't Mitsuru.
It's Mitsuru!
HE IS POPULAR.
BUT...
VEEN

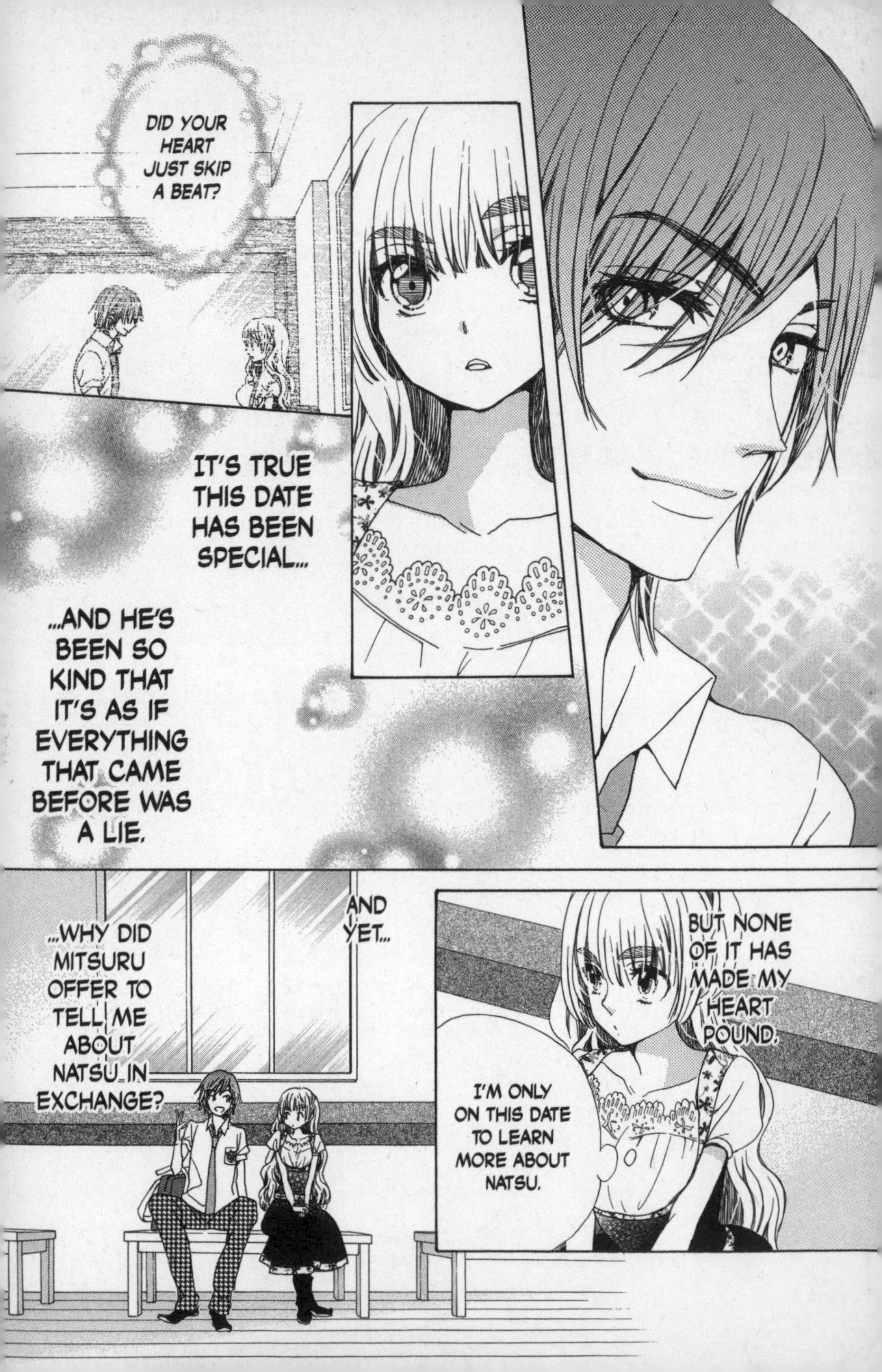
DID YOUR HEART JUST SKIP A BEAT?
IT'S TRUE THIS DATE HAS BEEN SPECIAL...
...AND HE'S BEEN SO KIND THAT IT'S AS IF EVERYTHING THAT CAME BEFORE WAS A LIE.
BUT NONE OF IT HAS MADE MY HEART POUND.
I'M ONLY ON THIS DATE TO LEARN MORE ABOUT NATSU.
AND YET...
...WHY DID MITSURU OFFER TO TELL ME ABOUT NATSU IN EXCHANGE?

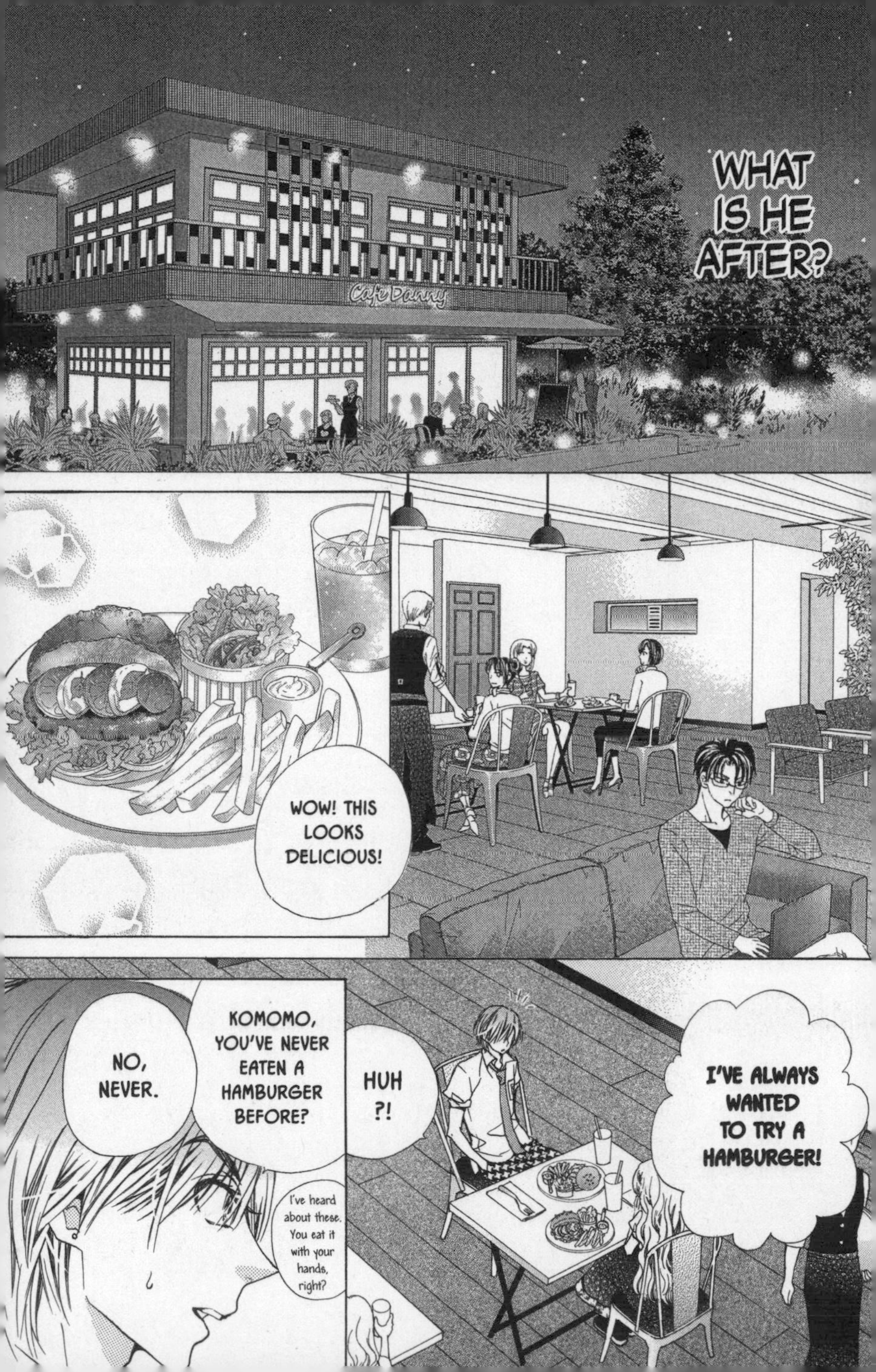
WHAT IS HE AFTER?
Cafe Danny
WOW! THIS LOOKS DELICIOUS!
I'VE ALWAYS WANTED TO TRY A HAMBURGER!
HUH ?!
KOMOMO, YOU'VE NEVER EATEN A HAMBURGER BEFORE?
NO, NEVER.
I've heard about these. You eat it with your hands, right?

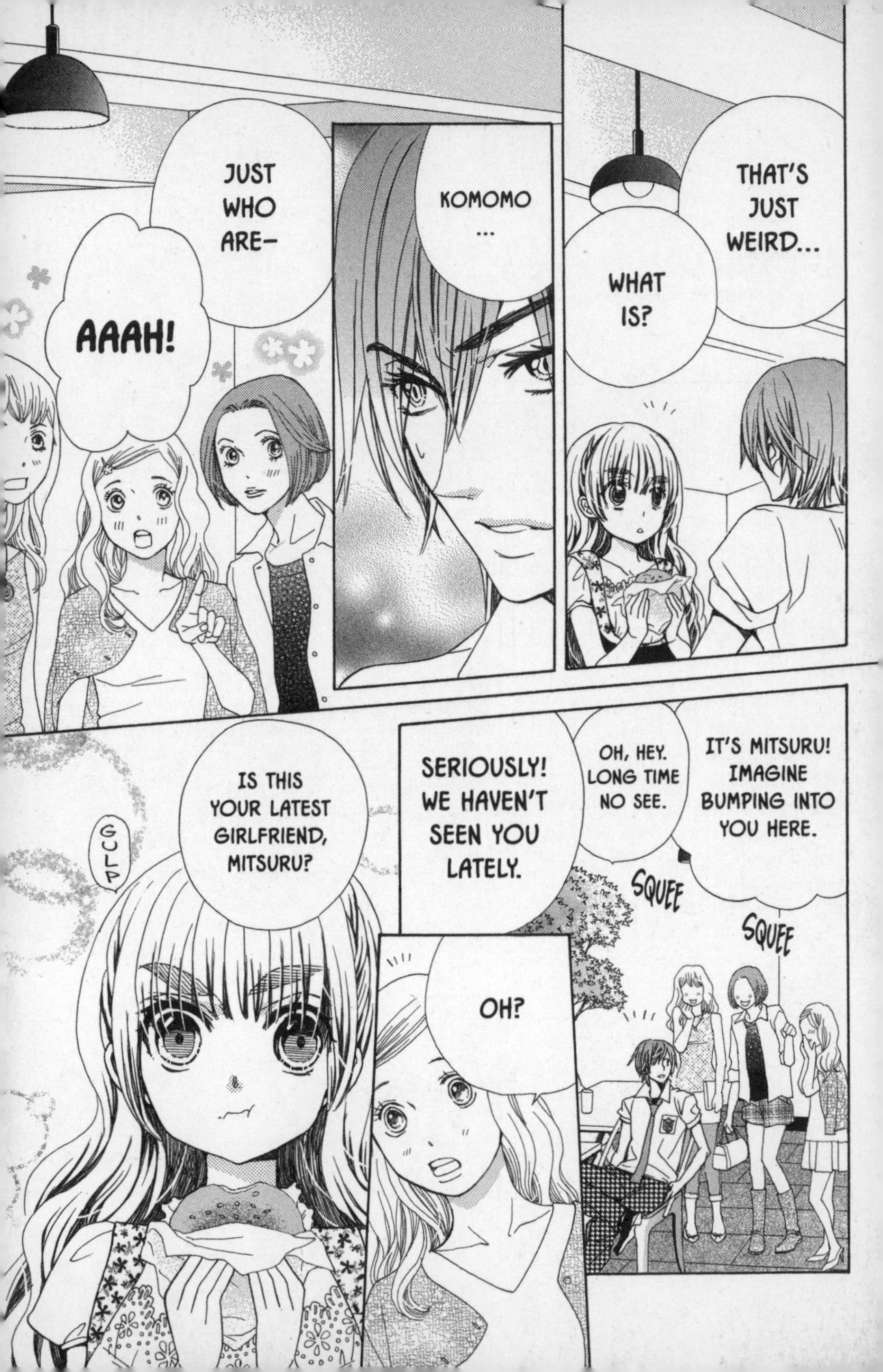
THAT'S JUST WEIRD...
WHAT IS?
KOMOMO ...
JUST WHO ARE–
AAAH!
IT'S MITSURU! IMAGINE BUMPING INTO YOU HERE.
OH, HEY. LONG TIME NO SEE.
SERIOUSLY! WE HAVEN'T SEEN YOU LATELY.
SQUEE
SQUEE
OH?
IS THIS YOUR LATEST GIRLFRIEND, MITSURU?
GULP

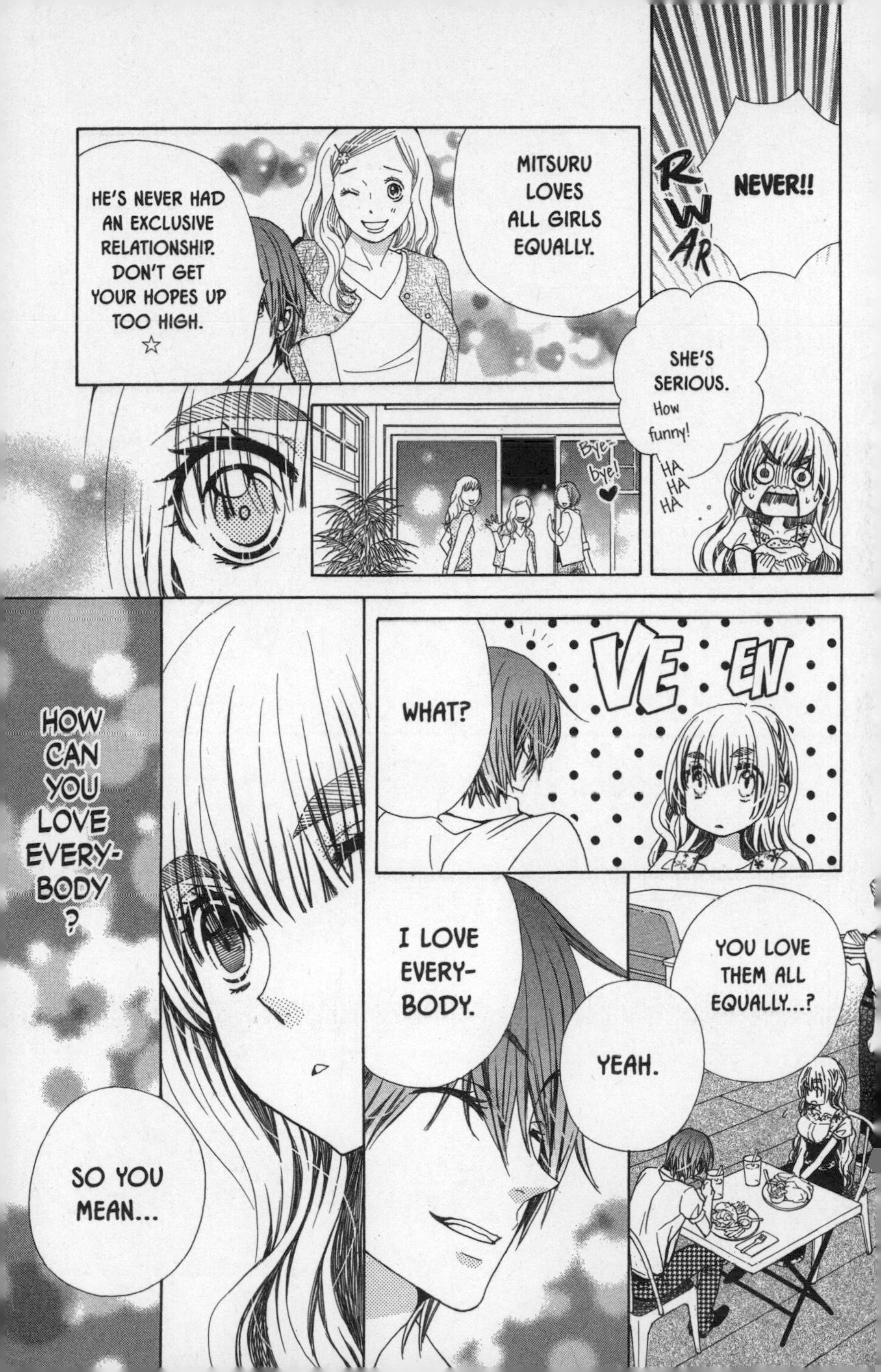
RWAR
NEVER!!
SHE'S SERIOUS.
How funny!
HA HA HA
MITSURU LOVES ALL GIRLS EQUALLY.
HE'S NEVER HAD AN EXCLUSIVE RELATIONSHIP. DON'T GET YOUR HOPES UP TOO HIGH. ☆
Bye-bye!
VE EN
WHAT?
YOU LOVE THEM ALL EQUALLY...?
YEAH.
I LOVE EVERY-BODY.
HOW CAN YOU LOVE EVERY-BODY?
SO YOU MEAN...

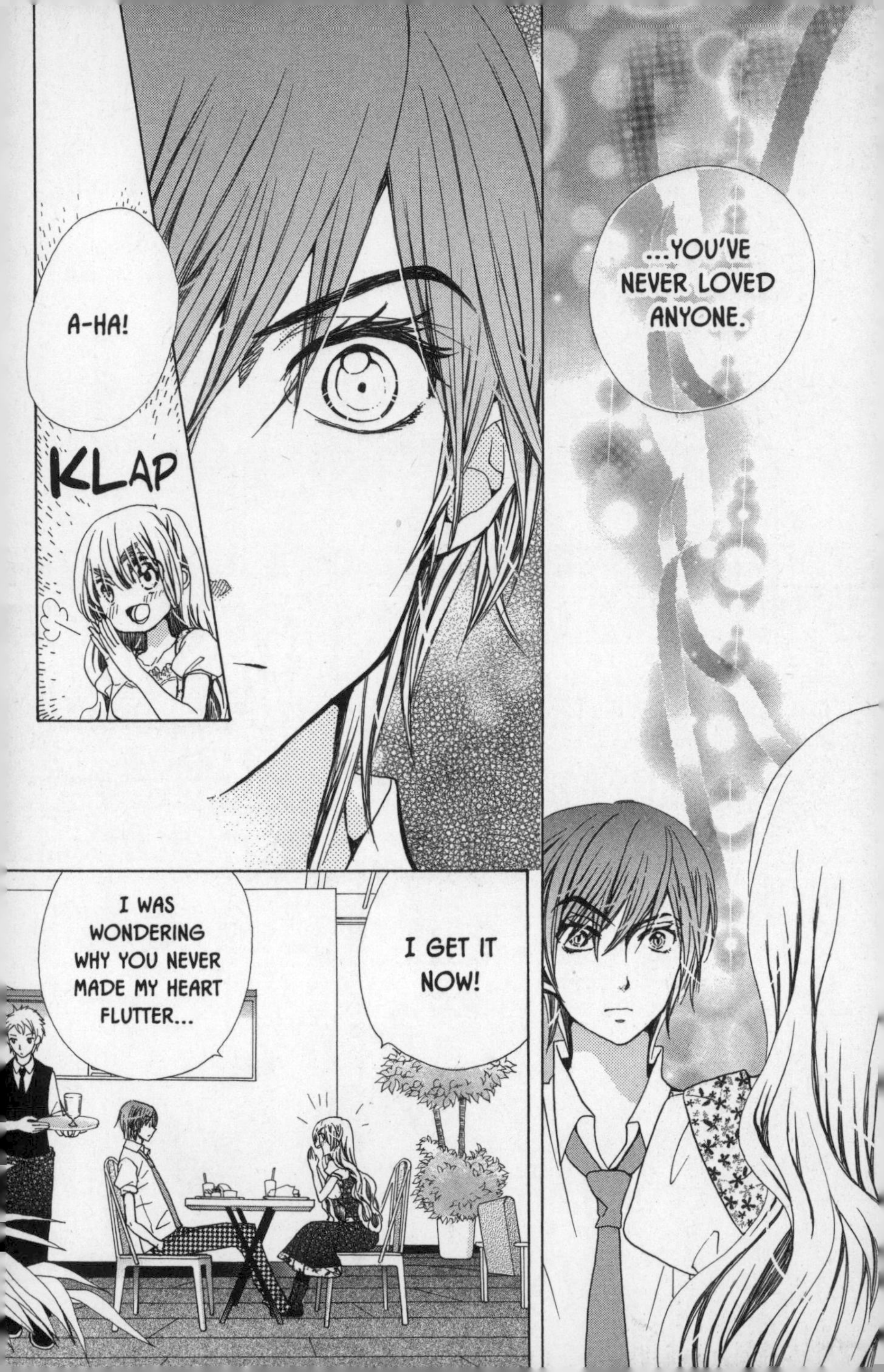
...YOU'VE NEVER LOVED ANYONE.
A-HA!
KLAP
I GET IT NOW!
I WAS WONDERING WHY YOU NEVER MADE MY HEART FLUTTER...

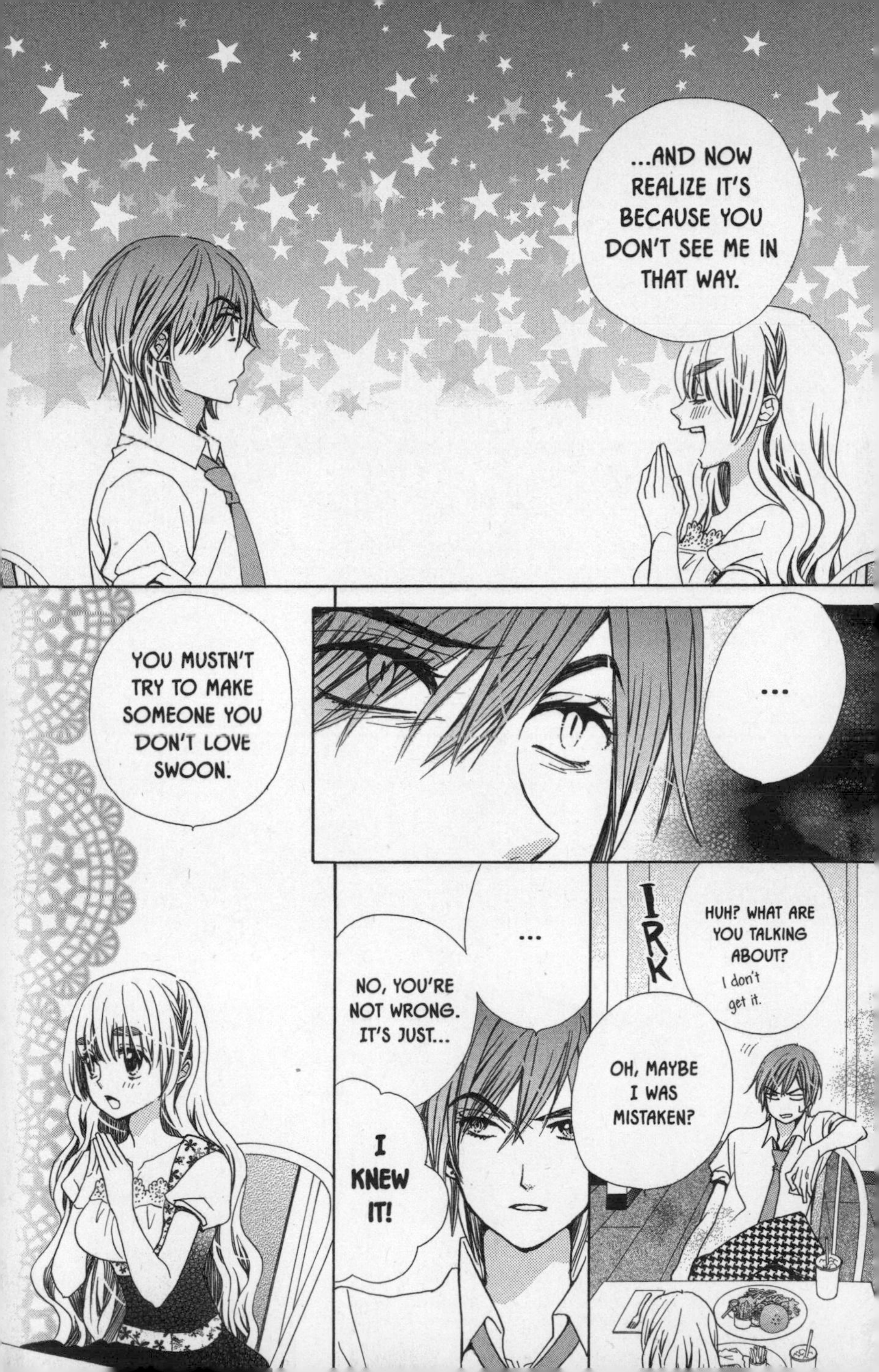
...AND NOW REALIZE IT'S BECAUSE YOU DON'T SEE ME IN THAT WAY.
...
HUH? WHAT ARE YOU TALKING ABOUT?
I don't get it.
IRK
OH, MAYBE I WAS MISTAKEN?
...
NO, YOU'RE NOT WRONG. IT'S JUST...
I KNEW IT!
YOU MUSTN'T TRY TO MAKE SOMEONE YOU DON'T LOVE SWOON.

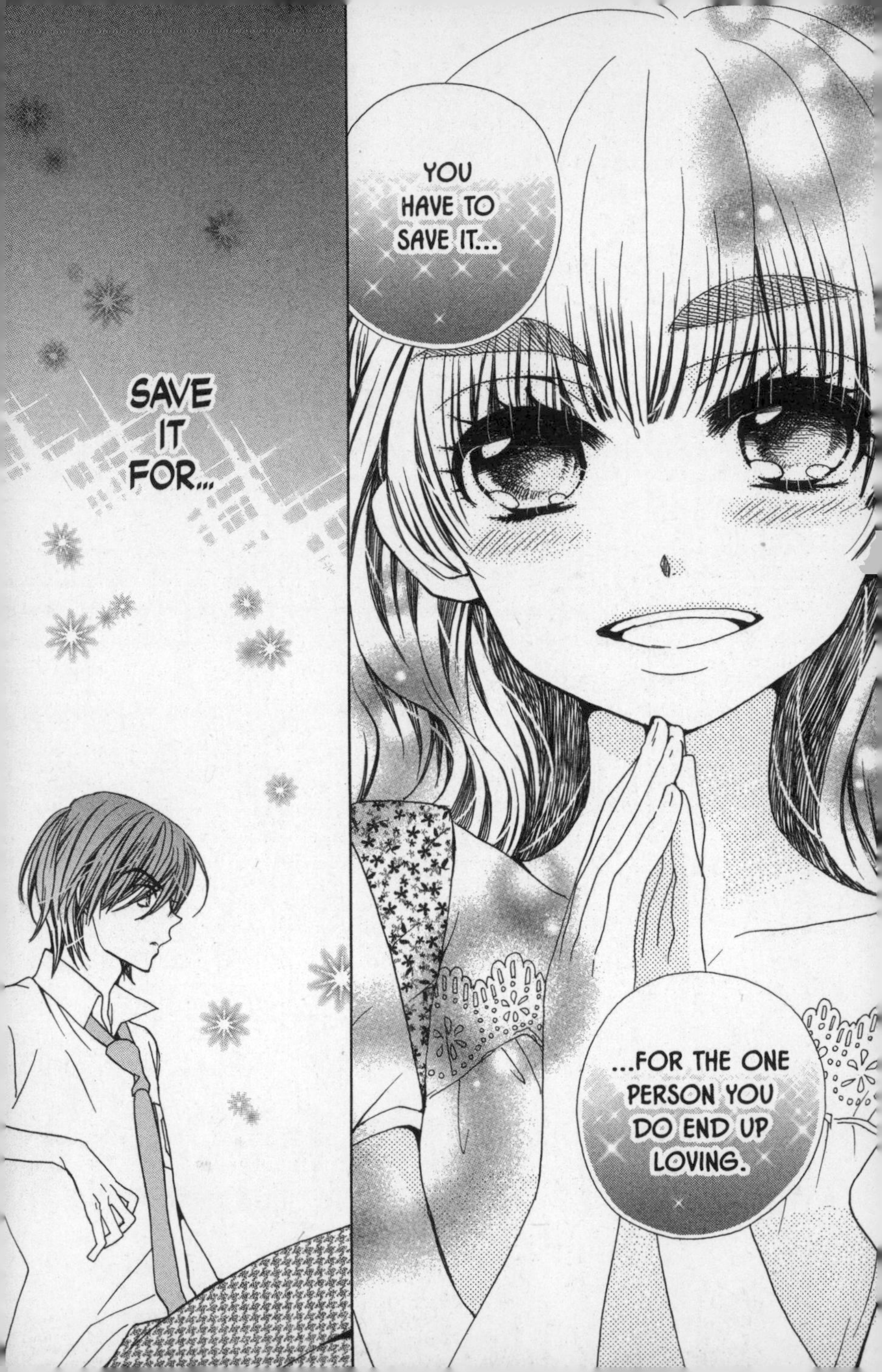
YOU HAVE TO SAVE IT...
...FOR THE ONE PERSON YOU DO END UP LOVING.
SAVE IT FOR...

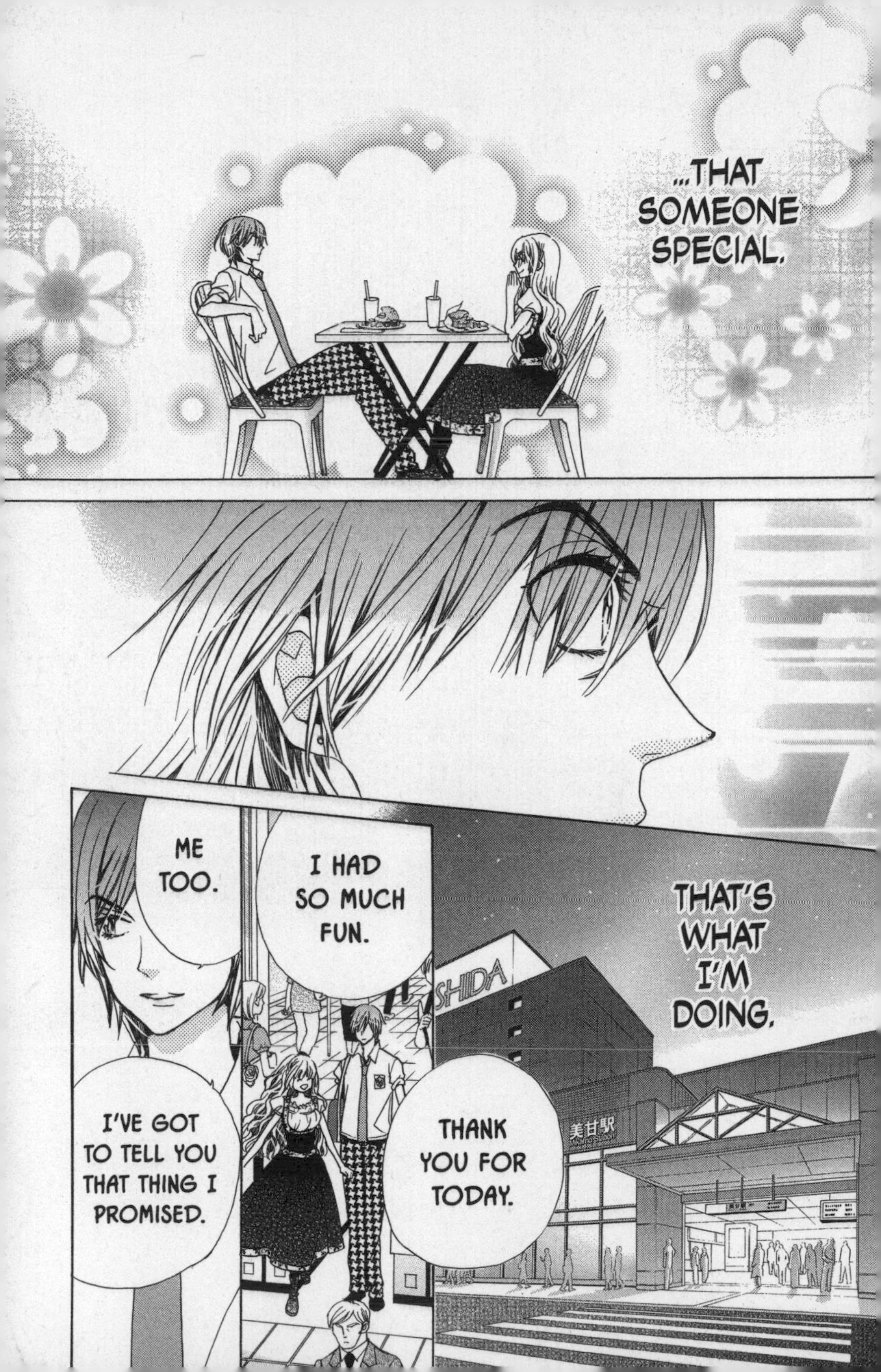
...THAT SOMEONE SPECIAL.
THAT'S WHAT I'M DOING.
SHIDA
美甘駅
I HAD SO MUCH FUN.
THANK YOU FOR TODAY.
ME TOO.
I'VE GOT TO TELL YOU THAT THING I PROMISED.

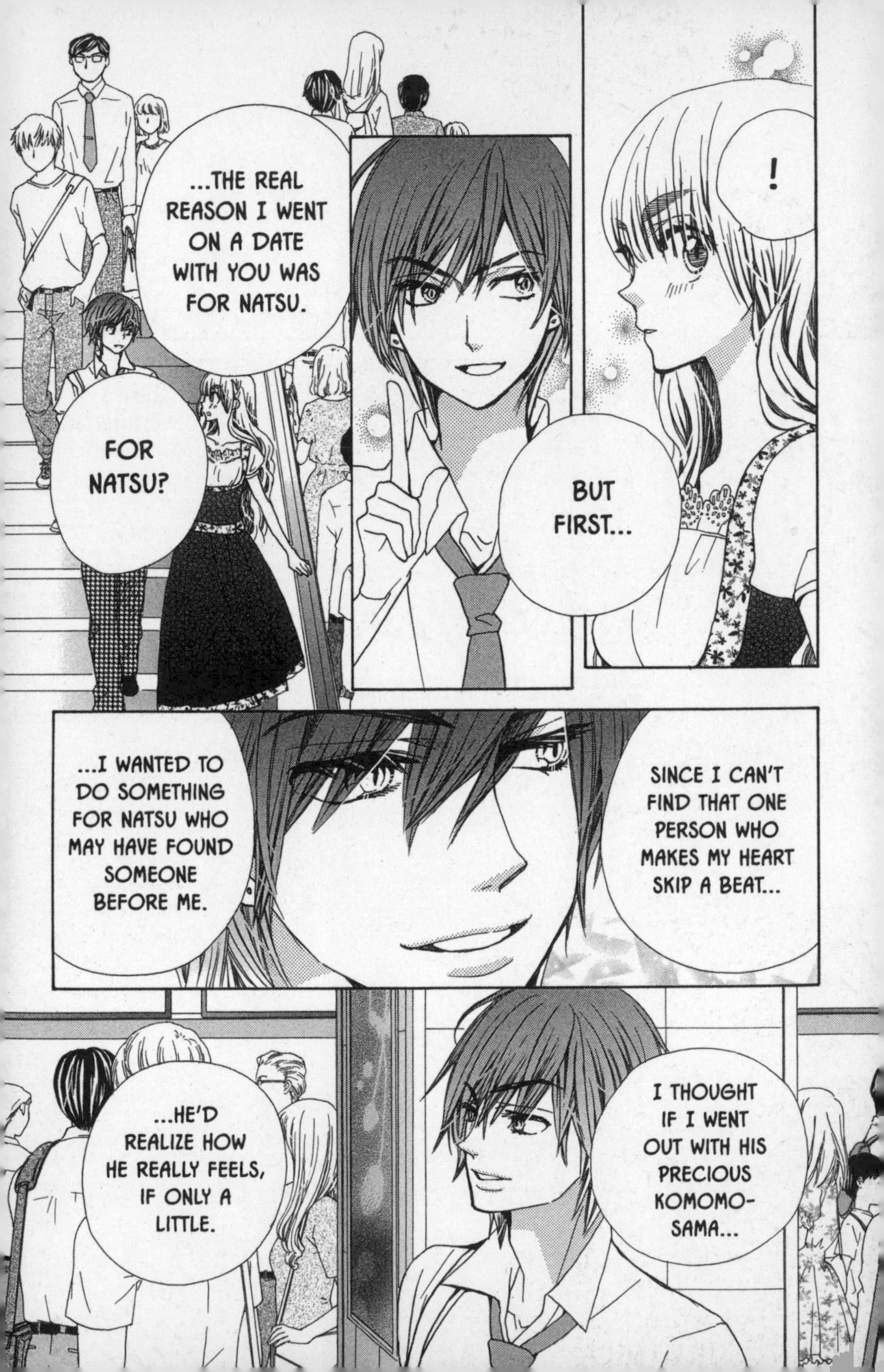
!
BUT FIRST...
...THE REAL REASON I WENT ON A DATE WITH YOU WAS FOR NATSU.
FOR NATSU?
SINCE I CAN'T FIND THAT ONE PERSON WHO MAKES MY HEART SKIP A BEAT...
...I WANTED TO DO SOMETHING FOR NATSU WHO MAY HAVE FOUND SOMEONE BEFORE ME.
I THOUGHT IF I WENT OUT WITH HIS PRECIOUS KOMOMO-SAMA...
...HE'D REALIZE HOW HE REALLY FEELS, IF ONLY A LITTLE.

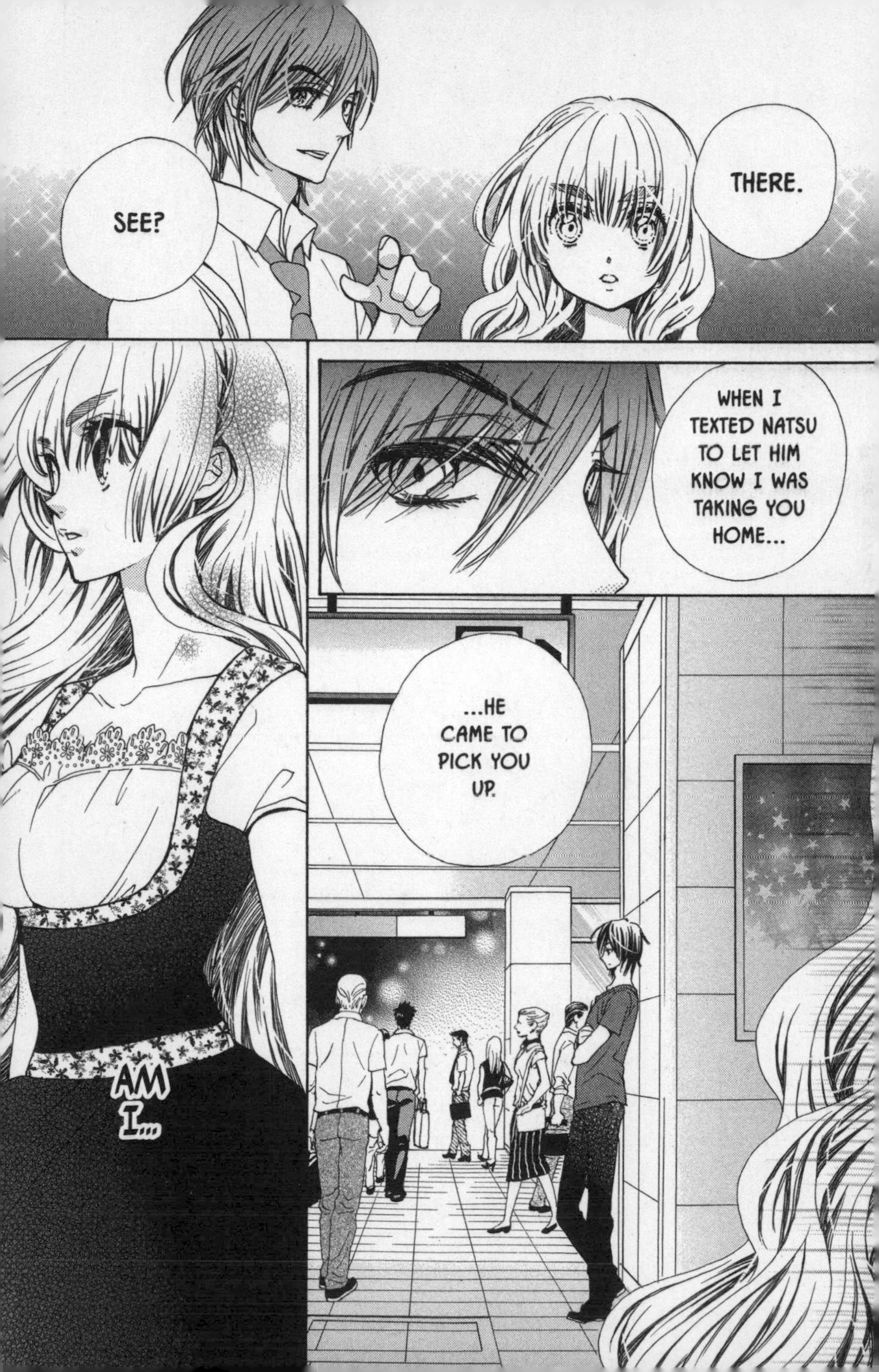
THERE.
SEE?
WHEN I TEXTED NATSU TO LET HIM KNOW I WAS TAKING YOU HOME...
...HE CAME TO PICK YOU UP.
AM I...

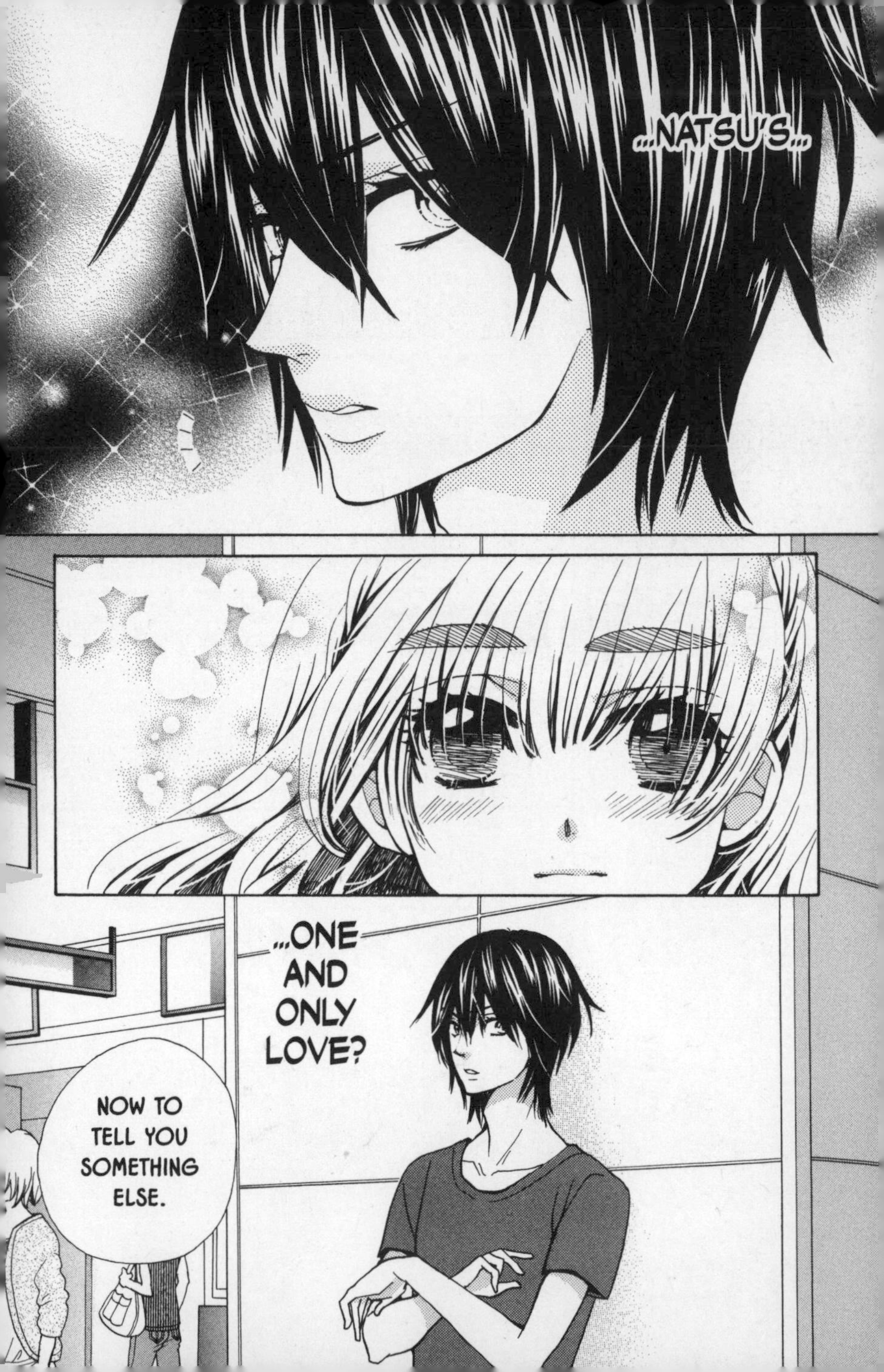
...NATSU'S...
...ONE AND ONLY LOVE?
NOW TO TELL YOU SOMETHING ELSE.

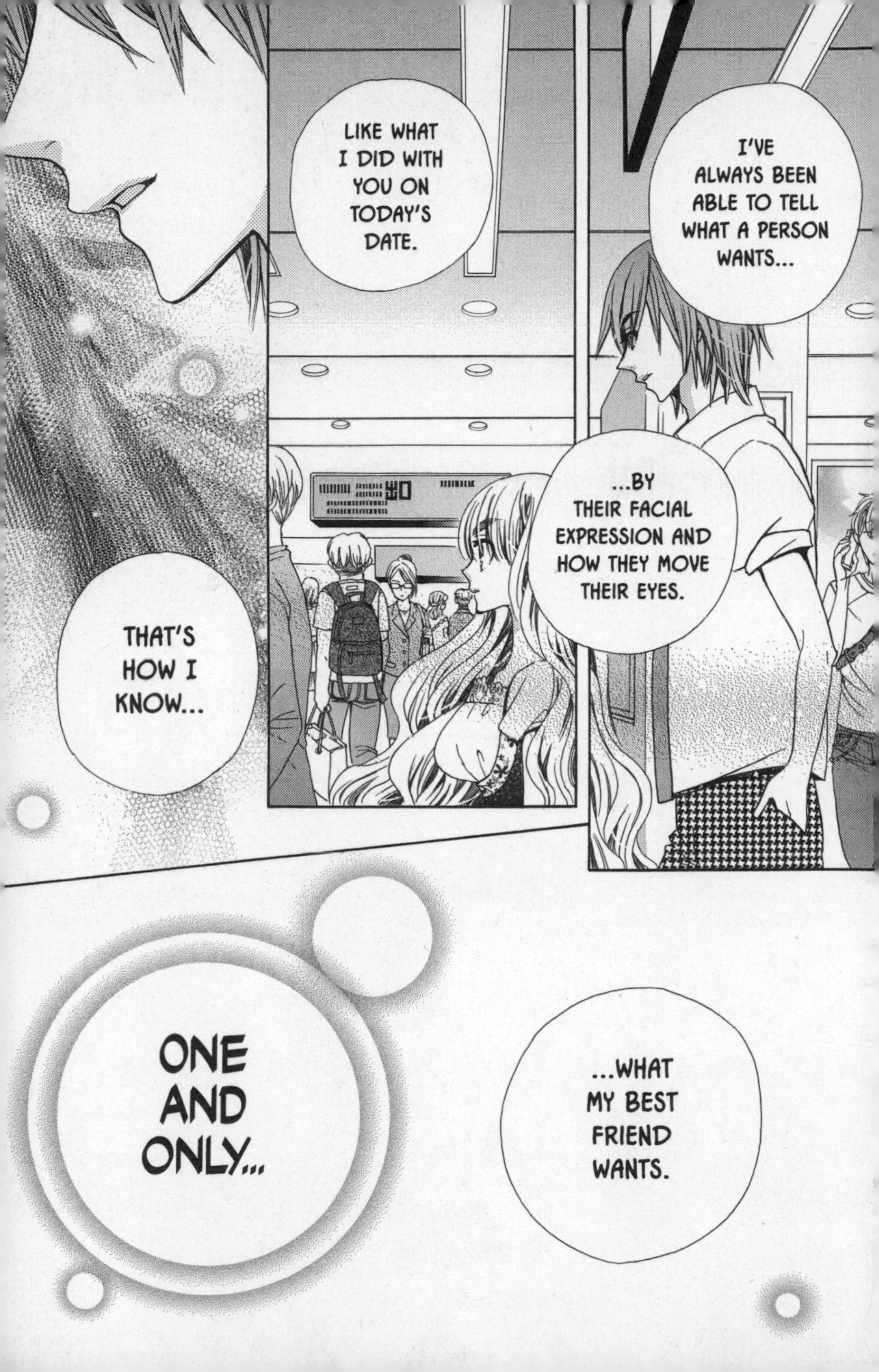
I'VE ALWAYS BEEN ABLE TO TELL WHAT A PERSON WANTS...
...BY THEIR FACIAL EXPRESSION AND HOW THEY MOVE THEIR EYES.
LIKE WHAT I DID WITH YOU ON TODAY'S DATE.
THAT'S HOW I KNOW...
...WHAT MY BEST FRIEND WANTS.
ONE AND ONLY...

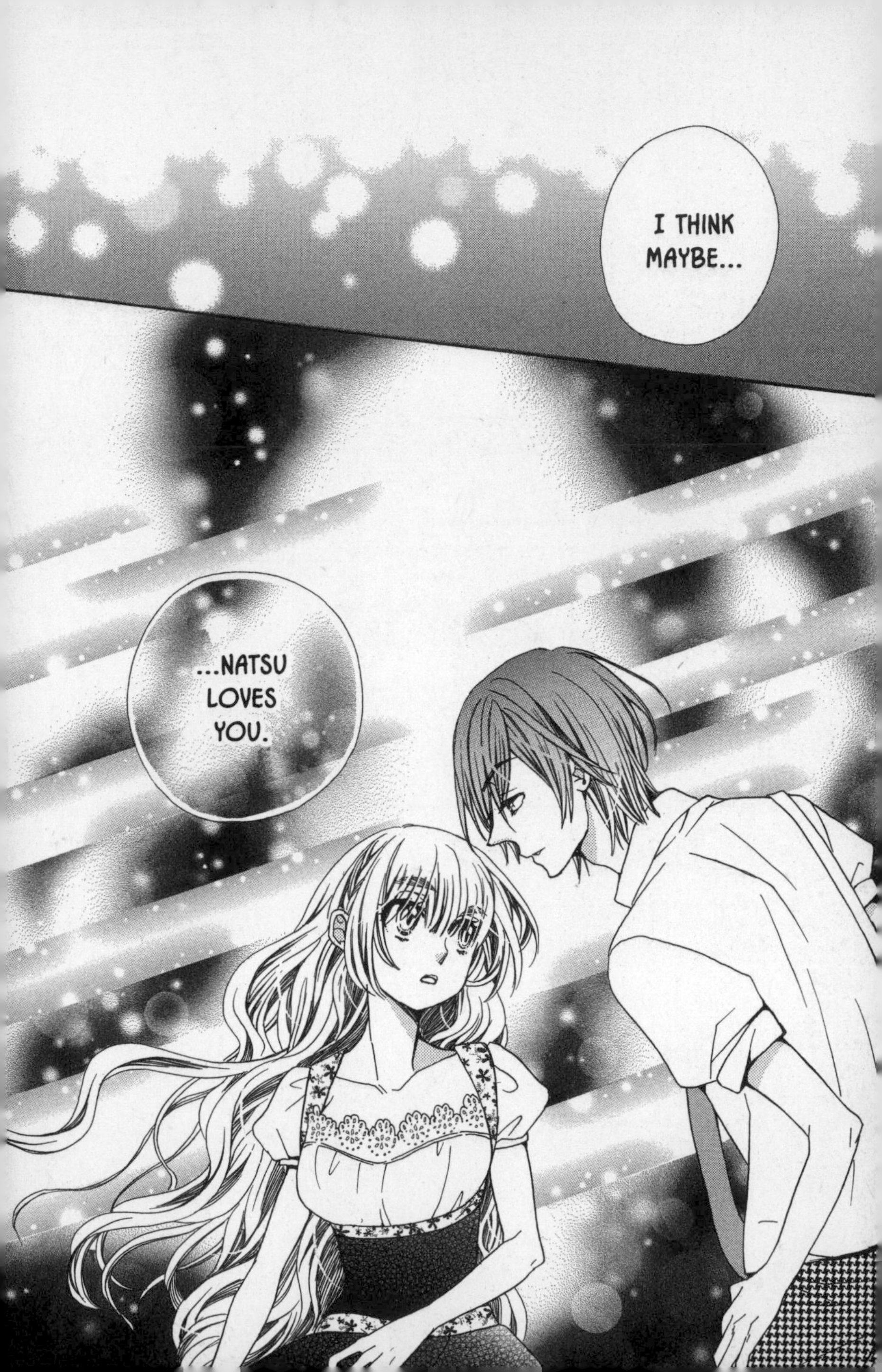
I THINK MAYBE...
...NATSU LOVES YOU.

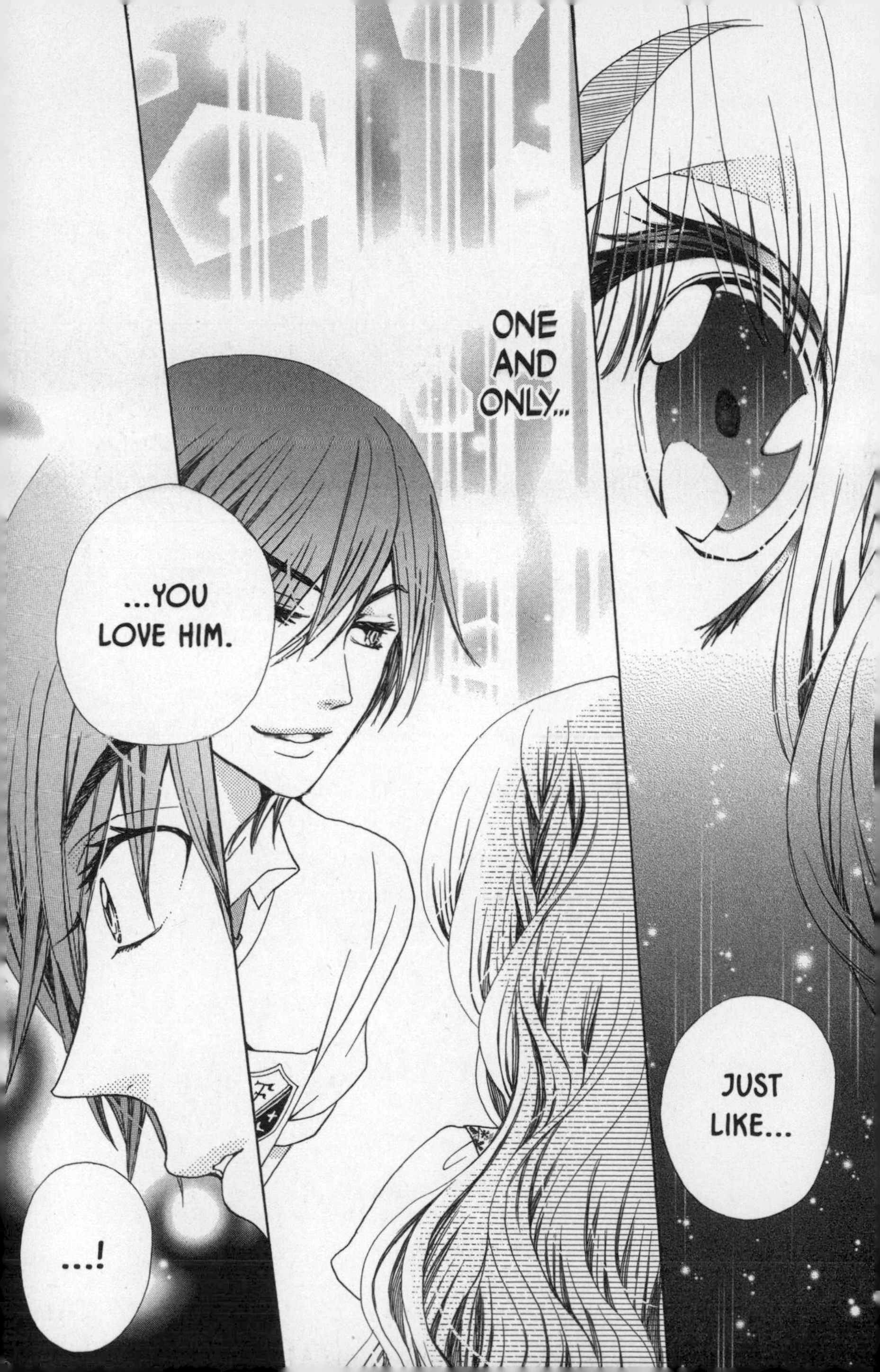
JUST LIKE...
ONE AND ONLY...
...YOU LOVE HIM.
...!

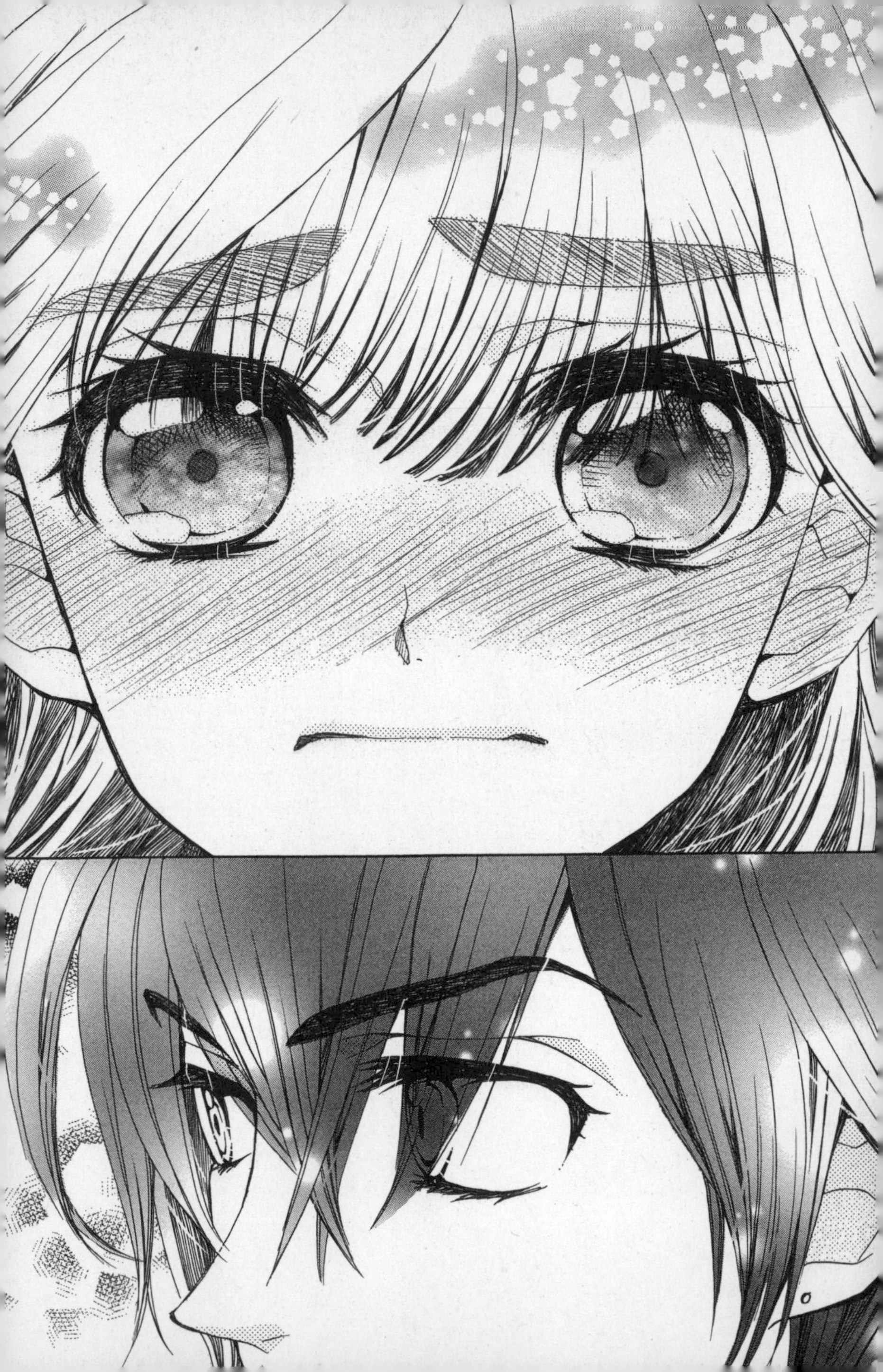

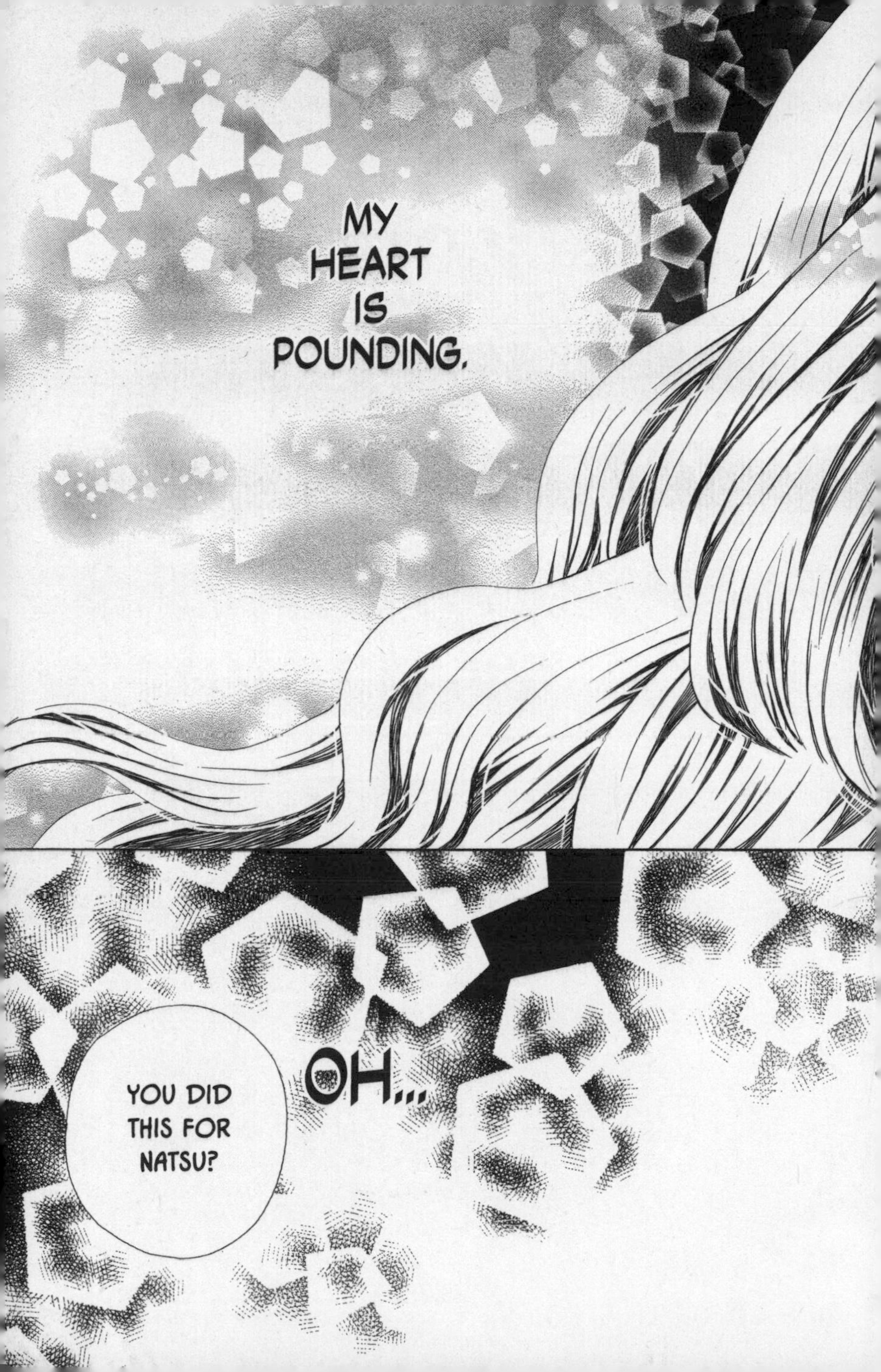
MY HEART IS POUNDING.
OH...
YOU DID THIS FOR NATSU?

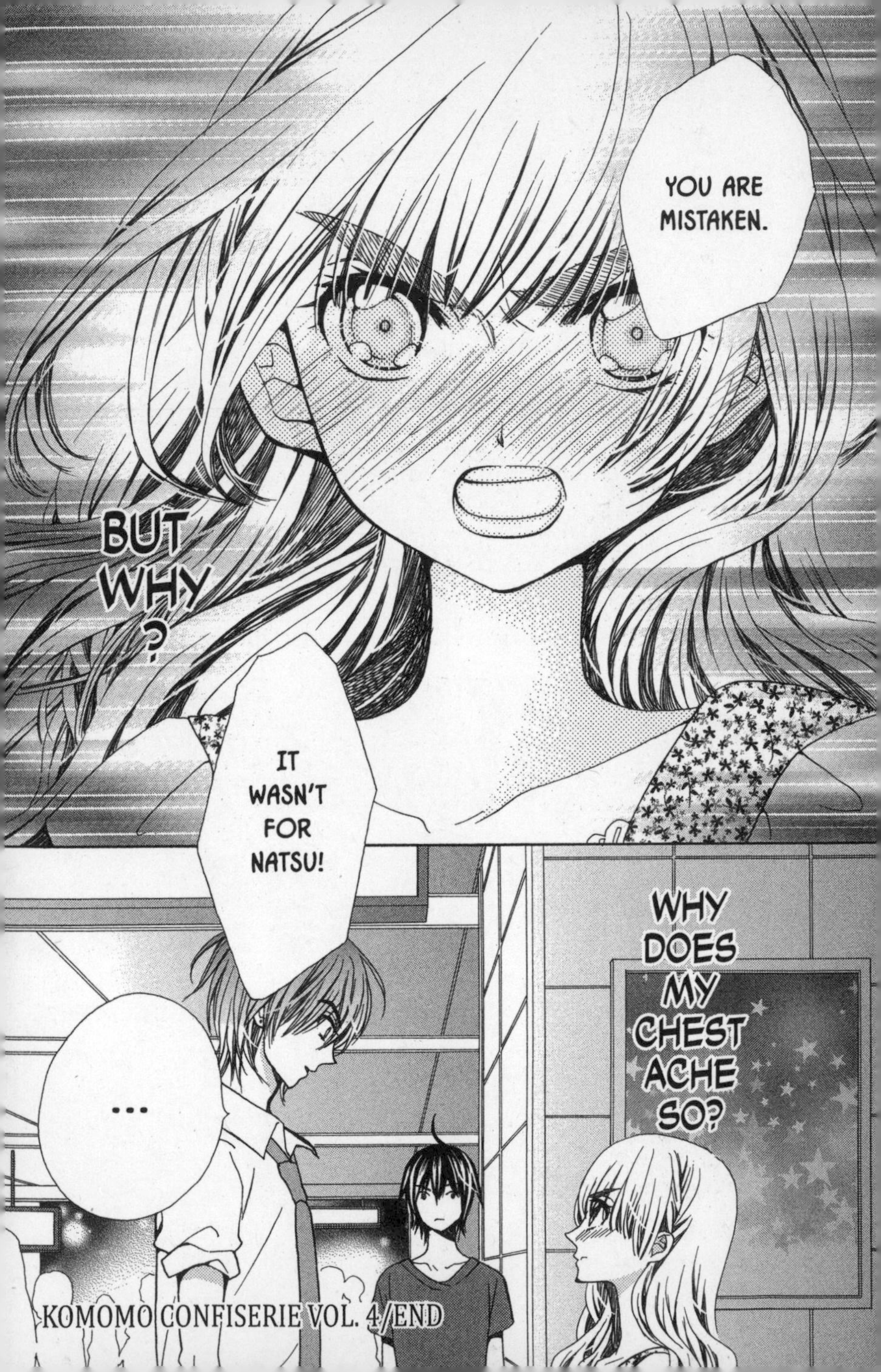
YOU ARE MISTAKEN.
IT WASN'T FOR NATSU!
BUT WHY ?
WHY DOES MY CHEST ACHE SO?
...
KOMOMO CONFISERIE VOL. 4/END

~ My Personal Takes on Different Pastries ~

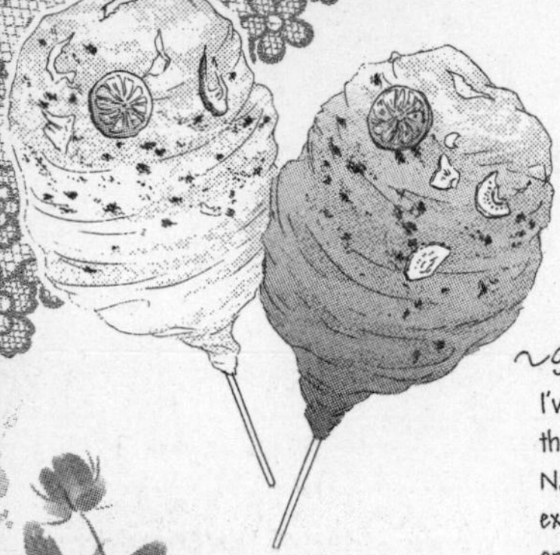

~Barbe á papa~

Also known as cotton candy. Sometimes they're made by crushing flavored candies to whip into cotton candy. I've had it garnished with dried fruits before, which really changes the texture and makes it very delicious. I also love the cotton candy they sell at festivals!!

~gelée de champagne~

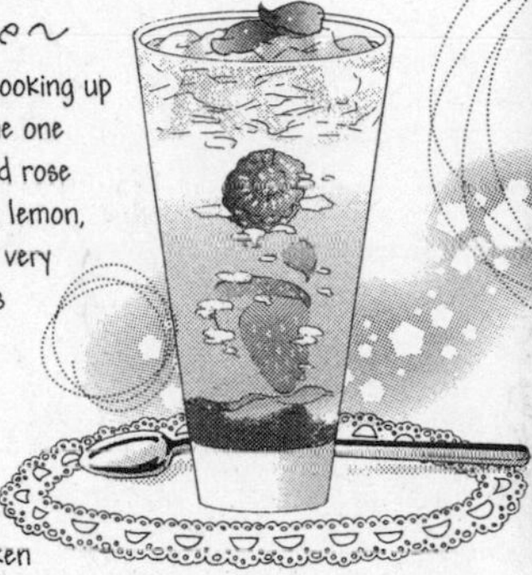

I've never tried this, so I tried looking up the recipe to make it myself. The one Natsu made used framboise and rose extract, but the one I made had lemon, orange, and grapefruit. It was a very strong drink. I got drunk. It was a stiff drink in the end, but I really enjoyed it.

le sandwich

(eggplant, smoked chicken and tomato sandwich)

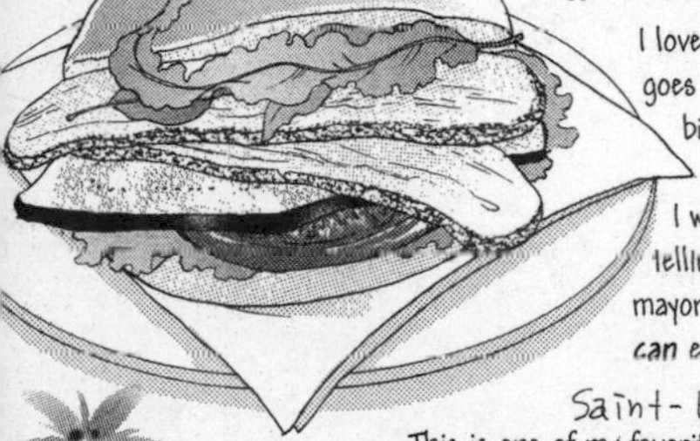

I love this combination. The chicken goes very well with basil or teriyaki! But since I'm not a big fan of mayonnaise, when I bought the sandwich and asked if they had any mayo-free versions of it, I was told a flat-out no. So I ate the sandwich while telling myself, "That white stuff isn't actually mayonnaise." It was pretty tough for me. *Wait...maybe I can eat this... No, I can't...*

Saint-Honoré

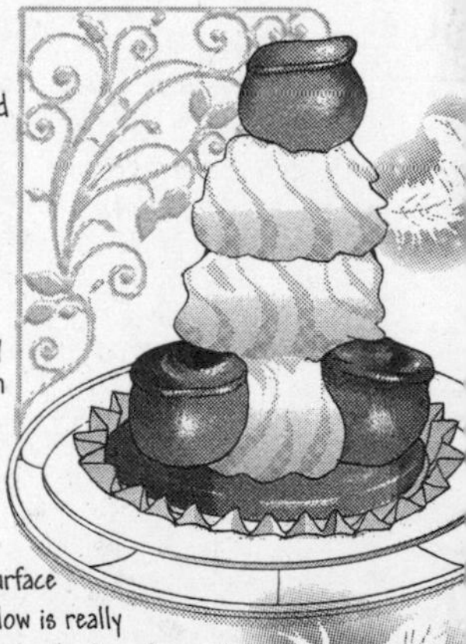

This is one of my favorite cakes. There's vanilla bean custard cream inside small puff pastries that are coated with crunchy candy. It's particularly delicious when topped with a generous helping of whipped cream. For some reason, the cake shop near my house only sells them on Saturdays and Sundays. I wonder why that is? Also, and this is unrelated, the "H" is silent in French, but when I first saw the name I didn't think it'd actually be pronounced "nore." Now I'm not sure what I'm saying anymore.

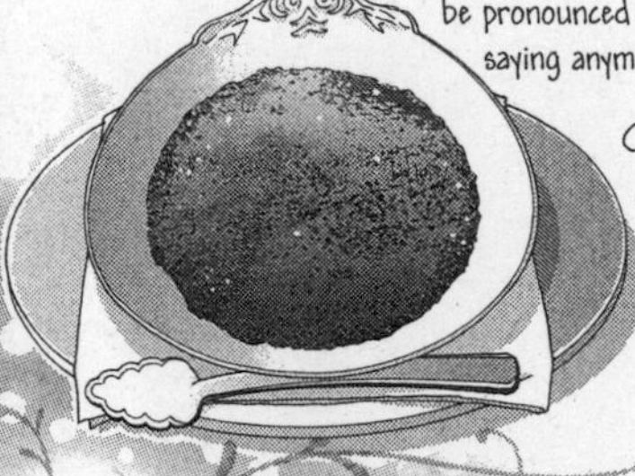

Crème brûlée

A pudding-like dessert. The crunchy caramel crust on the surface is delicious, and the pudding below is really smooth. I confess that I'm not much of a fan of smooth textures, so when the crunchy caramel is gone, it's actually a very trying confection for me to eat. I like my puddings to be firmer. But I still think it's delicious.

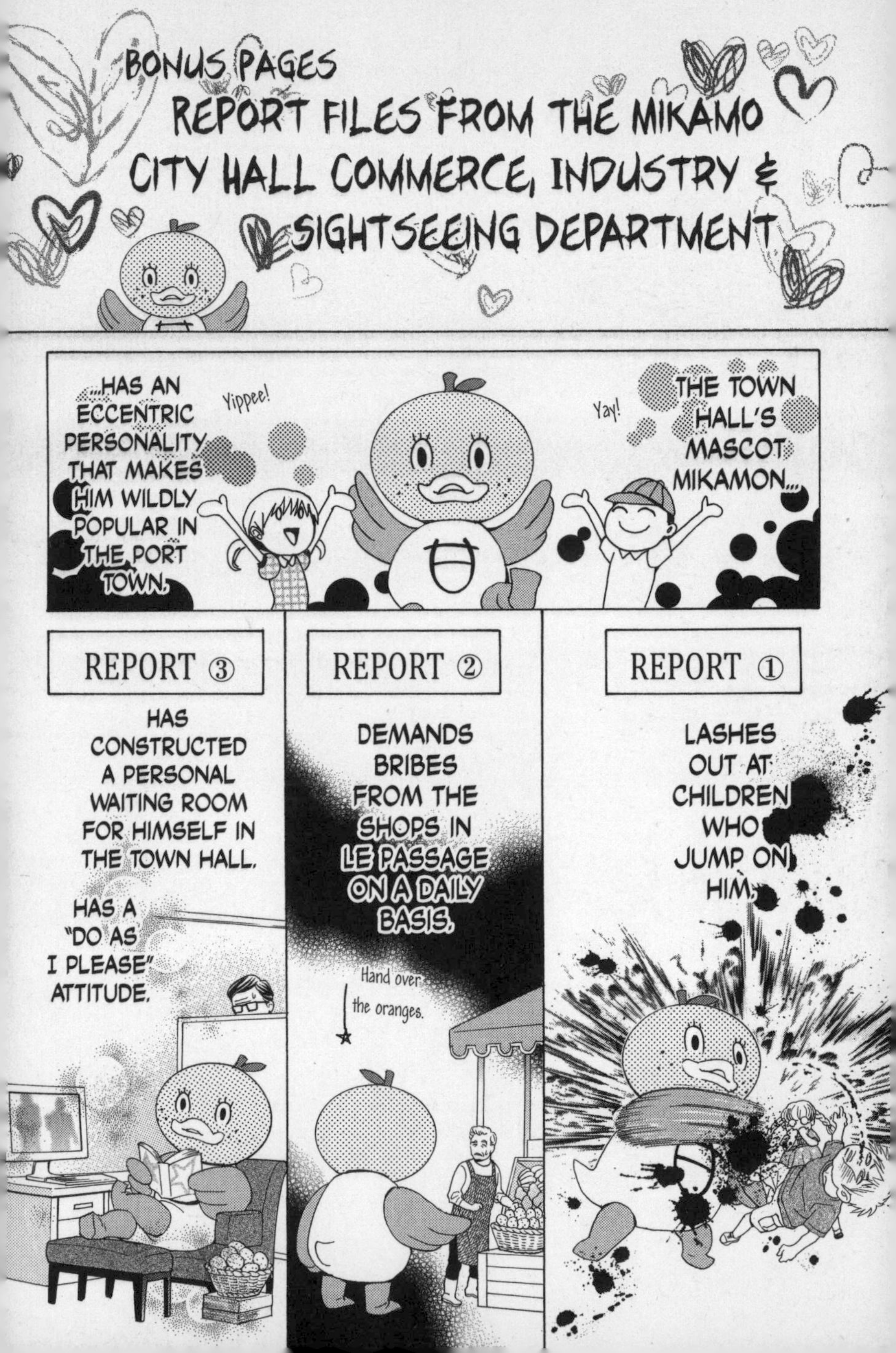
BONUS PAGES
REPORT FILES FROM THE MIKAMO CITY HALL COMMERCE, INDUSTRY & SIGHTSEEING DEPARTMENT
THE TOWN HALL'S MASCOT MIKAMON...
Yay!
Yippee!
...HAS AN ECCENTRIC PERSONALITY THAT MAKES HIM WILDLY POPULAR IN THE PORT TOWN.
REPORT ①
LASHES OUT AT CHILDREN WHO JUMP ON HIM.
REPORT ②
DEMANDS BRIBES FROM THE SHOPS IN LE PASSAGE ON A DAILY BASIS.
Hand over the oranges.
REPORT ③
HAS CONSTRUCTED A PERSONAL WAITING ROOM FOR HIMSELF IN THE TOWN HALL.
HAS A "DO AS I PLEASE" ATTITUDE.

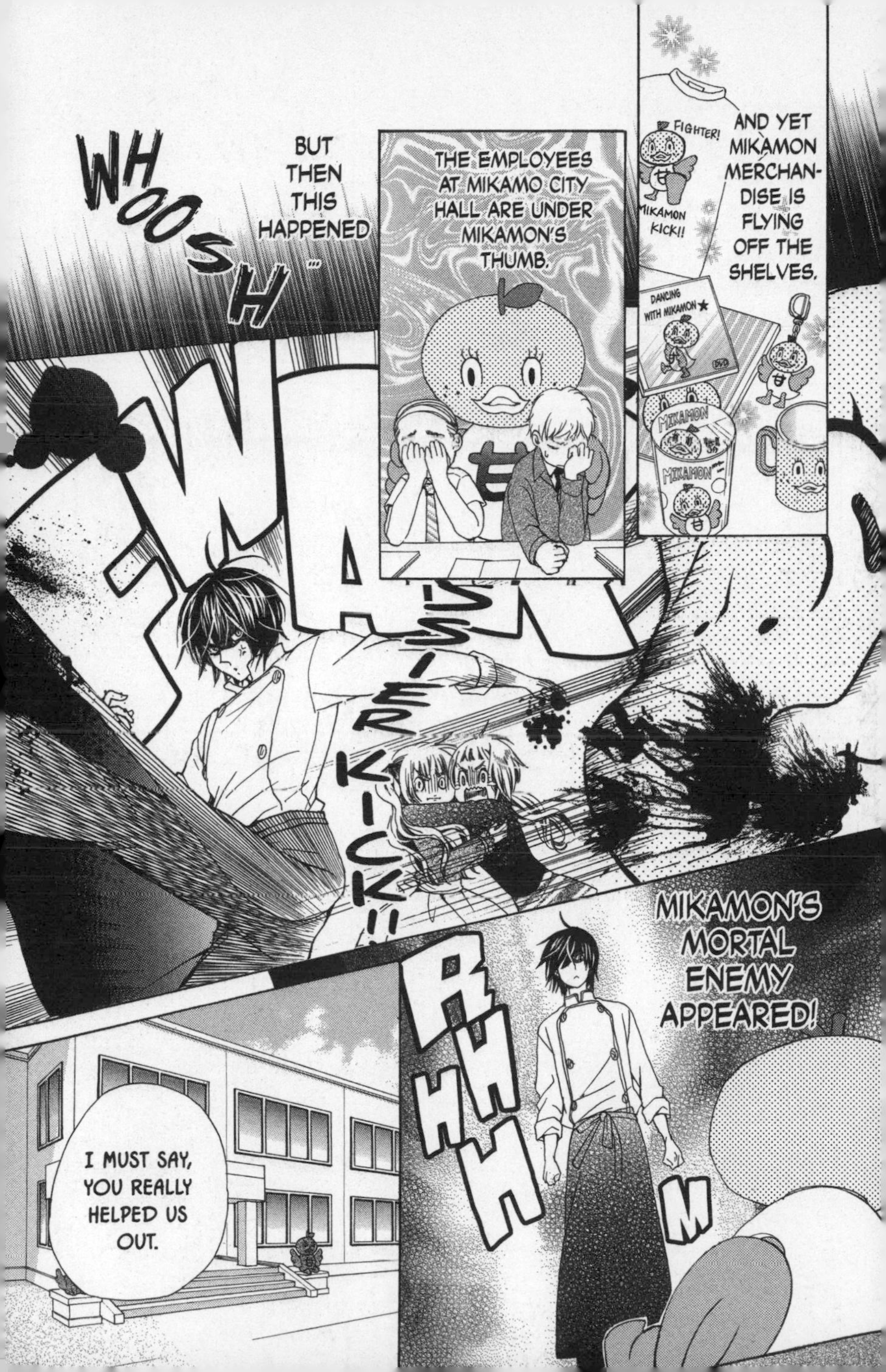
AND YET MIKAMON MERCHANDISE IS FLYING OFF THE SHELVES.
FIGHTER!
MIKAMON KICK!!
DANCING WITH MIKAMON ★
DVD
MIKAMON
MIKAMON
THE EMPLOYEES AT MIKAMO CITY HALL ARE UNDER MIKAMON'S THUMB.
BUT THEN THIS HAPPENED
WHOOSH...
SSIER KICK!!
MIKAMON'S MORTAL ENEMY APPEARED!
RHHHHM
I MUST SAY, YOU REALLY HELPED US OUT.

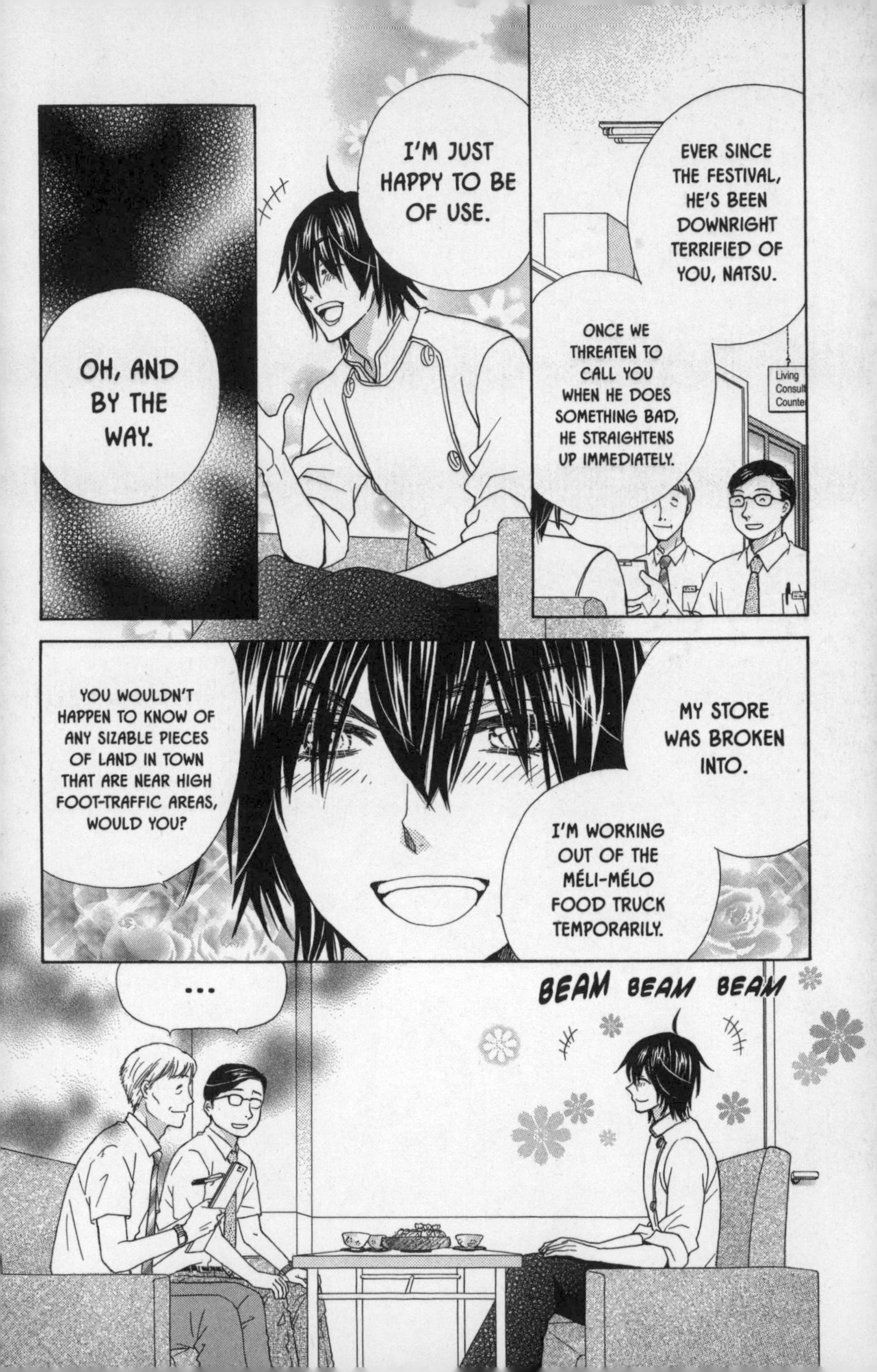
EVER SINCE THE FESTIVAL, HE'S BEEN DOWNRIGHT TERRIFIED OF YOU, NATSU.
ONCE WE THREATEN TO CALL YOU WHEN HE DOES SOMETHING BAD, HE STRAIGHTENS UP IMMEDIATELY.
Living Consult Counte
I'M JUST HAPPY TO BE OF USE.
OH, AND BY THE WAY.
MY STORE WAS BROKEN INTO.
I'M WORKING OUT OF THE MÉLI-MÉLO FOOD TRUCK TEMPORARILY.
YOU WOULDN'T HAPPEN TO KNOW OF ANY SIZABLE PIECES OF LAND IN TOWN THAT ARE NEAR HIGH FOOT-TRAFFIC AREAS, WOULD YOU?
BEAM BEAM BEAM
...

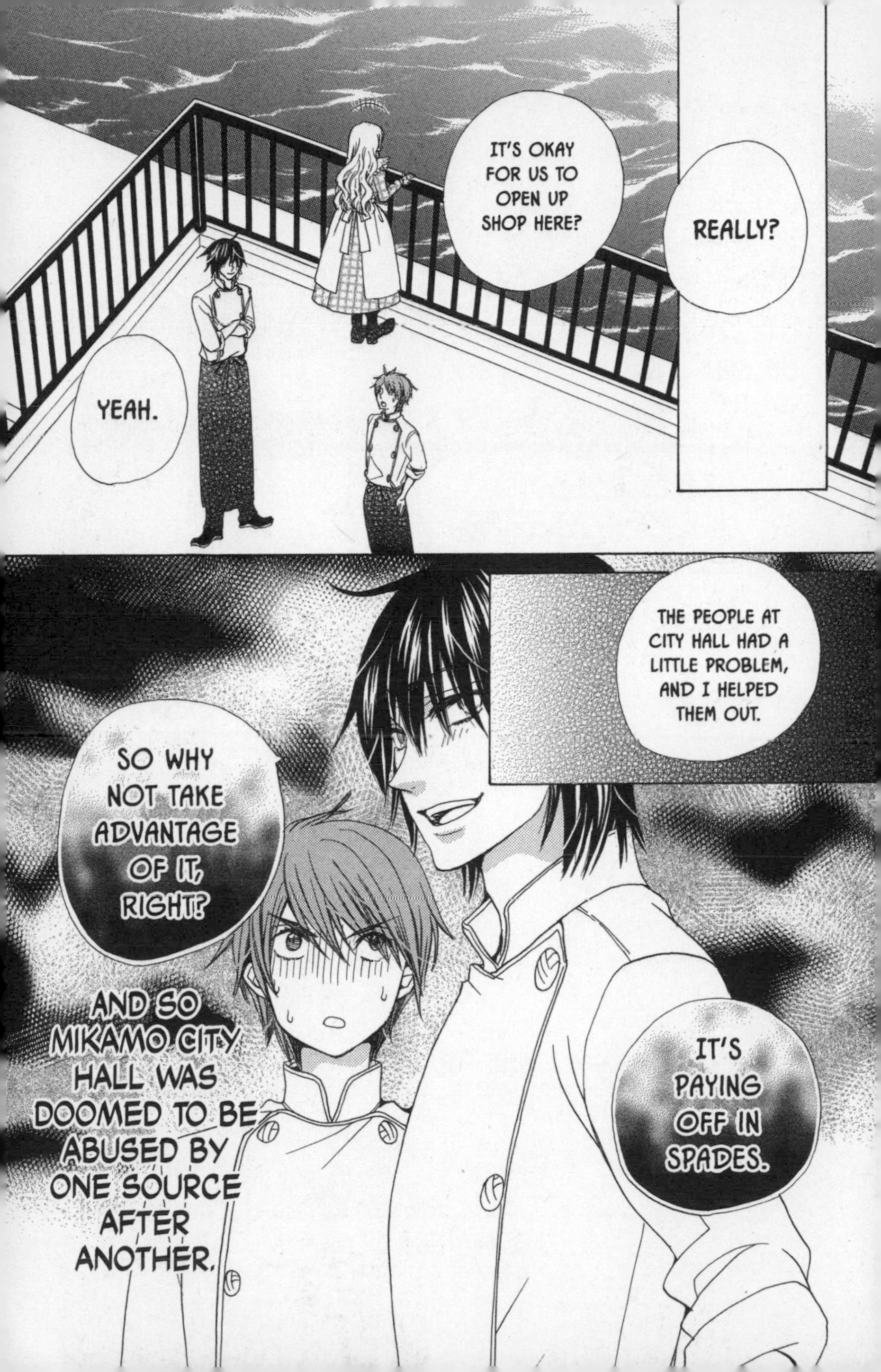
REALLY?
IT'S OKAY FOR US TO OPEN UP SHOP HERE?
YEAH.
THE PEOPLE AT CITY HALL HAD A LITTLE PROBLEM, AND I HELPED THEM OUT.
SO WHY NOT TAKE ADVANTAGE OF IT, RIGHT?
IT'S PAYING OFF IN SPADES.
AND SO MIKAMO CITY HALL WAS DOOMED TO BE ABUSED BY ONE SOURCE AFTER ANOTHER.

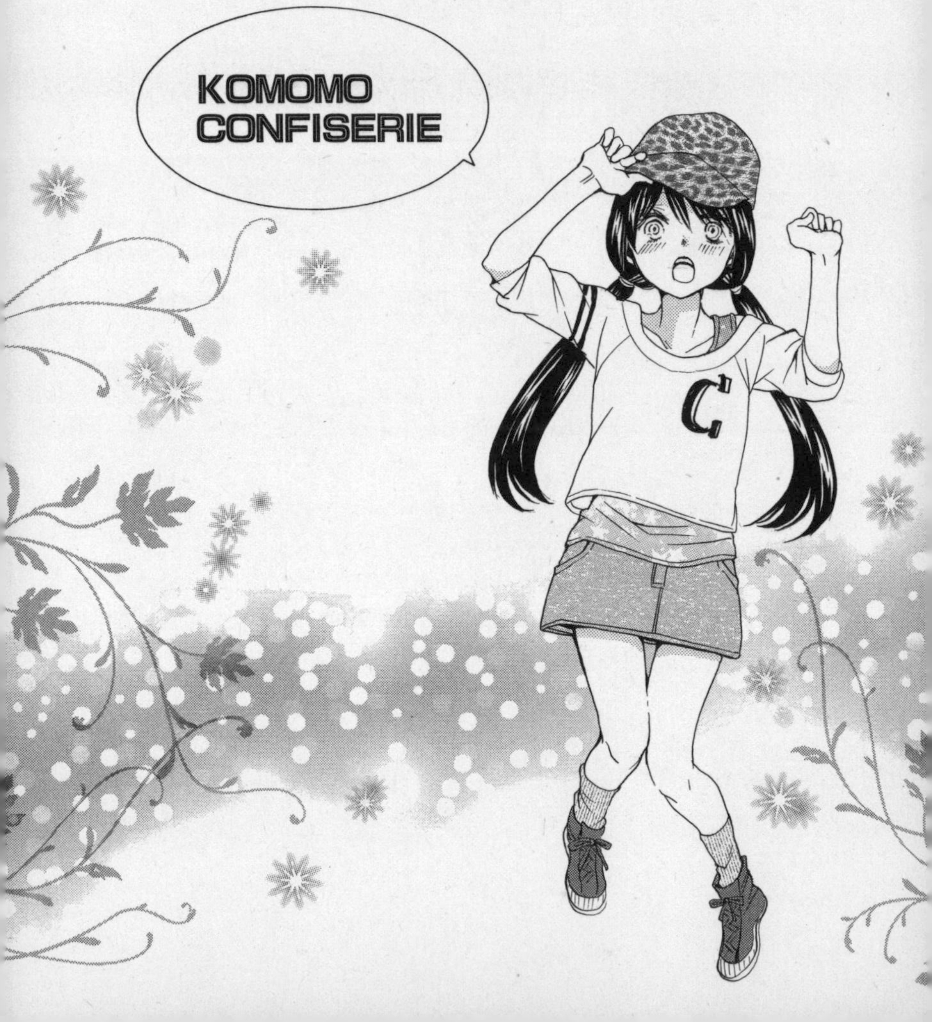
KOMOMO CONFISERIE

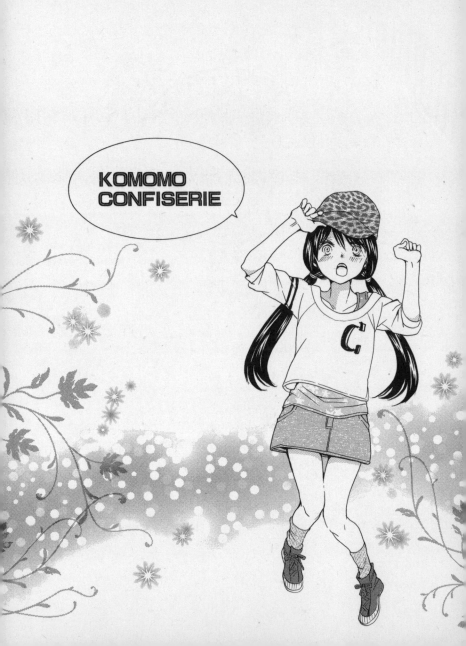

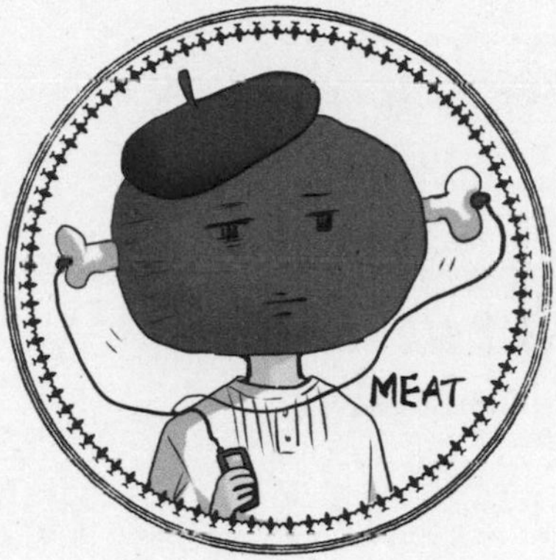
MEAT

Maki Minami is from Saitama Prefecture in Japan. She debuted in 2001 with *Kanata no Ao* (Faraway Blue). Her other works include *Kimi wa Girlfriend* (You're My Girlfriend), *Mainichi ga Takaramono* (Every Day Is a Treasure) and *Yuki Atataka* (Warm Winter). *S•A* and *Voice Over! Seiyu Academy* are published in English by VIZ Media.

Komomo Confiserie
Shojo Beat Edition
Volume 4

STORY AND ART BY
Maki Minami

Supervisor: Tsuji Shizuo Ryori Kyoiku Kenkyujo/Hiromi Kosaka
Special thanks to Tsujicho Group

Translation/Christine Dashiell
Touch-Up Art & Lettering/John Hunt
Design/Yukiko Whitley
Editor/Nancy Thistlethwaite

Komomo Confiserie by Maki Minami
© Maki Minami 2014
All rights reserved.
First published in Japan in 2014 by HAKUSENSHA, Inc., Tokyo.
English language translation rights arranged with HAKUSENSHA, Inc.,
Tokyo.

Printed in the U.S.A.

Published by VIZ Media, LLC
P.O. Box 77010
San Francisco, CA 94107

10 9 8 7 6 5 4 3 2 1
First printing, June 2016

www.viz.com   www.shojobeat.com

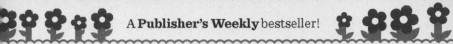

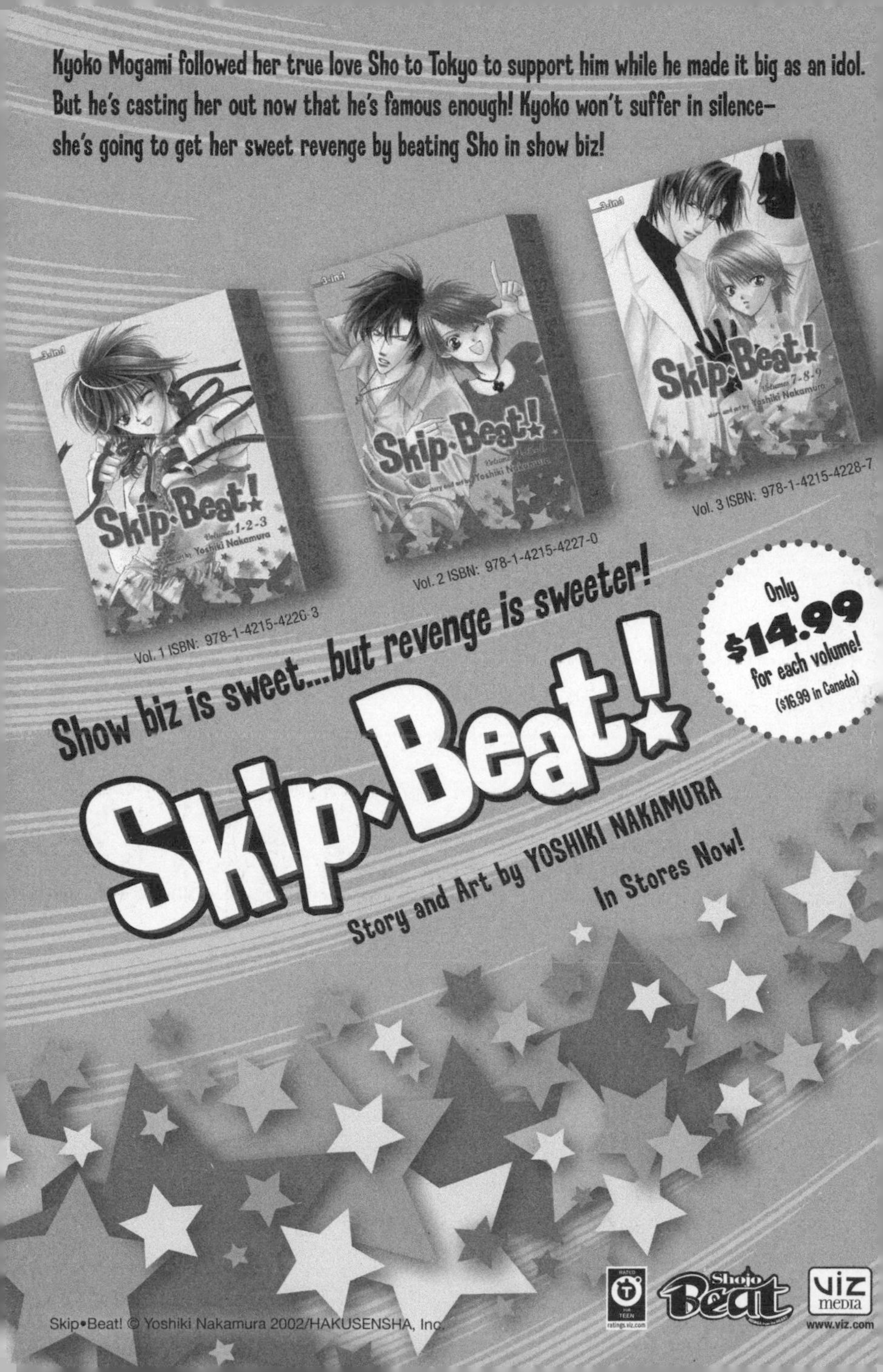
Kyoko Mogami followed her true love Sho to Tokyo to support him while he made it big as an idol. But he's casting her out now that he's famous enough! Kyoko won't suffer in silence– she's going to get her sweet revenge by beating Sho in show biz!
Vol. 1 ISBN: 978-1-4215-4226-3
Vol. 2 ISBN: 978-1-4215-4227-0
Vol. 3 ISBN: 978-1-4215-4228-7
Show biz is sweet...but revenge is sweeter!
Only $14.99 for each volume! ($16.99 in Canada)
Skip·Beat!
Story and Art by YOSHIKI NAKAMURA
In Stores Now!
Skip•Beat! © Yoshiki Nakamura 2002/HAKUSENSHA, Inc.
Shojo Beat
viz media
www.viz.com

Shojo Beat

S·A
Special.A

by Maki Minami

Manga series on sale now

Her whole life, Hikari Hanazono has been consumed with the desire to win against her school rival, Kei Takishima—at anything. He always comes out on top no matter what he does, and Hikari is determined to do whatever it takes to beat him!

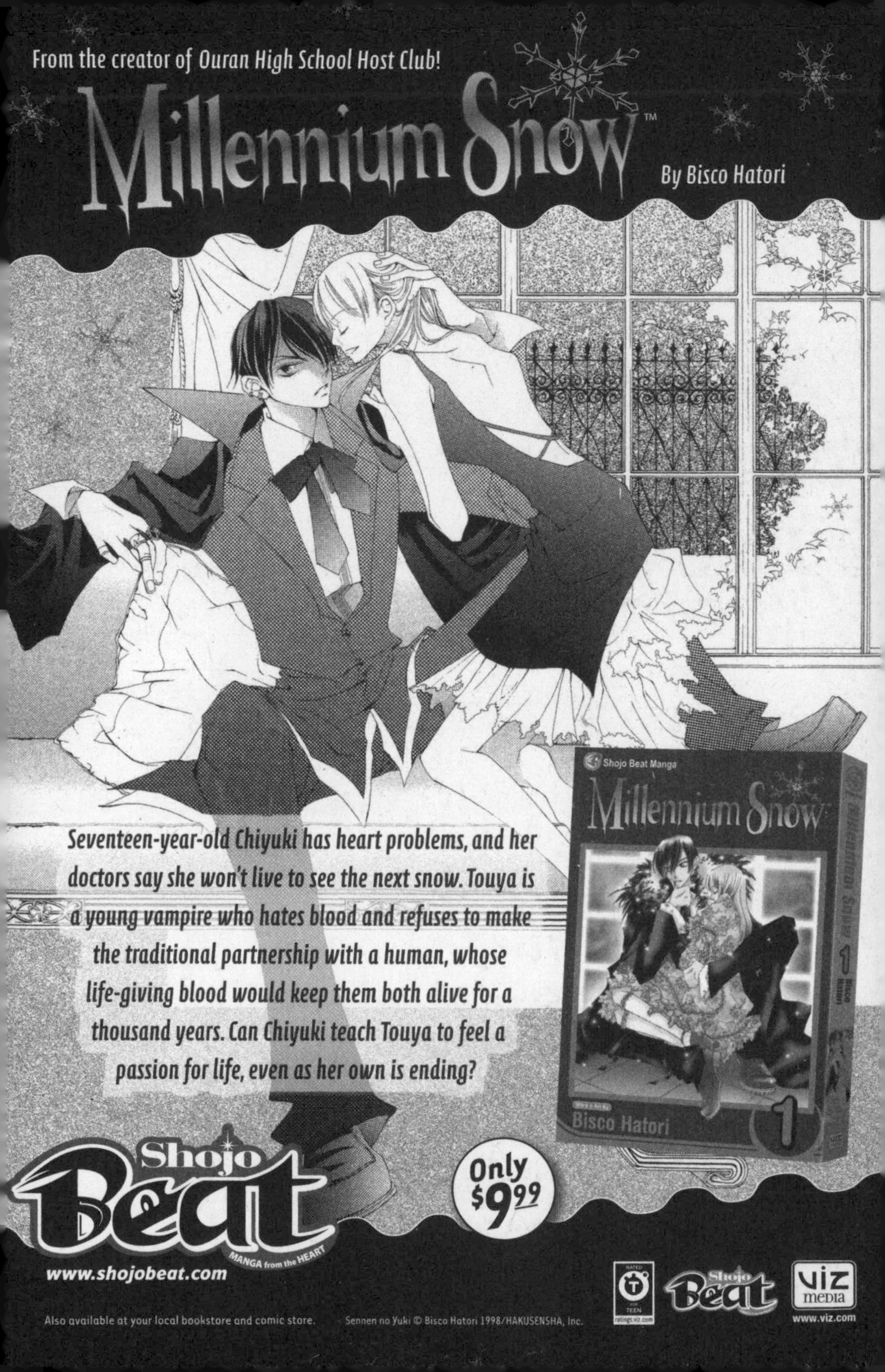

You may be reading the wrong way!

In keeping with the original Japanese comic format, this book reads from right to left, so action, sound effects and word balloons are reversed. This preserves the orientation of the original artwork. Check out the diagram below to get the order of things, and then turn to the other side of the book to get started!

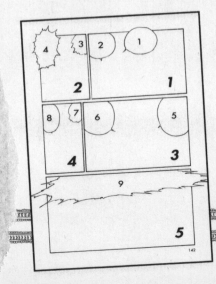